Basic
READING
Comprehension
Level G

Master the Basics One Step at a Time

edited by
Bearl Brooks
Daniel R. Burdyshaw
and
Marie-Jose Shaw

Student's Edition

ESP Publishing, Inc.
Largo, Florida

The Authors: **Basic Reading Comprehension is a compilation of reading and language arts materials written by professional classroom teachers.**

Book Design: **Bearl Brooks**

Editors: **Bearl Brooks, Daniel R. Burdyshaw, and Marie-Jose Shaw**

Cover Design: **Barbara K. Heer**

Graphic Arts Credits: **Melinda A. Baker, Nancy Baldridge, Rebecca L. Brown, Barbara K. Heer, Lesa Henson, Margie Luster, Donna Morrow, James D. Redding, Sheila Shockley, Robin Sydorenko, Janet E. Thiel, Judy Warren**

Student's Edition

Order number: BRC-G

ISBN 0-8209-0655-7

Published by
ESP Publishing, Inc.

Copyright ® 1993

Printed in the United States of America.

The Aardwolf

Study the spelling and meaning of each word. These words are used in today's story. Connect each word with its definition.

1. confuse   a. abandoned; left behind
2. crafty   b. not often
3. deserted   c. to make uncertain
4. frightened   d. cunning
5. seldom   e. easily frightened
6. shy   f. made afraid

Read the story carefully and remember the details.

In Dutch the words "aard wolf" mean "earth wolf." The aardwolf is a shy creature which looks and sounds much like a hyena.

The aardwolf is a native of south and east Africa. Its home is a hole in the ground which it digs itself or which was deserted by some other animal.

Because it stays hidden in its home during the daytime, the aardwolf is seldom seen by humans. Its main food is insects, especially white ants. The aardwolf usually lives in a small group.

When frightened, the aardwolf emits a foul-smelling odor. The aardwolf is not a fighter. Its teeth are small, and its jaws are weak.

Many people hunt the aardwolf for sport. The aardwolf is crafty, often traveling in circles to confuse the hunter.

A. Underline the correct answers about today's story.

1. In Dutch "aard" means (a) "earth"   (b) "false"   (c) "dangerous."
2. Which word describes the aardwolf? (a) aggressive   (b) shy   (c) friendly
3. The aardwolf eats (a) meat   (b) vegetables   (c) insects.
4. When frightened, the aardwolf (a) fights   (b) runs and hides   (c) emits an odor.
5. When hunted, the aardwolf is (a) crafty   (b) helpless   (c) inexperienced.

B. Reread the story and write the answers to these questions.

1. Where can the aardwolf be found during the day?

   In its home

3. In what country does the aardwolf live?

   south and east Africa

2. What other animal does the aardwolf resemble?

   cat

4. Where is the home of the aardwolf?

   hole

Consonants

A consonant sound is made by stopping air with the tongue, the teeth, or the lips. There are 21 consonants.

b c d f g h j k l m n p q r s t v w x y z

A. Add the missing consonants.

1. de_l_iver
2. fa_m_ous
3. ho__est
4. jo__e
5. _h_ey
6. _S_outh
7. peo_p_le
8. _g_arden
9. _n_eedle
10. zo__e
11. __uest
12. bo_n_us
13. __ude

14. ca__in
15. do__en
16. __ecision
17. _c_artoon
18. li__ense
19. kni__e
20. noi_g_e
21. __esult
22. li__erty
23. _l_ift
24. me__maid
25. __imple
26. va__uable
27. __onvince

28. po__ite
29. bree__e
30. __antastic
31. glo_b_e
32. to_d_ay
33. si__ent
34. mo_n_ey
35. _p_uzzle
36. o__inion
37. pa__ic
38. wi__dom
39. lea__er
40. pro__ise
41. i__em

42. pu_r_pose
43. dan_g_erous
44. _S_ecret
45. re__ard
46. __ecessary
47. perso_n_
48. pa__ade
49. _n_ewspaper
50. _c_ow

B. Add the missing consonants.

1. a_b_ _s_ent
2. adve____ure
3. e___ape
4. su___ound
5. lu___aby
6. mi___lace
7. no___ense
8. my___ery
9. adu___
10. e___ort
11. wi___out
12. ___ueeze

13. a_l_ _l_ow
14. ba_t_ _t_le
15. di_f_ _f_icult
16. exce_l_ _l_ent
17. fina_l_ _l_y
18. si___al
19. inco___ect
20. su___er
21. tale___
22. e___o
23. the___
24. forbi___en
25. go___ip

26. a___ident
27. hi___
28. cru___
29. co___ect
30. toge_t_ _h_er
31. nu___e
32. se_c_ _r_et
33. conde___
34. o___ect
35. a___iversary
36. sma_l_ _l_
37. tha___
38. a___roximate

39. de_s_ _s_ert
40. fo_l_ _l_ow
41. wa___
42. an___y
43. a___omplish
44. a___ention
45. e___ty
46. tomo___ow
47. wi_l_ _l_om
48. he_l_ _p_ful
49. a___er
50. u_g_ _l_y

6

The Addax

Study the spelling and meaning of each word. These words are used in today's story. Connect each word with its definition.

1. adapted   a. circumstances
2. Bedouins   b. adjusted
3. conditions   c. surroundings
4. dweller   d. one who resides
5. environment   e. very cautious
6. wary   f. nomadic Arabs

Read the story carefully and remember the details.

The addax is a true desert dweller. It survives under conditions that would be impossible for most other animals. The addax receives its moisture from plants.

In the summer the addax is a sandy color. In winter it wears a gray coat. The addax is well adapted to its environment. Its big hoofs make it easy to walk on the sand.

The addax is a shy and wary antelope. Its horns twist spirally up to a height of forty inches.

The addax is known for its speed. In olden times the Bedouins used the addax to test the speed of their horses. If the horses could overtake the addax, then the Bedouins considered them excellent runners.

A. Underline the correct answers about today's story.

1. Where does the addax live?   (a) desert   (b) mountains   (c) jungle
2. The addax is a/an   (a) horse   (b) antelope   (c) camel.
3. Bedouins used the addax   (a) as a work animal   (b) for food   (c) to test the speed of their horses.
4. In winter the addax is   (a) gray   (b) sandy   (c) black.
5. Which word describes the addax?   (a) shy   (b) aggressive   (c) fierce

B. Reread the story and write the answers to these questions.

1. What gives the addax its moisture?

_____

_____

_____

2. What makes it easy for the addax to walk on the sand?

_____

_____

_____

3. What characteristic of the addax changes?

_____

_____

_____

4. What people, in olden times, used the addax and what was the purpose?

_____

_____

_____

Unit 2 cont'd ☞

Using Consonants

A. Cross out the letters which are not consonants.

a   b   c   d   e   f   g   h   i   j   k   l   m   n

o   p   q   r   s   t   u   v   w   x   y   z

B. Underline the words which begin with consonants.

1. <u>music</u>	11. around	21. smoke	31. rain
2. fun	12. tooth	22. flower	32. nurse
3. orange	13. jump	23. eat	33. ate
4. ground	14. ago	24. hat	34. different
5. easy	15. people	25. oil	35. again
6. ice	16. barn	26. up	36. money
7. doctor	17. open	27. town	37. library
8. house	18. number	28. zoo	38. inside
9. game	19. use	29. cat	39. work
10. obey	20. cry	30. over	40. quiet

C. Place a consonant in each blank to make a complete word.

1. _b_ ook	16. ___ ire	31. ___ other	46. ___ ose
2. ___ elly	17. ___ oom	32. ___ ump	47. ___ould
3. ___ og	18. ___ onkey	33. ___ at	48. ___ ater
4. ___ anana	19. ___ irl	34. ___ ox	49. ___ eason
5. ___ alk	20. ___ aby	35. ___ uler	50. ___ ush
6. ___ ife	21. ___ est	36. ___ olor	51. ___ ame
7. ___ o	22. ___ ilk	37. ___ uppy	52. ___ ouse
8. ___ and	23. ___ agon	38. ___ ove	53. ___ armer
9. ___ ace	24. ___ encil	39. ___ ugar	54. ___ ecause
10. ___ ity	25. ___ ime	40. ___ ay	55. ___ arty
11. ___ us	26. ___ oat	41. ___ uilding	56. ___ ound
12. ___ un	27. ___ axi	42. ___ ake	57. ___ ard
13. ___ aint	28. ___ ong	43. ___ iver	58. ___ ree
14. ___ eed	29. ___ ice	44. ___ ool	59. ___ olice
15. ___ ow	30. ___ amily	45. ___ amp	60. ___ ind

African Elephants

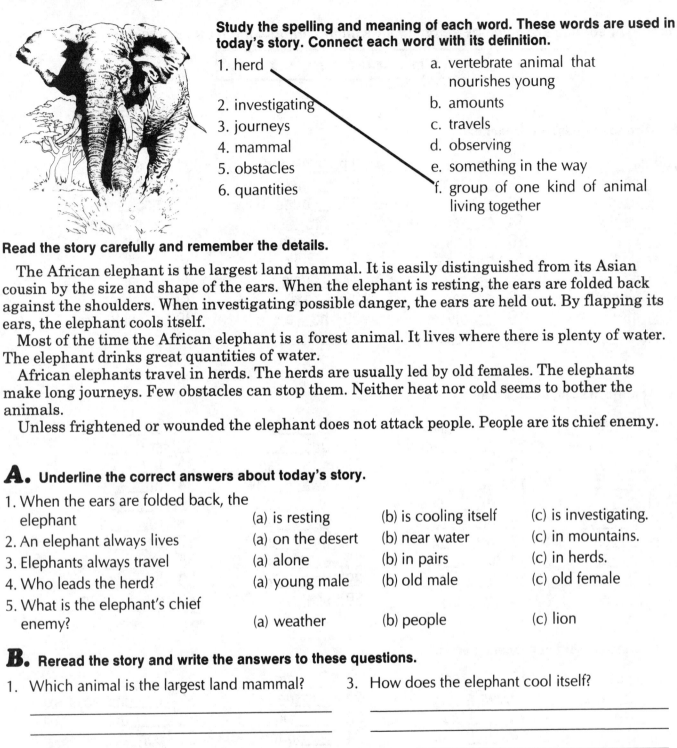

Study the spelling and meaning of each word. These words are used in today's story. Connect each word with its definition.

1. herd
2. investigating
3. journeys
4. mammal
5. obstacles
6. quantities

a. vertebrate animal that nourishes young
b. amounts
c. travels
d. observing
e. something in the way
f. group of one kind of animal living together

Read the story carefully and remember the details.

The African elephant is the largest land mammal. It is easily distinguished from its Asian cousin by the size and shape of the ears. When the elephant is resting, the ears are folded back against the shoulders. When investigating possible danger, the ears are held out. By flapping its ears, the elephant cools itself.

Most of the time the African elephant is a forest animal. It lives where there is plenty of water. The elephant drinks great quantities of water.

African elephants travel in herds. The herds are usually led by old females. The elephants make long journeys. Few obstacles can stop them. Neither heat nor cold seems to bother the animals.

Unless frightened or wounded the elephant does not attack people. People are its chief enemy.

A. Underline the correct answers about today's story.

1. When the ears are folded back, the elephant   (a) is resting   (b) is cooling itself   (c) is investigating.
2. An elephant always lives   (a) on the desert   (b) near water   (c) in mountains.
3. Elephants always travel   (a) alone   (b) in pairs   (c) in herds.
4. Who leads the herd?   (a) young male   (b) old male   (c) old female
5. What is the elephant's chief enemy?   (a) weather   (b) people   (c) lion

B. Reread the story and write the answers to these questions.

1. Which animal is the largest land mammal?

_____

_____

_____

2. How is the African elephant distinguished from the Asian?

_____

_____

_____

3. How does the elephant cool itself?

_____

_____

_____

4. When is the only time elephants attack people?

_____

_____

_____

Unit 3 cont'd ☞

Adding Consonants

Consonant sounds are made by stopping air with the tongue, the teeth, or the lips.

b c d f g h j k l m n p q r s t v w x y z

A. Add the missing consonants.

1. wor_m_
2. __alue
3. __eason
4. e__ergy
5. __ind
6. re__ult
7. __ile
8. __omplete
9. __ift
10. woma__

11. en__er
12. __asket
13. __usy
14. ca__el
15. __orest
16. hun__ry
17. __ud
18. o__ean
19. __adio
20. poc__et

21. __elephone
22. __oise
23. __ound
24. firs__
25. __outh
26. __ook
27. __usic
28. __axi
29. ho__e
30. finis__

31. __ear
32. dan__er
33. goo__
34. __ewspaper
35. __ome
36. __ait
37. __oo
38. nu__ber
39. __ecide
40. pi__e

B. Add the missing double consonants.

1. a_r__r_ow
2. ha____en
3. a____ress
4. bo____le
5. cro____
6. fina____y
7. le____on
8. bo____om
9. va____ey
10. la____er

11. di____erent
12. pa____word
13. je____y
14. bu____er
15. ro____er
16. discu____
17. wa____et
18. ca____y
19. li____le
20. si____y

21. bi____er
22. gue____
23. su____er
24. swa____ow
25. le____er
26. da____y
27. ha____er
28. e____
29. pe____y
30. spe____

31. su____enly
32. stu____
33. fi____le
34. bu____y
35. u____er
36. ru____er
37. be____er
38. gra____
39. fa____er
40. me____age

C. Add the missing consonant blends.

1. _gr_een
2. ri____
3. ____ee
4. ____y
5. ____eat
6. pu____
7. wa____
8. ____oe
9. ____at
10. ____eel

11. ____eak
12. wi____
13. ____ag
14. ____urch
15. ____ick
16. ____ow
17. ____ort
18. ____amp
19. ____eese
20. ____end

21. ____om
22. ____ue
23. ____ain
24. ____ound
25. ____air
26. ____ip
27. ____ep
28. ____eam
29. ____ese
30. ____oke

31. ____ea
32. ____ink
33. ____arp
34. por____
35. ____easure
36. ____ant
37. ____all
38. ____esh
39. ____ad
40. ____own

10

The Age of Reptiles

Study the spelling and meaning of each word. These words are used in today's story. Connect each word with its definition.

1. armored
2. enormous
3. fossil
4. preserved
5. reptile
6. roamed

a. great in size
b. air-breathing, scaly vertebrate
c. having a protective cover
d. wandered
e. kept from decaying
f. an impression preserved in the earth's crust

Read the story carefully and remember the details.

Millions of years ago dinosaurs roamed the earth. They were the kings and queens of the world. Some were enormous. Some were very small. Some had horns. Some had armored bodies. Dinosaurs were of many kinds.

The name "dinosaur" means "terrible lizard," but the word "lizard" is not entirely accurate. Dinosaurs were reptiles.

No animal today is like a dinosaur. What we know about the dinosaur comes from fossils. Fossils are records of the past that have been preserved in stone.

The things we know about dinosaurs are really educated guesses made by scientists who spend their lives studying fossils. No one can be positively certain about what happened during the age of reptiles.

A. Underline the correct answers about today's story.

1. "Dinosaur" means   (a) "terrible"   (b) "big lizard"   (c) "terrible lizard."
2. Dinosaurs were really   (a) reptiles   (b) lizards   (c) snakes.
3. Fossils tell us about the   (a) future   (b) present   (c) past.
4. Who was king during the age of the reptiles? (a) dinosaurs   (b) people   (c) lions
5. Our information on the past is   (a) accurate   (b) uncertain   (c) complete.

B. Reread the story and write the answers to these questions.

1. When did dinosaurs roam the earth?

_____
_____
_____

2. Were all of the dinosaurs large?

_____
_____
_____

3. What animals of today are like dinosaurs?

_____
_____
_____

4. How do we know about dinosaurs?

_____
_____
_____

Unit 4 cont'd ☞

Consonant Sounds

Most consonants spell their own sounds. Some, however,
may spell more than one sound.

(a) The "j" sound can be spelled with a "j" or a "g."
(b) The "s" sound can be spelled with a "c" or an "s."
(c) The "f" sound can be spelled with an "f," a "ph," or a "gh."
(d) The "k" sound can be spelled with a "k," "c," "ch," or "ck."
(e) The "kw" sound can be spelled with a "qu."
(f) The "ks" sound can be spelled with an "x."
(g) The "z" sound can be spelled with a "z" or an "s."

 What are the sounds of the underlined letters?

EXAMPLES:

<u>j</u> 1. arrange
<u>f</u> 2. cough
<u>b</u> 3. balloon

____ 1. certain	____ 26. enough	____ 51. journey	____ 76. museum
____ 2. dozen	____ 27. texture	____ 52. fox	____ 77. quiet
____ 3. box	____ 28. camera	____ 53. visitor	____ 78. sponge
____ 4. passing	____ 29. citizen	____ 54. necklace	____ 79. phase
____ 5. price	____ 30. circle	____ 55. garage	____ 80. hot
____ 6. costume	____ 31. zoo	____ 56. bugle	____ 81. window
____ 7. seven	____ 32. people	____ 57. kitten	____ 82. teeth
____ 8. danger	____ 33. raise	____ 58. organize	____ 83. tuxedo
____ 9. lights	____ 34. gang	____ 59. banquet	____ 84. huge
____ 10. music	____ 35. future	____ 60. medicine	____ 85. checkers
____ 11. does	____ 36. phone	____ 61. object	____ 86. surface
____ 12. needless	____ 37. best	____ 62. listen	____ 87. ripe
____ 13. elephant	____ 38. kitchen	____ 63. watch	____ 88. neat
____ 14. jewelry	____ 39. yellow	____ 64. tougher	____ 89. inquire
____ 15. taxi	____ 40. pleasure	____ 65. sax	____ 90. surprise
____ 16. bucket	____ 41. voice	____ 66. persuade	____ 91. captain
____ 17. unusual	____ 42. scheme	____ 67. wizard	____ 92. boots
____ 18. extra	____ 43. junk	____ 68. slip	____ 93. dictionary
____ 19. quick	____ 44. fix	____ 69. parent	____ 94. freedom
____ 20. seldom	____ 45. gallon	____ 70. dime	____ 95. yes
____ 21. testing	____ 46. reason	____ 71. cannon	____ 96. sixteen
____ 22. fancy	____ 47. wax	____ 72. square	____ 97. record
____ 23. never	____ 48. spook	____ 73. ache	____ 98. around
____ 24. sometimes	____ 49. begin	____ 74. word	____ 99. cabin
____ 25. person	____ 50. foxes	____ 75. feet	____ 100. young

The Albatross

Study the spelling and meaning of each word. These words are used in today's story. Connect each word with its definition.

1. favorite
2. glide
3. instinct
4. narrow
5. require
6. soars

a. to move smoothly, effortlessly
b. most preferred
c. natural response
d. of slender width
e. flies
f. to insist upon

Read the story carefully and remember the details.

Large but graceful, the albatross soars above the sea. The sea is its home. The albatross seldom comes to land.

Over the ocean the albatross can glide for hours. Its long and narrow wings spread twelve feet, the record wingspread of all birds. The albatross's long wings require a long runway. That runway is the ocean. The bird is able to light on the water and take off from there.

The ocean is also the bird's source of food. There it finds its favorite diet of squid.

When instinct urges the albatross to mate and breed, the bird heads for land. Large colonies then gather on islands.

Sailors have long considered the albatross a sign of good luck. Killing the bird meant misfortune.

A. Underline the correct answers about today's story.

1. The albatross makes its home   (a) in trees   (b) on land   (c) on the sea.
2. The albatross has the biggest   (a) wingspread   (b) body   (c) beak.
3. The bird's runway is   (a) the ocean   (b) a passing ship   (c) a nearby island.
4. The bird seeks land only for   (a) food   (b) breeding   (c) rest.
5. The albatross is a sign of   (a) bad luck   (b) good luck   (c) misfortune.

B. Reread the story and write the answers to these questions.

1. Does the albatross often come to land?

_____

_____

_____

2. What is the wingspread of the albatross?

_____

_____

_____

3. What is the favorite diet of the albatross?

_____

_____

_____

4. What do sailors believe it means when an albatross is killed?

_____

_____

_____

13

Unit 5 cont'd ☛

Consonant Blends

A consonant blend occurs when two consonants spell one sound.

sh dr pr tr br pl fl bl sl ch th wh sc sm st

A. Which consonant blends are in the words? Write them in the blanks.

1. bring *br*
2. drive ____
3. steak ____
4. plant ____
5. while ____

6. fly ____
7. scale ____
8. blank ____
9. shoe ____
10. prove ____

11. slow ____
12. thin ____
13. choose ____
14. train ____
15. show ____

16. draw ____
17. branch ____ ____
18. this ____
19. mesh ____
20. stop ____

B. Add a consonant blend to complete each word.

1. *sl* eep
2. mu____
3. ____ere
4. ____an
5. ____urch
6. ____ing
7. ____oor
8. ____oe
9. bu____
10. ____y

11. ____ue
12. ____eam
13. ____oke
14. ____en
15. ____udy
16. tea____
17. ____ant
18. ____ick
19. ____ove
20. ____eese

21. ____ural
22. wi____
23. ____ought
24. ____ip
25. ____ack
26. ____um
27. ____ite
28. ____ut
29. ____ey
30. ____ag

31. ____at
32. ____out
33. ea____
34. ____ow
35. ____all
36. di____
37. ____amp
38. ____em
39. ri____
40. ____ince

C. Write one word that begins with the same consonant blend as each of these words.

1. though *these*
2. whistle ____
3. brought ____
4. blew ____
5. proud ____

6. shade ____
7. stay ____
8. chase ____
9. plum ____
10. flea ____

11. truck ____
12. thank ____
13. sheep ____
14. drink ____
15. slip ____

16. wheel ____
17. school ____
18. small ____
19. they ____
20. chain ____

Comprehension Check

Ⓐ Add the missing consonants.

1. aa _r_ _d_ wolf
2. A _ _ ican
3. grou _ _
4. hi _ _ en
5. se _ _ om
6. e _ _ ecially
7. _ _ oup
8. fri _ _ tened
9. peo _ _ e
10. hu _ _ er

11. impo _ _ ible
12. moi _ _ ure
13. _ _ ants
14. su _ _ er
15. wi _ _ er
16. hei _ _ t
17. _ _ eed
18. ove _ _ ake
19. di _ _ ingui _ _ ed
20. re _ _ ing

21. inve _ _ igating
22. da _ _ er
23. _ _ inks
24. jou _ _ eys
25. _ _ avel
26. ob _ _ acles
27. nei _ _ er
28. a _ _ ack
29. _ _ ief
30. a _ _ ored

31. eno _ _ ous
32. fo _ _ ils
33. prese _ _ ed
34. mi _ _ ions
35. te _ _ ible
36. liza _ _
37. reco _ _ s
38. in _ _ inct
39. _ _ aceful
40. alba _ _ oss

Ⓑ Which words begin with consonants? Underline them. .

1. shy
2. seldom
3. addax
4. earth
5. country

6. crafty
7. desert
8. sandy
9. spirally
10. Bedouins

11. herd
12. obstacles
13. elephant
14. usually
15. attack

16. armored
17. fossils
18. enormous
19. kings
20. queens

21. graceful
22. able
23. breed
24. instinct
25. luck

Ⓒ Add a consonant blend to each word.

1. _sh_ y
2. ___ eature
3. sou ___
4. ___ ound
5. ___ ay

6. ___ en
7. A ___ ican
8. ___ ape
9. ele ___ ant
10. ___ apping

11. ___ op
12. bo ___ er
13. ob ___ acles
14. ___ ief
15. ear ___

16. ___ all
17. ___ eserved
18. ___ one
19. ___ ings
20. alba ___ oss

Ⓓ Complete these sentences.

1. "Dinosaur" means " __terrible lizard__ . "
2. The addax is known for its _____ .
3. The African elephant is the largest _____ mammal.
4. An old _____ elephant is the leader.
5. Aardwolves travel in _____ to confuse the hunter.
6. _____ are records of the past.
7. The addax receives moisture from _____ .

8. The albatross lives at _____ .
9. The word "aardwolf" means " _____ ."
10. African elephants travel in _____ .
11. Dinosaurs were _____ .
12. The aardwolf is _____ seen by people.
13. An albatross loves to eat _____ .
14. The albatross is a sign of _____ luck.
15. The addax is a true _____ dweller.
16. Bedouins used the addax to test their horses' _____ .

Test 1 cont'd ☞

Comprehension Check (continued)

(E) Match these words and their definitions. These words appeared in the reading selections from units 1-5.

<u>g</u> 1. environment   ____ 7. obstacles   a. wandered   h. vertebrate animal that
____ 2. wary   ____ 8. roamed   b. very cautious   nourishes young
____ 3. seldom   ____ 9. fossil   c. to make uncertain   i. a natural response
____ 4. crafty   ____ 10. reptile   d. most preferred   j. something in the way
____ 5. confuse   ____ 11. favorite   e. cunning   k. air-breathing, scaly
____ 6. mammal   ____ 12. instinct   f. not often   vertebrate
    g. surroundings   l. an impression preserved in the earth's crust

(F) Underline the correct answers.

1. What does "aardwolf" mean?   (a) <u>"earth wolf"</u>   (b) "earth pig"
2. In what country does the aardwolf live?   (a) Africa   (b) Asia
3. What color is the addax in winter?   (a) black   (b) gray
4. What gives the addax its moisture?   (a) animals   (b) plants
5. When do elephants attack people?   (a) when wounded   (b) when hungry
6. Who leads the elephant's herd?   (a) old female   (b) young female
7. Were all of the dinosaurs large?   (a) yes   (b) no
8. What does "dinosaur" mean?   (a) "big lizard"   (b) "terrible lizard"
9. Does the albatross often come to land?   (a) yes   (b) no
10. What does the albatross eat?   (a) squid   (b) sea gulls

Choose one of the following topics and write a paragraph.

(1) It is said that killing an albatross means misfortune. This is a superstition. Are you superstitious? Why or why not?

(2) It is thought that dinosaurs died out millions of years ago. Would life as we know it be possible if dinosaurs were still in existence?

_____

_____

_____

_____

_____

_____

_____

_____

_____

The American Badger

Study the spelling and meaning of each word. These words are used in today's story. Connect each word with its definition.

1. burrowing
2. consists
3. fierce
4. peaceful
5. powerful
6. prefers

a. serene
b. ferocious
c. is made up of
d. desires over something else
e. digging
f. strong

Read the story carefully and remember the details.

The American badger is a large and powerful member of the weasel family. It may be seen during the day, but usually it prefers to hunt for food in the late afternoon. Its diet consists of ground squirrels, mice, prairie dogs, and pocket gophers. The European badger's habits are similar to those of its American cousin.

The badger is a burrowing animal. Its front claws are excellent for digging. The badger looks for holes made by other burrowing animals. When it finds a hole, it begins to dig. When the badger is frightened, it digs its own hole.

Few animals attack the badger. It is known as a tough and fierce fighter. Once the badger begins fighting, it never gives up. However, the animal is quite peaceful unless attacked.

A. Underline the correct answers about today's story.

1. The badger is related to the   (a) fox   (b) weasel   (c) mouse.
2. When does the badger hunt?   (a) daytime   (b) in the dark   (c) late afternoon
3. The badger's home is a   (a) hollow tree   (b) burrow   (c) cave.
4. As a fighter, the badger is   (a) tough   (b) defensless   (c) weak.
5. Which word describes a badger?   (a) helpless   (b) always mean   (c) usually peaceful

B. Reread the story and write the answers to these questions.

1. Name three of the things that badgers eat.

_____

_____

_____

2. What does the badger do when frightened?

_____

_____

3. Do many animals attack the badger?

_____

_____

_____

4. When is the animal not a peaceful one?

_____

_____

_____

   Unit 6 cont'd ☞

Vowels

A vowel represents a sound which is made by allowing air to flow.

A. What are the five letters which are always vowels?

___ ___ ___ ___ ___

B. Underline the words which begin with vowels.

1. us
2. empty
3. gift
4. people
5. zero
6. again
7. rain
8. until
9. off
10. each
11. cry
12. because
13. add
14. even
15. quiet
16. ear
17. answer
18. nap
19. under
20. other
21. voice
22. island
23. flower
24. office
25. tooth
26. when
27. and
28. eleven
29. orange
30. laugh
31. if
32. sunshine
33. lake
34. eye
35. rabbit
36. always
37. candy
38. mother
39. mouse
40. over
41. sand
42. orange
43. carrot
44. nurse
45. extra
46. ice
47. earth
48. alone
49. yard
50. pet
51. often
52. into
53. weed
54. above
55. box

C. Supply the missing vowels.

1. p_u_ppy
2. b__rd
3. p__sh
4. w__ll
5. th__se
6. __nce
7. b__rn
8. fl__g
9. __t
10. kn__fe
11. r__de
12. __pple
13. p__t
14. wh__n
15. c__ty
16. l__mp
17. th__nk
18. g__t
19. n__se
20. w__lk
21. s__ng
22. h__r
23. __m
24. cl__wn
25. br__ve
26. d__d
27. __pon
28. m__tch
29. y__s
30. j__mp
31. m__rning
32. w__
33. f__n
34. v__ry
35. sk__n
36. t__wn
37. y__llow
38. h__me
39. __ld
40. __gg

The American Bittern

Study the spelling and meaning of each word. These words are used in today's story. Connect each word with its definition.

1. buff
2. illusive
3. loner
4. patiently
5. rely
6. remarkable

a. depend
b. light brownish yellow
c. noteworthy
d. deceptive
e. tolerating delay
f. one who prefers being alone

Read the story carefully and remember the details.

The American bittern is a bird that is most often heard but not seen. Shy and illusive, the bittern has a remarkable talent for self-concealment.

The bittern is a loner. Except for mating season the bittern does not even mix with birds of its own kind.

Buff and brown feathers protect the bird from many enemies. However, the bittern does not rely totally on its protective plumage. The bird lies very close to the ground when an enemy approaches. The foe may come very near before the bittern bolts quickly into the air. It is able to move swiftly.

The bittern's home is always near a swamp. There it patiently hunts for fish, frogs, and insects. The bittern is more active during the early morning hours of the day.

A. Underline the correct answers about today's story.

1. Which word does not describe the bittern? (a) shy   (b) illusive   (c) bold
2. The bittern lives   (a) in flocks   (b) in pairs   (c) alone.
3. For protection the bird relies on   (a) claws   (b) coloring   (c) its sharp beak.
4. Where is the bittern's home?   (a) swamp   (b) desert   (c) sea
5. As a flier, the bittern is   (a) slow   (b) awkward   (c) swift.

B. Reread the story and write the answers to these questions.

1. Name a remarkable talent of the bittern.

_____

_____

2. Where does the bittern go as the enemy approaches?

_____

_____

3. What does the bittern hunt?

_____

_____

4. When is the bittern most active?

_____

_____

Unit 7 cont'd

Adding Vowels

A. Add the missing vowel to complete each word.

1. f_i_sh
2. v__ry
3. y__rd
4. w__rk
5. t__ll
6. j__mp
7. st__ry
8. __wn
9. t__day
10. p__ncil
11. addr__ss
12. b__nk
13. gr__w
14. br__dge
15. c__mp

16. w__rm
17. b__sy
18. j__lly
19. m__d
20. n__ws
21. __pen
22. st__ne
23. sm__le
24. pl__ce
25. s__gn
26. __rrive
27. str__ng
28. gr__de
29. j__st
30. wh__t

31. __ften
32. st__dy
33. b__by
34. s__mmer
35. h__ppy
36. __f
37. __sk
38. __range
39. p__sh
40. w__th
41. r__place
42. __nce
43. l__nd
44. __very
45. p__ll

46. __bove
47. d__rty
48. pr__tty
49. h__ngry
50. w__
51. __ncle
52. st__ff
53. ph__ne
54. d__fferent
55. m__ybe
56. ch__ll
57. ours__lf
58. br__ng
59. __nder
60. th__

B. Add the vowels.

1. gr_e_e_n
2. b___k
3. ___rth
4. cart___n
5. s___d
6. l___n
7. ___ch
8. g___ng
9. cl___r
10. wh___l

11. t___th
12. d___s
13. l___ked
14. f___d
15. r___nd
16. l___rn
17. rad___
18. mov___
19. tr___
20. cl___

21. h___lth
22. sch___l
23. sw___t
24. fr___nd
25. br___ze
26. fr___
27. pl___se
28. f___t
29. ag___n
30. sm___th

31. p___no
32. betw___n
33. ___nt
34. agr___
35. sl___p
36. alr___dy
37. t___cher
38. br___d
39. y___
40. c___kie

20

The American Elk

Study the spelling and meaning of each word. These words are used in today's story. Connect each word with its definition.

1. civilization
2. detect
3. graze
4. keen
5. reduced
6. troubled

a. acute; sensitive
b. place with socially developed people
c. discover
d. feed on grasses
e. bothered
f. lessened

Read the story carefully and remember the details.

The Indians called the American elk the wapiti. Today the name "wapiti" is still commonly used.

Wapiti are mountain dwellers. During the winter they often move to the valleys to find food. Their winter coats of long, gray hair protect them from the cold.

The American elk are herd animals. They graze on grasses. Their keen hearing and sense of smell help detect the coming of an enemy. Their huge branching antlers make excellent weapons.

The elk are good swimmers. When troubled by summer insects, the elk often stand in water.

Today laws protect the animal which once wandered freely over the land. The elk's numbers have been greatly reduced by civilization.

A. Underline the correct answers about today's story.

1. The Indian name for elk is	(a) wapiti	(b) tundra	(c) apache.
2. Elk prefer to live in the	(a) forests	(b) mountains	(c) desert.
3. What is the elk's weapon?	(a) hoofs	(b) antlers	(c) teeth
4. To ward off insects, the elk	(a) swings its tail	(b) rolls in mud	(c) stands in water.
5. What has reduced the number of elk?	(a) disease	(b) cold weather	(c) civilization

B. Reread the story and write the answers to these questions.

1. When did the Indian stop calling the elk wapiti?

_____

_____

_____

2. Where do the elk go in the winter?

_____

_____

_____

3. What protects wapiti from cold?

_____

_____

_____

4. What now protects the wapiti?

_____

_____

_____

Unit 8 cont'd ☞

More Vowels

A vowel sound is made by allowing air to flow. The vowels include "a," "e," "i," "o," and "u."

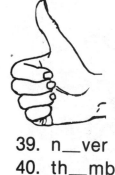

A. Add the missing vowels.

1. y_e_s
2. s__ggest
3. b__rthday
4. b__lance
5. __njoy
6. tr__st
7. l__cense
8. c__nfuse
9. __pinion
10. l__xury
11. gl__mpse
12. s__ldom
13. ch__nce
14. c__me
15. m__rning
16. w__nter
17. ch__rch
18. pr__tty
19. n__rmal
20. st__pid
21. com__dian
22. im__gine
23. l__yal
24. ex__rcise
25. alm__nac
26. __lways
27. f__nce
28. b__cause
29. m__ny
30. n__mber
31. h__ppy
32. __dentify
33. v__sible
34. __bility
35. v__yage
36. myst__ry
37. uns__fe
38. f__nally
39. n__ver
40. th__mb
41. __fter
42. kn__fe
43. w__gon
44. cl__mb
45. m__nkey
46. t__rtle
47. f__rmer
48. cl__thes
49. b__cycle
50. spl__ndid

B. Add the missing vowels.

1. br_e_ _a_kfast
2. capt___n
3. fr___dom
4. c___se
5. fam___s
6. g___nt
7. l___gh
8. ___tline
9. us___lly
10. l___f
11. h___vy
12. p___no
13. b___uty
14. fr___t
15. c___nt
16. ___gle
17. v___ce
18. d___ghter
19. f___r
20. gr___dy
21. d___dline
22. tr___ble
23. j___rney
24. p___ce
25. quest___n
26. th___gh
27. id___
28. r___n
29. f___lish
30. val___ble
31. r___son
32. r___ch
33. rec___ve
34. str___ght
35. h___r
36. bel___ve
37. th___ght
38. s___n
39. sh___t
40. sl___p
41. b___ng
42. w___gh
43. cl___n
44. sp___k
45. d___ble
46. thr___gh
47. y___ng
48. pr___d
49. y___rself
50. anx___us

22

Antbirds

Study the spelling and meaning of each word. These words are used in today's story. Connect each word with its definition.

1. depends
2. find
3. flush
4. method
5. races
6. snatch

a. grab
b. moves swiftly
c. relies on
d. drive out
e. locate the place of
f. procedure

Read the story carefully and remember the details.

One would think that a bird named the antbird got its name because it ate ants, but the antbird does not eat ants. It depends on ants to find its food.

The antbird follows army ants. The army ants march through the jungle and villages. Nothing stops or detours the ants. As they march, they flush out insects and small creatures. The antbird waits for these insects to come out of their hiding places. Then it races to snatch the insects before the ants do.

The antbirds depend exclusively on this method for finding their food. When a swarm of ants no longer furnish a sufficient supply of food, the antbirds leave and look for a new benefactor. Antbirds are found only in the jungles of South America.

A. Underline the correct answers about today's story.

1. Antbirds follow   (a) army ants   (b) insects   (c) the sun.
2. Antbirds eat   (a) ants   (b) insects   (c) birds.
3. The ants lead the antbirds to   (a) food   (b) water   (c) their homes.
4. The antbird is found in   (a) Asia   (b) Africa   (c) South America.
5. The benefactor is   (a) an enemy   (b) a giver   (c) a receiver.

B. Reread the story and write the answers to these questions.

1. What detours army ants?

_____

_____

_____

2. Who does the antbird compete with for food?

_____

_____

_____

3. What other methods are used for finding food?

_____

_____

_____

4. When do antbirds look for a new benefactor?

_____

_____

_____

23   **Unit 9 cont'd** ☞

Vowels Followed by "r"

A. Complete each word by adding a vowel in front of the "r."

1. st_o_re
2. anoth__r
3. __round
4. c__rl
5. f__re
6. flow__r
7. z__ro
8. n__rse
9. __range
10. h__rd
11. f__r
12. numb__r
13. ov__r

14. b__rn
15. d__rk
16. h__rse
17. p__rty
18. w__rd
19. m__re
20. s__re
21. ev__ry
22. h__rt
23. bef__re
24. c__re
25. f__r
26. h__re

27. diff__rent
28. __rrive
29. p__rson
30. aft__r
31. c__rn
32. ord__r
33. cha__r
34. ev__r
35. lett__r
36. t__rn
37. g__rl
38. e__rly
39. high__r

40. st__rt
41. pict__re
42. g__rden
43. und__r
44. y__rd
45. p__rk
46. col__r
47. th__re
48. teach__r
49. th__rd
50. t__rkey

B. Complete each sentence by underlining the correctly spelled word in the parentheses.

1. Who is that (gurl, girl)?
2. The (answer, answur) is "no."
3. Which (color, colur) do you like?
4. The (teachur, teacher) is Ms. Adams.
5. I sit in the (thurd, third) row.
6. It looks (different, diffurent).
7. The (watur, water) is cold.
8. What's for (supper, suppir)?
9. (Hur, Her) name is Sarah.
10. The (nurse, nerse) smiled.
11. I will see you (after, aftur) class.
12. The dog ran (undir, under) the porch.
13. Write him a (letter, lettir).
14. She (niver, never) came.
15. I am a (purson, person).
16. We will go (together, togethir).
17. (Wintar, Winter) is here.

18. I (lurned, learned) my lesson.
19. Is it my (tirn, turn)?
20. What is (yur, your) name?
21. The (river, rivir) is too wide.
22. He is my (brothir, brother).
23. Your (dinnar, dinner) is cold now.
24. Can you (cerry, carry) it?
25. The (fer, fur) is soft.
26. Don't run (ovir, over) the bridge.
27. What did you (ordur, order)?
28. Let me take your (picture, pictere).
29. What (are, ere) you doing?
30. A rose is a (flower, flowir).
31. I missed (numbir, number) six.
32. This feels (bettur, better).
33. Call (before, befere) you come.
34. Can you spell the (wurd, word)?

The Apatosaurus

Study the spelling and meaning of each word. These words are used in today's story. Connect each word with its definition.

1. completely
2. describe
3. enormous
4. offered
5. proof
6. real

a. presented
b. tell about
c. evidence
d. fully; entirely
e. true; genuine
f. huge

Read the story carefully and remember the details.

If one word were needed to describe the apatosaurus (uh•pat′•uh•saw′•ruhs), it would be enormous. This dinosaur was the biggest of all, that is, the biggest for which there is any real proof.

For all its size, the apatosaurus was really quite harmless. Its teeth were blunt and weak. It ate the softest plants that grew in the water. In fact, it spent most of its life just standing in the water eating. It took a lot of plants to fill such a big animal.

The water offered the apatosaurus protection. In deep water the apatosaurus was safe from the flesh-eaters. The apatosaurus had nostrils on the top of its head so it could stand completely underwater.

At seventy feet the apatosaurus was the biggest animal to walk on land. Its name means "unreal lizard."

A. Underline the correct answers about today's story.

1. Which word describes the apatosaurus?   (a) minute   (b) dwarfish   (c) enormous
2. What did the apatosaurus eat?   (a) meat   (b) water plants   (c) eggs
3. The dinosaur spent most of its life   (a) in water   (b) in forests   (c) on land.
4. Against other dinosaurs, the apatosaurus was   (a) fierce   (b) helpless   (c) always a winner.
5. The name "apatosaurus" means   (a) "big lizard"   (b) "real lizard"   (c) "unreal lizard."

B. Reread the story and write the answers to these questions.

1. Where did the animal spend most of its time?

_____

_____

_____

2. Describe the animal's teeth.

_____

_____

_____

3. What did the animal's nostrils help it to do?

_____

_____

_____

4. How long could the dinosaur grow?

_____

_____

_____

Unit 10 cont'd ☞

Long and Short Vowel Sounds

What is the main vowel sound of each word?
For long vowels use ā, ē, ī, ō, or ū.
For short vowels use ă, ĕ, ĭ, ŏ, or ŭ.

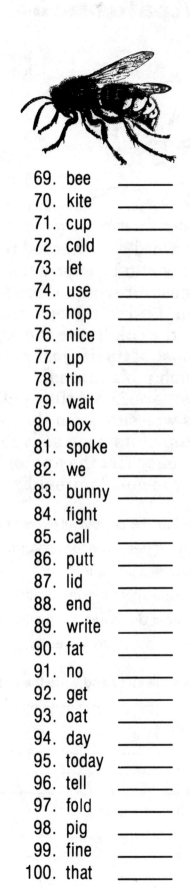

1. make   ā
2. me
3. cut
4. low
5. sad
6. age
7. sit
8. red
9. slide
10. own
11. pile
12. hat
13. beat
14. it
15. lake
16. met
17. hot
18. hose
19. fudge
20. fun
21. fire
22. farm
23. little
24. nose
25. jump
26. way
27. frog
28. best
29. people
30. hope
31. kind
32. man
33. wish
34. go

35. music
36. grade
37. bug
38. note
39. bite
40. net
41. had
42. sold
43. easy
44. sun
45. he
46. fit
47. right
48. weed
49. bat
50. know
51. under
52. base
53. wax
54. crop
55. size
56. step
57. sick
58. say
59. rug
60. home
61. pen
62. hill
63. very
64. nine
65. she
66. rock
67. like
68. egg

69. bee
70. kite
71. cup
72. cold
73. let
74. use
75. hop
76. nice
77. up
78. tin
79. wait
80. box
81. spoke
82. we
83. bunny
84. fight
85. call
86. putt
87. lid
88. end
89. write
90. fat
91. no
92. get
93. oat
94. day
95. today
96. tell
97. fold
98. pig
99. fine
100. that

Comprehension Check

Ⓐ Add the missing vowel(s).

1. Am _e_ ric _a_ n
2. we __ sel
3. f ___ rce
4. pock __ t
5. c __ ns __ sts
6. b __ rr __ wing
7. pat ___ ntly
8. sw __ mp
9. se __ son
10. bitt __ rn
11. fe __ th __ rs
12. __ lways
13. d __ tect
14. tr ___ bled
15. wap __ t __
16. mo __ nt __ in
17. pr __ tect
18. gr __ atly
19. meth __ d
20. sn __ tch
21. thr __ ugh
22. v __ llage
23. suff __ ci __ nt
24. fo __ nd
25. c __ mplet __ ly
26. d __ scr __ be
27. pr ___ f
28. dinos ___ r
29. h __ rml __ ss
30. und __ rw __ ter

Ⓑ Underline the words which begin with vowels.

1. <u>animals</u>
2. during
3. afternoon
4. cousin
5. excellent
6. powerful
7. own
8. badger
9. attacked
10. American
11. buff
12. illusive
13. rely
14. often
15. except
16. enemies
17. able
18. foe
19. approach
20. Indians
21. keen
22. detect
23. graze
24. reduced
25. antlers
26. insects
27. freely
28. ate
29. jungle
30. Africa
31. snatch
32. march
33. longer
34. enormous
35. size
36. offered
37. eating
38. all
39. lizard
40. unreal

Ⓒ Which words are spelled correctly? Underline them.

1. <u>weasel</u>, weesel
2. squrrels, squirrels
3. fierce, fearce
4. badgur, badger
5. rely, rily
6. bittern, bitturn
7. approach, upproach
8. swomp, swamp
9. graize, graze
10. trubled, troubled
11. montin, mountain
12. ensects, insects
13. depinds, depends
14. detours, detures
15. because, becuse
16. creatures, creetures
17. prufe, proof
18. really, reelly
19. hormless, harmless
20. describe, discribe

Ⓓ Underline the words which contain long vowel sounds.

1. <u>mice</u>
2. powerful
3. American
4. late
5. holes
6. frightened
7. tough
8. quite
9. buff
10. illusive
11. talent
12. loner
13. feathers
14. plumage
15. home
16. active
17. graze
18. reduced
19. keen
20. good
21. summer
22. insects
23. branching
24. freely
25. find
26. races
27. snatch
28. through
29. flush
30. waits
31. hiding
32. method
33. proof
34. real
35. which
36. harmless
37. plants
38. underwater
39. just
40. softest

Test 2 cont'd 👉

Comprehension Check (continued)

(E) **Match these words and their definitions. These words appeared in the reading selections from units 6-10.**

_j_ 1. prefers

___ 2. fierce

___ 3. buff

___ 4. illusive

___ 5. loner

___ 6. rely

___ 7. keen

___ 8. reduced

___ 9. find

___ 10. flush

___ 11. proof

___ 12. real

a. true; genuine

b. depend

c. ferocious

d. brownish yellow

e. deceptive

f. evidence

g. locate the place of

h. one who prefers being alone

i. to drive from cover

j. desires over something else

k. sharp

l. lessened

(F) **Underline the correct answers.**

1. When is the badger not peaceful?   (a) when attacked   (b) when hungry
2. What is a relative of the badger?   (a) weasel   (b) fox
3. Where is the bittern's home?   (a) swamp   (b) desert
4. When is the bittern most active?   (a) early daytime   (b) nighttime
5. What is the elk's weapon?   (a) hoofs   (b) antlers
6. Where do the elk go in winter?   (a) desert   (b) valleys
7. Where are antbirds found?   (a) South America   (b) Africa
8. What do antbirds follow?   (a) army ants   (b) the sun
9. What did the apatosaurus eat?   (a) water plants   (b) eggs
10. How long did the apatosaurus grow?   (a) seventy feet   (b) one hundred feet

Choose one of the following topics and write a paragraph.

(1) "Wapiti" is the Indian name for the American elk. Many words in the English language are actually foreign. List several and define them.

(2) Describe the antbird's method for finding food.

_____

_____

_____

_____

_____

_____

_____

_____

_____

_____

Asian Elephants

Study the spelling and meaning of each word. These words are used in today's story. Connect each word with its definition.

1. behaves
2. gentle
3. mainly
4. memory
5. nature
6. slightly

a. a small amount
b. primarily
c. character; disposition
d. mild; serene
e. acts; conducts itself
f. what one remembers

Read the story carefully and remember the details.

The Asian elephant is also called the Indian elephant. It is slightly smaller than its cousin, the African elephant.

The Asian elephant behaves much like the African elephant. It is mainly a forest animal. The Asian elephant travels less than the African one.

Many Asians use the elephant as a work animal. It has a gentle nature and is easily trained. For this reason the Asian elephant is often chosen for zoos and circuses.

The elephant rarely attacks people. It usually runs away from danger.

The old saying that an elephant never forgets is neither completely true nor completely false. An elephant does have a good memory and remembers those who were kind as well as those who were cruel.

A. Underline the correct answers about today's story.

1. Compared to the African elephant, the Asian elephant is   (a) bigger   (b) safe   (c) meaner.
2. The elephant's disposition is   (a) unpleasant   (b) offensive   (c) gentle.
3. When danger approaches, the elephant   (a) attacks   (b) runs away   (c) charges.
4. Where does the elephant live?   (a) forests   (b) desert   (c) mountains
5. An elephant never   (a) sleeps   (b) eats peanuts   (c) forgets

B. Reread the story and write the answers to these questions.

1. How do the Asians use the elephant?

_____
_____
_____

2. Why are Asian elephants often found in zoos?

_____
_____
_____

3. Which of the two elephants travels more?

_____
_____
_____

4. What does the elephant remember?

_____
_____
_____

Unit 11 cont'd ☞

Beginning Sounds

Write two words that begin with the same two-letter sound as the given one.

1. church
   a. ch ___*ain*___
   b. ch ___*eck*___
2. drop
   a. dr _____
   b. dr _____
3. clean
   a. cl _____
   b. cl _____
4. also
   a. al _____
   b. al _____
5. friend
   a. fr _____
   b. fr _____
6. shoe
   a. sh _____
   b. sh _____
7. cream
   a. cr _____
   b. cr _____
8. grape
   a. gr _____
   b. gr _____
9. quit
   a. qu _____
   b. qu _____
10. plain
    a. pl _____
    b. pl _____
11. score
    a. sc _____
    b. sc _____
12. know
    a. kn _____
    b. kn _____

13. tree
    a. tr _____
    b. tr _____
14. sky
    a. sk _____
    b. sk _____
15. story
    a. st _____
    b. st _____
16. flow
    a. fl _____
    b. fl _____
17. blue
    a. bl _____
    b. bl _____
18. glad
    a. gl _____
    b. gl _____
19. what
    a. wh _____
    b. wh _____
20. smoke
    a. sm _____
    b. sm _____
21. pretty
    a. pr _____
    b. pr _____
22. them
    a. th _____
    b. th _____
23. inside
    a. in _____
    b. in _____
24. often
    a. of _____
    b. of _____
25. report
    a. re _____
    b. re _____

26. snow
    a. sn _____
    b. sn _____
27. action
    a. ac _____
    b. ac _____
28. extra
    a. ex _____
    b. ex _____
29. enjoy
    a. en _____
    b. en _____
30. because
    a. be _____
    b. be _____
31. awful
    a. aw _____
    b. aw _____
32. space
    a. sp _____
    b. sp _____
33. improve
    a. im _____
    b. im _____
34. decide
    a. de _____
    b. de _____
35. unkind
    a. un _____
    b. un _____
36. onto
    a. on _____
    b. on _____
37. adverb
    a. ad _____
    b. ad _____
38. each
    a. ea _____
    b. ea _____

39. goat
    a. go _____
    b. go _____
40. sweet
    a. sw _____
    b. sw _____
41. high
    a. hi _____
    b. hi _____
42. measure
    a. me _____
    b. me _____
43. write
    a. wr _____
    b. wr _____
44. habit
    a. ha _____
    b. ha _____
45. television
    a. te _____
    b. te _____
46. road
    a. ro _____
    b. ro _____
47. hereby
    a. he _____
    b. he _____
48. lake
    a. la _____
    b. la _____
49. size
    a. si _____
    b. si _____
50. word
    a. wo _____
    b. wo _____

The Assyrians

Study the spelling and meaning of each word. These words are used in today's story. Connect each word with its definition.

1. change———————— a. variety
2. comfortably   b. not capable of being
3. impossible   c. knowing; well informed
4. intelligent   d. raising grazing animals
5. invent   e. to think up and devise
6. pasturing   f. in a satisfying way

Read the story carefully and remember the details.

The Assyrians were a farming and pasturing people that lived in the upper valley of the Tigris River. They were a very intelligent people who learned to live comfortably using what materials were available to them.

Assyria was a very warm country. The Assyrians were the first people to invent air conditioning. The richer Assyrians sat inside a thick wool tent. Servants poured water over the tent. They kept the tent wet. While the sun dried off the water, the inside of the tent was cool.

Assyrian houses had flat roofs. On hot nights Assyrians used the roofs to sleep on. The weather of Assyria wasn't always pleasing to the Assyrians, but they made the best of what was impossible to change.

A. Underline the correct answers about today's story.

1. Most Assyrians were   (a) fisherman   (b) farmers   (c) nomads.
2. The climate of Assyria was   (a) cold   (b) windy   (c) warm.
3. The first air conditioner was a (a) tent   (b) metal box   (c) grass hut.
4. On hot nights Assyrians slept   (a) under trees (b) near a river   (c) on the roof.
5. The Assyrians lived near the   (a) Tigris River (b) Nile River   (c) Amazon River.

B. Reread the story and write the answers to these questions.

1. What materials were used to live comfortably?

_____

_____

_____

2. What was invented by the Assyrians?

_____

_____

_____

3. What was the tent made of?

_____

_____

_____

4. Describe the roof of an Assyrian's house.

_____

_____

_____

Unit 12 cont'd ☞

Silent Letters

Silent letters are written but not pronounced.

A. Underline the words which contain silent letters.

1. <u>night</u>	16. hat	31. know	46. lost
2. baby	17. bright	32. never	47. folk
3. sign	18. life	33. cake	48. knew
4. mad	19. song	34. music	49. pan
5. knight	20. fun	35. mile	50. radio
6. we	21. thumb	36. lamb	51. could
7. ghost	22. me	37. taxi	52. plant
8. water	23. make	38. knife	53. wife
9. silent	24. island	39. cat	54. honor
10. stove	25. list	40. ink	55. trip
11. hit	26. would	41. knee	56. high
12. rock	27. it	42. box	57. leg
13. right	28. knot	43. write	58. wrong
14. show	29. bone	44. red	59. mind
15. value	30. sent	45. answer	60. note

B. Identify the silent letter or letters in each word.

1. often ___*t*___	14. thought _____	
2. stove _____	15. could _____	28. write _____
3. honor _____	16. cake _____	29. knee _____
4. climb _____	17. note _____	30. right _____
5. knit _____	18. knife _____	31. lake _____
6. high _____	19. wife _____	32. half _____
7. island _____	20. safe _____	33. should _____
8. calf _____	21. value _____	34. honest _____
9. know _____	22. sign _____	35. life _____
10. make _____	23. night _____	36. knock _____
11. echo _____	24. mouse _____	37. take _____
12. would _____	25. rode _____	38. light _____
13. thumb _____	26. wrist _____	39. ghost _____
	27. knight _____	40. side _____

The Aztecs

Study the spelling and meaning of each word. These words are used in today's story. Connect each word with its definition.

1. accomplished
2. conquered
3. highly
4. legend
5. powerful
6. search

a. very
b. defeated
c. strong
d. a story of an event
e. educated; polished
f. to explore

Read the story carefully and remember the details.

Long ago the Aztecs lived in Mexico. They were a highly intelligent and powerful group of people.

The legend of the Aztecs began when the people left their home in the desert to find a better place to live. Their chief god told them to search for a place until they found his sign. That sign was a rock from which a cactus grew.

The people wandered about for centuries. Finally they found their home. There was the rock. On the rock grew a cactus. On the cactus stood an eagle holding a live snake in its beak.

The Aztecs built their city. They were accomplished in war and government. Soon they conquered many of their neighbors and became the most powerful group of people in Mexico.

A. Underline the correct answers about today's story.

1. Where did the Aztecs live?　(a) Africa　(b) Mexico　(c) Spain
2. In the beginning the Aztecs' home was the　(a) mountains　(b) desert　(c) forest.
3. The chief god's sign was a　(a) rock and cactus　(b) rock and eagle　(c) eagle and snake.
4. After seeing the sign the Aztecs　(a) died　(b) went home　(c) built their city.
5. Which word does not describe the Aztecs?　(a) powerful　(b) intelligent　(c) weak

B. Reread the story and write the answers to these questions.

1. When did the legend of the Aztecs begin?

_____

_____

_____

2. When would the Aztecs stop looking for a place to live?

_____

_____

_____

3. How long did the people wander?

_____

_____

_____

4. What stood on the cactus?

_____

_____

_____

Unit 13 cont'd

Identifying Silent Letters

 Say each word softly. If the word contains any silent letters, write them in the blank. If the word has no silent letters, place a (✓) in the blank.

1. nap _____
2. wife _____
3. talk _____
4. two _____
5. fire _____
6. night _____
7. home _____
8. sand _____
9. knew _____
10. for _____
11. rope _____
12. think _____
13. live _____
14. bone _____
15. pens _____
16. give _____
17. cake _____
18. pond _____
19. light _____
20. man _____
21. high _____
22. make _____
23. ago _____
24. horse _____
25. knot _____
26. fun _____
27. before _____
28. win _____
29. bright _____
30. pipe _____
31. and _____
32. pole _____
33. city _____

34. open _____
35. cave _____
36. knife _____
37. long _____
38. game _____
39. calf _____
40. under _____
41. mark _____
42. walk _____
43. life _____
44. hole _____
45. east _____
46. right _____
47. no _____
48. sun _____
49. safe _____
50. star _____
51. lamb _____
52. know _____
53. mule _____
54. take _____
55. fudge _____
56. done _____
57. bus _____
58. dime _____
59. push _____
60. water _____
61. eight _____
62. race _____
63. wet _____
64. half _____
65. out _____
66. wrote _____
67. sigh _____

68. write _____
69. knee _____
70. never _____
71. snake _____
72. test _____
73. smoke _____
74. hero _____
75. brave _____
76. fight _____
77. gate _____
78. come _____
79. window _____
80. it _____
81. house _____
82. lake _____
83. red _____
84. mile _____
85. late _____
86. thumb _____
87. hide _____
88. tight _____
89. mouse _____
90. knob _____
91. find _____
92. comb _____
93. arm _____
94. with _____
95. none _____
96. knit _____
97. help _____
98. date _____
99. word _____
100. island _____

The Bandicoot

Study the spelling and meaning of each word. These words are used in today's story. Connect each word with its definition.

1. adaptable	a. surroundings
2. danger	a. hazard; risk
3. environment	c. capable of being made suitable
4. nocturnal	d. distinct kind of animal
5. relentlessly	e. pertaining to the night
6. species	f. in an unpitying way

Read the story carefully and remember the details.

Bandicoots are found in Australia and nearby islands. There are many kinds of bandicoots.

The bandicoot hops around on its hind legs like a kangaroo. Its front claws dig into the earth for food. These claws are also used to dig the animal's home.

A nocturnal animal, the bandicoot is highly adaptable to its environment. At night it hunts for food. The bandicoot's diet consists of worms, insects, mice, and roots. The bandicoot has a strange habit of beating its food on the ground before eating it.

The bandicoot was once hunted relentlessly for its meat and furry coat. Now it is protected by law, but many species of the bandicoot are in danger of extinction.

A. Underline the correct answers about today's story.

1. How does the bandicoot get
   around?   (a) crawls   (b) hops   (c) runs

2. At night the bandicoot   (a) hides   (b) sleeps   (c) hunts food.

3. Before eating, the bandicoot   (a) beats its food   (b) washes its food   (c) cooks its food.

4. The bandicoot is a native of   (a) Australia   (b) Canada   (c) the United States.

5. "Relentlessly" means   (a) "carefully"   (b) "with control"   (c) "without mercy."

B. Reread the story and write the answers to these questions.

1. How does the bandicoot move about?

   _____

   _____

   _____

2. Name two uses for the animal's claws.

   _____

   _____

   _____

3. Why was the bandicoot hunted?

   _____

   _____

   _____

4. What threatens some species of the animal?

   _____

   _____

   _____

Unit 14 cont'd ☛

The "ǝr" Ending

The "ǝr" ending may be spelled three ways.

-er   *writer*   *stranger*   *winter*

-ar   *cellar*   *collar*   *regular*

-or   *doctor*   *tractor*   *humor*

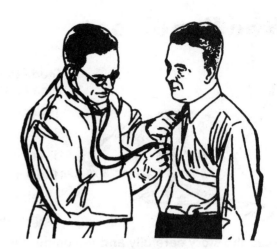

A. Supply the correct spellings of the "ǝr" endings.

1. whisp _er_
2. arm ____
3. particul ____
4. rath ____
5. flav ____
6. daught ____
7. maj ____
8. surrend ____
9. cent ____
10. edit ____

11. prison ____
12. terr ____
13. alt ____
14. forev ____
15. deliv ____
16. od ____
17. bewild ____
18. vig ____
19. newspap ____
20. chatt ____

21. summ ____
22. err ____
23. discov ____
24. ord ____
25. popul ____
26. famili ____
27. remaind ____
28. laught ____
29. may ____
30. publish ____

31. horr ____
32. prosp ____
33. eag ____
34. simil ____
35. unfamili ____
36. hunt ____
37. partn ____
38. protect ____
39. togeth ____
40. mirr ____

B. Complete each sentence with a word from part A.

1. Every _summer_ my family and I go to Florida.
2. Dianna is very _____ with everyone at school.
3. The _____ will try to escape at midnight tonight.
4. When did Christopher Columbus _____ America?
5. Mr. Samson has one _____ and three sons.
6. After dinner my parents relax and read the _____.
7. _____ the secret in my ear.
8. Anthony is my _____ for the science project.
9. Mike's uncle works for a magazine _____.
10. Will you _____ this package to Dr. Robinson?
11. We will work _____ as a team.
12. Parts of John's story sound _____.
13. Chocolate is my favorite _____ of ice cream.
14. Allen looked in the _____ while he combed his hair.
15. The _____ of the money will be donated to charity.

36

Basilisks

Study the spelling and meaning of each word. These words are used in today's story. Connect each word with its definition.

1. ability
2. balancing
3. characteristic
4. functions
5. length
6. peculiar

a. equalizing
b. distinguishing feature
c. normal action of something
d. distinctive
e. how long something is
f. power to do

Read the story carefully and remember the details.

The basilisk is a peculiar lizard which lives in South America and Central America. When the basilisk is in a hurry, it rises on its hind legs and runs. Its long tail functions as a balancing device.

The most unusual characteristic of the basilisk is its ability to walk on water. The lizard's feet are large, and its body is light. Because of its great speed, the lizard is able to skim across the surface of water. If the basilisk slows down, it sinks into the water. The basilisk is also a good swimmer.

The basilisk is a large lizard. It grows to be about three feet long. Most of the length is the lizard's tail.

Many people fear the basilisk because they think the lizard is dangerous. The basilisk is really harmless.

A. **Underline the correct answers about today's story.**

1. The basilisk is a   (a) snake   (b) lizard   (c) fish.
2. To move faster, the basilisk   (a) glides   (b) flies   (c) runs on its hind legs.
3. The basilisk is able to walk on   (a) water   (b) hot sand   (c) quicksand.
4. Most of the basilisk is   (a) fat   (b) its head   (c) its tail.
5. Which word describes the basilisk?   (a) dangerous   (b) harmless   (c) slow

B. **Reread the story and write the answers to these questions.**

1. Where does the basilisk live?

_____

_____

_____

2. What is the function of the lizard's tail?

_____

_____

_____

3. How long does the basilisk grow?

_____

_____

_____

4. How do many people feel about the lizard?

_____

_____

_____

Unit 15 cont'd ☞

The " əl" Ending

There are six ways to spell the " əl" ending.

"el" as in "bushel"   "al" as in "hospital"
"ul" as in "careful"   "ol" as in "pistol"
"le" as in "trouble"   "il" as in "pencil"

A. Complete each word with the correct spelling.

1. funn _el_
2. nation ____
3. unc ____
4. cast ____
5. purp ____
6. grav ____
7. turt ____
8. riv ____
9. leg ____
10. speci ____
11. anim ____
12. triang ____

13. examp ____
14. ridd ____
15. barr ____
16. app ____
17. surviv ____
18. nick ____
19. cam ____
20. nation ____
21. tab ____
22. dev ____
23. batt ____
24. valuab ____

25. pick ____
26. nov ____
27. pudd ____
28. need ____
29. sprink ____
30. shov ____
31. freck ____
32. kenn ____
33. buck ____
34. trav ____
35. chann ____
36. loc ____

37. eag ____
38. illeg ____
39. eas ____
40. musc ____
41. knuck ____
42. tick ____
43. terrib ____
44. norm ____
45. ment ____
46. commerci ____
47. tunn ____
48. tit ____

B. Complete each sentence with a word from part A.

1. A _triangle_ has three sides.
2. My _____ is a rancher.
3. I'll help you _____ the snow.
4. I'm reading a _____ about war.
5. He fell in a mud _____.
6. Bring me a _____ and thread.
7. _____ is my favorite color.
8. I made a _____ dessert for you.
9. Put the bag on the _____.
10. What is the _____ of the book?

11. A _____ needs little water.
12. I want a dill _____.
13. Stealing is _____.
14. Gene was eating an _____.
15. _____ his feet with a feather.
16. Our team's _____ is the Lions.
17. A _____ is five cents.
18. The jewel is very _____.
19. Henry plans to _____ to Europe.
20. Turn the television to _____ two.

Comprehension Check

(A) What is the beginning sound of each word?

_b_	1. bandicoot	___	6. people	___	11. acre	___	16. garage
___	2. sound	___	7. elephants	___	12. basilisks	___	17. teeth
___	3. various	___	8. ocean	___	13. reading	___	18. house
___	4. count	___	9. desert	___	14. fish	___	19. music
___	5. never	___	10. ice	___	15. listen	___	20. summer

(B) Identify the silent letter(s) in each word.

1. wrong _w_	11. night ___	21. salmon ___
2. lamb ___	12. bridge ___	22. write ___
3. knew ___	13. scissors ___	23. comb ___
4. condemn ___	14. debt ___	24. window ___
5. dumb ___	15. line ___	25. sigh ___
6. talk ___	16. know ___	26. gnu ___
7. wrist ___	17. walk ___	27. badge ___
8. ridge ___	18. autumn ___	28. knit ___
9. knee ___	19. knead ___	29. thumb ___
10. shadow ___	20. high ___	30. tomb ___

(C) Spell the " ə r" ending of each word.

1. weath _er_	11. lawy ___
2. pap ___	12. pitch ___
3. farm ___	13. doct ___
4. riv ___	14. auth ___
5. whisp ___	15. butl ___
6. bright ___	16. tart ___
7. may ___	17. read ___
8. flow ___	18. nev ___
9. listen ___	19. mot ___
10. sist ___	20. lay ___

(D) Spell the " ə l" ending of each word.

1. whist _le_	11. vow ___
2. wrink ___	12. reg ___
3. tow ___	13. troub ___
4. app ___	14. nov ___
5. shov ___	15. cor ___
6. knuck ___	16. litt ___
7. need ___	17. music ___
8. coup ___	18. puzz ___
9. dent ___	19. comic ___
10. plur ___	20. jing ___

(E) Complete these sentences.

1. The Assyrians invented _air conditioning_ .
2. The basilisk is a _____ .
3. Bandicoots live in _____ .
4. Many Asians use elephants as _____ animals.
5. The Aztec's sign was a rock from which a _____ grew.
6. Long ago the Aztecs lived in _____ .
7. Assyrians were a _____ people.
8. To get around, bandicoots _____ .
9. The Asian elephant is also called the _____ elephant.
10. The basilisk is able to walk on _____ .

Test 3 cont'd ☞

Comprehension Check (continued)

(F) Match these words and their definitions. These words appeared in the reading selections from units 11-15.

_a_ 1. mainly   ____ 7. danger

____ 2. memory   ____ 8. nocturnal

____ 3. intelligent   ____ 9. ability

____ 4. invent   ____ 10. balancing

____ 5. accomplished   ____ 11. characteristic

____ 6. conquered   ____ 12. functions

a. primarily

b. hazard; risk

c. knowing; well informed

d. defeated

e. equalizing

f. pertaining to the night

g. what one remembers

h. distinguishing feature

i. to think up and devise

j. educated; polished

k. power to do

l. normal action of something

(G) Underline the correct answers.

1. Where does the elephant live?   (a) <u>forests</u>   (b) mountains
2. How is the Asian elephant used?   (a) for food   (b) work animal
3. What was invented by the Assyrians?   (a) air-conditioning   (b) farming tools
4. Describe the roof of an Assyrian house.   (a) flat   (b) peaked
5. Where did the Aztecs live?   (a) Spain   (b) Mexico
6. How long did the Aztecs wander?   (a) centuries   (b) eight years
7. Why was the bandicoot hunted?   (a) furry coat   (b) claws
8. How does the bandicoot move about?   (a) hops   (b) slithers
9. Which word describes the basilisk?   (a) slow   (b) harmless
10. Where does the basilisk live?   (a) Central America   (b) Canada

Choose one of the following topics and write a paragraph.

(1) Elephants are often found in circuses. Describe a circus. What do you like best about a circus and why?

(2) Animals in zoos are constantly watched by people walking by. Write a creative paragraph about what one particular animal might think as it is being watched. Select any animal you like.

_____

_____

_____

_____

_____

_____

_____

_____

The Basking Shark Unit 16

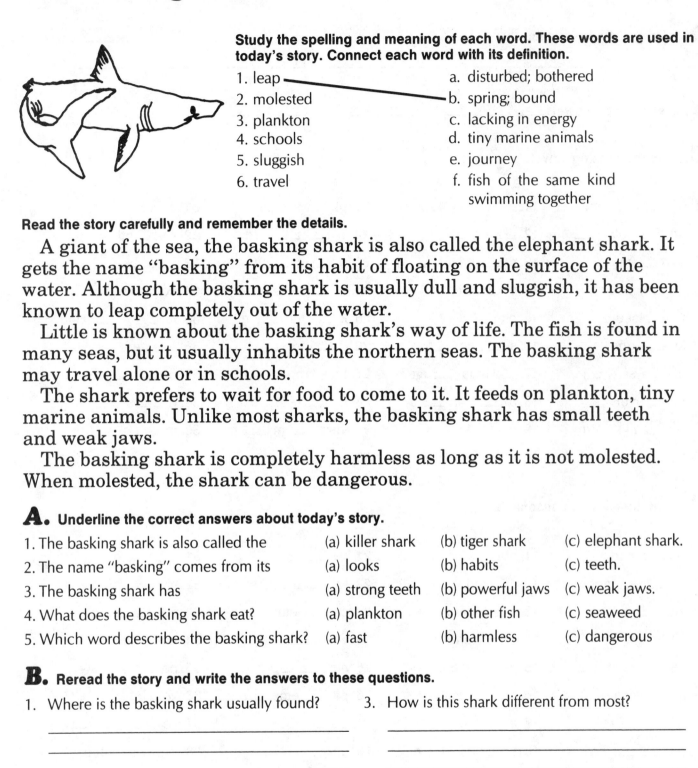

Study the spelling and meaning of each word. These words are used in today's story. Connect each word with its definition.

1. leap
2. molested
3. plankton
4. schools
5. sluggish
6. travel

a. disturbed; bothered
b. spring; bound
c. lacking in energy
d. tiny marine animals
e. journey
f. fish of the same kind swimming together

Read the story carefully and remember the details.

A giant of the sea, the basking shark is also called the elephant shark. It gets the name "basking" from its habit of floating on the surface of the water. Although the basking shark is usually dull and sluggish, it has been known to leap completely out of the water.

Little is known about the basking shark's way of life. The fish is found in many seas, but it usually inhabits the northern seas. The basking shark may travel alone or in schools.

The shark prefers to wait for food to come to it. It feeds on plankton, tiny marine animals. Unlike most sharks, the basking shark has small teeth and weak jaws.

The basking shark is completely harmless as long as it is not molested. When molested, the shark can be dangerous.

A. Underline the correct answers about today's story.

1. The basking shark is also called the   (a) killer shark   (b) tiger shark   (c) elephant shark.
2. The name "basking" comes from its   (a) looks   (b) habits   (c) teeth.
3. The basking shark has   (a) strong teeth   (b) powerful jaws   (c) weak jaws.
4. What does the basking shark eat?   (a) plankton   (b) other fish   (c) seaweed
5. Which word describes the basking shark?   (a) fast   (b) harmless   (c) dangerous

B. Reread the story and write the answers to these questions.

1. Where is the basking shark usually found?

_____

_____

_____

2. What two ways does the shark travel?

_____

_____

_____

3. How is this shark different from most?

_____

_____

_____

4. When is the shark dangerous?

_____

_____

_____

Unit 16 cont'd ☞

Vowels and Consonants

A. List the 21 consonants. _____

_____

B. List the main vowels. _____

C. Add the missing vowels.

1. v _i_ s _i_ tor
2. ch __ colat __
3. wh __ m
4. l __ b __ rty
5. m __ seum
6. kn __ ght
7. sc __ ss __ rs
8. m __ rror
9. pr __ bl __ m
10. t __ m __ rr __ w

11. c __ mer __
12. __ nough
13. s __ ndw __ ch
14. p __ blic
15. gh __ st
16. s __ cc __ ss
17. __ mus __ ment
18. h __ ndr __ d
19. c __ py
20. t __ xi

21. pl __ t __
22. w __ z __ rd
23. d __ z __ n
24. z __ ne
25. k __ tch __ n
26. c __ rcl __
27. f __ rn __ ture
28. m __ s __ c
29. instr __ m __ nt
30. sh __ d __ w

31. q __ __ ck
32. n __ nth
33. l __ br __ ry
34. sc __ r __
35. m __ g __ zine
36. __ pera
37. pr __ __ f
38. d __ s __ rt
39. m __ st __ ry
40. cl __ th __ ng

D. Add the missing consonants.

1. hea _v_ en
2. di __ __ ance
3. stu __ __ orn
4. e __ ge
5. ma __ eria __
6. si __ ewa __ __
7. e __ __ ra
8. pa __ __ ern
9. __ __ oulder
10. co __ __ on

11. ou __ __
12. __ lind
13. s __ uare
14. __ itizen
15. g __ oce __ y
16. pa __ ace
17. e __ ual
18. s __ ien __ e
19. fo __ __ ive
20. bu __ iness

21. na __ ion
22. fu __ u __ e
23. ca __ ete __ ia
24. wi __ __ er
25. em __ __ y
26. pa __ eme __ __
27. jea __ ous
28. uni __
29. le __ el
30. a __ __ ange

31. __ __ eed
32. me __ ici __ e
33. au __ __ or
34. to __ el
35. na __ __ ow
36. vo __ e
37. ye __ __ erday
38. __ o __ ads
39. __ unshi __ e
40. __ ee __ ive

E. What two consonants are sometimes used as vowels? _____

42

Bedouin Arabs **Unit 17**

Study the spelling and meaning of each word. These words are used in today's story. Connect each word with its definition.

1. constantly	a. pursuit
2. members	b. facing
3. primitive	c. without stopping
4. search	d. of the earliest times
5. toward	e. those who belong to something
6. treasure	f. prize

Read the story carefully and remember the details.

Arabia is a hot and dry country where it hardly ever rains. Most of Arabia is desert.

Bedouin Arabs move about the desert in search of grass and water. They do not stay in one place for very long. Some people call the Bedouins the only true Arabs because of their primitive way of life.

The Bedouins treasure camels. They constantly guard their camels from other Arab thieves.

Some members of the group scout ahead for grass and water. The others follow their lead. When they find water, they set up camp. The Bedouins live in tents made of black goat hair. The back of the tent is toward the wind to keep sand from blowing in.

A. Underline the correct answers about today's story.

1. Which word describes Arabia? (a) cold (b) wet (c) dry
2. Most of Arabia is (a) mountains (b) desert (c) water.
3. The Bedouins treasure the (a) camel (b) sun (c) goat.
4. The Bedouins live in (a) stone huts (b) palaces (c) tents.
5. Which word describes the Bedouins? (a) modern (b) primitive (c) lazy

B. Reread the story and write the answers to these questions.

1. What do the Bedouin Arabs search?

_____

_____

_____

2. Why do some people call the Bedouins the only true Arabs?

_____

_____

_____

3. What is their home?

_____

_____

_____

4. How is their home positioned and why?

_____

_____

_____

Unit 17 cont'd ☞

Arranging Letters into a Word

The letters in a word are arranged in a definite order.

A. Unscramble each group of letters
to form a word.

1. giwn ___wing___
2. rfma _____
3. rtwei _____
4. ese _____
5. lwla _____
6. snig _____
7. kobo _____
8. erda _____
9. lkei _____
10. ksy _____
11. whso _____
12. tca _____
13. rac _____
14. kdse _____
15. hfsi _____
16. ntwo _____
17. phle _____
18. emho _____
19. nwok _____
20. enw _____

21. kate _____
22. owod _____
23. pnoe _____
24. ooz _____
25. tiwh _____
26. nuf _____
27. odrw _____
28. ppaer _____
29. fael _____
30. neli _____
31. lelt _____
32. nca _____
33. rfie _____
34. vrrie _____
35. droa _____
36. leub _____
37. kmae _____
38. eter _____
39. yee _____
40. fsto _____

41. ainr _____
42. wsno _____
43. ymna _____
44. mrof _____
45. nbar _____
46. vaec _____
47. nsu _____
48. eht _____
49. hswi _____
50. dwni _____
51. lslam _____
52. rglae _____
53. esbt _____
54. uyo _____
55. psto _____
56. ebtla _____
57. ehro _____
58. rmeo _____
59. lypa _____
60. omec _____

B. Complete each sentence by unscrambling
the word in parentheses.

(sucmi) 1. Do you like the ___music___?
(rweat) 2. Drink some _____.
(lweofr) 3. Who picked the _____?
(tseret) 4. I live across the _____.
(reibdg) 5. We must cross the _____.
(rftui) 6. An apple is a _____.
(eclpni) 7. I need a _____.
(glhits) 8. Turn on the _____.
(drneif) 9. He is my _____.
(coshlo) 10. Jan went to _____.

(gdrnae) 11. We planted a _____.
(tretel) 12. Mail this _____.
(ntari) 13. She rode the _____.
(gbein) 14. You may _____ now.
(puritec) 15. This is his _____.
(mseil) 16. Will you _____?
(lylweo) 17. I ride a _____ bus.
(cotdro) 18. My neighbor is a _____.
(toermh) 19. Ask your _____.
(higet) 20. He has _____ sisters.

44

Beehive Houses

Study the spelling and meaning of each word. These words are used in today's story. Connect each word with its definition.

1. abundant
2. almost
3. brighter
4. collected
5. smoother
6. spread

a. nearly
b. plentiful
c. gathered
d. more radiant
e. distributed
f. less rough

Read the story carefully and remember the details.

Beehive houses were first made by Italians who lived in the southern part of Italy. The builders collected loose stones which were abundant in the area. The stones were used to build thick stone walls. No mortar or cement held the stones together. The walls were built in a circle until they came almost to a point at the top. Some beehive houses are still used today.

Some owners did not sweep the roof. Dust collected so heavily that sometimes grass and flowers grew on the roof.

Inside the home the walls were often painted white. The white walls made the rooms brighter for there were few windows. The floor was of stone. Grass was spread over the floor to make it smoother.

A. Underline the correct answers about today's story.

1. Beehive houses were first made by the   (a) Greeks   (b) Russians   (c) Italians.
2. Beehive houses were made of   (a) grass   (b) stones   (c) mud.
3. What shape was the house?   (a) square   (b) circle   (c) triangle
4. What made the room brighter?   (a) hole in roof   (b) big windows   (c) white walls
5. What was used to cover the floor?   (a) grass   (b) mud   (c) flat stones

B. Reread the story and write the answers to these questions.

1. Where did the builders of the beehive houses live?

_____

_____

_____

2. What was often on the roof?

_____

_____

3. What was the floor made of?

_____

_____

_____

4. What was the purpose of the floor covering?

_____

_____

_____

Unit 18 cont'd ☛

Word Building

Make new words by changing the beginning of each word.

EXAMPLES: *pair   hair   fair*

a. may
1. ____ay
2. ____ay
3. ____ay
4. ____ay
5. ____ay

b. rat
6. ____at
7. ____at
8. ____at
9. ____at
10. ____at

c. bad
11. ____ad
12. ____ad
13. ____ad
14. ____ad
15. ____ad

d. best
16. ____est
17. ____est
18. ____est
19. ____est
20. ____est

e. cow
21. ____ow
22. ____ow
23. ____ow
24. ____ow
25. ____ow

f. cold
26. ____old
27. ____old
28. ____old
29. ____old
30. ____old

g. bake
31. ____ake
32. ____ake
33. ____ake
34. ____ake
35. ____ake

h. park
36. ____ark
37. ____ark
38. ____ark
39. ____ark
40. ____ark

i. none
41. ____one
42. ____one
43. ____one
44. ____one
45. ____one

j. cross
46. ____oss
47. ____oss
48. ____oss
49. ____oss
50. ____oss

k. pen
51. ____en
52. ____en
53. ____en
54. ____en
55. ____en

l. met
56. ____et
57. ____et
58. ____et
59. ____et
60. ____et

m. head
61. ____ead
62. ____ead
63. ____ead
64. ____ead
65. ____ead

n. need
66. ____eed
67. ____eed
68. ____eed
69. ____eed
70. ____eed

o. light
71. ____ight
72. ____ight
73. ____ight
74. ____ight
75. ____ight

p. call
76. ____all
77. ____all
78. ____all
79. ____all
80. ____all

q. place
81. ____ace
82. ____ace
83. ____ace
84. ____ace
85. ____ace

r. care
86. ____are
87. ____are
88. ____are
89. ____are
90. ____are

s. sound
91. ____ound
92. ____ound
93. ____ound
94. ____ound
95. ____ound

t. flowers
96. ____owers
97. ____owers
98. ____owers
99. ____owers
100. ____owers

The Black Rhinoceros

Study the spelling and meaning of each word. These words are used in today's story. Connect each word with its definition.

1. fortunate   a. lacking
2. keen   b. treasured
3. poor   c. lucky
4. prized   d. perception
5. readily   e. sharp
6. sense   f. willingly

Read the story carefully and remember the details.

In the brushy country of central and southern Africa lives the black rhinoceros. A big animal, the black rhinoceros is aggressive. It can be very dangerous, readily attacking man and even moving vehicles. The two horns on its head are powerful weapons.

The black rhinoceros has a keen sense of hearing which is fortunate since its eyesight is very poor. Its tiny eyes are surrounded by deep folds of skin.

The mother rhinoceros is a loving parent. She ferociously defends her young from all dangers.

The rhinoceros has always been hunted. Its meat is edible, and its hide is used in making many products. The most prized part of the rhinoceros is its horns.

A. Underline the correct answers about today's story.

1. Which word describes the rhinoceros?   (a) aggressive   (b) friendly   (c) shy
2. The rhinoceros has a keen sense of   (a) sight   (b) smell   (c) hearing.
3. As a parent, the mother is   (a) lazy   (b) loving   (c) unfit.
4. The rhino's weapon is its   (a) size   (b) hoofs   (c) horns.
5. The prized part of the rhinoceros is the   (a) meat   (b) horns   (c) hide.

B. Reread the story and write the answers to these questions.

1. Where does the black rhino live?

_____

_____

2. Name two things the rhinoceros might attack.

_____

_____

3. Describe the rhino's eyesight.

_____

_____

4. Name two reasons the animal is hunted.

_____

_____

Unit 19 cont'd

Writing Words

Arrange each set of letters into a word.

1. clwno   *clown*
2. udm
3. pnoe
4. nbka
5. sbuy
6. wno
7. ttelbo
8. rwrao
9. wte
10. lsseon
11. cmap
12. lljey
13. dnaec
14. tsneo
15. orcnre
16. hdie
17. rcko
18. gwor
19. cheo
20. eewlh
21. mkea
22. efre
23. dwro
24. dmni
25. rclae
26. nvree
27. tjsu
28. miet
29. vtsii
30. ysk
31. wtaer
32. nta
33. brid
34. fncee

35. thwi
36. reeht
37. ingeb
38. nosei
39. xmi
40. aneol
41. eht
42. ghhi
43. nsog
44. thnig
45. etnh
46. waay
47. teroh
48. ookl
49. vrrie
50. dtoay
51. drmea
52. flga
53. nnfyu
54. hvae
55. pemty
56. oospn
57. sreett
58. ycti
59. oorm
60. otu
61. mslie
62. ntaw
63. atls
64. oen
65. kwno
66. rryca
67. lphe
68. htwa

69. smlla
70. oochse
71. ghtli
72. rwok
73. pcsae
74. rtfiu
75. yver
76. ttllie
77. pnnye
78. mnyoe
79. bleta
80. fdni
81. turlte
82. finred
83. flerow
84. btahi
85. llyeow
86. nmalia
87. bccyile
88. rdnou
89. wgaon
90. oomn
91. tsra
92. veol
93. ppera
94. oofd
95. klea
96. ebe
97. twia
98. afrm
99. atuo
100. wton

The Black Widow

Study the spelling and meaning of each word. These words are used in today's story. Connect each word with its definition.

1. avoids	a. result
2. effect	b. companion
3. lessens	c. shy
4. mate	d. reduces
5. timid	e. keeps clear of
6. usually	f. most often

Read the story carefully and remember the details.

Of all spiders in the world, the black widow has earned a reputation as a deadly foe. In reality, however, the widow's poison is rarely fatal to humans, although it is serious. If the wound is properly treated, the ill effect soon lessens.

The black widow does not get her name from her poisonous bite. The name comes from the fact that the female black widow sometimes kills her mate.

The widow's web is usually close to the ground. The web is always found in a dark location.

Like other spiders the black widow is timid. It avoids contact with people. If it is hurt or frightened, however, it inflicts its bite.

The spider is more helpful than most people realize. It destroys many insects.

A. Underline the correct answers about today's story.

1. The black widow has a reputation as a   (a) foe   (b) friend   (c) helper.
2. The widow's bite is rarely   (a) harmful   (b) painful   (c) fatal.
3. The widow's web is always   (a) in a sunny place   (b) underground   (c) in a dark place.
4. Spiders are helpful because they   (a) spin webs   (b) eat insects   (c) dislike humans.
5. Unless threatened, the widow is   (a) very shy   (b) aggressive   (c) friendly.

B. Reread the story and write the answers to these questions.

1. What happens if a spider bite is treated?

_____

_____

_____

2. Where does the widow's name come from?

_____

_____

3. What does the black widow avoid?

_____

_____

_____

4. When does the spider attack?

_____

_____

_____

Unit 20 cont'd ☞

Adding Letters to Make New Words

 Add the letter or letters to the given word. Then write the new word in the blank to complete each sentence.

1. g + round
   The __ground__ is too wet.

2. new + s
   Did you hear the _____?

3. heal + th
   I have lost my _____ book.

4. b + ranch
   That _____ is too weak.

5. sp + ring
   Flowers bloom in the _____.

6. non + sense
   All of this is _____.

7. yell + ow
   Sam bought a _____ hat.

8. f + lower
   A daisy is a _____.

9. s + care
   Ghosts _____ me.

10. ho + nest
    She seems _____ to me.

11. p + each
    The _____ is not ripe.

12. a + cross
    We drove _____ the bridge.

13. p + rice
    What is the _____ of the car?

14. t + rust
    Can we _____ him?

15. s + mile
    Do you ever _____?

16. car + toon
    The _____ made me laugh.

17. b + us
    I will ride the _____ home.

18. w + itch
    I play the part of the _____.

19. c + over
    The _____ is bright green.

20. us + e
    Don't _____ Ken's tools.

21. of + f
    Turn the lights _____.

22. en + joy
    Did you _____ the game?

23. c + old
    The weather is turning _____.

24. b + right
    The light is too _____.

25. a + sleep
    Are you _____ yet?

26. w + ink
    I saw you _____ at him.

27. st + and
    _____ in the corner.

28. c + lock
    Does that _____ work?

29. hop + e
    I _____ Alice wins.

30. d + own
    Did you write _____ the number?

31. n + ever
    Henry has _____ seen a cow.

32. k + now
    I _____ all of the answers.

33. m + any
    Dave has _____ friends.

Comprehension Check

(A) Add the vowels.

1. _a_ ble
2. j ___ lly
3. r ___ ce
4. ___ cean
5. ___ pper
6. ___ mbrella
7. c ___ mmon
8. wh ___ te
9. l ___ tters
10. v ___ wels
11. sp ___ der
12. r ___ sh
13. sh ___ rk
14. bl ___ ck
15. beeh ___ ves
16. f ___ mous
17. ___ dentify
18. bl ___ nder
19. ___ nding
20. rhin ___ ceros

(B) Add the consonants.

1. _m_ oney
2. ___ inutes
3. ___ ouses
4. ___ idow
5. a ___ imal
6. de ___ ert
7. sta ___ ion
8. ___ ight
9. te ___ evision
10. ___ onsonant
11. ___ edicine
12. ___ aseball
13. ___ orth
14. ___ icycle
15. ___ uilding
16. ___ istory
17. e ___ tra
18. ___ agazine
19. ___ umber
20. cho ___ olate

(C) Arrange each set of letters into a word.

1. wsho _show_
2. xta _____
3. kcne _____
4. tbael _____
5. snwe _____
6. erlya _____
7. vfie _____
8. poen _____
9. rdao _____
10. lsmei _____
11. tmae _____
12. sholco _____
13. thngi _____
14. mage _____
15. rstoe _____
16. mtha _____
17. sett _____
18. syea _____
19. wdin _____
20. dogo _____
21. yllewo _____
22. psetor _____
23. sdtunet _____
24. rtseet _____
25. ftoers _____
26. tyic _____
27. weart _____
28. iemt _____
29. seatt _____
30. wteir _____

(D) Read each definition. Then unscramble the word.

1. the state or condition of being free — drefemo — _freedom_
2. very pleasing to taste or smell — dliicesou — _____
3. of or having to do with the United States — micanAre — _____
4. a man who is honorable and well-bred — mgetlenna — _____
5. having to do with electricity — eericltc — _____
6. the inner surface or part — tinerrio — _____
7. to observe a special time or day — bcleeraet — _____
8. the written story of a person's life — bogphyria — _____

(E) Complete these sentences.

1. The black widow has a reputation as a ___ _deadly_ ___ foe.
2. Most of Arabia is _____ .
3. Beehive houses were first made in _____ .
4. The black rhinoceros has excellent _____ .
5. The basking shark is also called the _____ shark.
6. The most prized part of the rhinoceros is its _____ .
7. The basking shark feeds on _____ .
8. The black widow is a _____ .
9. Bedouins treasure their _____ .
10. The walls of a beehive house form a _____ .

51

Test 4 cont'd ☞

Comprehension Check (continued)

(F) Match these words and their definitions. These words appeared in the reading selections from units 16-20.

_g_ 1. leap   ___ 7. collected

___ 2. molested   ___ 8. keen

___ 3. plankton   ___ 9. readily

___ 4. constantly   ___ 10. avoids

___ 5. toward   ___ 11. mate

___ 6. abundant   ___ 12. timid

a. tiny marine animals

b. gathered

c. without stopping

d. sharp

e. facing

f. companion

g. spring; bound

h. plentiful

i. willingly

j. shy

k. disturbed; bothered

l. keeps clear of

(G) Underline the correct answers.

1. What is another name for the basking shark?   (a) killer shark   (b) <u>elephant shark</u>
2. What does the basking shark eat?   (a) plankton   (b) other fish
3. What do Bedouin Arabs treasure?   (a) camels   (b) the sun
4. How are the Bedouins described?   (a) primitive   (b) lazy
5. Who first made beehive houses?   (a) Italians   (b) Romans
6. What was used to cover the floor?   (a) flat stones   (b) grass
7. How does the rhinoceros protect itself?   (a) horns   (b) hoofs
8. Describe the rhino's eyesight.   (a) keen   (b) poor
9. Where are black widow's webs?   (a) sunny porches   (b) dark places
10. Describe the black widow's personality.   (a) timid   (b) friendly

Choose one of the following topics and write a paragraph.

(1) The Bedouin Arabs used camels for transportation; people today use various animals for different reasons. Write about four animals and how they are used.

(2) Describe a beehive house.

(3) How does the black widow spider get her name?

_____

_____

_____

_____

_____

_____

_____

_____

_____

Blackfoot Indians

Study the spelling and meaning of each word. These words are used in today's story. Connect each word with its definition.

1. changed
2. crude
3. ornaments
4. settlers

5. wandered
6. weapons

a. fighting instruments
b. altered
c. decorations
d. persons who make homes in a new place
e. rough or clumsy
f. roamed

Read the story carefully and remember the details.

Before white settlers began moving across the Great Plains, the Blackfoot Indians wandered over the land. They traveled in small groups and carried with them their tents and supplies.

The Blackfoot Indians' tools and weapons were crude. Their arrow points and knives were made of stone. Their spoons and cups were made of buffalo horns. Their bowls were made of wood.

The Blackfoot Indians wore clothes made of deerskins. They wore ornaments of bear claws or buffalo teeth.

The Blackfoot Indians hunted the buffalo on foot. They drove the herd over a cliff. Until the white settlers came, the Blackfoot Indians were people of the open country. Their lives changed completely with the arrival of the white man.

A. Underline the correct answers about today's story.

1. Where did the Blackfoot live?   (a) Mexico   (b) Great Plains   (c) desert
2. The knives were made of   (a) wood   (b) teeth   (c) stone.
3. Clothes were made of   (a) deerskins   (b) grass   (c) feathers.
4. The Blackfoot hunted the   (a) buffalo   (b) eagle   (c) horse.
5. What changed their way of life?   (a) weather   (b) food supply   (c) white settlers

B. Reread the story and write the answers to these questions.

1. When did the Blackfoot Indians wander the Great Plains?

   _____

   _____

   _____

2. How did the Blackfoot Indians travel?

   _____

   _____

3. Describe their tools and weapons.

   _____

   _____

   _____

4. What items were made of bear claws or buffalo teeth?

   _____

   _____

   _____

Unit 21 cont'd ☞

Singular and Plural

"Singular" means "one."
"Plural" means "more than one."

A. Write "s" for singular and "p" for plural.

_p_ 1. facts	___ 16. offices	___ 31. mice	___ 46. minutes
___ 2. newspaper	___ 17. piano	___ 32. opinion	___ 47. voice
___ 3. promises	___ 18. reward	___ 33. secrets	___ 48. halves
___ 4. adventures	___ 19. vacations	___ 34. ponies	___ 49. matches
___ 5. potato	___ 20. boxes	___ 35. books	___ 50. vines
___ 6. question	___ 21. adult	___ 36. market	___ 51. tooth
___ 7. reasons	___ 22. ghosts	___ 37. telephone	___ 52. daughter
___ 8. thought	___ 23. umbrella	___ 38. fence	___ 53. juice
___ 9. cacti	___ 24. television	___ 39. knives	___ 54. owner
___ 10. necklace	___ 25. examples	___ 40. candle	___ 55. fears
___ 11. key	___ 26. stories	___ 41. blankets	___ 56. ideas
___ 12. giant	___ 27. favorite	___ 42. eagle	___ 57. jewel
___ 13. parachute	___ 28. habits	___ 43. jobs	___ 58. signatures
___ 14. holiday	___ 29. chances	___ 44. sandwiches	___ 59. deadlines
___ 15. castle	___ 30. crowd	___ 45. contests	___ 60. excuse

B. Write the plural of each word.

1. captain _captains_	15. change _____	29. guest _____
2. country _____	16. joke _____	30. mistake _____
3. grade _____	17. leaf _____	31. tomato _____
4. sheep _____	18. laugh _____	32. day _____
5. library _____	19. machine _____	33. password _____
6. tunnel _____	20. wrench _____	34. zoo _____
7. highway _____	21. sky _____	35. chief _____
8. boss _____	22. man _____	36. lady _____
9. monkey _____	23. answer _____	37. picture _____
10. word _____	24. child _____	38. breeze _____
11. watch _____	25. branch _____	39. tax _____
12. life _____	26. number _____	40. foot _____
13. spoon _____	27. ox _____	
14. family _____	28. cabin _____	

The Blue Men

Study the spelling and meaning of each word. These words are used in today's story. Connect each word with its definition.

1. independence
2. mystery
3. nomads
4. possession
5. referred
6. valuable

a. of considerable worth
b. people without permanent homes
c. something not known
d. directed attention to
e. a reliance on oneself
f. an owned item

Read the story carefully and remember the details.

The Blue Men of the Sahara are often referred to as the last great nomads of the world. The most valuable possession of the Blue Men is their independence.

The Blue Men receive their name from the blue color of their skin. For many years the skin color presented quite a mystery. Blue is not the real color of their skin. It is the color of their clothing. The blue dye in the clothing stains the skin. The dye helps protect the Blue Men from the sun.

The Blue Men take great pride in their hair. The hair is never cut. Not only does it adorn the head, but it often serves as a pillow.

The Blue Men lead a hard life. They are deep-rooted in the traditions of their ancestors. For them the outside world does not exist.

A. Underline the correct answers about today's story.

1. The Blue Men value   (a) independence   (b) money   (c) education.
2. Nomads are   (a) city dwellers   (b) wanderers   (c) farmers.
3. Which color identifies these people? (a) brown (b) green   (c) blue
4. The color of the skin is caused by the (a) sun (b) sand   (c) dye in clothing.
5. Which word describes the Blue Men? (a) lazy   (b) traditional (c) modern

B. Reread the story and write the answers to these questions.

1. How did the Blue Men receive their name?

_____

_____

_____

2. What purpose does the blue skin serve?

_____

_____

_____

3. In what do the Blue Men take great pride?

_____

_____

_____

4. Describe the life of the Blue Men.

_____

_____

_____

Unit 22 cont'd ☞

Rules for Forming the Plural

Rule 1 Most nouns form the plural by adding "s."

Rule 2 If a noun ends in "ch," "sh," "x," "z," "s," or "ss," form the plural by adding "es."

Rule 3 If a noun ends with a vowel plus "y," add "s" to form the plural.

Rule 4 If a noun ends with a consonant plus "y," change the "y" to "i" and add "es" to form the plural.

Rule 5 If a noun ends in "f" or "fe," change the "f" or "fe" to "v" and add "es" to form the plural.

Rule 6 If a noun ends in a vowel plus "o," add "s" to form the plural.

Rule 7 If a noun ends in a consonant plus "o," add "es" to form the plural.

Rule 8 Some nouns change their spellings to form the plural.

 Write the number of the rule which was used to form the plural of each noun.

EXAMPLES: __5__ a. wolves __2__ c. boxes __6__ e. radios
 __1__ b. friends __4__ d. ponies __3__ f. days

____ 1. children	____ 26. zoos	____ 51. sketches	____ 76. highways
____ 2. kittens	____ 27. women	____ 52. dresses	____ 77. boys
____ 3. rodeos	____ 28. secrets	____ 53. eyes	____ 78. branches
____ 4. plays	____ 29. kidneys	____ 54. cacti	____ 79. puppies
____ 5. bushes	____ 30. decisions	____ 55. potatoes	____ 80. selves
____ 6. tomatoes	____ 31. memories	____ 56. flowers	____ 81. accidents
____ 7. families	____ 32. trios	____ 57. toys	____ 82. men
____ 8. wives	____ 33. zeroes	____ 58. calves	____ 83. volcanoes
____ 9. chances	____ 34. peaches	____ 59. glasses	____ 84. businesses
____ 10. examples	____ 35. libraries	____ 60. knives	____ 85. centuries
____ 11. cameos	____ 36. lives	____ 61. cities	____ 86. voices
____ 12. holidays	____ 37. daughters	____ 62. adventures	____ 87. buses
____ 13. countries	____ 38. opinions	____ 63. keys	____ 88. copies
____ 14. geese	____ 39. guests	____ 64. inches	____ 89. reasons
____ 15. mistakes	____ 40. skies	____ 65. treaties	____ 90. finches
____ 16. monkeys	____ 41. attorneys	____ 66. mosquitoes	____ 91. flies
____ 17. leaves	____ 42. lice	____ 67. berries	____ 92. halves
____ 18. watches	____ 43. buffaloes	____ 68. taxes	____ 93. birthdays
____ 19. beaches	____ 44. axes	____ 69. foxes	____ 94. careers
____ 20. ideas	____ 45. scarves	____ 70. thieves	____ 95. folios
____ 21. teeth	____ 46. promises	____ 71. cabins	____ 96. fields
____ 22. echoes	____ 47. dishes	____ 72. oxen	____ 97. crosses
____ 23. loaves	____ 48. feet	____ 73. sandwiches	____ 98. parties
____ 24. churches	____ 49. mice	____ 74. ghosts	____ 99. turkeys
____ 25. ladies	____ 50. journeys	____ 75. babies	____ 100. losses

The Blue Whale

Study the spelling and meaning of each word. These words are used in today's story. Connect each word with its definition.

1. commonly
2. enormous
3. needless
4. supports
5. surface
6. weighs

a. not required
b. upholds; sustains
c. usually
d. measured heaviness
e. to rise to the top
f. larger than usual

Read the story carefully and remember the details.

Today there lives an animal that is bigger than the biggest dinosaur was. The animal lives in the sea. Sometimes called the sulfur-bottom, it is most commonly referred to as the blue whale.

The blue whale weighs almost three times as much as the biggest dinosaur did. On land the blue whale would be too heavy to move about. In the sea, the blue whale moves at a speed of fourteen miles an hour. It can even race at thirty miles an hour. The water supports the whale's bulk.

The blue whale is not a fish. It is a mammal. It must surface every half hour to breathe.

Needless to say, the blue whale requires an enormous amount of food. It easily travels hundreds of miles in search of food.

A. Underline the correct answers about today's story.

1. The blue whale is _____ than dinosaurs were.   (a) smaller   (b) bigger   (c) taller
2. What supports the whale's weight?   (a) water   (b) big feet   (c) air
3. The blue whale is a   (a) fish   (b) mammal   (c) reptile.
4. The blue whale travels in search of   (a) protection   (b) other whales   (c) food.
5. The blue whale lives   (a) in the sea   (b) on land   (c) in rivers.

B. Reread the story and write the answers to these questions.

1. What is the blue whale sometimes called?

_____
_____
_____

2. Why could the animal not live on land?

_____
_____
_____

3. What purpose does the water serve?

_____
_____
_____

4. How far might the blue whale search for food?

_____
_____
_____

Unit 23 cont'd ☞

Plural Nouns

Singular	Plural
alumnus	alumni
analysis	analyses
batch	batches
belief	beliefs
brother	brethren
bunny	bunnies
day	days
dish	dishes
echo	echoes
elf	elves
half	halves
knife	knives
lady	ladies
leaf	leaves
navy	navies
pass	passes

 Fill in the blanks. Then complete the puzzle.

Across

2. _j_ _o_ _y_ _s_ glad feelings; expressions of happiness

4. _ _ _ _ _ young foxes, lions, tigers, bears, or other wild animals

5. _ _ _ _ _ _ automobiles for hire

6. _ _ _ _ _ _ animals raised for wool, meat, or skins

9. _ _ _ _ _ _ women who have husbands; married women

12. _ _ _ _ _ small insects that infest the hair or skin of people

19. _ _ _ _ adult male persons

20. _ _ _ _ _ _ _ ornaments or belts worn around the waists of women

Down

1. _ _ _ _ _ _ heavenly bodies appearing as bright points in the sky at night

3. _ _ _ _ _ full-grown males of domestic cattle

4. _ _ _ _ _ _ _ _ _ young boys or girls; sons and daughters

7. _ _ _ _ _ _ _ records, recitals, narratives, fibs, lies, and newspaper articles

8. _ _ _ _ _ _ hard, bonelike parts in the mouth used for biting

10. _ _ _ _ _ _ _ the four periods of the year

11. _ _ _ _ _ _ wild or tame birds like ducks; ganders

13. _ _ _ _ _ _ _ young cows or bulls; young elephants or whales

14. _ _ _ _ _ end parts of legs that a person or animal stands on

15. _ _ _ _ _ _ monies paid by people for support of government

16. _ _ _ _ _ small, gnawing rodents found around the world

17. _ _ _ _ _ tools with sharp blades fastened to handles used for chopping

18. _ _ _ _ _ male children; male descendants

58

The Bobcat

Study the spelling and meaning of each word. These words are used in today's story. Connect each word with its definition.

1. active
2. camouflage
3. constantly
4. prowler
5. silently
6. warns

a. informs of danger
b. in an unchanging way
c. a disguise
d. one that wanders
e. making no sound
f. energetic

Read the story carefully and remember the details.

The bobcat lives anywhere in North America where there is enough brush land to provide food and shelter. The bobcat is a member of the cat family, deriving its name from its short tail.

The bobcat is a prowler. It moves about silently. The bobcat often waits for its prey to come to it. When the prey comes near, the bobcat attacks from an overhanging ledge or limb.

The bobcat constantly moves about in search of food. Its coat provides an excellent camouflage. The animal is most active at night.

The bobcat is aware of the slightest movement. Its keen eyesight not only helps it locate its prey but also warns it of coming danger. The bobcat is hunted for sport.

A. Underline the correct answers about today's story.

1. Where does the bobcat live?	(a) jungle	(b) forest	(c) mountains
2. The bobcat's name comes from its	(a) tail	(b) habits	(c) coloring.
3. The bobcat moves about in search of	(a) water	(b) shelter	(c) food.
4. When is the bobcat active?	(a) morning	(b) night	(c) evening
5. The bobcat is hunted for	(a) sport	(b) food	(c) fur.

B. Reread the story and write the answers to these questions.

1. What purpose is served by brush land?

_____

_____

_____

2. How does the bobcat move?

_____

_____

_____

3. What purpose is served by the animal's coat?

_____

_____

_____

4. How does the cat's eyesight help it?

_____

_____

_____

Unit 24 cont'd ☞

Writing Plurals

"Plural" means "more than one."

 Write the plural of each word.

1. sister _____sisters_____
2. box _____
3. highway _____
4. mouse _____
5. room _____
6. life _____
7. child _____
8. flower _____
9. pony _____
10. clock _____
11. tree _____
12. key _____
13. body _____
14. wheel _____
15. eye _____
16. paper _____
17. woman _____
18. ocean _____
19. way _____
20. orange _____
21. city _____
22. show _____
23. place _____
24. story _____
25. forest _____
26. bush _____
27. apple _____
28. window _____
29. bridge _____
30. lady _____
31. road _____
32. witch _____
33. wife _____
34. berry _____

35. foot _____
36. word _____
37. toy _____
38. calf _____
39. fox _____
40. rock _____
41. picture _____
42. dress _____
43. turkey _____
44. car _____
45. doctor _____
46. letter _____
47. boy _____
48. church _____
49. gift _____
50. dog _____
51. wolf _____
52. finger _____
53. candy _____
54. dream _____
55. monkey _____
56. page _____
57. lesson _____
58. bottle _____
59. bell _____
60. inch _____
61. teacher _____
62. country _____
63. jungle _____
64. sky _____
65. friend _____
66. bus _____
67. wall _____
68. girl _____

69. garden _____
70. leaf _____
71. tooth _____
72. wish _____
73. family _____
74. glass _____
75. game _____
76. smile _____
77. fruit _____
78. baby _____
79. flag _____
80. student _____
81. cowboy _____
82. house _____
83. puppy _____
84. cross _____
85. man _____
86. arrow _____
87. match _____
88. pal _____
89. dish _____
90. sign _____
91. door _____
92. bench _____
93. number _____
94. day _____
95. light _____
96. book _____
97. cow _____
98. fly _____
99. school _____
100. branch _____

The Bobwhite

Study the spelling and meaning of each word. These words are used in today's story. Connect each word with its definition.

1. bold	a. bashful
2. coy	b. brave
3. distinctive	c. regarded with preference
4. favorite	d. protected from injury
5. sheltered	e. divided from others
6. single file	f. one behind the other

Read the story carefully and remember the details.

The bobwhite is a favorite game bird. It is a plump chickenlike bird with a distinctive call. From this call the bobwhite gets its name.

The male bobwhite is often described as bold. The female is shy and coy. Together they build their nest in dry grass sheltered by tall weeds. The male shares the duties of housekeeping. He is a devoted mate, singing to the female as she sits on the nest.

Young bobwhites follow their parents in a single file. During the day the birds love to sun themselves. At night the family roosts in a tight circle. Their tails are to the inside and their heads face out.

The bobwhite must be constantly alert for predators. Their enemies include foxes, hawks, and owls. When danger approaches, the bobwhites take to the air.

A. Underline the correct answers about today's story.

1. The bobwhite's name comes from its	(a) call	(b) color	(c) habits.
2. Which word describes the female?	(a) bold	(b) shy	(c) rude
3. As a mate, the male bobwhite is	(a) lazy	(b) untrustworthy	(c) devoted.
4. The bobwhite roosts in	(a) trees	(b) old buildings	(c) a circle.
5. When danger approaches, the bobwhite	(a) is helpless	(b) flies away	(c) attacks.

B. Reread the story and write the answers to these questions.

1. Describe the bobwhite's appearance.

_____

_____

_____

2. How are the male and female different?

_____

_____

_____

3. What do bobwhite's love to do during the day?

_____

_____

_____

4. Name the enemies of the bobwhite.

_____

_____

_____

Unit 25 cont'd ☞

Forming Plural Nouns

A. Fill in the blank in each sentence with the plural form of the word written before the sentence.

1. teacher   He has many _____ at his school.
2. dress   She has several pink _____.
3. fish   The boys caught four _____.
4. child   A few _____ were playing on the street.
5. tooth   She lost her two front _____.

B. Look at each word on the left. Draw a line under its correct plural form on the right.

1. lady   ladys   <u>ladies</u>
2. thief   thieves   thiefs
3. family   families   familys
4. mouse   mouses   mice
5. church   churchs   churches
6. peach   peachs   peaches
7. box   boxes   boxs
8. foot   foots   feet
9. goose   gooses   geese
10. wolf   wolves   wolfs

C. Count nouns stand for things that can be counted. Noncount nouns stand for things that cannot be counted. Look at the examples in the following lists; then write the letter "c" on the line before the count nouns. Write the letter "n" on the line before the noncount nouns.

<u>Count Nouns</u>

five dogs
eight cats
three persons

<u>Noncount Nouns</u>

steel
math
wool

_c_ 1. pencils
____ 2. children
____ 3. hay
____ 4. dirt

____ 5. steel
____ 6. feet
____ 7. water
____ 8. sugar

Comprehension Check

Ⓐ Write "s" for singular and "p" for plural.

_s_ 1. library	___ 11. model	___ 21. mountains	___ 31. owners
___ 2. notebooks	___ 12. ticket	___ 22. pictures	___ 32. rocket
___ 3. sandwich	___ 13. rules	___ 23. fireplace	___ 33. trays
___ 4. morning	___ 14. actors	___ 24. alarm	___ 34. sweater
___ 5. teeth	___ 15. persons	___ 25. spiders	___ 35. telephones
___ 6. address	___ 16. desks	___ 26. offices	___ 36. dance
___ 7. records	___ 17. building	___ 27. tournament	___ 37. coach
___ 8. pages	___ 18. Indians	___ 28. dinners	___ 38. partners
___ 9. mouse	___ 19. room	___ 29. letters	___ 39. ranches
___ 10. passenger	___ 20. reporters	___ 30. textbook	___ 40. friend

Ⓑ Fill in the blanks.

1. "Singular" means " ____ _one_ ____ ."
2. "Plural" means " _____ ."
3. Most nouns add ____ to form the plural.
4. Nouns ending in "ch," "sh," "s," "ss," "x," or "z" add ____ .
5. Nouns ending in a vowel plus "y" add ____ .
6. Nouns ending in a consonant plus "y" change the ____ to ____ and add ____ .
7. Nouns ending in a vowel plus "o" add ____ .
8. Nouns ending in a consonant plus "o" add ____ .
9. Some nouns change their _____ to form the plural.
10. Some nouns stay the _____ in both the singular and the plural.

Ⓒ Write the plural of each word.

1. child _children_	9. bus _____	17. branch _____
2. bobcat _____	10. man _____	18. whale _____
3. bird _____	11. hill _____	19. radio _____
4. nest _____	12. beach _____	20. family _____
5. color _____	13. cherry _____	21. wolf _____
6. monkey _____	14. ocean _____	22. sheep _____
7. life _____	15. wish _____	23. lunch _____
8. news _____	16. class _____	24. journey _____

Ⓓ Complete these sentences.

1. The bobwhite family roosts in a ____ _circle_ ____ .
2. The Blackfoot Indians wandered over the _____ .
3. The bobcat gets its name from its _____ .
4. Blue Men do not cut their _____ .
5. The sulfur-bottom whale is also called the _____ whale.
6. Blue Men value their _____ .
7. The bobcat is most active at _____ .
8. The Blackfoot Indians hunted _____ .
9. The blue whale is not a _____ , but a mammal.
10. The bobwhite gets its name from its _____ .

Test 5 cont'd ☞

Comprehension Check (continued)

(E) **Match these words and their definitions. These words appeared in the reading selections from units 21-25.**

_a_ 1. changed   ___ 7. supports

___ 2. wandered   ___ 8. silently

___ 3. independence   ___ 9. warns

___ 4. valuable   ___ 10. bold

___ 5. commonly   ___ 11. coy

___ 6. needless   ___ 12. favorite

a. altered

b. a reliance on oneself

c. usually

d. upholds; sustains

e. roamed

f. brave

g. not required

h. making no sound

i. of considerable worth

j. bashful

k. informs of danger

l. regarded with preference

(F) **Underline the correct answers.**

1.	What did the Blackfoot Indians hunt?	(a)	eagles	(b)	buffalo
2.	How did the Blackfoot travel?	(a)	on foot	(b)	on donkey
3.	What purpose did the Blue Men's skin color serve?	(a)	protection	(b)	decoration
4.	What did the Blue Men value?	(a)	jewels	(b)	independence
5.	What is the blue whale?	(a)	fish	(b)	mammal
6.	Give another name for the blue whale.	(a)	elephant whale	(b)	sulfur-bottom
7.	How does the bobcat move?	(a)	clumsily	(b)	silently
8.	Where does the bobcat live?	(a)	mountains	(b)	forest
9.	Describe the bobwhite's appearance.	(a)	plump	(b)	trim
10.	How does the bobwhite roost?	(a)	in a circle	(b)	upside down

Choose one of the following topics and write a paragraph.

(1) The Blackfoot Indians traveled on foot. Write about how your life would change without the invention of the automobile.

(2) Describe a day in the life of a bobcat.

_____

_____

_____

_____

_____

_____

_____

_____

_____

The Burglar and the Mud Dauber

Study the spelling and meaning of each word. These words are used in today's story. Connect each word with its definition.

1. burglar ——————— a. one who steals
2. constructed   b. goes somewhere
3. countless   c. unable to move
4. moist   d. slightly wet
5. paralyzed   e. too many to count
6. visits   f. built

Read the story carefully and remember the details.

There are many kinds of mud daubers. They get their name from their homes which are constructed of mud.

The common mud dauber builds its home on porch ceilings or under eaves. To build its nest, the mud dauber visits ponds and mud puddles. With its mouth and forefeet it collects the moist soil. The mud dauber makes countless trips to finish one cell of the home. When a cell is finished, the wasp carries in a paralyzed spider on which she lays her eggs. Then the cell is sealed.

The burglar mud dauber does not build a nest of its own. It waits until the other wasps have finished a cell. Then it breaks into the cell, throws out the spider, and restocks the nest with its own spider and eggs. The burglar then reseals the cell which others have worked so hard to make.

A. Underline the correct answers about today's story.

1. Mud daubers get their name from their   (a) looks   (b) homes   (c) eating habits.
2. In the cell the mud dauber places a/an   (a) dead wasp   (b) spider   (c) egg.
3. The mud dauber lays its eggs   (a) in the water   (b) in the mud   (c) on the spider.
4. The mud dauber's nest is built   (a) under eaves   (b) in trees   (c) in the ground.
5. The burglar mud dauber steals the   (a) eggs   (b) spider   (c) nest.

B. Reread the story and write the answers to these questions.

1. What material makes up the mud dauber's home?

_____

_____

_____

2. Why does the mud dauber visit ponds and mud puddles?

_____

_____

_____

3. What happens after the wasp lays eggs?

_____

_____

_____

4. Why does the burglar not build a nest of its own?

_____

_____

_____

       Unit 26 cont'd ☞

Plurals

A. Underline the plural nouns.

1. <u>students</u>
2. peach
3. bicycles
4. brother
5. chairs
6. clouds
7. windows
8. road
9. letters
10. glass
11. plant
12. girls
13. buildings
14. floor
15. farmers
16. test
17. words
18. pictures
19. lamp
20. animals
21. jackets
22. buses
23. book
24. stars
25. street
26. flags
27. games
28. birds
29. table
30. month
31. orange
32. coat
33. yards
34. days
35. penny
36. cups
37. movie
38. trucks
39. page
40. eyes

B. Underline each correctly spelled plural. Then write the plural noun in the blank to complete the sentence.

1. class — <u>classes</u> classs
   Classes begin tomorrow.
2. kitten — kittenes kittens
   My cat had four _____.
3. friend — friends friendes
   His _____ gave him a party.
4. box — boxs boxes
   Those _____ are filled with books.
5. light — lightes lights
   Please turn out the _____.
6. train — trains traines
   The _____ are late again.
7. plant — plantes plants
   These _____ need water.
8. wish — wishs wishes
   All your _____ will come true.
9. leaf — leaves leafs
   The _____ are turning green.
10. man — mans men
    Who are those _____?
11. child — children childs
    The _____ are asleep.
12. flower — flowers floweres
    Don't pick the _____.
13. desk — deskes desks
    Clear your _____.
14. dress — dresses dresss
    Their _____ are made of paper.
15. mouse — mouses mice
    Two _____ live in this cage.
16. banana — bananaes bananas
    I ate five _____.
17. brush — brushes brushs
    Those _____ are dirty.
18. tooth — tooths teeth
    Brush your _____.
19. seed — seedes seeds
    Now plant the _____.
20. coin — coins coines
    I found four _____.

66

The Capybara

Study the spelling and meaning of each word. These words are used in today's story. Connect each word with its definition.

1. aquatic
2. clumsy
3. coarse
4. destructive
5. tamed
6. vegetarian

a. awkward
b. tearing down
c. pertaining to water
d. one who eats no meat
e. harsh to the touch
f. changed to a domestic animal

Read the story carefully and remember the details.

The capybara is an aquatic rodent which lives in Central and South America. It is one of the largest rodents. Many capybaras are the size of small pigs.

The capybara makes its home on the shores of streams and rivers. When it is frightened, it dives into the water. The capybara is more at home in the water than on land. It has strong webbed feet and is able to swim underwater for long distances. On land, the capybara is clumsy. Its webbed feet make walking and running awkward.

The capybara is a vegetarian. It has coarse brown hair and no tail. Although most rodents are destructive, the capybara is not. It is a good-natured animal and easily tamed.

A. Underline the correct answers about today's story.

1. Of all rodents the capybara is one of the   (a) meanest   (b) largest   (c) most destructive.
2. The capybara lives   (a) near water   (b) in trees   (c) on the desert.
3. On land, the capybara is   (a) fast   (b) clumsy   (c) graceful.
4. A vegetarian eats   (a) meat   (b) no vegetables   (c) only vegetables.
5. Which word describes a capybara?   (a) destructive   (b) dangerous   (c) good-natured

B. Reread the story and write the answers to these questions.

1. What type of rodent is the capybara?

_____

_____

_____

2. What animal is similar in size to the capybara?

_____

_____

_____

3. What does the animal do when frightened?

_____

_____

_____

4. Where is the capybara more at home?

_____

_____

_____

    Unit 27 cont'd ☛

Positions of Nouns

A. Mark an "x" on the line before each sentence that has a noun in the wrong position, and underline that noun.

_____ 1. Peter is breakfast eating.
_____ 2. The work children.
_____ 3. The girl likes the boy.
_____ 4. The student letter writes a.
_____ 5. I pencil dropped a.

B. Underline the subject of each sentence. Remember that the subject of any sentence is the doer of the action.

1. The <u>horse</u> races.
2. The elephant drinks with his trunk.
3. Lee ate lunch.
4. Dorothea made the tree house.
5. Zelda wants some money.
6. The ball broke the window.

C. Underline the object of each sentence. Remember that the object of any sentence is the receiver of the action

1. I hit <u>Mary</u>.
2. The children play ball every night.
3. Mom pays the bills.
4. She likes the sandwich.
5. The lady bakes the cookies.
6. My brother likes cars.

The Cardinal

Study the spelling and meaning of each word. These words are used in today's story. Connect each word with its definition.

1. beneficial ——————— a. useful
2. devoted   b. dull
3. drab   c. feathers of a bird
4. harmful   d. causing hurt
5. plumage   e. given up to a purpose
6. serenades   f. sings

Read the story carefully and remember the details.

Named for his beautiful cardinal red color, the male cardinal proudly earns the credit as one of America's most handsome birds. The male is the only crested red bird in America. Many states have named the cardinal as their state's bird.

The cardinal's song is heard throughout the year. The female, whose plumage is drab, has a much prettier song than the male.

The male cardinal is a devoted mate and father. He serenades the female as she builds the nest and sits on the eggs. He carries food to the female. When the young are hatched, the male helps the female feed and care for them.

The cardinal is a beneficial bird to farmers and gardeners. This bird eats many harmful insects.

A. Underline the correct answers about today's story.

1. Which cardinal is the prettier?	(a) female	(b) male	(c) neither
2. What color is cardinal?	(a) green	(b) yellow	(c) red
3. As a mate, the male cardinal is	(a) devoted	(b) lazy	(c) irresponsible.
4. Farmers consider the bird	(a) a pest	(b) helpful	(c) harmful.
5. The cardinal's song is heard	(a) in spring	(b) in fall	(c) all year round.

B. Reread the story and write the answers to these questions.

1. How do some states honor the cardinal?

_____

_____

_____

2. Describe the female's plumage.

_____

_____

_____

3. What does the male do when the young are hatched?

_____

_____

_____

4. What does the cardinal do for farmers and gardeners?

_____

_____

_____

Unit 28 cont'd ☞

Nouns of Ownership

A. Underline the nouns which show ownership.

1. day's
2. hours
3. Williams
4. books'
5. Mrs. Rogers
6. dog's
7. shows
8. city's
9. homes
10. Tim's
11. Betty's
12. tables
13. Americans'
14. spider's
15. pictures
16. monkey's
17. pins
18. kittens'
19. pitcher's
20. lions
21. Martins
22. Jones
23. rabbits'
24. fox's
25. Mr. Bridges
26. houses
27. Terry's
28. boxes
29. Mrs. Wilson's
30. Chris
31. Ms. Davis
32. Adams
33. clown's
34. Dr. James
35. eyes
36. coach's
37. flowers
38. Ned's
39. Miss Baker's
40. drivers
41. Sandra's
42. friends
43. earth's
44. friends'
45. ghost's
46. months
47. today's
48. player's
49. Dr. Stevens
50. rivers
51. owners'
52. buses
53. Capt. Sands
54. man's
55. Bess
56. ears
57. song's
58. hills
59. Mr. Carson's
60. Ross

B. Write the possessive form of the word in parentheses to complete each sentence.

(teacher) 1. This is the _____*teacher's*_____ desk.

(boys) 2. The _____ room is upstairs.

(aunt) 3. My _____ car is blue.

(Ralph) 4. _____ book is on the table.

(sisters) 5. Your _____ eyes are brown.

(children) 6. This is the _____ room.

(Ms. Kent) 7. Where is _____ coat?

(uncle) 8. Here is your _____ hat.

(Kevin) 9. _____ bike was stolen.

(turtles) 10. We tried to find the _____ nests.

(Jane) 11. I am _____ friend.

(mother) 12. Where is _____ pen?

(book) 13. What is the _____ title?

(story) 14. The _____ ending was sad.

(girls) 15. She's a member of the _____ club.

(bug) 16. Count the _____ legs.

(Billy) 17. _____ teacher is Ms. Murdock.

(king) 18. Bring me the _____ crown.

(parents) 19. My _____ friends are here.

(Mr. Fish) 20. These are _____ keys.

Cassowaries

Study the spelling and meaning of each word. These words are used in today's story. Connect each word with its definition.

1. designed   a. particularly
2. illusive   b. misleading
3. never   c. not ever
4. solitude   d. offensive
5. specifically   e. being alone
6. unpleasant   f. formed

Read the story carefully and remember the details.

Many people have never heard of a cassowary. It is a large bird that resembles an ostrich. The cassowary is a bird that cannot fly.

Often described as shy and illusive, the cassowary has earned an unpleasant reputation. It travels in pairs but often prefers solitude. It is usually heard but not seen.

The cassowary is specifically designed for its life in the rain forest. Instead of feathers, the bird has quills. Its main diet consists of vegetation.

The female cassowary is bigger than the male. The male sits on the nest and cares for the young.

When danger approaches, the cassowary runs away. Its long legs allow the bird to run very quickly.

A. **Underline the correct answers about today's story.**

1. The cassowary resembles   (a) an ostrich   (b) a duck   (c) a penguin.
2. "Solitude" means   (a) "social"   (b) "isolation"   (c) "friendly."
3. Where does the cassowary live? (a) desert   (b) rain forests   (c) Arctic
4. Who cares for the young?   (a) male   (b) female   (c) both parents
5. When danger is near, the cassowary   (a) hides in sand   (b) attacks   (c) runs away.

B. **Reread the story and write the answers to these questions.**

1. How is the cassowary unlike most birds?

_____

_____

_____

2. How does the bird travel?

_____

_____

_____

3. What does the bird eat?

_____

_____

_____

4. How does the female compare to the male physically?

_____

_____

_____

71   Unit 29 cont'd ☞

Forming Possessive Nouns

A. Each group of sentences tells you that someone has or owns something. Fill in each blank with the correct possessive form of the noun. Look at the example.

EXAMPLE: *The boy owns a dog. It is the **boy's** dog.*

1. The lady owns a horse. It is the _____ horse.
2. The man has a hat. It is the _____ hat.
3. The teachers own a boat. It is the _____ boat.
4. The neighbors have a swimming pool. It is the _____ pool.
5. The women own a store. It is the _____ store.
6. The children own a tree house. It is the _____ tree house.

B. Look at the noun tree. The plural and the possessive forms of the regular noun "boy" and the irregular noun "man" are written correctly in the boxes of the tree. Use these words as models to form the plural and possessive forms of the regular noun "lady" and the irregular noun "child."

Noun Tree

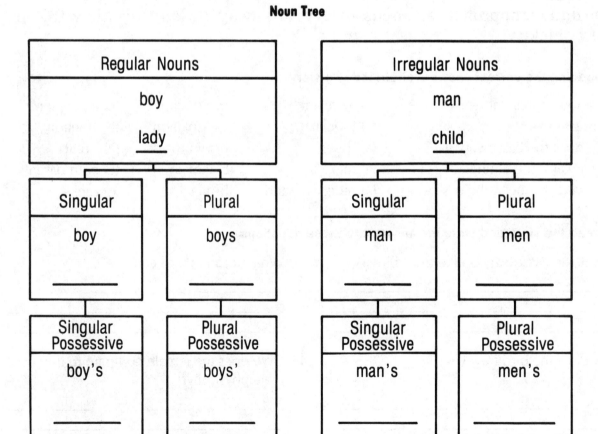

Castles of Old

Study the spelling and meaning of each word. These words are used in today's story. Connect each word with its definition.

1. always
2. comfortable
3. drawbridge
4. exciting
5. fort
6. moat

a. a bridge that can be raised
b. all the time
c. a ditch around a castle
d. providing ease
e. an enclosed place built for defense
f. thrilling

Read the story carefully and remember the details.

Long ago people were not too friendly with one another. To protect themselves, they built castles which were like forts.

Around the castle was a tall, thick wall of stone. Around the wall was a ditch. The ditch was called a moat. The only way to get inside the castle was over a drawbridge.

The castle was made of heavy stone. In the winter the castle was cold and drafty. The only way to heat the rooms was with a fireplace, but the fireplace was too small to heat the large rooms. The stone floors were usually cold, even though they were piled deep with straw.

The stories about castle life are usually exciting. However, the people who lived in castles were not always comfortable.

A. **Underline the correct answers about today's story.**

1. A castle resembles a   (a) town   (b) village   (c) fort.
2. A moat is a   (a) wall   (b) ditch   (c) bridge.
3. To get inside, one crossed a   (a) drawbridge   (b) wall   (c) river.
4. The castle was made of   (a) mud   (b) wood   (c) stone.
5. The castle was heated by   (a) fireplaces   (b) gas stoves   (c) candles.

B. **Reread the story and write the answers to these questions.**

1. How did people protect themselves in days of old?

_____

_____

_____

2. What was around the castle?

_____

_____

_____

3. What covered the floors of the castle?

_____

_____

_____

4. How are stories about castle life usually written?

_____

_____

_____

Unit 30 cont'd ☞

Plurals and Possessives

"Plural" means "more than one."

A. Write the plural of each word.

1. banana   *bananas* _____
2. business _____
3. author _____
4. wolf _____
5. copy _____
6. sandwich _____
7. scissors _____
8. library _____
9. envelope _____
10. circle _____
11. knife _____
12. witch _____
13. victory _____
14. berry _____
15. attorney _____
16. leaf _____
17. magazine _____
18. ghost _____
19. theory _____
20. buffalo _____
21. class _____
22. news _____
23. museum _____
24. deadline _____
25. sky _____

26. mouse _____
27. child _____
28. mosquito _____
29. radio _____
30. company _____
31. visitor _____
32. sign _____
33. delay _____
34. pants _____
35. skeleton _____
36. wife _____
37. sketch _____
38. zoo _____
39. breeze _____
40. fox _____
41. branch _____
42. ox _____
43. tomato _____
44. insect _____
45. problem _____
46. volunteer _____
47. thief _____
48. table _____
49. pencil _____
50. potato _____

51. cactus _____
52. life _____
53. cuff _____
54. enemy _____
55. chimney _____
56. city _____
57. spoon _____
58. house _____
59. half _____
60. trousers _____
61. echo _____
62. lunch _____
63. shelf _____
64. book _____
65. lamp _____
66. watch _____
67. animal _____
68. bus _____
69. window _____
70. day _____
71. luxury _____
72. box _____
73. loaf _____
74. highway _____
75. chair _____

Possessive words show ownership.

B. Write the possessive form of each word.

1. he   *his* _____
2. children _____
3. Cathi _____
4. we _____
5. baby _____
6. car _____
7. Mr. Kent _____
8. fox _____

9. Tony _____
10. citizen _____
11. you _____
12. George _____
13. wind _____
14. monkeys _____
15. tree _____
16. mother _____

17. chimney _____
18. river _____
19. puppy _____
20. ant _____
21. Mark _____
22. Jones _____
23. hero _____
24. mouse _____

Comprehension Check

A Underline the plural nouns.

1. <u>lessons</u>
2. castles
3. quarrel
4. televisions
5. exercises
6. flowers
7. submarine
8. mud daubers
9. cassowaries
10. teeth
11. homes
12. spider
13. capybaras
14. rivers
15. animals
16. stories
17. vegetarian
18. governments
19. friend
20. appointments

B Write 1 if the noun is plural and 2 if the noun shows possession.

_1 & 2_ 1. Americans'
_____ 2. captain's
_____ 3. families
_____ 4. teachers'
_____ 5. vehicle's
_____ 6. beliefs
_____ 7. officers'
_____ 8. treaty's
_____ 9. Ms. Smith's
_____ 10. Diane's

_____ 11. President's
_____ 12. reporters
_____ 13. country's
_____ 14. woman's
_____ 15. record's
_____ 16. soldiers'
_____ 17. movie's
_____ 18. leader's
_____ 19. magazines
_____ 20. Roger's

_____ 21. windows
_____ 22. workers'
_____ 23. birds
_____ 24. enemies
_____ 25. mountains
_____ 26. men
_____ 27. stories'
_____ 28. Melinda's
_____ 29. bicycles'
_____ 30. Mr. Hoover's

C Write each phrase using a noun which shows possession.

1. keys of Greg   _Greg's keys_
2. office of Dr. Greene _____
3. books of the students _____
4. home of the animal   _____
5. gift of Mrs. Brown   _____
6. works of the members _____
7. painting of Monet   _____
8. apology of Keith   _____
9. money of the people   _____
10. bite of the ant   _____

11. song of a cardinal   _____
12. parents of the child   _____
13. owner of the castle   _____
14. leaves of the trees   _____
15. house of Tony   _____
16. doors of the building _____
17. switch of the machine _____
18. vacation of Edna   _____
19. music of Bach   _____
20. speech of Horace   _____

D Complete these sentences.

1. A cassowary resembles an ___ostrich___ .
2. The cardinal is named for its _____ .
3. Castles were made of heavy _____ .
4. Capybaras are _____ rodents.
5. The ditch around a castle is a _____ .
6. The capybara is more at home in _____ .

7. Mud daubers get their names from their ___oss___ .
8. A cassowary is a large _____ .
9. Mud daubers' homes are made of _____ .
10. The male cardinal is _____ than the female.

Test 6 cont'd ☞

Comprehension Check (continued)

(E) Match these words and their definitions. These words appeared in the reading selections from units 26-30.

_c_ 1. aquatic	___ 7. devoted	a. feathers of a bird	g. not ever	
___ 2. paralyzed	___ 8. burglar	b. unable to move	h. one who steals	
___ 3. plumage	___ 9. never	c. pertaining to water	i. given up to a	
___ 4. moat	___ 10. solitude	d. providing ease	purpose	
___ 5. coarse	___ 11. countless	e. harsh to the touch	j. too many to count	
___ 6. comfortable	___ 12. destructive	f. a ditch around	k. tearing down	
		a castle	l. being alone	

(F) Underline the correct answers.

1. Where do mud daubers get their name?	(a) looks	(b) <u>habits</u>
2. What feeds the newborn mud daubers?	(a) soil	(b) spiders
3. Where is the capybara more at home?	(a) on land	(b) in water
4. What do vegetarians eat?	(a) plants	(b) animals
5. What color is the male cardinal?	(a) red	(b) brown
6. How do cardinals help farmers?	(a) eat seeds	(b) eat insects
7. How does a cassowary handle danger?	(a) It attacks.	(b) It runs away.
8. Which other bird does a cassowary resemble?	(a) ostrich	(b) goose
9. Of what were castles built?	(a) stone	(b) wood
10. What covered the castle floors?	(a) wool rugs	(b) straw

Choose one of the following topics and write a paragraph.

(1) Describe the building of a mud dauber's nest.

(2) Describe a castle. Would you have liked to live in one? Why or why not?

_____

_____

_____

_____

_____

_____

_____

_____

_____

The Cat Family

Study the spelling and meaning of each word. These words are used in today's story. Connect each word with its definition.

1. ferocious
2. includes
3. playful
4. prey
5. silent
6. various

a. no sound
b. several different
c. fierce; savage
d. animal hunted for food
e. frisky; lively
f. has as part

Read the story carefully and remember the details.

The cat family includes a wide variety of different-sized, different temperament animals. The members range from the ferocious "king of the beasts," the lion, to the friendly and playful family pet.

All members of the cat family, however, share many characteristics. Their bodies are supple. Their muscles are well-developed. Their coats of fur are beautiful and well-groomed. The coats are designed to camouflage the cats. The cats that hunt in the open have coats which are various shades of brown. Those that hunt in the forests have spotted or striped coats.

The cat's movements are silent. The cat often approaches the prey without being noticed until it is far too late. Its claws and canine teeth are superb weapons. All cats are supreme hunters.

A. Underline the correct answers about today's story.

1. The "king of the beasts" is the   (a) leopard   (b) tiger   (c) lion.
2. The fur of the cat is designed to   (a) camouflage   (b) repel water   (c) keep the cat warm.
3. Cats which hunt in the forests have   (a) brown coats   (b) no fur   (c) spotted and striped coats.
4. When moving, the cat is   (a) easily heard   (b) silent   (c) easily seen.
5. All cats are excellent   (a) pets   (b) hunters   (c) helpers.

B. Reread the story and write the answers to these questions.

1. What is the range of the cat family?

_____

_____

_____

2. Describe the coats of cats that hunt in the open.

_____

_____

_____

3. Describe the cat's movements.

_____

_____

_____

4. What are the cat's weapons?

_____

_____

_____

Unit 31 cont'd ☞

Capital Letters Signal Nouns

A. Mark an "X" on the line next to each noun that is written correctly.

  _X_   1. restaurant
_____ 2. Judge
_____ 3. san francisco
_____ 4. Plaza
_____ 5. writer
_____ 6. Howard Johnson
_____ 7. Empire State Building
_____ 8. magazine
_____ 9. The New York Times
_____ 10. Democratic
_____ 11. the Declaration of
                Independence
_____ 12. the Arctic Circle
_____ 13. the middle east
_____ 14. East
_____ 15. Apache
_____ 16. Christmas
_____ 17. Buddhism
_____ 18. the Pacific coast
_____ 19. the house of representatives

B. Underline all the common nouns in each of the following sentences.

1. <u>Professors</u> who study English found that some <u>languages</u> are related.
2. The teachers concluded that English grew from a language spoken by some people who lived in Europe and the Near East.
3. As the cultures grew, the people moved to many places such as England where our language began.
4. One of the forces that changed our language was the invasion by outside tribes.
5. The Roman invasion gave us the word "candle."
6. The Vikings gave us some words such as "sister."
7. The French gave us some words such as "government."
8. Scholars often turn Latin and Greek into new English words.
9. The word "automobile" came from the Greek word "auto" and the Latin word "mobile."
10. The word "umbrella" came from Latin; "umbra" means "shade," and "ella" means "little."
11. Explorers discovered new things in foreign lands.
12. The explorers used the words of the culture to describe the things they saw.
13. Some words explorers gave us are "igloo," "karate," "banana," and "boomerang."

78

The Celts

Study the spelling and meaning of each word. These words are used in today's story. Connect each word with its definition.

1. evil   a. adored with reverence
2. festival   b. wicked, corrupt
3. nature   c. happy holiday
4. prisoner   d. reasoned
5. thought   e. one in custody
6. worshipped   f. natural scenery

Read the story carefully and remember the details.

In the land which is now called Great Britain and northern France there once lived a group of people called the Celts. These people worshipped nature.

The Celts had many gods. The favorite was the sun god. The sun god gave the earth life. He made the crops grow.

The Celts did not know that the earth moved around the sun. They thought that the sun god disappeared every winter. The sun god was attacked by the evil powers of cold and darkness. These evil powers held the sun god prisoner for six months. The sun god fought the powers and won. He returned to the earth and made everything bright again.

Each year on November 1 the Celts held a big festival. The celts celebrated the end of the season of the sun. In the spring they celebrated the sun's return.

A. Underline the correct answers about today's story.

1. The Celts worshipped   (a) nature   (b) light   (c) death.
2. Their favorite god was the   (a) sun god   (b) god of coldness   (c) god of darkness.
3. Every winter the sun   (a) appeared   (b) disappeared   (c) was reborn.
4. Darkness was considered   (a) as life   (b) good   (c) evil.
5. On November 1, the Celts
   celebrated the   (a) evil powers   (b) sun's return   (c) sun's departure.

B. Reread the story and write the answers to these questions.

1. What is the land on which the Celts lived now called?

_____

_____

_____

2. What did the sun god do?

_____

_____

_____

3. How long was the sun god thought to be held prisoner?

_____

_____

_____

4. What did the Celts celebrate in the spring?

_____

_____

_____

Unit 32 cont'd ☞

Noun Adjuncts

A. Underline the noun adjunct or adjuncts in each of the following sentences. Remember, noun adjuncts modify or describe other nouns.

EXAMPLE: *The <u>newspaper</u> boy left.*

1. The apple pie tasted delicious.
2. Her sun hat had a wide brim.
3. An American dollar is almost worthless.
4. That lady is a ballet dancer.
5. Each person has a ticket to the picture show.
6. All china and silverware imports are banned.
7. Our mother has an antique clock.
8. Let's all move to the ballroom floor.

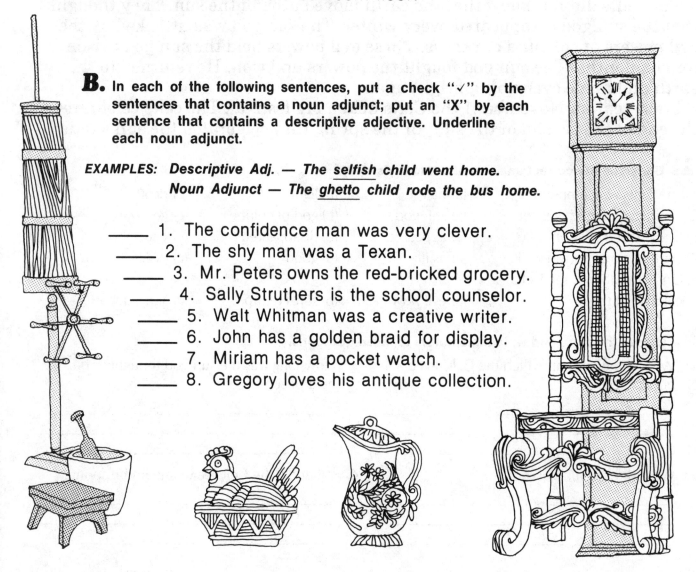

B. In each of the following sentences, put a check "✓" by the sentences that contains a noun adjunct; put an "X" by each sentence that contains a descriptive adjective. Underline each noun adjunct.

EXAMPLES: *Descriptive Adj. — The <u>selfish</u> child went home.*
Noun Adjunct — The <u>ghetto</u> child rode the bus home.

_____ 1. The confidence man was very clever.
_____ 2. The shy man was a Texan.
_____ 3. Mr. Peters owns the red-bricked grocery.
_____ 4. Sally Struthers is the school counselor.
_____ 5. Walt Whitman was a creative writer.
_____ 6. John has a golden braid for display.
_____ 7. Miriam has a pocket watch.
_____ 8. Gregory loves his antique collection.

The Chevrotain

Study the spelling and meaning of each word. These words are used in today's story. Connect each word with its definition.

1. aloof
2. bigger
3. combination
4. defends
5. habitat
6. pairs

a. guards
b. union
c. larger
d. natural home
e. groups of two
f. showing no interest

Read the story carefully and remember the details.

The chevrotain is a tiny animal that is a combination of many animals. It has the legs of a deer, the body shape of a mouse, the teeth of a wild pig, and the stomach of a camel. Some people call the chevrotain a deer mouse.

The chevrotain is not much bigger than a large rabbit. It makes its way through the forest without a sound. The chevrotain's habitat is in Africa.

During the day the chevrotain sleeps. At night it hunts for berries and leaves. The chevrotain lives alone or in pairs.

The chevrotain is really a helpless animal. It defends itself by hiding, climbing onto low tree branches, or jumping into the water.

The chevrotain is shy and aloof. Its cry is a weak noise.

A. **Underline the correct answers about today's story.**

1. The chevrotain has the legs of a   (a) mouse   (b) wild pig   (c) deer.
2. The chevrotain is active   (a) at night   (b) in the daytime   (c) at dusk.
3. The chevrotain defends itself   (a) by hiding   (b) with its sharp claws   (c) with its sharp teeth.
4. Which word describes the chevrotain?   (a) dangerous   (b) aloof   (c) social
5. Where does the chevrotain live?   (a) Africa   (b) United States   (c) Europe

B. **Reread the story and write the answers to these questions.**

1. What does the chevrotain do during the day?

_____
_____
_____

2. What does it do at night?

_____
_____
_____

3. How large is the chevrotain?

_____
_____
_____

4. How does the chevrotain defend itself?

_____
_____
_____

Unit 33 cont'd

Nouns

A. Unscramble each set of letters to make a word.

1. miet   *time*
2. nmyoe _____
3. eter _____
4. ccklo _____
5. lrgi _____

6. wkor _____
7. tdyoa _____
8. onno _____
9. trehe _____
10. rtus _____

11. nbuerm _____
12. ptnuea _____
13. mgea _____
14. wndiow _____
15. ppliu _____

B. Write "c" for "common noun." Write "p" for "proper noun."

___c___ 1. dime
_____ 2. Monday
_____ 3. gorilla
_____ 4. professor
_____ 5. Chevrolet

_____ 6. California
_____ 7. weather
_____ 8. Omaha
_____ 9. river
_____ 10. home

_____ 11. Ms. Watson
_____ 12. mountain
_____ 13. Dr. Stevens
_____ 14. December
_____ 15. newspaper

_____ 16. capital
_____ 17. orchestra
_____ 18. children
_____ 19. Pacific Ocean
_____ 20. artichoke

C. Underline the words which should be capitalized.

1. i was born in denver, colorado.
2. my cousin's name is cynthia.
3. louis is talking to frank.
4. i won't be back until thursday.
5. have you read huckleberry finn?
6. it is six o'clock.
7. brenda is carla's best friend.
8. let's sing ''on top of old smokey.''
9. you shouldn't work so hard.
10. who was that man?
11. she will visit me in july.
12. we have nothing to do but wait.
13. who wrote the poem ''the snail''?
14. terry and i went to the show.
15. how did you know the answer?
16. don't tell anyone else.
17. look at that!
18. yesterday was wednesday.
19. jackie introduced mr. thompson.
20. may i sit down and rest?

D. Which two nouns make up each compound word?

1. toothache   *tooth*   *ache*
2. flashlight _____ _____
3. switchboard _____ _____
4. firecracker _____ _____
5. sunshine _____ _____
6. carwash _____ _____
7. seashore _____ _____
8. downhill _____ _____
9. textbook _____ _____
10. bumblebee _____ _____

E. Write either "a" or "an" before each noun.

1. __a__ diamond
2. _____ aardvark
3. _____ novel
4. _____ squeak
5. _____ exam
6. _____ pretzel
7. _____ umbrella
8. _____ orchestra
9. _____ lesson
10. _____ earache

11. _____ invitation
12. _____ pineapple
13. _____ storm
14. _____ broom
15. _____ account
16. _____ whistle
17. _____ island
18. _____ allowance
19. _____ officer
20. _____ circle

Cheyenne

Study the spelling and meaning of each word. These words are used in today's story. Connect each word with its definition.

1. appointed ——————— a. named officially
2. entire   b. whole or all
3. interested   c. concerned
4. nomad   d. wanderer
5. rare   e. seldom met with
6. stalked   f. approached

Read the story carefully and remember the details.

In Cheyenne society every member had an appointed place. The society was a close-knit community. The Cheyenne shared hardships and sorrows. The society was a happy and orderly one where crime was rare.

Every tribe had a number of chiefs. No single man could ever speak for the entire tribe.

The Cheyenne were nomads. They roamed freely over the Great Plains. They stalked the grazing buffalo herds.

Everything the Cheyenne possessed was suited to their roving lives. Cheyenne were not interested in collecting material things. They treasured freedom and independence. When the white settlers began their westward migration, the Cheyenne's orderly way of life ended.

A. Underline the correct answers about today's story.

1. The Cheyenne community was   (a) disorderly   (b) uncaring   (c) close-knit.
2. In Cheyenne society crime was   (a) rare   (b) common   (c) frequent.
3. The tribe was led by   (a) one man   (b) a priest   (c) many chiefs.
4. The Cheyenne treasured   (a) freedom   (b) wars   (c) material things.
5. What disrupted the Cheyenne's way of life?   (a) buffalo   (b) white settlers   (c) weather

B. Reread the story and write the answers to these questions.

1. What did the Cheyenne share?

_____

_____

_____

2. Where did the Cheyenne roam?

_____

_____

_____

3. What did not interest the Cheyenne?

_____

_____

_____

4. Why could no single man speak for the tribe?

_____

_____

_____

Unit 34 cont'd ☛

A Noun Puzzle

1. s	2.	3.	4.				5.
e		6.			7.	8.	
9. c	10.		11.				12.
u	13.	14.	15.	16.			
r	17.		18.				
i		19.		20.			
21. t	22.	23.	24.				
y			25.	26.			
27.							

Fill in the blanks. Then complete the puzzle.

Down

1. <u>s e c u r i t y</u> feeling of being safe; surety

2. _ _ _ automobile

3. _ _ _ _ _ group of animals of one kind herded together

4. _ _ _ opening; unfilled space; empty part

5. _ _ _ _ _ _ _ _ _ _ process of changing food so the body can absorb it

6. _ _ _ _ _ means of fastening doors, windows, or boxes

7. _ _ _ _ passageway; way through a building

8. _ _ _ _ _ farm implement; machine for moving snow

9. _ _ _ worthless dog of mixed breed

11. _ _ _ _ person who carries parcels, delivers messages

12. _ _ _ _ story of romance in verse; tale

13. _ _ _ _ _ look long with eyes wide open

16. _ _ _ _ _ _ _ nap or rest taken at noon or in the afternoon

17. _ _ _ _ substance obtained by distillation of wood or coal

19. _ _ _ _ short seam to make a garment fit better

23. _ _ _ painting, drawing, and sculpture

Across

4. _ _ _ _ _ _ small mallet used by presiding officer

6. _ _ _ _ _ _ the act or sounds made that show one is happy

8. _ _ ratio of the circumference of a circle to its diameter

9. _ _ _ _ _ plants grown or gathered; especially as food

10. _ _ _ _ _ strong, thick line or cord

11. _ _ _ _ _ _ part of a flower that is usually colored

14. _ _ _ _ _ money in the form of coins or bills

15. _ _ _ _ shade tree with tough wood

18. _ _ _ _ _ part of a fish that enables it to breathe in water

19. _ _ _ _ _ brave, skillful or unusual act

20. _ _ _ _ _ the line or place where something ends

21. _ _ _ _ _ device for catching animals

22. _ _ _ _ a quick, light blow; light, sharp knock

24. _ _ _ _ _ _ a sacred song or poem

25. _ _ _ _ _ _ _ slice of beef, especially cut from the hindquarter

26. _ _ _ _ _ heavy, resinous wood of great strength and durability

27. _ _ _ _ _ _ _ _ _ _ _ combination of circumstances; job or position

The Chimney Swift

Study the spelling and meaning of each word. These words are used in today's story. Connect each word with its definition.

1. arranges
2. favorite
3. resembles
4. saliva
5. separate
6. suitable

a. most preferred
b. prepares; puts in order
c. watery liquid in the mouth
d. individual; distinct
e. looks like
f. appropriate

Read the story carefully and remember the details.

The chimney swift gets its name from its favorite home, the chimney. It is a small bird whose coloring of dark gray resembles the sooty walls of its home.

After finding a suitable chimney, the chimney swift begins to build the nest. It collects dead twigs and arranges them into a half circle. The twigs are glued together with the bird's saliva. The nest is attached to the inside wall of the chimney. Saliva is again used to hold the nest in place.

The chimney swift has small legs and feet, but it is strong enough to hold on to the walls of the chimney. Even baby birds instinctively know how to climb the walls.

The chimney swift may also nest in hollow trees, barns, silos, and old wells. Its preference, however, is for chimneys. Each pair of chimney swifts sets up housekeeping in a separate chimney.

A. Underline the correct answers about today's story.

1. The chimney swift gets its name from its   (a) coloring   (b) size   (c) home.
2. The nest is made of   (a) twigs   (b) ashes   (c) grass.
3. The twigs are held together with   (a) string   (b) feathers   (c) saliva.
4. Chimney swifts nest in   (a) pairs   (b) large flocks   (c) groups of ten.
5. What color is the chimney swift?   (a) white   (b) gray   (c) black

B. Reread the story and write the answers to these questions.

1. What does the color of the chimney swift resemble?

_____

_____

_____

2. Where does the chimney swift attach its nest?

_____

_____

_____

3. How do baby birds know to climb the walls?

_____

_____

_____

4. Name alternate nesting places for the bird.

_____

_____

_____

Unit 35 cont'd ☞

Common Nouns

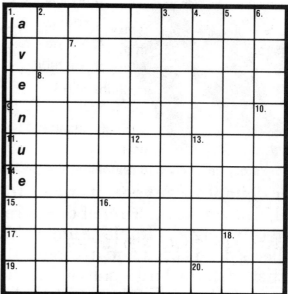

Other Common Nouns

girl	uncle
day	aunt
country	theater
holiday	lake
nation	building
autumn	south
fall	boy
summer	railroad
document	sea

 Fill in the blanks. Then complete the puzzle.

Down

1. _a v e n u e_ city thoroughfare

2. _ _ _ _ _ shed for small animals

3. _ _ _ _ _ _ _ _ _ periodical

4. _ _ _ _ _ quick, sharp sound

5. _ _ _ _ _ _ _ public road in a city

6. _ _ _ _ _ heavenly body appearing at night

10. _ _ _ _ _ _ large, natural stream of water

12. _ _ _ _ _ _ sent to find the enemy

13. _ _ _ _ _ important town

18. _ _ mother (informal)

Across

2. _ _ _ _ _ same as "13" down

7. _ _ _ _ _ _ great body of salt water

8. _ _ _ _ _ people working together, especially in a game

9. _ _ _ _ _ _ _ _ _ _ sheets of printed paper telling the news

11. _ _ _ _ _ thin, long bone of the forearm

14. _ _ _ _ _ large, red deer

15. _ _ _ _ _ land used to raise crops

16. _ _ _ _ _ _ one-twelfth of a year

17. _ _ _ _ _ permanent military station

19. _ _ _ _ _ _ _ property; possessions

20. _ _ _ _ automobile

Comprehension Check

(A) Underline the nouns.

1. circle
2. freedom
3. freely
4. home
5. arranges
6. muscles
7. hunter
8. and
9. French
10. winter
11. family
12. things
13. Katherine
14. treasured
15. chiefs
16. through
17. earth
18. chevrotain
19. aloof
20. movements
21. where
22. community
23. speak
24. members
25. migration
26. weapons
27. resembles
28. westward
29. together
30. Great Britain

(B) Connect each noun with its definition.

1. saliva
2. forest
3. crime
4. nature
5. prey
6. chimney
7. combination
8. characteristics
9. prisoner
10. society
11. preference
12. earth
13. habitat
14. nomads
15. independence

a. an act that is against the law
b. large areas of land covered with trees
c. liquid produced in the mouth
d. animal hunted for food
e. the part of a fireplace that rises through the roof
f. person kept shut up against his will
g. all things except those made by people
h. special qualities or features
i. the act of liking better
j. things joined together for a common purpose
k. people joined together by a common interest
l. the planet on which we live
m. people that move from place to place
n. freedom from influence or control of others
o. place where one naturally lives

(C) Underline the nouns which should be capitalized.

1. cheyenne
2. dr. gladen
3. november
4. boston
5. sweden
6. atlantic ocean
7. english
8. mr. stevenson
9. winter
10. territory
11. mrs. adams
12. shawn
13. language
14. celts
15. secret
16. africa
17. tuesday
18. easter
19. lawyer
20. annette

(D) Complete these sentences.

1. Some call the chevrotain the ___*deer mouse*___ .
2. The chimney swift lives in a _____ .
3. The chevrotain is a _____ animal.
4. All cats are supreme _____ .
5. The Cheyenne community was _____ .
6. A cat's movements are _____ .

7. The Celts worshipped _____ .
8. The Cheyenne treasured _____ .
9. The color of a chimney swift resembles _____ .
10. On November 1 the Celts celebrated the end of the season of the _____ .

Test 7 cont'd 👉

Comprehension Check (continued)

(E) Match these words and their definitions. These words appeared in the reading selections from units 31-35.

_**b**_ 1. nomads   ___ 7. defends   a. approached   g. distinct

___ 2. stalked   ___ 8. habitat   b. wanderers   h. most preferred

___ 3. ferocious   ___ 9. pairs   c. fierce   i. protects

___ 4. playful   ___ 10. favorite   d. respected reverently   j. frisky

___ 5. prisoner   ___ 11. resembles   e. groups of two   k. looks like

___ 6. worshipped   ___ 12. separate   f. one held captive   l. natural home

(F) Underline the correct answers.

1. Where did the Cheyenne roam?   (a) Smoky Mountains   (b) <u>Great Plains</u>
2. What did not interest the Cheyenne?   (a) material things   (b) independence
3. Describe a cat's movements.   (a) silent   (b) clumsy
4. What are a cat's weapons?   (a) claws, teeth   (b) guns
5. What was the Celt's favorite god?   (a) god of the ocean   (b) sun god
6. What was celebrated on November 1?   (a) sun's departure   (b) harvest
7. What does the chevrotain do during the day?   (a) hunt   (b) sleep
8. What is the chevrotain's defense?   (a) clawing   (b) hiding
9. What composes the chimney swift's nest?   (a) dead twigs   (b) wet leaves
10. Name one alternate home for the chimney swift.   (a) old well   (b) drain pipe

Choose one of the following topics and write a paragraph.

(1) The Cheyenne's community was happy and orderly. Crime was rare. What could be done today to return to this way of life?

(2) Many animals, such as wild cats, are hunted for sport. Some are in danger of extinction. Should such hunting be allowed? Why or why not?

_____
_____
_____
_____
_____
_____
_____
_____
_____

Climbing Perch

Study the spelling and meaning of each word. These words are used in today's story. Connect each word with its definition.

1. accustomed
2. loss
3. migrates
4. periodic
5. prevented
6. strange

a. odd
b. used to
c. happening repeatedly
d. decrease in amount
e. kept from happening
f. moves from one place to another

Read the story carefully and remember the details.

The climbing perch is a strange fish with some unusual habits. The climbing perch is one of the few fish that can live out of the water.

The climbing perch can live for hours out of the water. It has a very thick skin which slows down the loss of moisture. In fact, the fish is so accustomed to its periodic trips out of water that it would drown if prevented from doing so. The climbing perch has the habit of resting on tree trunks which stick out above the water.

When a pond dries up, the perch migrates to a new home. It usually travels at night.

The climbing perch makes a wonderful pet. It can be kept in an aquarium that has water on one end and dry sand on the other.

A. Underline the correct answers about today's story.

1. How long can the fish stay out
   of water?   (a) days   (b) hours   (c) weeks
2. To keep in moisture, the fish has   (a) thick skin   (b) water bags   (c) thin skin.
3. Where does the fish rest?   (a) on river banks (b) in water   (c) on tree trunks
4. When a pond dries up, the fish   (a) migrates   (b) dies   (c) buries itself.
5. When does the perch travel?   (a) on rainy days (b) during the day   (c) at night

B. Reread the story and write the answers to these questions.

1. What is unusual about the climbing perch?

_____
_____
_____

2. What would happen to the fish if prevented from leaving the water?

_____
_____
_____

3. When does the fish seek a new home?

_____
_____
_____

4. What would an aquarium require to be a home for the fish?

_____
_____
_____

Proper Nouns

 Fill in the blanks. Then complete the puzzle.

Across

1. _W_ _h_ _i_ _g_ was a name for political parties in England, Scotland, and America.

2. Henry _ _ _ _ _ led the National League in home runs in 1957, 1963, 1966, and 1967.

4. Eastman _ _ _ _ _ Company is one of the world's largest manufacturers of photographic equipment.

5. The Striped _ _ _ _ _ of South America, somewhat like a frog, has dry, warty skin.

7. _ _ _ _ _ _ is the second largest state in the United States.

10. The Tiger _ _ _ _ _ is a tall garden flower that originally grew in eastern Asia.

11. _ _ _ _ _ was the eldest son of Adam and Eve.

12. _ _ _ _ _ His wife is a countess.

15. _ _ _ _ _ _ _ The basic unit of money of this country is the franc.

16. _ _ _ _ Mahal is one of the most beautiful and costly tombs in the world.

18. English _ _ _ _ Spaniel—There are four kinds of these small dogs.

19. Alexander Graham _ _ _ _ _ invented the telephone.

21. The Purebred _ _ _ _ _ _ Cattle Association is an organization of about 25 dairy farmers.

22. _ _ _ _ is the fifth sign of the zodiac.

23. _ _ _ _ _ _ _ is a Christian festival that celebrates the resurrection of Jesus Christ.

24. The New England _ _ _ _ _ _ has deep purple flowers.

25. _ _ _ _, Nevada, is the center of one of the great mining districts in the United States.

26. _ _ _ _ _ _ This month honors Mars, the Roman god of war.

27. Gateway _ _ _ _ _ , in St. Louis, ranks as the tallest monument constructed in the United States.

Down

3. _ _ _ _ _ _ _ _ is the capital of and largest city in Georgia.

6. Elfreth's _ _ _ _ _ _, in Philadelphia, is one of the oldest streets in the United States.

8. _ _ _ _ _ Germany surrounds the city of Berlin.

9. The Red _ _ _ has been the great waterway between Europe and the Orient.

13. _ _ _ _ _ Julius Caesar was born during this month.

14. The _ _ _ _ _ _ is the most sacred book of the Jewish and Christian religions.

17. _ _ _ _ _ and Eve were the parents of the human race, according to the Bible.

20. Robert E. _ _ _ _ commanded the Confederate Army during the Civil War.

The Cormorant

Study the spelling and meaning of each word. These words are used in today's story. Connect each word with its definition.

1. agile
2. awkward
3. importantly
4. rewarded
5. tamed
6. trained

a. given something in return for good
b. significantly
c. brisk; active
d. not having grace
e. changed from wild
f. taught

Read the story carefully and remember the details.

The cormorant is a bird that has often been called the living submarine. It is an excellent swimmer and diver. The cormorant has been known to dive over 100 feet deep.

Like other water birds, the legs of the cormorant are far back on the body. On land, the bird is awkward; but on the sea it is agile.

In China and Japan the cormorant has been trained to fish with people. The fisherman ties a strap around the bird's throat. The strap keeps the bird near its owner, but more importantly, it keeps the bird from swallowing the fish. When the bird brings in a supply of fish, it is rewarded. The cormorant is easily tamed.

A. Underline the correct answers about today's story.

1. The cormorant is a	(a) ship	(b) fish	(c) bird.
2. On land, the cormorant is	(a) agile	(b) awkward	(c) graceful.
3. The cormorant can be trained to work with	(a) fishermen	(b) sailors	(c) other birds.
4. The cormorant is not a good	(a) swimmer	(b) diver	(c) land bird.
5. What does the cormorant eat?	(a) fish	(b) seeds	(c) insects

B. Reread the story and write the answers to these questions.

1. What is the cormorant often called?

_____

_____

_____

2. How deep has the cormorant been known to dive?

_____

_____

_____

3. How is the bird kept near its owner when fishing?

_____

_____

_____

4. What happens when the cormorant brings in a supply of fish?

_____

_____

_____

Unit 37 cont'd ☞

Noun Markers

Noun markers help to identify nouns. Almost all sentences contain noun markers. They point out that a noun is to follow. A noun marker is an excellent way of telling whether a word is a noun.

✴ **Fill in the blanks. Then complete the puzzle.**

Down

1. _a l l_ every one of; the whole of; every kind or sort

2. _ _ _ _ everyone considered separately or one by one

3. _ _ _ _ the two; the one and the other

4. _ _ _ _ certain or particular but not known or named

5. _ _ _ _ indicating the nearer of two

7. _ _ _ single unit or individual; single kind

8. _ _ _ _ pointing out a certain one

9. _ _ _ _ _ _ _ _ one more; not the same; a different one

10. _ _ word used to say you can't or won't

11. _ _ _ _ greatest in amount, quantity, measure, degree, or number

12. _ _ _ _ one more than one; a set of one and one

15. _ _ _ _ _ remaining; different; additional or further

16. _ _ _ _ numerous; considering a great number

19. _ _ _ not many; amounting to a small number

24. _ indefinite article; one like; another

Across

5. _ _ _ _ _ _ indicating the ones nearest

6. _ _ _ _ greater in amount, quantity, measure, degree, or number

13. _ _ _ _ used in asking questions about people or things

14. _ _ _ _ _ _ pointing out or indicating certain ones

17. _ _ _ shows that a certain one is meant

18. _ _ _ _ indicating a certain one

20. _ _ _ one out of many; no matter how great or how small

21. _ _ _ _ _ referring to the one or ones specified

22. _ _ _ _ _ _ _ being more than two or three

23. _ _ _ _ _ each one of the entire number

24. _ _ indefinite article; one; any; each

Crabs

Study the spelling and meaning of each word. These words are used in today's story. Connect each word with its definition.

1. caught
2. discarded
3. maturity
4. molts
5. pincers
6. protective

a. gripping tools
b. taken captive
c. that guards or protects
d. fully grown
e. thrown away
f. sheds outer covering

Read the story carefully and remember the details.

Most animals run forward, but the crab is not like most animals. It runs sideways.

The crab has eight legs and two big pincers. If a pincer is lost, the crab is able to grow a new one.

The crab lives in or near the sea. It eats old or dead sea animals. The crab is always hungry. It helps keep the water clean by eating the dead animals. The crab is caught each year for food.

The crab has a protective shell. When the crab grows, the shell becomes too tight. The old shell is discarded. Meanwhile, the crab has grown a new shell. At first this shell is soft but it soon hardens. Until this hardening process is finished, the crab hides under rocks. The changing of the shells is called molting. The young crab molts often to reach full maturity.

A. Underline the correct answers about today's story.

1. Crabs run	(a) forward	(b) sideways	(c) backward.
2. Crabs live in or near the	(a) sea	(b) rivers	(c) desert.
3. While the shell hardens, the crab	(a) hides in water	(b) burrows in sand	(c) hides under rocks.
4. The changing of the shell is called	(a) molting	(b) shedding	(c) shelling.
5. When a crab loses a pincer, it	(a) hides	(b) dies	(c) grows a new one.

B. Reread the story and write the answers to these questions.

1. How many legs does the crab have?

_____

_____

_____

2. What does the crab eat?

_____

_____

_____

3. How is the crab a helpful animal?

_____

_____

_____

4. As the crab grows, what happens to its shell?

_____

_____

_____

Unit 38 cont'd ☞

Pronouns

Most pronouns have a different form for the subject form and the object form. The subject form is used when it functions as the subject or as a linking-verb complement. The object form is used when the pronoun functions as the direct object or as the object of a preposition.

 Fill in the blanks. Then complete the puzzle.

Across

3. _t_ _h_ _e_ _m_ objective case of "they"

7. _ _ _ _ used in asking questions about a person or persons

9. _ _ _ possessive form of the thing, part, animal or person spoken about

10. _ _ _ _ _ used when asking questions about persons or things

12. _ _ _ _ _ the one or ones belonging to her

13. _ _ objective form of the word "I"

16. _ _ _ _ _ _ _ no one; no person

18. _ _ _ _ of him; belonging to him

19. _ _ _ _ _ _ _ any person; anybody

20. _ _ first person, subjective plural of "I"

21. _ _ _ _ _ the subjective plural of "he," "she," or "it"

22. _ _ _ singular, subjective form; female spoken about or mentioned before

23. _ _ _ _ _ _ used when asking questions about persons or things

Down

1. _ _ _ _ _ _ _ possessive form of "they"; belonging to them

2. _ _ _ _ _ _ possessive form of "you"; the ones belonging to you

4. _ _ _ _ objective case of "he"

5. _ _ _ _ _ _ _ _ _ _ each person; every person, grammatically singular

6. _ _ possessive form of "I"; belonging to me

8. _ _ _ _ _ of or belonging to you

11. _ _ the thing, part, animal, or person spoken about

14. _ _ _ _ _ the one or ones belonging to me

15. _ _ _ _ _ _ possessive form of "they"; belonging to them

17. _ _ _ _ the person or persons spoken to

94

The Crayfish

Study the spelling and meaning of each word. These words are used in today's story. Connect each word with its definition.

1. behind   a. depending on
2. entrance   b. in back of
3. relying   c. animal that is hunted
4. scarce   d. takes hold of
5. seizes   e. entry passageway
6. victim   f. not plentiful

Read the story carefully and remember the details.

The crayfish is also called the crawfish. It lives in ponds, rivers, streams, and lakes. Its home is a burrow in the sand or mud.

At night the crayfish hides at the entrance of its home or behind some cover. It waits patiently for its prey. When its victim swims by, the crayfish seizes it with its powerful pincers. The victim is torn to pieces and immediately eaten. The crayfish prefers to eat meat which it has caught. However, when food is scarce, it will feed on plants or dead animals.

The crayfish usually avoids its enemies by relying on its coloring. When alarmed, the crayfish can shoot backwards at surprising speed. The crayfish spends much of its time hiding beneath rocks on the stream's bottom.

A. Underline the correct answers about today's story.

1. Where is the crayfish's home?   (a) in a burrow   (b) in a cave   (c) under rocks
2. When does the crayfish hunt food?   (a) night   (b) early morning   (c) afternoon
3. The crayfish seizes its prey with its (a) teeth   (b) long arms   (c) pincers.
4. To avoid enemies, the crayfish relies on its (a) power (b) coloring   (c) speed.
5. Which word does not describe the
   crayfish?   (a) patient   (b) helpless   (c) powerful

B. Reread the story and write the answers to these questions.

1. What is another name for the crayfish?

   _____

   _____

   _____

2. Name the bodies of water in which a crayfish might live.

   _____

   _____

   _____

3. What does the crayfish eat when food is scarce?

   _____

   _____

   _____

4. Where does the crayfish spend much of its time?

   _____

   _____

   _____

Unit 39 cont'd ☞

Indefinite Pronouns

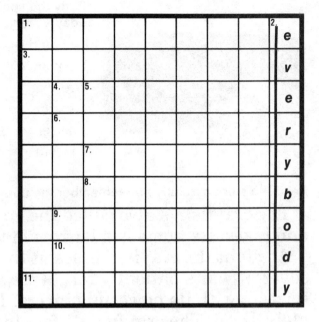

Pronouns that refer to no special person or thing are indefinite pronouns. Other indefinite pronouns are as follows: no one, one, many, none, some, both, and everything.

 Fill in the blanks. Then complete the puzzle.

Down

2. _e_ _v_ _e_ _r_ _y_ _b_ _o_ _d_ _y_ every person, grammatically singular, sometimes used as collective

3. _ _ _ _ _ _ _ _ some person; somebody

4. _ _ _ _ _ every one of two or more persons or things considered separately or one by one

Across

1. _ _ _ _ _ _ _ _ _ _ often two words; particular thing not mentioned; a certain amount

3. _ _ _ _ _ _ _ _ _ a person not known or named; some person; someone

5. _ _ _ _ _ _ _ _ any person, written as one word when the stress is put on the first of the word

6. _ _ _ _ _ _ _ _ any person; any one

7. _ _ _ _ _ _ _ one or the other of two; each of two; this word can be used as an adjective, pronoun, adverb, or conjunction

8. _ _ _ _ _ _ _ no one; no person; a person of no importance

9. _ _ _ _ _ _ _ one more; not the same; different; one of the same kind

10. _ _ _ _ _ _ _ _ not either

11. _ _ _ _ _ _ _ _ _ every person, grammatically singular, sometimes used as collective; when "one" is stressed, written as two words

96

The Crested Porcupine

Study the spelling and meaning of each word. These words are used in today's story. Connect each word with its definition.

1. appetite
2. considerable
3. relative
4. scarce
5. several
6. social

a. noteworthy
b. not plentiful
c. associating in groups
d. connected by blood or marriage
e. desire for food or drink
f. many

Read the story carefully and remember the details.

A close relative of the American porcupine is the crested porcupine. The crested porcupine is a native of Africa, Asia, and Europe.

The crested porcupine lives in an underground nest at the end of a long tunnel. The home is usually in an area where there is plenty of underbrush or rocks to hide the animal. The crested porcupine is very social. Often several live together.

The crested porcupine eats grasses and vegetables. It has a large appetite and often does considerable damage to crops. It eats corn, potatoes, pumpkins, and fruits. When food is scarce, the crested porcupine is able to live on tree bark.

The crested porcupine has long quills which lie flat except when the animal is excited. It fights by turning its back on its opponent and slapping it with its tail.

A. Underline the correct answers about today's story.

1. The crested porcupine is a native of   (a) America   (b) Europe   (c) Australia.
2. The animal lives where there is plenty of   (a) underbrush   (b) water   (c) sun.
3. To its own kind, the crested porcupine is   (a) deadly   (b) antisocial   (c) social.
4. When not excited, the quills   (a) lie flat   (b) stand erect   (c) are hidden.
5. The crested porcupine fights by   (a) shooting quills   (b) clawing   (c) slapping.

B. Reread the story and write the answers to these questions.

1. Describe the crested porcupine's personality.

_____

_____

_____

2. What does the animal usually eat?

_____

_____

_____

3. What happens to the animal's quills when he is excited?

_____

_____

_____

4. When food is scarce, what does the porcupine live on?

_____

_____

_____

Unit 40 cont'd ☞

Positions of Adjectives

A. Underline the attributive adjectives in the following sentences.

1. The workers buy lunch from <u>vending</u> machines.
2. That large house was listed in the paper.
3. The restaurant served excellent chicken.
4. We go to our beach house every summer.
5. There was a terrible snowstorm in the northern states.
6. I will go to the fall carnival.

B. Underline the predicate adjectives in the following sentences.

1. The perfume smells sweet.
2. He looks pale.
3. Many children are tall.
4. The teacher seems happy today.
5. His hair was short.

C. Show what position the underlined adjective takes in each of the following sentences. Write the correct letter on the line before each sentence. Follow the example.

Positions

A - attributive   *EXAMPLES:*   *a. Mary wants <u>chocolate</u> milk.*

B - predicate   *b. I feel <u>good</u>.*

____ 1. The lawyer is wearing a <u>light</u> coat.
____ 2. Margaret became <u>lonely</u> in the hospital.
____ 3. Mindy looks very <u>tired</u> today.

Comprehension Check

(A) **Match each proper noun with its definition.**

1. Whig
2. Texas
3. Kodak
4. France
5. Easter
6. Atlanta
7. March
8. Adam
9. July
10. Taj Mahal

a. one of the world's largest manufacturers of photo equipment
b. second largest state in the United States
c. country whose basic monetary unit is the franc
d. Christian holiday that celebrates the resurrection of Christ
e. a political party
f. month that honors Mars, the Roman god of war
g. capital and largest city in Georgia
h. one of the most beautiful and costly tombs of the world
i. month in which Julius Caesar was born
j. male parent of the human race, according to the Bible

(B) **Underline the pronouns.**

1. you
2. our
3. we
4. them
5. thing
6. he
7. mine
8. ask
9. they
10. noun
11. your
12. it
13. person
14. I
15. who
16. everyone
17. their
18. us
19. him
20. before

(C) **Add the indefinite pronouns.**

1. _____Someone_____ is at the door.
2. _____ agreed with Ted.
3. Don't say _____ .
4. _____ has stolen the money!
5. Has _____ seen my pencil?
6. _____ was at home.
7. Did _____ see them?
8. _____ is wrong.

9. _____ likes Jeremy.
10. _____ was given his allowance.
11. _____ was willing to help.
12. Did _____ call me?
13. _____ will talk to me!
14. _____ is fine with me.
15. I have _____ to do.
16. _____ signed the petition.

(D) **Complete these sentences.**

1. On the sea the cormorant is _____agile_____ .
2. Crested porcupines are very _____ .
3. A crab runs _____ .
4. When alarmed, the crayfish moves _____ .
5. Crested porcupines often damage _____ .
6. The climbing perch often stays out of the _____ .

7. Some train the cormorant to _____ .
8. The climbing perch is a _____ .
9. A crab is always _____ .
10. Crayfish are also called _____ .
11. Crested porcupines eat _____ .
12. The cormorant has often been called a living _____ .

 Test 8 cont'd ☛

Comprehension Check (continued)

E Match these words and their definitions. These words appeared in the reading selections from units 36-40.

_h_ 1. periodic   ____ 7. maturity
____ 2. accustomed   ____ 8. relying
____ 3. strange   ____ 9. scarce
____ 4. agile   ____ 10. behind
____ 5. trained   ____ 11. considerable
____ 6. discarded   ____ 12. several

a. in back of   g. able to move quickly
b. depending on   h. happening repeatedly
c. fully grown   i. taught
d. not plentiful   j. used to
e. thrown away   k. many; quite a few
f. odd   l. large in extent

F Underline the correct answers.

1. Where does the climbing perch rest?   (a) <u>tree trunks</u>   (b) in the water
2. When does the perch travel?   (a) spring   (b) at night
3. What does the cormorant eat?   (a) seeds   (b) fish
4. What is the cormorant often called?   (a) land bird   (b) living submarine
5. What is the changing of a crab's shell called? (a) molting   (b) harvesting
6. How many legs does the crab have?   (a) six   (b) eight
7. When does the crayfish hunt food?   (a) at night   (b) during the day
8. What is another name for the crayfish?   (a) crawfish   (b) mudfish
9. What does the crested porcupine eat?   (a) vegetables   (b) rodents
10. What country is home to the porcupine?   (a) Mexico   (b) Africa

Choose one of the following topics and write a paragraph.

(1) Just as the climbing perch is a fish with habits different than most, there are also people with habits different than most. How do you react to people from different cultures? Why?

(2) The crab does its part to keep the ocean clean by eating dead animals. Do you think people do enough to keep the ocean and beaches clean?

_____
_____
_____
_____
_____
_____
_____
_____
_____
_____
_____

Dall Sheep

Study the spelling and meaning of each word. These words are used in today's story. Connect each word with its definition.

1. choice
2. elevation
3. game
4. influenced
5. migrate
6. presence

a. place where animal is
b. preference
c. controlled; affected by
d. a high place on the earth
e. move from one place to another
f. animal hunted for food or sport

Read the story carefully and remember the details.

Like other mountain sheep, Dall sheep do not travel or migrate unless food supply or weather conditions force them. Dall sheep are grazing animals.

During the summer, Dall sheep live at higher elevations. When colder weather sets in, the sheep move down the mountain.

The sheep's choice of a home is also influenced by the presence of wolves. When wolves are around, the sheep live at higher elevations.

The melting snow is a source of water for the Dall sheep. Water is also available from mountain springs.

Dall sheep depend on keen eyesight and sense of smell to protect them from their main enemy, the timber wolf. Dall sheep are game animals, highly prized by people.

A. Underline the correct answers about today's story.

1. Where do Dall sheep live?   (a) open range   (b) forests   (c) mountains
2. What forces the sheep to move?   (a) food supply   (b) weather   (c) both a and b
3. When wolves are near, the sheep move   (a) lower   (b) higher   (c) to a different mountain.
4. What is the sheep's main enemy?   (a) wolf   (b) man   (c) weather
5. Dall sheep are hunted for   (a) food   (b) fur   (c) sport.

B. Reread the story and write the answers to these questions.

1. Name something that influences where the sheep live.

_____
_____
_____

2. Name two sources of water for the sheep.

_____
_____
_____

3. How do the sheep protect themselves?

_____
_____
_____

4. Who is their main enemy?

_____
_____
_____

Unit 41 cont'd ☞

Order of Adjectives

A. Write phrases for each group of words, placing the adjectives in the proper order. Follow the example.

noun	adjectives	phrase
EXAMPLE: man	other, the	the other man
1. people	these, three	_____
2. horse	girl's, the	_____
3. books	three, which	_____
4. work	ladies', several	_____
5. clothes	her, other	_____
6. soldier	U.S., third, a	_____
7. restaurant	Italian, which	_____
8. toys	boy's, each	_____

B. Put a plus sign (+) before each sentence that uses proper adjective word order.

_____ 1. The jackrabbit is known for quick his hopping.

_____ 2. A young elephant needs his parents' help to grow.

_____ 3. Barn the swallow sings.

_____ 4. My family went to horse the races.

_____ 5. There is a big swimming pool down the block.

_____ 6. Our house has large three bedrooms.

_____ 7. Six children watched their favorite TV show.

_____ 8. The judges were given ten the best manuscripts.

_____ 9. The expensive, stylish clothes are sold in that store.

_____ 10. A shy, soft-spoken, well-mannered man was the leader.

The Discovery of Fire

Study the spelling and meaning of each word. These words are used in today's story. Connect each word with its definition.

1. doubt ——————————— a. question; uncertainty
2. experimentation b. one who knows
3. imagine c. frightened
4. shock d. the act of trying
5. terrified e. surprise
6. witness f. to picture in the mind

Read the story carefully and remember the details.

No one knows exactly how people discovered fire, but one can imagine what a shock such a discovery was. No doubt, a fire must have terrified its first witnesses. Certainly the first people did not know what to do with fire.

Soon, however, whether by accident or experimentation, people learned the value of fire. They felt its warmth. They saw how it frightened the wildest of beasts. Before fire, people went to bed at sunset and awoke at sunrise. With fire the night was not so dark, and people stayed awake later. Before fire, food was eaten raw. With the discovery of fire, people soon learned to cook their food. The first cooked meat was roasted.

Because a fire was so difficult to make, people kept it burning constantly. Fire was a person's most valuable possession.

A. **Underline the correct answers about today's story.**

1. What probable reaction did the
   first people have to fire?   (a) shock   (b) none   (c) happiness
2. Before fire, people ate   (a) raw foods   (b) only plants (c) only roots.
3. The first cooked meat was   (a) roasted   (b) baked   (c) fried.
4. Before fire, people retired at   (a) sunrise   (b) sunset   (c) dawn.
5. To prehistoric people, fire was (a) unimportant (b) useless   (c) most valuable.

B. **Reread the story and write the answers to these questions.**

1. How was fire discovered?

   _____

   _____

   _____

2. What did the first people do with fire?

   _____

   _____

   _____

3. How was food cooked before fire?

   _____

   _____

   _____

4. Why were fires kept burning constantly?

   _____

   _____

   _____

Unit 42 cont'd ☞

Types of Adjectives

A. Underline the descriptive adjectives in the following sentences.

1. The <u>restless</u> boy wriggled around in the <u>big</u> chair.
2. The full moon shone on the small lake.
3. The pine trees lined the country road.
4. Snakes are slimy, slithering reptiles.
5. You should put a gauze Band-Aid on the wound.
6. Polluted air may cause watery eyes.
7. Many American people watch detective stories on TV.
8. The rapid river flowed through the little village.
9. Peggy saw a white cat being stroked by a happy little girl.
10. Sad children played indoors on the rainy day.
11. Music lessons are during a bad time of day.
12. The huge crowd cheered the basketball players.
13. You are not supposed to wear your good clothes to the football game.
14. That is a bacon, lettuce, and tomato sandwich.
15. The hungry man ate ten doughnuts.

B. Underline the limiting adjectives in these sentences. Use the list of examples to complete the exercise.

limiting adjectives

articles — a, the, an

demonstratives — this, that, these, those

numbers — one, two, three, etc.

relatives — which, what, whose, whatever, whichever

interrogatives — which, what, whose

1. <u>Several</u> men sailed <u>that</u> boat.
2. She would like these jars and those jars.
3. Which one do you want?
4. A cow is an animal.
5. The teacher, whose day had been ruined, left early.
6. Many women talked about what meeting time would be the best.
7. The coach told a player which play to use next.
8. Come at whatever time is best for you.
9. This cat had twelve kittens.
10. Some students were wondering which questions would be asked.
11. How many of these pens do you want?
12. Those adults came to the picnic.
13. Give me the paper whose edges are torn.
14. Each child has some candy.
15. What time is it?

The Dodo Bird

Study the spelling and meaning of each word. These words are used in today's story. Connect each word with its definition.

1. abundant
2. attempt
3. extinct
4. skeletons
5. source
6. wastefulness

a. bony frameworks
b. plentiful
c. using more than needed
d. try
e. no longer in existence
f. place where something is acquired

Read the story carefully and remember the details.

The dodo bird was a flightless bird that was once abundant on the islands in the Indian Ocean. It is now extinct.

The dodo bird was about the twice the size of a goose. When sailors landed on the islands, they killed the bird for food. The dodo bird was easily killed with a club. It made little attempt to escape. The sailors killed so many birds that soon the dodo bird had died out.

The last records of the bird were in 1681. The only source of its existence was in the journals of sailors. Some museums have skeletons of dodo birds. The dodo bird was a funny-looking bird.

The dodo bird's existence was ended because of wastefulness. This can happen when man is not careful with the things around him.

A. Underline the correct answers about today's story.

1. Where did the dodo bird live?   (a) Australia   (b) Africa   (c) Indian Ocean

2. "Extinct" means   (a) "died out"   (b) "alive"   (c) "changed."

3. Who killed off the dodo birds?   (a) alligators   (b) sailors   (c) snakes

4. Why was the dodo bird killed?   (a) for food   (b) dangerous   (c) for feathers

5. The dodo bird was a _____ bird.   (a) tiny   (b) friendly   (c) funny-looking

B. Reread the story and write the answers to these questions.

1. How large was the bird?

_____

_____

_____

2. When was the last records of the bird written?

_____

_____

_____

3. Where is the only source of the bird's existence?

_____

_____

_____

4. Why did the dodo bird's existence end?

_____

_____

_____

Unit 43 cont'd ☞

Adjectives

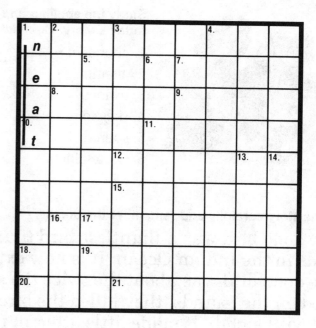

Words that are used to modify nouns are usually adjectives. The use of adjectives can often improve sentences by giving them clearer meanings. Usually adjectives come before the nouns they modify. When adjectives follow linking verbs, they function as complements.

✳ Fill in the blanks. Then complete the puzzle.

Down

1. _n_ _e_ _a_ _t_ clean and in order; well formed

2. _ _ _ _ having the color of a ruby

3. _ _ _ _ _ to blow with short, quick blasts

4. _ _ _ _ _ _ _ _ _ having the attitude of a person who knows and likes another

5. _ _ _ _ _ _ swift, fast and sudden; coming soon

6. _ _ _ _ great in amount or size

8. _ _ _ _ _ _ odd and amusing; quaint and laughable

10. _ _ _ _ _ domestic; not wild or savage

13. _ _ _ _ _ _ done or made in a hurry

14. _ _ _ _ _ _ _ full of juice; having much juice

17. _ _ _ _ having been for a long time; aged

Across

2. _ _ _ _ _ _ moving, acting, or doing with speed

7. _ _ _ _ _ color made by mixing black with white

9. _ _ _ _ _ having height; rising up; up above the ground

11. _ _ _ _ _ _ the color of most growing plants

12. _ _ _ _ _ small-minded; not noble; petty; unkind

15. _ _ _ _ _ having high quality; excellent; superior

16. _ _ _ _ _ _ not fastened; unbound; untied

18. _ _ _ _ _ merry; joyous; suitable for a feast

19. _ _ _ _ _ _ awkwardly long and thin

20. _ _ _ _ not as good as it ought to be; not good

21. _ _ _ _ _ _ glad; contented; well and having a good time

106

Dogs of Long Ago

Study the spelling and meaning of each word. These words are used in today's story. Connect each word with its definition.

1. bred ——————————	a. produced
2. continued	b. savage; wild
3. dependent	c. persisted
4. domestic	d. relying on another
5. eventually	e. tame
6. fierce	f. finally

Read the story carefully and remember the details.

The first animals to become friends with people were dogs. The first dogs were wild. They were fierce hunters which often followed people and ate whatever the people left behind.

Soon people discovered that the dog could help them hunt other animals. They began to take care of the dog and eventually the dog became dependent on people. In time the wild nature was bred out of the dog.

Since then people have continued to use the dog. Hunters use the dog to follow scents and lead the hunters to the prey. Bird hunters use the dog to fetch birds which have been shot. Shepherds use the dog to watch and round up sheep. Eskimos use the dog to pull sleds.

Today the dog is one of the most common domestic animals. It is often used to frighten away burglars. The most popular use is as a lovable pet.

A. Underline the correct answers about today's story.

1. The first dogs	(a) avoided people	(b) hunted people	(c) followed people.
2. Dogs were first used as	(a) hunters	(b) food	(c) beasts of burden.
3. Bird hunters use dogs to	(a) carry supplies	(b) fetch birds	(c) scare birds.
4. Today's dogs are	(a) wild	(b) domestic	(c) independent.
5. The most popular use is as a	(a) hunter	(b) watchdog	(c) pet.

B. Reread the story and write the answers to these questions.

1. What were the first animals to become friends with people?

_____
_____
_____

2. What helpful discovery was made about dogs?

_____
_____
_____

3. How do Eskimos use dogs?

_____
_____
_____

4. What is a burglar?

_____
_____
_____

Unit 44 cont'd ☛

Degrees of Comparison

A. Write the comparative forms for the following adjectives on the lines below. Follow this example.

positive
fuzzy

comparative
fuzzier

1. nice
2. smooth
3. sleek
4. silly
5. cloudy
6. nasty
7. tall
8. smart
9. loose
10. neat
11. shady
12. dark

_____
_____
_____
_____
_____
_____
_____
_____
_____
_____
_____
_____

B. Write the form of each underlined adjective in the blank provided. Follow the examples.

Example 1:   My house is the **biggest** of all.   _superlative_
Example 2:   My doll is **bigger** than yours is.   _comparative_

1. The freeway is <u>wider</u> than the road.
2. Our town is the <u>largest</u> in the state.
3. Summer is the <u>hottest</u> season in North America.
4. Winter is <u>warmer</u> than summer in South America.
5. Madge is <u>skinnier</u> than Georgia.
6. The tortoise is the <u>slowest</u> animal in the zoo.
7. Motorcycles go <u>faster</u> than bicycles.
8. The clown was the <u>funniest</u> act in the circus.
9. Is New York <u>bigger</u> than Los Angeles?
10. The Beatles are one of the <u>greatest</u> rock groups.
11. The witch costume is <u>scarier</u> than the goblin costume.
12. That girl can jump <u>higher</u> than her teammate.

_____
_____
_____
_____
_____
_____
_____
_____
_____
_____
_____
_____

Dolphins

Study the spelling and meaning of each word. These words are used in today's story. Connect each word with its definition.

1. contacts ———————— a. touches
2. highly   b. extremely; very
3. incredibly   c. things in the way
4. obstacles   d. more intelligent than
5. often   e. unbelievably
6. smarter   f. frequently

Read the story carefully and remember the details.

The dolphin is often called a fish. It is really a mammal that lives in the sea. The dolphin must come to the surface to breathe. It can stay underwater six minutes before returning for air.

Often referred to as the "prankster of the sea," the dolphin is a friendly animal. It seems to enjoy its contacts with humans.

The dolphin reaches a length of 8 to 12 feet. It swims incredibly fast at speeds up to thirty miles per hour. The animal makes a large number of sounds. These sounds help the dolphin get about. The sound waves tell the dolphin what obstacles are in its path.

Dolphins travel in schools. Highly social, the animals help each other.

Many scientists believe the dolphin is a highly intelligent animal. Some think it is smarter than the ape.

A. Underline the correct answers about today's story.

1. The dolphin is a/an   (a) fish   (b) amphibian   (c) mammal.
2. To get oxygen, the dolphin   (a) comes to the surface   (b) swallows water   (c) crawls on land.
3. A prankster is   (a) playful   (b) serious   (c) grouchy.
4. What helps the dolphin get about?   (a) sharp eyes   (b) sense of touch   (c) sound waves
5. Which word describes the dolphin?   (a) unsocial   (b) intelligent   (c) unintelligent

B. Reread the story and write the answers to these questions.

1. How long can a dolphin stay underwater at one time?

_____

_____

_____

2. How large are some dolphins?

_____

_____

3. How do dolphins travel?

_____

_____

_____

4. How do dolphins know something is in their path?

_____

_____

_____

Unit 45 cont'd ☞

Using "More" and "Most"

A. Underline the correct adjective forms in the following sentences.

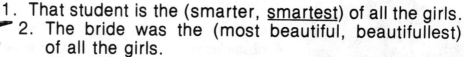

1. That student is the (smarter, <u>smartest</u>) of all the girls.
2. The bride was the (most beautiful, beautifullest) of all the girls.
3. This essay is (more interesting, most interesting) than the first one.
4. Michael is the (taller, tallest) of all the campers.
5. I like the morning paper (more, most) than the evening edition.
6. That ride is (more fun, most fun) than the carousel.
7. The last game was the (excitinger, most exciting) of the season.
8. This time, be (careful, carefuller).
9. There are (fewer, fewest) children in this class.
10. Night is the (more peaceful, most peaceful) time of day.
11. The sunset is (more gorgeous, most gorgeous) than yesterday.
12. Timothy is the (more alert, most alert) of the six children.

B. Write the superlative forms of the adjectives below. Follow the examples.

| EXAMPLES: | happy | more happy | most happy |
| | happy | less happy | least happy |

	positive	comparative	superlative
1.	popular	more popular	
2.	satisfied	more satisfied	
3.	horrible	less horrible	
4.	disappointed	less disappointed	
5.	quickly	less quickly	
6.	stubborn	more stubborn	
7.	tasty	more tasty	
8.	wonderful	more wonderful	
9.	laughable	more laughable	
10.	mountainous	less mountainous	
11.	defensive	less defensive	
12.	resentful	more resentful	

Comprehension Check

Ⓐ Match each adjective with its definition.

1. good		a. domestic; not wild or savage
2. neat		b. clean and in order; well formed
3. big		c. great in amount or size
4. tame		d. having high quality excellent
5. loose		e. well and having a good time; glad
6. old		f. moving, acting, or doing with speed
7. rapid		g. not fastened; unbound; untied
8. happy		h. having been for a long time; aged
9. hasty		i. done or made in a hurry
10. juicy		j. awkwardly long and thin
11. lanky		k. full of juice; having much juice
12. quick		l. odd and amusing; quaint and laughable
13. droll		m. swift, fast, and sudden; coming soon
14. bad		n. not as good as it ought to be
15. friendly		o. knowing or liking another

Ⓑ Underline the adjectives.

1. <u>careful</u>	6. chocolate	11. dry	16. cooked
2. first	7. green	12. always	17. sweet
3. difficult	8. never	13. pretty	18. and
4. underline	9. wide	14. watery	19. even
5. hungry	10. bright	15. large	20. softer

Ⓒ Write the comparative and superlative forms of each adjective.

1. large	*larger*	*largest*	6. smart	_____	_____
2. great	_____	_____	7. expensive	_____	_____
3. stubborn	_____	_____	8. dark	_____	_____
4. peaceful	_____	_____	9. popular	_____	_____
5. happy	_____	_____	10. sweet	_____	_____

Ⓓ Complete these sentences.

1. The dolphin is the "_____*prankster*_____ of the sea."
2. The dodo bird is now _____ .
3. The first dogs were _____ .
4. Dall sheep live in the _____ .
5. Fire provided _____ and _____ .
6. The dodo bird was a _____ bird.
7. Dolphins travel in _____ .
8. Before fire, food was eaten _____ .
9. Today most dogs are _____ .
10. Dall sheep are _____ animals.

Test 9 cont'd ☞

Comprehension Check (continued)

(E) Match these words and their definitions. These words appeared in the reading selections from units 41-45.

_g_ 1. choice   ___ 7. domestic   a. plentiful   g. selection

___ 2. influence   ___ 8. eventually   b. finally   h. surprise

___ 3. doubt   ___ 9. fierce   c. control   i. tame

___ 4. shock   ___ 10. highly   d. question; uncertainty   j. savage; wild

___ 5. abundant   ___ 11. incredibly   e. extremely; very   k. frequently

___ 6. extinct   ___ 12. often   f. no longer in existence   l. unbelievably

(F) Underline the correct answers.

1. Where do dall sheep live?   (a) <u>mountains</u>   (b) open range
2. What is the sheep's main enemy?   (a) timber wolf   (b) weather
3. How was the first meat cooked?   (a) roasted   (b) fried
4. How was fire first discovered?   (a) experimentation   (b) No one knows.
5. Where did the dodo bird live?   (a) Indian Ocean   (b) Hawaii
6. When were the last records of the dodo bird written?   (a) 1981   (b) 1681
7. How were dogs first used?   (a) hunters   (b) beasts of burden
8. How do Eskimos use dogs?   (a) pull sleds   (b) fetch birds
9. How do dolphins travel?   (a) schools   (b) alone
10. What helps the dolphin get about?   (a) sound waves   (b) sense of touch

Choose one of the following topics and write a paragraph.

(1) Fire was a very important discovery. Write about some of its uses.

(2) Dogs are one of the most popular pets. Do you have a dog? Write about an experience involving a dog.

_____

_____

_____

_____

_____

_____

_____

_____

_____

_____

_____

Domestic Cats

Study the spelling and meaning of each word. These words are used in today's story. Connect each word with its definition.

1. cautious
2. contentment
3. determinedly
4. facial
5. independent
6. pleasure

a. not relying on anything
b. careful
c. resolvedly
d. relating to the face
e. delight
f. feeling quiet satisfaction

Read the story carefully and remember the details.

One of the most popular and best-loved pets is the cat. Like its cousins, the wild cats, the cat is a beautiful but determinedly independent animal.

The cat is one of the few animals which show its feelings in its facial expression. It can show anger, fear, pain, and pleasure. When its ears point forward, it is happy. When they lie flat against its head, the cat is angry. A common sign of contentment is a purring noise.

The cat is able to move quickly. It is an excellent climber. Although cautious, the cat usually does not run away from danger.

There are many kinds of cats. They are divided into two groups, the longhaired and the shorthaired. Some cats are kept to catch mice and rats, but the majority are kept as family pets.

A. Underline the correct answers about today's story.

1. The cat is a cousin to the	(a) dog	(b) mouse	(c) wild cat.
2. When ears point forward, the cat is	(a) afraid	(b) happy	(c) angry.
3. When content, the cat	(a) purrs	(b) meows	(c) licks its paws.
4. When danger approaches, the cat	(a) stands its ground	(b) runs away	(c) hides.
5. Which word describes the cat?	(a) unlikeable	(b) independent	(c) dependent

B. Reread the story and write the answers to these questions.

1. How does the cat show its feelings?

_____

_____

_____

2. Name three of the emotions a cat can show.

_____

_____

_____

3. What are the two groups of cats?

_____

_____

_____

4. Why do most people have cats?

_____

_____

_____

Unit 46 cont'd

Irregular Comparison of Adjectives

A. Underline the correct irregular adjective forms in each of the following sentences. Choose the answer from the list below.

positive	comparative	superlative
bad, evil, ill	worse	worst
good, well	better	best
little	less, lesser	least
much, many, some	more	most

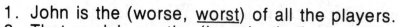

1. John is the (worse, <u>worst</u>) of all the players.
2. That model was the (late, last) of the series.
3. It certainly is the (best, better) of the group.
4. The rehearsal was (best, better) than yesterday.
5. Pierre is (older, oldest) than his sister.
6. The Mexican food had the (more, most) seasoning of all.
7. The northbound train was (later, last) than the southbound train.
8. The grocery store is (farthest, farther) away than the fruit stand.
9. All cruise ships are very (much, more) alike.
10. I like my Aunt Bessie (much, most) of all.
11. The Dead Sea Scrolls are the (oldest, old) of all written material yet found by man.
12. That restaurant is (worse, worst) than the one across the street.

B. Underline the irregular adjectives in each of the following sentences. Write the comparison form of positive, comparative, or superlative in the blank before each use. Use the list above to help you.

comparative 1. My sister has <u>more</u> dolls than anyone else.
_____ 2. That paper is the best one of all.
_____ 3. There is more milk in the carton than in the bottle.
_____ 4. The man was bad.
_____ 5. Our neighbors have many toys.
_____ 6. My friend has the most marbles of all the kids in the class.
_____ 7. Winter is the worst season of the year.
_____ 8. Summer is the best season of the year.
_____ 9. I feel worse today.

114

The Dress of Mexico

Study the spelling and meaning of each word. These words are used in today's story. Connect each word with its definition.

1. customs
2. forefathers
3. modern

4. rebozos
5. reflect
6. serapes

a. of present or recent times
b. common practices
c. colorful wool blankets worn by men
d. ancestors
e. to cast as a consequence
f. long shawls worn by women

Read the story carefully and remember the details.

Mexico is a land of many people and many customs. Although parts of Mexico have modern cities with people who dress the same as we, much of Mexico is made up of small villages. In these villages the people wear costumes which reflect their heritage.

Most men wear white pants and shirts. Many wear serapes, a colorful wool blanket which has a slit in the center to put the head through. The design of the serape indicates which region is the man's home. A sombrero, straw hat, is worn to shade oneself from the hot sun.

Many women wear full, brightly colored skirts with white blouses. Almost all wear rebozos, long shawls. The rebozos serve as wraps and as head coverings.

The villagers are proud people who strongly believe in the customs of their forefathers. Each village's style of dress is slightly different.

A. Underline the correct answers about today's story.

1. Mexico's heritage is reflected in the   (a) cities   (b) villages   (c) holidays.

2. A serape is a   (a) blanket   (b) shoe   (c) hat.

3. A sombrero is a   (a) kerchief   (b) hat   (c) belt.

4. A rebozo is a   (a) skirt   (b) shawl   (c) blouse.

5. Which words describe a Mexican?   (a) copies others   (b) hates the past   (c) proud of heritage

B. Reread the story and write the answers to these questions.

1. What do most Mexican men wear?

_____

_____

_____

2. What does the design of the serape indicate?

_____

_____

_____

3. What do almost all Mexican women wear?

_____

_____

_____

4. What strong belief do the villagers have?

_____

_____

_____

Unit 47 cont'd ☞

Comparative Adjectives

Most of the shorter adjectives form the comparative degree by adding "-er." Longer adjectives form the comparative degree by the use of "more" ("less") in front of them. A few adjectives have an irregular comparison. Some examples are: "warm," "warmer," "helpful," "less helpful," "beautiful," "more beautiful," "good," "better," "bad," and "worse."

 Fill in the blanks. Then complete the puzzle.

Down

2. _h_ _u_ _g_ _e_ _r_ unusually larger in size, bulk, or dimensions; larger in quantity or number

3. _ _ _ _ _ _ _ _ smaller; shorter; smaller in number; smaller in importance or interest

5. _ _ _ _ _ _ _ more excellent or useful than another

6. _ _ _ _ _ _ _ friendlier; more sympathetic; more gentle and humane

8. _ _ _ _ _ _ _ having more money, goods, or land than another

Across

1. _ _ _ _ _ _ _ _ more awkward; longer and thinner; taller and more ungraceful

4. _ _ _ _ _ _ _ _ more distant; farther; additional; more

7. _ _ _ _ _ _ prettier and dearer; more pleasing and attractive; more charming

8. _ _ _ _ _ _ more seldom seen or found; not happening often

9. _ _ _ _ _ _ more modern; more up-to-date; more recently

10. _ _ _ _ _ _ _ in a more natural or raw state; more unfinished

11. _ _ _ _ _ _ _ _ more contented; gladder; more cheerful; more elated

12. _ _ _ _ _ _ _ more slack; more unbound; more untied

13. _ _ _ _ _ _ more ill; less well; less good; more evil; more painful

14. _ _ _ _ _ smaller; of less width; not so much; lower in age, rank, etc.

116

Driver Ants Unit 48

Unit 48

Study the spelling and meaning of each word. These words are used in today's story. Connect each word with its definition.

1. entire
2. incredible
3. sensitive
4. swarm
5. troublesome
6. victim

a. unbelievable
b. whole or all
c. causing trouble
d. to appear in a crowd
e. one harmed by another
f. quick to feel

Read the story carefully and remember the details.

Among the most feared insects in all the world are the driver ants of Africa. A single ant is not dangerous, but the driver ants always move in great armies. Millions of ants travel together.

Driver ants are meat-eaters. The ants swarm over their victim. Because of their incredible numbers, they are able to overcome an elephant.

The ants are very sensitive to sunlight. Direct sunlight will kill them within a short period of time. Usually the ants travel at night or in the shadows.

Driver ants have been known to invade entire villages. The natives of the villages vacate their homes until the ants move on. Although the ants are troublesome, they are often welcomed by natives. While the ants are moving through the villages, they rid the villages of unwelcome insects and pests.

A. **Underline the correct answers about today's story.**

1. Driver ants are native to	(a) Africa	(b) Australia	(c) the United States.
2. Driver ants travel	(a) alone	(b) in pairs	(c) in armies.
3. Driver ants eat	(a) plants	(b) meat	(c) insects.
4. Driver ants are sensitive to	(a) water	(b) darkness	(c) direct sunlight.
5. Which word describes these ants?	(a) feared	(b) friendly	(c) harmless

B. **Reread the story and write the answers to these questions.**

1. How many ants travel together?

_____
_____
_____

2. What can direct sunlight do to the ants?

_____
_____
_____

3. When do the ants usually travel?

_____
_____
_____

4. How can these ants be helpful?

_____
_____
_____

Unit 48 cont'd ☞

Superlative Adjectives

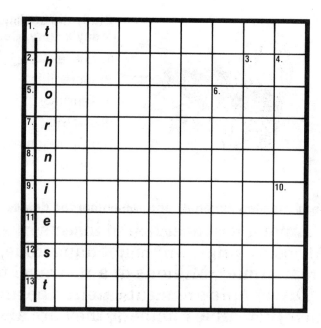

You should use the superlative degree of adjectives when comparing three or more persons or things.

 Fill in the blanks. Then complete the puzzle.

Down

1. <u>t h o r n i e s t</u> most spiny; most full of thorns; most overgrown with brambles

2. _ _ _ _ _ _ _ _ _ most calloused; most hard like a horn

3. _ _ _ _ _ _ _ _ _ most pleasing to the taste; most delicious; most appetizing

4. _ _ _ _ _ greatest in amount, quantity, measure, degree, or number; almost all

6. _ _ _ _ _ _ _ _ most large; most unusually large in size, bulk, or dimensions; most unusually large in quantity or number

10. _ _ _ _ _ _ most good, excellent, or useful; largest; greatest; chief; main hope

Across

1. _ _ _ _ _ _ _ _ _ _ _ most worthless; that which contains the most trash

2. _ _ _ _ _ _ _ _ _ most calloused; most hard like a horn; same as number two down

5. _ _ _ _ _ _ _ _ dating farther back than others; much more in age than others; most dilapidated, decayed, shabby, or outworn

7. _ _ _ _ _ _ _ _ most seldom seen or found; very unusual; not happening often; unusually good or greatest

8. _ _ _ _ _ _ _ _ most pleasing, agreeable, or satisfactory; most thoughtful and kind; most precise and exact

9. _ _ _ _ _ _ _ _ most like ice; most cold and slippery; having the most ice

11. _ _ _ _ _ _ _ oldest of a set of brothers and sisters or of a group

12. _ _ _ _ _ _ _ most free from harm, danger, or loss; most out of danger; most secure

13. _ _ _ _ _ _ _ _ _ most sticky or gummy

The Eastern Chipmunk

Study the spelling and meaning of each word. These words are used in today's story. Connect each word with its definition.

1. active
2. curious
3. dash
4. defense
5. rather
6. satisfy

a. move rapidly
b. means of protecting
c. more willingly
d. please; gratify
e. lively
f. strongly wanting to know

Read the story carefully and remember the details.

Although the eastern chipmunk is well-suited to life in the trees, it spends much of its time on the ground. The chipmunk is a curious little animal which would rather dash away than satisfy its curiousity.

The chipmunk gets its name from the chipping noise it makes. It is active during the day, gathering berries and seeds in its cheek pouches. The seeds are stored in preparation for the cold winter months when finding food is more difficult.

Eastern chipmunks which live in the northern states sleep most of the winter season. Those which live in the southern states are active the year round.

The chipmunk's enemies include the weasel, owl, and snake. Its only defense is its speed at getting away from danger.

A. Underline the correct answers about today's story.

1. The chipmunk spends most of the time   (a) in the trees   (b) on the ground   (c) in water.

2. The chipmunk's name comes from its   (a) home   (b) noise   (c) habits.

3. To prepare for winter, the chipmunk   (a) grows fur   (b) collects grass   (c) gathers seeds.

4. The chipmunk's defense is its   (a) sharp claws   (b) teeth   (c) speed.

5. Which word describes the chipmunk?   (a) curious   (b) careless   (c) lazy.

B. Reread the story and write the answers to these questions.

1. When is the chipmunk active?

_____

_____

_____

2. Where does it gather the berries and seeds?

_____

_____

_____

3. Name the chipmunk's enemies.

_____

_____

_____

4. What do Eastern chipmunks do in the winter?

_____

_____

_____

   Unit 49 cont'd ☛

Adverb Signals

A. Form adverbs by adding the suffix "-ly" to the adjectives below. Follow the example.

EXAMPLE: *nice*   _____*nicely*_____

adjective	adverb	adjective	adverb
1. loud	_____	6. quick	_____
2. soft	_____	7. hopeful	_____
3. noisy	_____	8. selfish	_____
4. rapid	_____	9. quiet	_____
5. beautiful	_____	10. peaceful	_____

B. Underline each correct word in parentheses. Remember that adjectives describe nouns and adverbs describe verbs.

1. The car's engine ran (smooth, <u>smoothly</u>).
2. The rabbits work (quick, quickly).
3. The soldiers were (brave, bravely).
4. The baseball team played (good, well).
5. That judge ruled (unfair, unfairly).
6. His work was done (careful, carefully).
7. Bears growl (loud, loudly).
8. Mary feels (miserable, miserably).
9. Those limes are (sour, sourly).
10. The train appeared (sudden, suddenly).
11. They work (good, well) together.
12. Many people were hurt (bad, badly).

The Egyptians

Study the spelling and meaning of each word. These words are used in today's story. Connect each word with its definition.

1. ancient   a. found
2. comfortable   b. of times long past
3. conveniences   c. to leak through pores
4. discovered   d. providing ease
5. evaporated   e. things that make life easier
6. seeped   f. changed from liquid to gas

Read the story carefully and remember the details.

The ancient Egyptians lived along the shores of the Nile River 6,000 years ago. They were an intelligent people who lived comfortable lives in a world with few conveniences.

The Egyptians had no ice, but they knew how to keep water cool. They kept their drinking water in clay jars. Some water seeped through the side of the jars. When this was water was evaporated into the air, the water inside the jars was cooled.

The Egyptians were the first people to make glass. They put sand and a special mineral into a kettle and heated the mixture until it turned into a liquid. The liquid was poured into molds. When it cooled, it was glass. Many of our modern conveniences were first discovered by the Egyptians.

A. Underline the correct answers about today's story.

1. Where did the Egyptians live?	(a) Nile River	(b) ocean	(c) desert
2. In what did the people keep water?	(a) clay jars	(b) metal tubs	(c) glass jars
3. A convenience is a	(a) home	(b) well	(c) comfort.
4. The Egyptians were the first to make	(a) houses	(b) glass	(c) money.
5. Which word describes the Egyptians?	a) lazy	(b) intelligent	(c) backwards

B. Reread the story and write the answers to these questions.

1. How long ago did the Egyptians live along the Nile?

_____

_____

_____

2. What final product came from sand and a special mineral?

_____

_____

_____

3. Who first discovered many of our modern conveniences?

_____

_____

_____

4. What modern day convenience did the story say Egyptians did without?

_____

_____

_____

Unit 50 cont'd ☞

Inflection of Adverbs

A. Underline the comparison forms of the adverbs in the sentences below.

1. Mark ran <u>more</u> <u>quickl</u>y than the champion.
2. My brother worked the hardest of all on the snowman.
3. The science professor spoke more clearly.
4. Sports cars go faster than sedans.
5. Sally looks better in blue than in pink.
6. She drove the best of all the drivers.
7. Basketball players must jump higher than baseball players.
8. Margaret came later than Peter.
9. These errands can be done the easiest of all.
10. My teacher talks faster than my mom.
11. Talk softer when the baby is asleep.
12. She hears better now.
13. Play more gently with my toys.
14. John has been working less regularly.

B. For each incorrect sentence write an "X" in the blank.

<u>_X_</u> 1. Speak to him more gentler.
___ 2. Whatever she does, she does the most best.
___ 3. That athlete performs the most gracefully.
___ 4. John drives more recklessly than ever.
___ 5. Pronounce words more clearer.
___ 6. The lady gave her money most willingly.
___ 7. She listened more carefuller.
___ 8. This plane lands more safely than that plane.

122

Comprehension Check

A Identify the form of each adjective. Write "p" for positive, "c" for comparative, and "s" for superlative.

_p_	1. sweet	____	11. happiest	____	21. better
____	2. nearest	____	12. cutest	____	22. richest
____	3. worse	____	13. newer	____	23. safe
____	4. smoother	____	14. wide	____	24. farthest
____	5. cheapest	____	15. most	____	25. nicer
____	6. least	____	16. taller	____	26. more
____	7. faster	____	17. oldest	____	27. shortest
____	8. sooner	____	18. loose	____	28. pretty
____	9. hot	____	19. higher	____	29. later
____	10. youngest	____	20. softest	____	30. easiest

B Write the comparative form of each adjective or adverb.

1. clearly ___*more clearly*___
2. quickly _____
3. cold _____
4. far _____
5. thin _____

6. big _____
7. narrow _____
8. long _____
9. poor _____
10. bad _____

11. clean _____
12. helpful _____
13. warm _____
14. safely _____
15. quietly _____

C Write the superlative form of each adjective or adverb.

1. kind ___*kindest*___
2. bright _____
3. good _____
4. sad _____
5. sure _____

6. carefully _____
7. cool _____
8. small _____
9. flat _____
10. curious _____

11. active _____
12. bravely _____
13. sharp _____
14. thick _____
15. beautiful _____

D Complete these sentences.

1. A cat is an ___*independent*___ animal.
2. Egyptians lived along the _____ .
3. Driver ants live in _____ .
4. Chipmunks are active during the _____ .
5. Egyptians were very _____ .
6. Most cats are kept as _____ .
7. A rebozo is a long _____ .
8. Driver ants travel at _____ .

9. A sombrero is a _____ .
10. When content, cats _____ .
11. A chipmunk's defense is _____ .
12. A serape is a _____ .
13. Egyptians made jars of _____ .
14. Driver ants are sensitive to _____ .
15. Chipmunks gather food in their _____ .
16. Egyptians were first to make _____ .

Test 10 cont'd ☛

Comprehension Check (continued)

E Match these words and their definitions. These words appeared in the reading selections from units 46-50.

_c_ 1. cautious   ____ 7. active

____ 2. pleasure   ____ 8. rather

____ 3. modern   ____ 9. satisfy

____ 4. rebozos   ____ 10. ancient

____ 5. entire   ____ 11. evaporated

____ 6. incredible   ____ 12. discovered

a. whole or all

b. of times long past

c. careful

d. delight

e. more willingly

f. of present or recent times

g. long shawls

h. found

i. unbelievable

j. lively

k. please; gratify

l. changed from liquid to gas

F Underline the correct answers.

1. What does a cat do when content?   (a) <u>purrs</u>   (b) claws
2. Which word describes a cat?   (a) independent   (b) dependent
3. What do most Mexican women wear?   (a) turbans   (b) rebozos
4. What is a serape?   (a) blanket   (b) shoe
5. What can direct sunlight do to driver ants?   (a) tan them   (b) kill them
6. When do driver ants usually travel?   (a) at night   (b) during the day
7. How does the chipmunk prepare for winter?   (a) gathers seeds   (b) builds a den
8. Name an enemy of the chipmunk.   (a) owl   (b) raccoon
9. Where did the Egyptians live?   (a) Nile River   (b) Amazon River
10. What did the Egyptians make before anyone else?   (a) glass   (b) jars

Choose one of the following topics and write a paragraph.

(1) Cats are some of the most loved pets. There are many kinds of cats. Write a paragraph which involves a cat. Be sure to include the kind and the color of the cat.

(2) The Egyptians lived without most of today's conveniences. Name one convenience missing from their life and how they dealt with it. Then, name three modern day conveniences and what life would be like without them.

_____

_____

_____

_____

_____

_____

_____

_____

_____

Elephant Seals

Study the spelling and meaning of each word. These words are used in today's story. Connect each word with its definition.

1. attempt
2. frantic
3. proboscis
4. roughly
5. sluggish
6. threatened

a. approximately or somewhat
b. expressed source of danger
c. greatly excited
d. try
e. snout
f. lacking in energy

Read the story carefully and remember the details.

The elephant seal gets its name from its proboscis, or snout, which roughly resembles the trunk of an elephant. Actually, only the male seal has the flabby snout which droops over his jaws.

On land, the elephant seal is sluggish. Its large bulky body makes it difficult for the animal to move around. It also makes it difficult for the animal to escape danger. When alarmed, the elephant seal panics and makes a frantic attempt to escape. However, it tires easily on land and usually loses.

In the sea the elephant seal hunts its food. There its only natural enemy is the killer whale. Once threatened by extinction, the elephant seal is now making a slow comeback.

A. Underline the correct answers about today's story.

1. A proboscis is a   (a) snout   (b) arm   (c) mouth.

2. On land the elephant sea is   (a) active   (b) sluggish   (c) energetic.

3. In the sea the seal's enemy is   (a) the octopus   (b) man   (c) the killer whale.

4. The seal's body is   (a) bulky   (b) streamlined   (c) dwarfish.

5. Which word describes the seal?   (a) extinct   (b) helpless   (c) dangerous

B. Reread the story and write the answers to these questions.

1. What once threatened the seal?

_____

_____

_____

2. What does the seal's proboscis resemble?

_____

_____

_____

3. What happens when the seal is alarmed?

_____

_____

_____

4. Where does the seal hunt for food?

_____

_____

_____

Unit 51 cont'd ☞

Adverbs

An adverb is a word that tells how, when, or where something happens. Adverbs tell how much or how little is meant. An adverb is used to extend or limit the meaning of a verb, an adjective, another adverb, or a phrase, clause, or even a whole sentence. Most adverbs are made up of adjectives or participles plus the ending "-ly." Many of the frequently used adverbs have no formal feature identifying them as adverbs.

✳ **Fill in the blanks. Then complete the puzzle.**

Across

1. _a_ _l_ _w_ _a_ _y_ _s_ every time; at all times

3. _ _ _ _ _ in a manner of taking a long time

4. _ _ _ _ _ _ in that place; at that place

5. _ _ _ _ in this place; at this place; this place; now

6. _ _ _ _ at or to a tall point, place, rank, amount, price, or pitch

7. _ _ _ _ _ _ very near to; nearly; all but

8. _ _ _ _ in what way or manner; by what means

11. _ _ _ _ a long way off in time or space

12. _ _ _ _ _ at that time; soon afterward

13. _ _ _ _ at the present time; at this moment

14. _ _ _ _ _ in a satisfactory, favorable, or good manner

16. _ _ _ _ _ _ _ _ on or for the day after today

17. _ _ _ _ _ _ rarely; not often

18. _ _ from a lower to a higher place

19. _ _ _ _ _ done, happening, or appearing every day

20. _ _ _ _ _ on or during this very day

21. _ _ _ _ _ with skill; in an able manner

Down

2. _ _ _ _ _ _ _ _ _ on the day before today

9. _ _ _ _ _ _ _ _ in a weary manner

10. _ _ _ _ _ afterward; subsequently

15. _ _ _ _ _ far; from a place to a distance

The European Hedgehog

Study the spelling and meaning of each word. These words are used in today's story. Connect each word with its definition.

1. beneath ————————————— a. courageous
2. confuse ————————————— b. directly under
3. daring   c. something done automatically
4. habit   d. sleep through winter
5. hibernate   e. notable
6. striking   f. to mix up

Read the story carefully and remember the details.

Many people confuse the European hedgehog with the porcupine. Although the two animals do bear a striking resemblance to one another, their habits and habitats are quite different.

Few people have rarely seen the hedgehog in motion. It is a nocturnal animal which spends its days sleeping beneath a hedge or bush. Usually a silent creature, the European hedgehog has been heard snoring.

The quills are the hedgehog's only defense. When attacked, the hedgehog rolls into a ball. In this position the quills are erect. They break away easily into the flesh of daring opponents. The hedgehog is vulnerable on its underside.

The hedgehog is a strong animal. It can survive cold temperatures and hot ones alike. In mild climates the hedgehog stays active year round. In very cold climates the hedgehog hibernates.

A. Underline the correct answers about today's story.

1. The hedgehog is often confused with the   (a) skunk   (b) pig   (c) porcupine.
2. During the day the hedgehog   (a) plays   (b) sleeps   (c) hunts for food.
3. The hedgehog's defense is its   (a) quills   (b) sharp teeth   (c) sharp claws.
4. "Vulnerable" means   (a) "safe"   (b) "stronger"   (c) "open to attack."
5. In which climate does the animal live? (a) hot   (b) cold   (c) all climates

B. Reread the story and write the answers to these questions.

1. What two things are different between the European hedgehog and the porcupine?

_____

_____

_____

2. What does the hedgehog do when attacked?

_____

_____

_____

3. What does the hedgehog do if the climate is mild?

_____

_____

_____

4. What does the hedgehog do in cold climates?

_____

_____

_____

Unit 52 cont'd ☛

Verbs

 Fill in the blanks. Then complete the puzzle.

Down

1. <u>s w a y</u> to swing back and forth

3. _ _ _ _ _ to form a circle around; to give forth a clear sound

5. _ _ _ _ _ _ _ _ to turn out well

7. _ _ _ _ _ _ had; possessed

9. _ _ _ to fold over and sew down

10. _ _ _ _ _ to place guards at a particular place

11. _ _ _ _ _ to carry in a vehicle with two wheels

12. _ _ _ _ to strike lightly so that one can hear

13. _ _ _ _ _ _ to speak or write in a friendly way

14. _ _ _ _ _ to open the mouth wide because of being sleepy

15. _ _ _ _ _ _ _ _ to speak well of; to worship in words or song

18. _ _ _ _ _ _ to lift up; to move to a higher place

19. _ _ _ _ _ _ to put clothes on; attire; garb

23. _ _ _ to annoy or irritate by peevish complaints

Across

2. _ _ _ _ _ _ _ _ stirred to action; excited

4. _ _ _ _ _ _ was put into action; practiced actively

6. _ _ to carry through to the end of the work; to perform

8. _ _ _ _ lash; flog; thrash; switch; to move suddenly

11. _ _ _ _ to divide, separate, open, or remove with a knife

16. _ _ _ _ _ _ _ _ _ _ flattered grossly; spread with butter

17. _ _ _ _ _ to speak; to make known; to express

20. _ _ _ _ _ to stop doing something; to pause; to tarry; to linger

21. _ _ _ _ _ to strike again and again; to whip; to thrash

22. _ _ _ to chew and swallow; to have a meal

23. _ _ _ _ _ _ fastened; closed; made secure with nails

24. _ _ _ to be ill; to feel sick; be indisposed

25. _ _ _ _ _ to plunge headfirst into water

26. _ _ _ _ _ _ _ _ tells confidently and positively

27. _ _ _ _ _ sleeps; is still and quiet

28. _ _ _ _ _ _ to seize and hold fast by closing the fingers around

29. _ _ _ _ _ to make a harsh, grating sound

30. _ _ _ _ _ _ to iron clothes

The European Stork

Study the spelling and meaning of each word. These words are used in today's story. Connect each word with its definition.

1. certain
2. flocks
3. furnish
4. protect
5. symbol
6. welcome

a. something that stands for something else
b. receive with gladness
c. provide
d. groups of birds of any kind
e. particular
f. keep from harm

Read the story carefully and remember the details.

The European stork builds its nest on a rooftop. Europeans welcome the stork. They believe that the stork is a symbol of good luck. If a stork builds a nest on a certain home, that home is supposed to have good luck in the coming year.

Most storks live in flocks. In the winter they migrate to Africa. In the spring they return to Europe. Their nests are made of sticks. The same nests are used year after year.

Europeans protect the stork. The return of the stork means the arrival of spring. Many Europeans furnish food for the birds. No one dares to destroy a stork's nest for fear of bringing bad luck to the household.

A. Underline the correct answers about today's story.

1. Where does the stork build its nest? (a) in a tree (b) on the ground (c) on a rooftop
2. The stork is a symbol of (a) good luck (b) death (c) fortune.
3. In winter the stork (a) sleeps (b) hibernates (c) migrates.
4. The stork's nest is made of (a) mud (b) sticks (c) stones.
5. The return of the stork is the arrival of (a) fall (b) spring (c) winter.

B. Reread the story and write the answers to these questions.

1. What does the building of a nest on a certain rooftop mean?

_____

_____

_____

2. How do Europeans feel about the stork?

_____

_____

_____

3. Where does the stork go in the winter?

_____

_____

_____

4. Why will no one destroy the stork's nest?

_____

_____

_____

Unit 53 cont'd ☛

Inflection of Regular Verbs

A regular verb adds "ed" to form the past tense. An irregular verb changes its spelling completely to form the past tense.

EXAMPLES: **regular:**
    a. **walk**   **walked**
    b. **study**   **studied**

irregular:
    a. **drive**   **drove**
    b. **eat**   **ate**

A. Mark a check on the line before each action verb in this list.

 ✓   1. walk
_____ 2. play
_____ 3. elephant
_____ 4. baby
_____ 5. sleep
_____ 6. drink
_____ 7. study
_____ 8. write
_____ 9. marshmallow
_____ 10. eat

B. Underline the correct verb form for each sentence.

1. The boy (<u>likes</u>, like) his new bike.
2. The men (wants, want) something to eat.
3. My mother (drives, drive) a station wagon to work.
4. The mice (eat, eats) the cheese.
5. The child (rides, ride) the skateboard down the hill.
6. The score (changes, change) each quarter.
7. The babies all (drinks, drink) their milk.
8. Many sheep (grazes, graze) on the hillside.
9. The women (attends, attend) the meeting.
10. Father (cooks, cook) the dinner.

C. Fill in the blanks with the past tense form of the regular verbs written before each sentence.

1. walk   She _____ yesterday.
2. climb   The guide _____ the mountain first.
3. play   The children _____ this morning.
4. cross   The woman _____ the street.
5. type   She _____ the paper for my class.

Falconry

Study the spelling and meaning of each word. These words are used in today's story. Connect each word with its definition.

1. centuries
2. obtain
3. often
4. popular
5. quiet
6. supremacy

a. acquire; get
b. periods of one hundred years each
c. frequently
d. high in quality
e. liked by many people
f. hushed

Read the story carefully and remember the details.

For centuries people have trained birds to help them obtain food. Most commonly used has been the falcon, a bird of prey which is still known for its supremacy as a hunter. Today falconry is still popular, though it has become more of a sport rather than a means to obtain food.

The falconer trains the bird with kindness and rewards of food. The bird is kept hungry just before training. It sits on the falconer's gloved fist. A hood is placed over its head to keep it quiet.

When the prey is spotted, the hood is removed. The falcon makes its attack. Bells on the bird tell the falconer where the bird is with the prey. After the kill the bird is rewarded with food.

Hawks are often used instead of falcons. The sport may be referred to as hawking.

A. Underline the correct answers about today's story.

1. Falconry was first popular	(a) to obtain food	(b) as a sport	(c) to find water.
2. The person who trains the bird is the	(a) falconer	(b) falcon	(c) falconry.
3. To keep the bird quiet, it is	(a) fed	(b) hooded	(c) put in a box.
4. The bird is rewarded with	(a) rest	(b) food	(c) the kill.
5. Which other bird is used instead of the falcon?	(a) owl	(b) vulture	(c) hawk

B. Reread the story and write the answers to these questions.

1. Why was the falcon used to hunt food?

_____

_____

_____

2. Why is falconry popular today?

_____

_____

_____

3. How is the bird trained?

_____

_____

_____

4. How does the falconer know where the bird is with the prey?

_____

_____

_____

 Unit 54 cont'd ☞

Inflection of Irregular Verbs

A. The three forms of the irregular verb "cut" are listed. All three forms are used in the example sentences. Fill in the blank in each of the following sentences with the correct form of "cut."

form 1 — cut   *The ladies cut now.*
form 2 — cuts   *The lady cuts now.*
form 3 — cut   *The lady cut yesterday.*

1. The children _____ the paper now.
2. The boy _____ his finger now.
3. The girl _____ her finger yesterday.

B. The three forms of the irregular verb "bend" are listed. All three forms are used in the example sentences. Fill in the blank in each of the following sentences with the correct form of "bend."

form 1 — bend   *The boys bend the stick now.*
form 2 — bends   *The boy bends the stick now.*
form 3 — bent   *The boys bent the stick yesterday.*

1. The children _____ the rope now.
2. The dog _____ the fence now.
3. She _____ her gold ring yesterday.

C. The three forms of the irregular verb "wind" are listed. All three forms are used in the example sentences. Fill in the blank in each of the following sentences with the correct form of "wind."

form 1 — wind   *They wind the string now.*
form 2 — winds   *He winds the string now.*
form 3 — wound   *She wound the string before.*

1. They _____ the rope around the tree now.
2. She _____ her watch now.
3. He _____ the music box last night.

D. The three forms of the irregular verb "buy" are listed. All three forms are used in the example sentences. Fill in the blank in each of the following sentences with the correct form of "buy."

form 1 — buy   *The women buy their groceries.*
form 2 — buys   *The man buys a newspaper.*
form 3 — bought   *Many tourists bought post cards.*

1. The men _____ their suits now.
2. The teacher _____ her lunch in the cafeteria now.
3. All my friends _____ new sweaters.

The Fiddler Crab

Study the spelling and meaning of each word. These words are used in today's story. Connect each word with its definition.

1. alone   a. gesture
2. easy   b. small portions
3. motion   c. away from others
4. particles   d. looks closely
5. peers   e. not difficult
6. pick   f. gather

Read the story carefully and remember the details.

The fiddler crab is an odd-looking marine animal. Its left claw is small. It is used to pick particles of food out of the mud and sand. The crab's right claw is very large. The crab sometimes waves the claw slowly back and forth. The motion resembles a person playing a fiddle. Thus the fiddler crab gets its name.

When danger is near, the fiddler crab runs sideways to its burrow in the sand. The crab always peers about cautiously before coming out again.

When two male crabs meet, they lock their two large claws together. Then they shake hands as if trying to break the other's claw. It is easy to see why the fiddler crab lives alone.

A. Underline the correct answers about today's story.

1. The fiddler crab gets its name
   from its   (a) home   (b) claw   (c) walk.
2. The right claw is   (a) larger   (b) smaller   (c) the same as the left.
3. The fiddler crab runs   (a) backwards   (b) forwards   (c) sideways.
4. The crab's home is   (a) on the shore   (b) a burrow   (c) under a rock.
5. Which word describes the
   fiddler crab?   (a) friendly   (b) cautious   (c) helpless

B. Reread the story and write the answers to these questions.

1. What kind of animal is the crab?

   _____

   _____

   _____

2. What does the crab do when danger is near?

   _____

   _____

   _____

3. What happens when two male crabs meet?

   _____

   _____

   _____

4. What does the fiddler crab do before coming out of its home?

   _____

   _____

   _____

Unit 55 cont'd ☞

Auxiliaries as Verb Markers

A. Underline the modals in the following sentences. The five modals are listed in their present and past tense forms. Use this list as a guide to complete the exercise.

present tense	past tense
can	could
will	would
shall	should
may	might
must	

1. The car <u>must</u> be taken to the garage.
2. Adults should never ask children silly questions.
3. My sister could walk home instead.
4. We shall go camping this weekend.
5. Margaret may have only one candy bar.
6. The President can veto laws passed by the Congress.
7. The principal will pass out report cards.
8. We might move to the state of Arizona.
9. I would go swimming if it were warmer.

B. Underline the auxiliaries in the following sentences. The three forms of the auxiliary are listed with examples. Use the list as a guide to complete the exercise.

modals ────────────────→ *shall, must, can, may, will*
have + participle ──────→ *have gone, have walked*
be + action verb ───────→ *is going, was walking*

1. You <u>are</u> learning English grammar.
2. Many stores will sell skateboards next spring.
3. Several airplane pilots have flown in that plane.
4. The whole class will want to be in the play.
5. The players might go out to eat after the play.
6. Those adults have gone to school for years without graduating.
7. All drivers must pass the written test and road test.
8. My brother would like to go to a big college.
9. The patient was resting in his room.
10. Many tourists have seen Yellowstone National Park.

Comprehension Check

(A) Match each adverb with its definition.

1.	now	a. in that place; at that place
2.	there	b. every time; at all times
3.	daily	c. at the present time; at this moment
4.	then	d. soon afterward
5.	always	e. on or during this very day
6.	today	f. very near to; nearly; all but
7.	here	g. done, happening, or appearing every day
8.	almost	h. in this place
9.	later	i. subsequently; afterward
10.	seldom	j. from a place to a distance; far
11.	wearily	k. in a weary manner
12.	easily	l. in an easy manner
13.	away	m. rarely; not often
14.	tomorrow	n. on the day before today
15.	yesterday	o. on the day after today

(B) Match each verb with its definition.

1.	yawn	a. to swing back and forth
2.	sway	b. to open the mouth wide
3.	raise	c. to annoy or irritate by peevish complaints
4.	nag	d. to move to a higher place; to lift up
5.	cut	e. to divide with a knife
6.	utter	f. to plunge headfirst into water
7.	eat	g. to iron clothes
8.	dive	h. to speak; to make known; to express
9.	ail	i. to chew and swallow; to have a meal
10.	press	j. to be ill; to feel sick
11.	grasp	k. to seize and hold fast with the hand
12.	greet	l. to speak or write in a friendly way
13.	praise	m. to put clothes on
14.	dress	n. to pause
15.	wait	o. to speak well of

(C) Complete these sentences.

1. The fiddler crab is a ___*marine*___ animal.
2. The stork symbolizes _____ luck.
3. On land, the elephant seal is _____ .
4. The hedgehog's defense is its _____ .
5. Falconry is a _____ .
6. The hedgehog resembles the _____ .

7. The elephant seal gets its name from its _____ .
8. After a kill the falcon is rewarded with _____ .
9. The fiddler crab runs _____ .
10. The return of the stork means the arrival of _____ .

135   **Test 11 cont'd** 👉

Comprehension Check (continued)

(D) Match these words and their definitions. These words appeared in the reading selections from units 51-55.

_g_ 1. frantic   ___ 7. certain

___ 2. proboscis   ___ 8. centuries

___ 3. sluggish   ___ 9. obtain

___ 4. daring   ___ 10. quiet

___ 5. striking   ___ 11. motion

___ 6. furnish   ___ 12. peer

a. snout

b. acquire; get

c. courageous

d. particular

e. hushed

f. lacking in energy

g. greatly excited

h. gesture

i. provide

j. periods of one hundred years

k. look closely

l. notable

(E) Underline the correct answers.

1. What is a "proboscis"?   (a) mouth   (b) <u>snout</u>
2. Which word describes an elephant seal?   (a) dangerous   (b) helpless
3. What animal does the European hedgehog resemble?   (a) skunk   (b) porcupine
4. What is the hedgehog's defense?   (a) quills   (b) claws
5. What did the European stork supposedly symbolize?   (a) good luck   (b) bad luck
6. Where does the stork build its nest?   (a) on the ground   (b) on a rooftop
7. Why was falconry first popular?   (a) to find water   (b) to obtain food
8. What is the falcon's reward?   (a) the kill   (b) food
9. Where does the fiddler crab live?   (a) in a burrow   (b) under a rock
10. How does the crab's right claw compare to the left?   (a) larger   (b) smaller

Choose one of the following topics and write a paragraph.

(1) The European stork supposedly symbolized good luck. Over time there have been many things that were supposed to symbolize or bring good luck. List three and discuss them, including how you feel about them.

(2) Falconry enjoyed considerable popularity with English royalty beginning almost a thousand years ago. Name and discuss a modern day sport.

The Fiji Islands

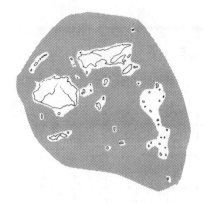

Study the spelling and meaning of each word. These words are used in today's story. Connect each word with its definition.

1. built
2. called
3. inhabited
4. island
5. near
6. simple

a. close to
b. lived in
c. formed; developed
d. referred to as
e. uncomplicated
f. pieces of land surrounded by water

Read the story carefully and remember the details.

The people of the Fiji Islands are called Fijians. They are a dark-skinned, fuzzy-haired people whose way of life has not changed much over the last few hundred years.

The Fiji Islands are a group of small islands. There are over 300 islands, but most of them are too small to be inhabited. Only a third of the islands is inhabited.

Most Fijians live in villages away from the towns. Their houses are built above the ground on blocks of stone. Those Fijians who live near the sea eat lots of fish.

Many Fijians are farmers. Some grow coconuts. Some grow bananas.

Many people consider the Fijians primitive. Fijians seem to be happy leading simple lives.

A. Underline the correct answers about today's story.

1. People of the Fiji Islands are called   (a) Fijilanders   (b) Fijians   (c) Islanders.

2. "Inhabited" means   (a) "connected"   (b) "lived on"   (c) "covered with water."

3. Most Fijians live   (a) in towns   (b) on the water   (c) in villages.

4. Many Fijians are   (a) farmers   (b) factory workers   (c) cattle ranchers.

5. Which word describes the Fijians?   (a) lazy   (b) modern   (c) primitive

B. Reread the story and write the answers to these questions.

1. How many islands make up the Fiji Islands?

_____

_____

_____

2. How many of the Fiji Islands are inhabited?

_____

_____

_____

3. Name two crops grown by Fiji farmers.

_____

_____

_____

4. Where do most Fijians live?

_____

_____

_____

 Unit 56 cont'd ☛

Auxiliaries

Auxiliaries are often called helping words. They are used with verbs to help express differences in time, intent, attitude, and condition. The auxiliary verb gives a sense of continuing or continued action. When an auxiliary and a verb are used in a question, the auxiliary comes before the subject or noun substitute.

Some auxiliaries are "am," "are," "can," "could," "did," "does," "get," "go," "had," "has," "have," "is," "keep," "may," "must," "shall," "should," "was," "were," "will," and "would."

 Fill in the blanks. Then complete the puzzle.

Across

2. _a r e_ used with plural nouns to show present tense

4. ___ ___ first and third person singular; past indicative of "be"

6. ___ ___ used with "I" in the present tense

8. ___ ___ ___ ___ the past tense of "will"

9. ___ ___ ___ ___ be forced to; ought to; obliged to

11. ___ ___ ___ to be able to; to know how to

13. ___ ___ third person singular, present indicative of "be"

15. ___ ___ ___ held in one's hand, in one's keeping

16. ___ ___ ___ carried through to the end; performed

17. ___ ___ ___ ___ am going to; is going to; are going to

18. ___ ___ ___ to reach; to arrive; to become; to come or go

19. ___ ___ ___ same as "15" across

20. ___ ___ ___ ___ third person singular, present indicative of "do"

Down

1. ___ ___ ___ ___ plural and second person singular past indicative of "be"

3. ___ ___ ___ ___ ___ ___ to express duty or obligation

5. ___ ___ ___ to be permitted or allowed to

7. ___ ___ to move along; to leave; to be in motion

10. ___ ___ ___ ___ used to express future time

11. ___ ___ ___ ___ used to convey a shade of doubt

12. ___ ___ ___ ___ to hold in one's keeping

14. ___ ___ ___ ___ to have for a long time, forever

15. ___ ___ ___ possesses an absolute quality or right

138

Fingerprints

Study the spelling and meaning of each word. These words are used in today's story. Connect each word with its definition.

1. distinctive   a. close likeness
2. distinguish   b. clearly different
3. outlines   c. examination
4. ridge   d. raised line
5. scrutiny   e. to recognize by some mark
6. similarities   f. marks

Read the story carefully and remember the details.

As we go through life, there are many things about us which change, but there are some things which do not change. One of these things is our fingerprints.

A fingerprint is the pattern made by the distinctive ridge outlines on each finger. No two people in all the world have the same pattern. There are many similarities in every fingerprint, but close scrutiny by an expert will distinguish one print from another.

The pattern never changes. When the skin is damaged, nature always restores the print to its original pattern.

Fingerprints were established as the official means of criminal identifications. Fingerprints are also valuable in identifying missing persons, amnesia victims, and unknown dead.

A. Underline the correct answers about today's story.

1. A fingerprint is a   (a) ridge pattern   (b) smudge   (c) distinct color.
2. The pattern is shared by   (a) no one   (b) blood relatives   (c) parents.
3. As we grow older, the pattern   (a) changes   (b) never changes   (c) gets smaller.
4. When the skin is damaged, the pattern   (a) changes   (b) is destroyed   (c) is restored.
5. Fingerprints are the official means of identifying   (a) unknown dead   (b) babies   (c) criminals.

B. Reread the story and write the answers to these questions.

1. As we go through life, what does not change?

_____

_____

_____

2. Who can distinguish one fingerprint from another?

_____

_____

_____

3. How often does the pattern change?

_____

_____

_____

4. How are fingerprints valuable?

_____

_____

_____

Unit 57 cont'd ☞

Position of Verbs

A. Unscramble each group of words into sentences. Write the sentences on the lines on the right side of the page.

1. she, listens
2. eats, Peter
3. girl, the, comes
4. the, bark, dogs
5. write, I

_____
_____
_____
_____
_____

B. Write the object of each verb in the blank.

1. Mary likes candy.   *candy*
2. The President vetoed the bill.
3. The coach used the first team for the whole game.
4. The cafeteria workers served lunch to the visitors.
5. The bank credited my account.
6. Trees beautify the countryside.
7. Exercise strengthens your body.
8. The judge announced his sentence.
9. That book simplifies the instructions.
10. All sentences have verbs.

C. Underline the verbs and the predicate nominatives in these sentences.

1. He is our hero.
2. Dishwashers are a convenience.
3. English is an easy language.
4. Today is the right time.
5. Kindness is a virtue.

D. Unscramble the following groups of words into good sentences. Write the sentences on the lines.

1. eat, lunch, I _____ *I eat lunch.*
2. actor, the, handsome, was_____
3. is, a, teacher, the, man _____
4. support, they, the, candidate _____
5. is, the, warm, room _____
6. model, is, a, the, woman _____

140

Fire Ants

Study the spelling and meaning of each word. These words are used in today's story. Connect each word with its definition.

1. dreaded ———————— a. feared greatly
2. gnaws   b. forming an opinion
3. harmless   c. causing no harm
4. judging   d. having bad habits
5. speculate   e. bites; nibbles
6. vicious   f. to make guesses

Read the story carefully and remember the details.

The fire ant is tiny, only one fourth of an inch long. Judging from its size, it would seem to be quite harmless. However, the fire ant is one of the most vicious and dreaded of insects.

The fire ant is also called the southern stinger. It lives in a colony. Most members of the colony are workers.

The fire ant damages livestock and crops. It gnaws at the roots of any growing plant. It preys on newborn fowl and calves. The ant is also dangerous to people. Its bites have been reported to cause death in humans.

Scientists speculate that fire ants were first brought the the United States on fruit boats from South America. Constant travel and rapid multiplication have spread the ants over much of the country.

A. Underline the correct answers about today's story.

1. Which word does not describe
   the fire ant?   (a) vicious   (b) dreaded   (c) harmless
2. The fire ant lives in   (a) colonies   (b) schools   (c) flocks.
3. Most fire ants are   (a) soldiers   (b) queens   (c) workers.
4. The fire ant constantly (a) eats   (b) travels   (c) drinks water.
5. The fire ant preys on   (a) newborn animals (b) humans   (c) other fire ants.

B. Reread the story and write the answers to these questions.

1. What is another name for the fire ant?

   _____

   _____

   _____

2. How did the ants get to the United States?

   _____

   _____

3. How small is the fire ant?

   _____

   _____

   _____

4. How have the ants spread throughout the country?

   _____

   _____

Unit 58 cont'd

Plain Form Verbs

¹b	l	o	²w	³	⁴		⁵
	⁶				⁷		
	⁸	⁹			¹⁰	¹¹	
		¹²	¹³		¹⁴		¹⁵
¹⁶	¹⁷				¹⁸		¹⁹
²⁰				²¹			
			²²		²³		²⁴
		²⁵					
²⁶			²⁷			²⁸	

 Fill in the blanks. Then complete the puzzle.

Across

1. <u>b l o w</u> to send forth a strong current of air
4. _ _ _ _ _ to stop until someone comes
6. _ _ _ _ _ to claw to pieces; to pull apart by force
7. _ _ _ to chew and swallow; to devour
9. _ _ _ _ _ _ to cause to come to pieces
14. _ _ _ _ _ to enclose; to put a circle around
18. _ _ to carry through to an end any action
20. _ _ _ _ _ _ to form thread into a fabric
21. _ _ _ _ to prepare for further use; to dress
22. _ _ _ _ _ _ to send through the air with force
23. _ _ _ to use oars to move a boat
25. _ _ _ _ _ _ to make letters, words, or symbols with a pen
26. _ _ _ _ _ to drop or come down from a higher place
27. _ _ _ _ _ to let another have or use for a time
28. _ _ _ _ to hunt or follow; to track; to pursue

Down

1. _ _ _ _ _ to seize, cut into, or cut off with the teeth
2. _ _ _ _ to fight
3. _ _ _ _ _ _ _ to be turned into ice; to become very cold
5. _ _ _ _ _ to make or cause to make a clear, ringing sound
8. _ _ _ _ _ to conceal; to put or keep out of sight
10. _ _ _ _ to tease playfully; to talk in a joking way
11. _ _ _ _ _ to be skilled in; to have the facts of
12. _ _ _ _ _ _ to place in classes; to make more nearly level
13. _ _ _ _ _ to hand over as a present without pay
14. _ _ _ _ to decay; to spoil; to become rotten
15. _ _ _ _ _ to become bigger by taking in food
16. _ _ _ _ _ to move on or in the water by using arms and legs
17. _ _ _ _ _ to have to do; to give a share to each; to distribute
18. _ _ _ _ _ to throw or shoot suddenly and swiftly
19. _ _ _ _ to arrange in a straight line
21. _ _ _ _ _ to make less crowded by removing some
24. _ _ _ to move from side to side or up and down

The First Hunters

Study the spelling and meaning of each word. These words are used in today's story. Connect each word with its definition.

1. crude
2. depend
3. entire
4. method
5. outwitting

6. popular

a. procedure; way
b. not refined
c. complete; total
d. to rely on
e. getting the better of by being smarter
f. common

Read the story carefully and remember the details.

Long ago people had few weapons. Those they had were simple and homemade. Thus people had to depend on their crude instruments and on outwitting the animals during a hunt. The invention of modern weapons made hunting much easier.

The first weapons were made of stone and wood. Most weapons were knives and spears.

The first hunters used fire to frighten the animals. They often built fires around entire herds.

Often hunters drove herds of animals over steep cliffs. At the bottom of the cliffs waited other hunters who finished killing the animals.

A popular method was to dig a deep pit. The pit was covered with branches and dirt. When an animal walked over the pit, it fell in and was trapped. Hunters rolled heavy stones on it and killed it.

A. Underline the correct answers about today's story.

1. The first weapons were made of (a) steel   (b) stone   (c) clay.

2. To frighten animals, the hunters (a) threw rocks   (b) screamed   (c) built fires.

3. Animals were often driven (a) into rivers   (b) into caves   (c) over steep cliffs.

4. The top of the pit was covered with   (a) animal skins   (b) branches   (c) rocks.

5. Which word describes the first weapons?   (a) simple   (b) modern   (c) complex

B. Reread the story and write the answers to these questions.

1. What made hunting much easier?

_____
_____
_____

2. Name two weapons.

_____
_____
_____

3. What did the hunters do when an animal fell into a pit?

_____
_____
_____

4. Why did hunters build fires?

_____
_____
_____

Unit 59 cont'd 🐾

Verb Form Shows Tense

These six forms are used in the language to divide time into six parts.

the time line	past perfect	past	present perfect	present	future perfect	future
	had walked	walked	has walked	walk	will have	will walk
			have walked	walks	walked	shall walk

A. Mark a check on the line before each sentence that uses an incorrect verb form. Remember that the past perfect is used for the action which happened first.

_____ 1. He had wanted (past perfect) the job before she came (past).

_____ 2. The teacher had explained (past perfect) things I heard (past) before.

_____ 3. I had stayed (past perfect) after I watched (past) TV.

_____ 4. There was (past) a parking lot where the building had been (past perfect).

B. Underline the verbs in these sentences. Write the tense of each verb on the line before the sentence. Choose your answers from the examples on the time line.

__*present perfect*__ 1. The definition of time has confused the greatest philosophers.

_____ 2. The verb form changes for each tense.

_____ 3. The two basic tenses are present and past.

_____ 4. Other tenses use forms of the auxiliary to show meaning.

_____ 5. Our language has changed over time.

_____ 6. The language changed with the culture of the people.

_____ 7. Perhaps the earliest beings on earth had communicated before man.

_____ 8. By the year 2000, linguists will have studied the language of the present times.

_____ 9. Our English language will change in the future.

_____ 10. Linguists will continue their study of the spoken language.

144

The Fisher

Study the spelling and meaning of each word. These words are used in today's story. Connect each word with its definition.

1. few
2. implies
3. instead
4. preys
5. sure
6. unlike

a. rather; in place of
b. small number
c. certain
d. suggests
e. different
f. hunts as food

Read the story carefully and remember the details.

Unlike its name implies, the fisher does not catch fish. Instead, the fisher, a member of the weasel family, preys on rodents and other small animals. The fisher is one of the few animals that can kill a porcupine. The fisher knocks the porcupine on its back and attacks the soft side.

The size of a fox, the fisher is the fastest tree traveler of all mammals. It is active the year round. It usually hunts at night.

The fisher lives in the cool forests of New England and Canada. Its den is usually a hollow log or tree.

No one is really sure how the fisher got its name. It likes to eat fish, but it is not a fisherman.

A. **Underline the correct answers about today's story.**

1. What is the fisher's main food?   (a) fish   (b) plants   (c) rodents
2. The fisher travels   (a) on the ground   (b) in trees   (c) underground.
3. When is the fisher active?   (a) summer   (b) winter   (c) year round
4. The fisher's home is   (a) a log or tree   (b) a cave   (c) a burrow.
5. When does the fisher hunt?   (a) at night   (b) daytime   (c) early morning

B. **Reread the story and write the answers to these questions.**

1. What is one thing the fisher can do that most animals cannot do?

_____

_____

_____

2. What other animal is the same size as the fisher?

_____

_____

3. What part of the year is the fisher active?

_____

_____

_____

4. What two countries does the fisher inhabit?

_____

_____

_____

Unit 60 cont'd ☞

Transitive and Intransitive Verbs

Write a "T" on the line before each sentence with a transitive verb and an "I" on the line before each sentence with an intransitive verb.

<u>T</u> 1. The businessman started the deal.

____ 2. The king lost his supremacy.

____ 3. The entire family arrived at six o'clock.

____ 4. Boeing is a large airplane manufacturer.

____ 5. Awards were announced at the assembly.

____ 6. My brother shares my room.

____ 7. She was liked by the group.

____ 8. Elizabeth Taylor is a famous actress.

____ 9. Lester's restaurant serves spaghetti on Thursday night.

____ 10. The balloon floats freely.

____ 11. The clerk scratched his nose with a pen.

____ 12. After school the teacher appears tired.

____ 13. His face looked old and wrinkled.

____ 14. Mom always fixes something special for dinner on Mondays.

____ 15. The mole buried himself in his hole.

____ 16. No answer came.

____ 17. The basketball players played the game like champions.

____ 18. It was difficult to settle down to study.

____ 19. The weather has been terrible.

____ 20. The class is studying psychology.

Comprehension Check

(A) Supply the auxiliary verbs.

1. ___Did___ he leave a message?
2. _____ you like to come too?
3. Sue _____ already gone home.
4. I _____ waiting for an answer.
5. She _____ reading a magazine.
6. _____ you want to dance?
7. Brad _____ work tonight.
8. _____ you go so soon?
9. Liz _____ not see me.
10. Nothing _____ been done.

11. John _____ not like beef stew.
12. You _____ going to hurt yourself.
13. I _____ go to the game after all.
14. No one _____ know about it.
15. They _____ lost the tournament.
16. It _____ not matter to James.
17. I _____ not say anything.
18. Something _____ happened to him.
19. The bus _____ arrived.
20. Louis _____ not doing his homework.

(B) Which tense is each verb?

1——present   2——past   3——future

_2_	1. drove	____	6. will move	____	11. studied	____	16. swims
____	2. sends	____	7. shall see	____	12. held	____	17. froze
____	3. will open	____	8. walked	____	13. finish	____	18. will believe
____	4. throws	____	9. needs	____	14. ate	____	19. wrote
____	5. is	____	10. will talk	____	15. will try	____	20. looks

(C) Underline the verb in each sentence. Write "t" for transitive and "i" for intransitive.

___t___ 1. No two people have the same set of fingerprints.
____ 2. The invention of modern weapons made hunting easier.
____ 3. The Fiji Islands are a group of small islands.
____ 4. Long ago people had few weapons.
____ 5. The fisher is the fastest tree traveler of all mammals.
____ 6. The pattern of a fingerprint never changes.
____ 7. The fisher lives in the cool forests of New England and Canada.
____ 8. The fire ant is one of the most vicious and dreaded of insects.

(D) Complete these sentences.

1. Many consider Fijians to be ___primitive___ .
2. The fisher is a _____ traveler.
3. Most fire ants are _____ .
4. Fingerprints serve as _____ .
5. First weapons were made of _____ and _____ .

6. Only a third of the Fiji Islands are _____ .
7. Fingerprint patterns are shared by _____ _____ .
8. Fire was once used to frighten _____ .
9. A fisher hunts _____ .
10. A fire ant is also called a southern _____ .

Test 12 cont'd ☞

Comprehension Check (continued)

(E) Match these words and their definitions. These words appeared in the reading selections from units 56-60.

<u>c</u> 1. near   ____ 7. harmless   a. not refined   g. causing no harm

____ 2. simple   ____ 8. crude   b. procedure; way   h. close likenesses

____ 3. distinctive   ____ 9. method   c. close to   i. clearly different

____ 4. distinguish   ____ 10. outwitting   d. feared greatly   j. suggests

____ 5. similarities   ____ 11. implies   e. uncomplicated   k. certain

____ 6. dreaded   ____ 12. sure   f. to recognize by some mark   l. getting the better of by being smarter

(F) Underline the correct answers.

1. Where do most Fijians live?   (a) on the water   <u>(b) in villages</u>
2. Name a crop grown by Fijians.   (a) oranges   (b) bananas
3. How often do fingerprints change?   (a) yearly   (b) never
4. Who shares a fingerprint?   (a) no one   (b) blood relatives
5. What is another name for the fire ant?   (a) flame thrower   (b) southern stinger
6. How have fire ants spread?   (a) constant travel   (b) wind blown
7. What was built to frighten animals?   (a) wooden dragons   (b) fires
8. What made hunting easier?   (a) winter   (b) weapons
9. What is the fisher's main food?   (a) rodents   (b) fish
10. Where is the fisher's home?   (a) log or tree   (b) burrow or cave

Choose one of the following topics and write a paragraph.

(1) Many of the Fiji Islands are not inhabited. If you were alone on one of them, what would you do? Why?

(2) The first hunters had to outwit the animals to trap them. This was made easier with the invention of weapons. Name three inventions that you use today and how they directly affect your life.

_____

_____

_____

_____

_____

_____

_____

_____

_____

The Flowerball Builders

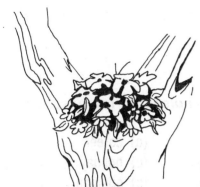

Study the spelling and meaning of each word. These words are used in today's story. Connect each word with its definition.

1. chosen
2. collect
3. deposited
4. formed
5. scoop
6. tropics

a. to dig out
b. selected
c. to gather in one place
d. tropical part of earth
e. put down
f. shaped

Read the story carefully and remember the details.

In the jungles of the tropics live ants which build a home called a flowerball. To begin, the ants scoop up the moist ground from the jungle floor. The soil is carried up the trunks of a chosen tree. There it is deposited and formed into a mound. Many ants are needed to build the home.

As soon as the ball of earth is large enough, workers begin to make tunnels and rooms. Meanwhile, other worker ants collect seeds from the flowers. These seeds are planted in the moist ball. When they sprout and grow, the ball is covered with colorful flowers and leaves.

The flowers are not mere decoration. They make up a protective covering against the rains of the wet season. To onlookers they are beautiful and decorative.

A. Underline the correct answers about today's story.

1. The flowerball builders are   (a) birds   (b) bees   (c) ants.
2. The flowerball is built   (a) on the ground   (b) in a tree   (c) near water.
3. Inside the ball are   (a) tunnels   (b) flowers   (c) stones.
4. Which ants build the home?   (a) queens   (b) soldiers   (c) workers
5. The flowers serve as   (a) protection   (b) decoration   (c) no purpose.

B. Reread the story and write the answers to these questions.

1. Where do the ants get the material to build their home?

_____

_____

_____

2. Where do the flowerball builders live?

_____

_____

_____

3. What are some worker ants doing while others are making tunnels?

_____

_____

_____

4. What is the flowerball to onlookers?

_____

_____

_____

Unit 61 cont'd ☞

Choosing Correctly Spelled Nouns

A noun names a person, place, or thing.

 Complete each sentence with the noun which is spelled correctly.

EXAMPLE: *That dog is getting to be a* __nuisance__. *(a) newsonce (b) nuisance (c) nuisence*

1. Jamie wants a _____ in medicine.   (a) carear (b) career (c) coreer
2. Christmas is my favorite _____.   (a) holliday (b) holaday (c) holiday
3. What's your _____?   (a) opinion (b) oppinion (c) openion
4. Is this his _____?   (a) signature (b) signeture (c) cignature
5. Let's watch _____.   (a) tellevision (b) television (c) televishun
6. The _____ happened yesterday.   (a) acksident (b) accidunt (c) accident
7. Do you know the _____?   (a) password (b) passwurd (c) pastword
8. _____ is important.   (a) Edukation (b) Education (c) Edducation
9. The _____ was found here.   (a) skeleton (b) skeletun (c) skellton
10. Repeat the _____.   (a) kwestion (b) queshton (c) question
11. May I have your _____?   (a) permission (b) purrmision (c) permishion
12. Ask Samuel for the _____.   (a) infurmation (b) information (c) infermation
13. Did you get an _____?   (a) invitation (b) invatation (c) envitation
14. Dave had another _____.   (a) nitmare (b) nightmare (c) nightmer
15. The _____ is up to you.   (a) decision (b) dicision (c) desishon
16. You have an _____ to fulfill.   (a) obligation (b) oblagation (c) oblegation
17. We are the new state _____.   (a) champeons (b) champions (c) champiens
18. Joel speaks a foreign _____.   (a) langauge (b) language (c) languag
19. Help me work this _____.   (a) problim (b) problum (c) problem
20. I have never broken a _____.   (a) promise (b) promus (c) promis
21. Don't forget to give her the _____.   (a) messege (b) message (c) mesage
22. Our _____ is a democracy.   (a) goverment (b) government (c) governmint
23. _____ filled the room.   (a) Laughter (b) Laufter (c) Laffter
24. It's only your _____.   (a) shaddow (b) shadowe (c) shadow
25. The party will be a _____.   (a) surprise (b) surprize (c) serprise
26. Their _____ forfeited.   (a) opponant (b) opponint (c) opponent
27. Lewis comes from a big _____.   (a) familly (b) famaly (c) family
28. I finished my _____.   (a) reporte (b) report (c) repourt
29. The coldest season is _____.   (a) wintur (b) winter (c) wintir
30. Kelly lives in an _____.   (a) apartmint (b) appartment (c) apartment
31. My _____ has a hole in it.   (a) pickit (b) pocket (c) pockut
32. Liza is _____ of the club.   (a) presedent (b) pressident (c) president
33. Who broke the _____?   (a) mirror (b) mirrer (c) miror
34. Which _____ did he go?   (a) direcktion (b) direction (c) direcshun
35. Wally's _____ is tomorrow.   (a) burthday (b) berthday (c) birthday

Flying Fish

Study the spelling and meaning of each word. These words are used in today's story. Connect each word with its definition.

1. escape
2. glide
3. incredible
4. rarely
5. sense
6. successful

a. not believable
b. get away
c. meaning
d. having a favorable result
e. moves smoothly
f. hardly ever

Read the story carefully and remember the details.

Would you believe that there is a fish that flies? Incredible as that may sound, there is. Its home is in the Atlantic Ocean.

The flying fish has winglike fins. Most of the time it swims underwater. However in order to escape its enemies, the fish swims quickly to the surface and out into the air. The flight does not last long, rarely more than half a minute. Yet the flying fish has been known to reach speeds up to 35 miles an hour. Thus it is often successful in escaping dolphins and other large fish looking for their dinners.

The flying fish really does not fly in the true sense of the word. It glides. The fish travels in large schools and is sometimes seen following a ship out to sea.

A. Underline the correct answers about today's story.

1. "Incredible" means   (a) "silly"   (b) "true"   (c) "not believable."

2. Flying fish live in   (a) rivers   (b) oceans   (c) streams.

3. The fish comes out of the water to   (a) breathe   (b) eat   (c) escape enemies.

4. Instead of flying, the fish really   (a) glides   (b) jumps   (c) swims fast.

5. Flying fish usually travel   (a) alone   (b) in schools   (c) in pairs.

B. Reread the story and write the answers to these questions.

1. Where is the home of the flying fish?

_____

_____

_____

2. How long does its flight usually last?

_____

_____

_____

3. How fast has it been known to fly?

_____

_____

_____

4. Name an animal that the flying fish must sometimes escape.

_____

_____

_____

Unit 62 cont'd ☞

Choosing Correctly
Spelled Adjectives

An adjective is a word which tells which one, what kind, what color, or how many.

 Complete each sentence with the adjective which is spelled correctly.

EXAMPLE: *Yellow is my favorite color.*   *(a) faverite   (b) favorit   (c) favorite*

1. The whale is an _____ animal.	(a) enormus	(b) enormous	(c) enormis
2. You have made an _____ choice.	(a) excellent	(b) ekscellent	(c) excellint
3. Your story is very _____ .	(a) inturesting	(b) interresting	(c) interesting
4. The diamond is a _____ stone.	(a) valluable	(b) valuable	(c) valuble
5. Did you hear a _____ noise?	(a) strange	(b) strainge	(c) strang
6. Mr. Cook is a _____ businessman.	(a) prosperous	(b) properus	(c) prosperis
7. This is not a _____ line.	(a) straght	(b) straigt	(c) straight
8. The sunset was _____ .	(a) beutiful	(b) beautiful	(c) beautifel
9. She is _____ and trustworthy.	(a) honest	(b) onest	(c) honist
10. That sounds _____ !	(a) terribul	(b) terrible	(c) terribel
11. Quincy is my _____ brother.	(a) yungest	(b) youngist	(c) youngest
12. Do you have a _____ size?	(a) larger	(b) largger	(c) largeer
13. The food was _____ .	(a) delishus	(b) delicious	(c) delecious
14. Jean was _____ about the trial.	(a) nervous	(b) nerveous	(c) nurvous
15. Paul is a _____ dancer.	(a) terific	(b) terrifik	(c) terrific
16. Many people are _____ .	(a) discontent	(b) discontint	(c) discontant
17. We're all part of a _____ team.	(a) wining	(b) winning	(c) winnin
18. Katie always looks _____ .	(a) chearful	(b) cheerful	(c) cheerfull
19. I need a _____ suitcase.	(a) broun	(b) browen	(c) brown
20. _____ students were absent.	(a) Twenty	(b) Twinty	(c) Twente
21. I've never visited a _____ country.	(a) foriegn	(b) foreign	(c) forun
22. My parents were _____ .	(a) furus	(b) furrious	(c) furious
23. You can't see an _____ man.	(a) invisible	(b) innvisible	(c) invisibul
24. The _____ lot has been sold.	(a) vakant	(b) vacant	(c) vacent
25. Newton was a _____ scientist.	(a) famus	(b) fammous	(c) famous
26. He collected _____ signatures.	(a) seventeen	(b) seventene	(c) sevinteen
27. My grandmother is a _____ woman.	(a) wize	(b) wise	(c) whise
28. Fred lives in a _____ house.	(a) haunted	(b) hanted	(c) hauntid
29. The cars' lights were _____ .	(a) brit	(b) bright	(c) brigt
30. Tim is an _____ boy.	(a) intelligent	(b) inteligent	(c) intelligant
31. What is the _____ answer?	(a) corect	(b) correct	(c) coreck
32. May I have a _____ one?	(a) diffrent	(b) differint	(c) different
33. Pam baked a _____ cake.	(a) choclate	(b) chocolate	(c) choklat
34. Steve is in the _____ grade.	(a) fourth	(b) forthe	(c) foreth

The Flying Squirrel

Study the spelling and meaning of each word. These words are used in today's story. Connect each word with its definition.

1. branch
2. curious
3. friendly
4. hind
5. hollow
6. steers

a. having a desire to learn
b. control
c. limb; twig
d. kind; showing good feelings
e. rear
f. empty on the inside

Read the story carefully and remember the details.

The flying squirrel is a nocturnal animal that belongs to the rodent family. Its home is a hollow tree.

Although called the flying squirrel, the animal does not really fly. It glides. A loose piece of skin stretches between the front and hind legs. When the squirrel jumps from one branch to another, the skin serves as wings. The squirrel steers by raising or lowering its legs.

The flying squirrel is a curious animal. Its curiousity often brings trouble. The squirrel is friendly with people and sometimes becomes a pet.

In the wild, the squirrel gathers nuts, mostly acorns. It also eats fruits and insects.

A. Underline the correct answers about today's story.

1. The flying squirrel is active   (a) during the day   (b) at night   (c) at dawn.

2. What is the squirrel's home?   (a) tunnel   (b) burrow   (c) hollow tree

3. Instead of flying, the squirrel really   (a) glides   (b) jumps   (c) runs fast.

4. What is the squirrel's main food? (a) meat   (b) grass   (c) nuts

5. Which word describes the squirrel?   (a) curious   (b) unfriendly   (c) dangerous

B. Reread the story and write the answers to these questions.

1. What does "nocturnal" mean?

_____

_____

_____

2. What purpose does the stretched skin between the squirrels front and hind legs serve?

_____

_____

_____

3. What sometimes comes about as a result of its curiousity?

_____

_____

_____

4. What alternate foods does the squirrel eat?

_____

_____

_____

     Unit 63 cont'd ☞

Choosing Correctly Spelled Adverbs

An adverb is a word which shows when, where, why, or how.

✳ Complete each sentence with the adverb which is spelled correctly.

> EXAMPLE: **Our next meeting is <u>tomorrow</u> at noon.**
> **(a) tumorrow   (b) tommorrow   (c) tomorrow**

1. _____ I argue with myself.
   (a) Sumtimes   (b) Sometimes   (c) Somtimes

2. Henry _____ wears that red cap.
   (a) always   (b) allways   (c) alsways

3. _____ was Wednesday.
   (a) Yesturday   (b) Yestirday   (c) Yesterday

4. The front lock was fastened _____.
   (a) sekurely   (b) securly   (c) securely

5. Paper was flying _____.
   (a) everwhere   (b) everywhere   (c) everywher

6. I _____ wonder what happened to him.
   (a) ofen   (b) often   (c) offten

7. Please try to come _____.
   (a) early   (b) urly   (c) earley

8. Finish your work _____.
   (a) qwickly   (b) quickly   (c) kwickly

9. Adam has _____ been to Mexico.
   (a) never   (b) niver   (c) nevur

10. He was _____ to be found.
    (a) nowher   (b) nowhere   (c) no where

11. _____ we gave up.
    (a) Finaly   (b) Finally   (c) Finnally

12. She smiled _____.
    (a) saddly   (b) sadly   (c) sadley

13. _____ Don accepted the proposal.
    (a) Eagerly   (b) Egerly   (c) Eagurly

14. Brad is _____ asking questions.
    (a) forevir   (b) forevor   (c) forever

15. The mountain towered _____.
    (a) majestically (b) magestically (b) majestikally

16. Mom waited _____.
    (a) patently   (b) patiently   (c) patintly

17. I _____ regret my decision.
    (a) sincerely   (b) sincerly   (c) sincerelly

18. John _____ lifted the box.
    (a) carfully   (b) carefuly   (c) carefully

19. I waited _____ for the mail.
    (a) anxshusly   (b) anxiously   (c) anxiusly

20. Les _____ drinks milk for lunch.
    (a) usually   (b) ussualy   (c) usualy

21. Spread the paint _____.
    (a) evinly   (b) evenly   (c) evenlly

22. I'll call you _____.
    (a) tunight   (b) tonit   (c) tonight

23. She answered each one _____.
    (a) korrectly   (b) corectly   (c) correctly

24. _____ it began to rain.
    (a) Suddenly   (b) Suddinly   (c) Sudenly

25. Won't you come _____?
    (a) innside   (b) inside   (c) insside

26. Your room is _____.
    (a) upstares   (b) upstairz   (c) upstairs

27. The boy _____ speaks.
    (a) selldom   (b) seldom   (c) seldim

28. Step _____.
    (a) forward   (b) forword   (c) forwerd

29. School begins _____.
    (a) tuday   (b) todaey   (c) today

30. Paul comes here _____.
    (a) frequently   (b) freqwently   (c) frequintly

31. The man spoke _____.
    (a) tactlessly   (b) taklessly   (c) tactlesly

32. You were _____ responsible.
    (a) direkly   (b) directly   (c) directley

33. _____ it's not too late.
    (a) Hopefuly   (b) Hopefully   (c) Hopfully

34. _____ he opened the door.
    (a) Cautiously   (b) Cautiusly   (c) Cawtiously

Foxes

Study the spelling and meaning of each word. These words are used in today's story. Connect each word with its definition.

1. craftiness
2. deserted
3. desperate
4. noted
5. similar
6. vary

a. almost beyond hope
b. almost the same
c. of different kinds
d. skill; cunning
e. well known for
f. left behind

Read the story carefully and remember the details.

The fox is a member of the dog family. It is an intelligent animal, often noted for its craftiness and slyness. Thus comes the saying, "sly as a fox."

The fox may live in open areas, but always near rocks and bushes where it can hide. Its home is a burrow which it has dug itself or found deserted by another animal.

The fox does its hunting at night. It eats insects, mice, and moles. When desperate, the fox may raid poultry yards.

There are many kinds of foxes. They all vary in size and color. Their habits are similar. The best known foxes are the red foxes. Basically shy animals , the foxes stay away from people. Many foxes are raised on farms for their furs.

A. **Underline the correct answers about today's story.**

1. The fox is a member of the   (a) cat family   (b) mouse family   (c) dog family.

2. Why does the fox live
   near bushes?   (a) to hide   (b) for food   (c) to make a home

3. When does the fox hunt?   (a) morning   (b) at night   (c) afternoon

4. Which word describes the fox?   (a) simple   (b) unskilled   (c) crafty

5. Foxes are often raised for   (a) meat   (b) furs   (c) protection.

B. **Reread the story and write the answers to these questions.**

1. What saying comes from the fox?

_____

_____

_____

2. Where does the fox live?

_____

_____

_____

3. What does the fox usually eat?

_____

_____

_____

4. What is the best known fox?

_____

_____

_____

    Unit 64 cont'd ☛

Choosing Correctly Spelled Verbs

A verb shows action or state of being.

❋ **Complete each sentence with the verb which is spelled correctly.**

EXAMPLE: I <u>advise</u> you to tell Ms. Fisher.
(a) advize (b) addvise (c) advise

1. _____ the next chapter.
   (a) Owtline (b) Outline (c) Outlin

2. Did you _____ to call Chuck?
   (a) remimber (b) remember (c) remembur

3. Anna is _____ her grandmother.
   (a) viseting (b) viziting (c) visiting

4. Joey _____ newspapers.
   (a) delivurs (b) delivors (c) delivers

5. I've _____ my mind.
   (a) changed (b) chanjed (c) changd

6. _____ parts ''A'' and ''B.''
   (a) Seperate (b) Sepurate (c) Separate

7. Bears _____ in the winter.
   (a) hiburnate (b) hibernate (c) hibernat

8. Don't _____ to call.
   (a) hesitate (b) hessitate (c) hesatate

9. The city should _____ the building.
   (a) condemn (b) condem (c) condimn

10. Donna _____ home.
    (a) hurryed (b) hurryied (c) hurried

11. My brother _____ the car.
    (a) wrecked (b) recked (c) wreckt

12. Millie _____ with the officer.
    (a) argueed (b) argued (c) aregued

13. It was _____.
    (a) rainning (b) raining (c) rayning

14. Let's _____ the barn green.
    (a) paynt (b) paint (c) paent

15. Terry _____ to wait for us.
    (a) decided (b) desided (c) decidded

16. Dad _____ the bicycle.
    (a) asembled (b) assembled (c) asembuld

17. The ghost _____.
    (a) vanushed (b) vanished (c) vannished

18. This shield will _____ your eyes.
    (a) protect (b) pertect (c) protek

19. I _____ the assignment.
    (a) undirstand (b) understan (c) understand

20. Columbus _____ America.
    (a) disscovered (b) discovired (c) discovered

21. The dog _____ me home.
    (a) folowed (b) followed (c) folloed

22. George _____ on the door.
    (a) nocked (b) knocked (c) knoked

23. Zeke _____ to come early.
    (a) promised (b) promized (c) promused

24. I _____ we reconsider.
    (a) seggest (b) suggest (c) suggist

25. Would you _____ it again?
    (a) eksplain (b) explane (c) explain

26. _____ your name at the top.
    (a) Rite (b) Write (c) Wright

27. Mr. Thompson _____ at the bakery.
    (a) wurks (b) werks (c) works

28. Betty _____ for the job.
    (a) applyed (b) applyied (c) applied

29. We are _____ our history.
    (a) studying (b) studdying (c) studiing

30. No one _____ my story.
    (a) beleives (b) beleves (c) believes

31. Roy and I will _____ the floor.
    (a) skrub (b) scrubb (c) scrub

32. Mr. Weston _____ the truck.
    (a) bot (b) boutgh (c) bought

33. The man _____ us for a dime.
    (a) begged (b) beged (c) beggd

34. Clark _____ at the dog.
    (a) wistled (b) whistled (c) whisled

The Frigate Bird

Study the spelling and meaning of each word. These words are used in today's story. Connect each word with its definition.

1. badgers ————————— a. annoys
2. devours   b. most recent
3. enormous   c. showy
4. latter   d. fly
5. soar   e. eats greedily
6. spectacular   f. huge

Read the story carefully and remember the details.

The frigate bird is a large, spectacular air bird with an enormous wingspread. It is often referred to as a "feathered airplane." The frigate bird can soar for hours without moving its wings.

The frigate bird spends most of its life flying about over the sea. The bird eats almost anything it can find. One frigate bird sometimes steals from another. The thief badgers the bird until the latter drops its prey. Then the thief grabs the prey and devours it.

At dusk the frigate bird retires to the trees near the coast to roost. Here the bird builds its nest of sticks. The frigate bird makes an excellent parent. Both the male and female are always guarding the nest.

The frigate bird is also called a man-of-war bird. Both names refer to the bird's size and habitat.

A. Underline the correct answers about today's story.

1. The frigate bird spends its life   (a) on land   (b) in trees   (c) over the sea.

2. The birds roost   (a) on the coast   (b) over the water   (c) on marshes.

3. As a parent, the frigate bird is   (a) careless   (b) watchful   (c) negligent.

4. The bird's name refers to its   (a) size   (b) habits   (c) feeding.

5. Which word describes the bird?   (a) puny   (b) spectacular   (c) weak

B. Reread the story and write the answers to these questions.

1. What is the frigate bird's "nickname"?

_____

_____

_____

2. Where does this bird spend most of its life?

_____

_____

_____

3. What does the frigate bird do at dusk?

_____

_____

_____

4. What material makes up the bird's nest?

_____

_____

_____

          Unit 65 cont'd ☞

Changing Parts of Speech

Sometimes the same word can function as different parts of speech. It may have to take on additional prefixes and suffixes, but its part of speech is determined by its use in a sentence. For example, notice how the word "order" changes from a noun to a verb to an adjective in these three sentences:

> *I gave you an order.*
> *Kevin did order the tuna salad.*
> *Fill out the order blank.*

✱ **Identify the part of speech of each underlined word. Write "1" for noun, "2" for verb, and "3" for adjective.**

_1_ 1. A small crowd gathered around us.
____ 2. I felt uncomfortable in the crowded room.
____ 3. Ten people crowded into the elevator.

____ 4. He is an escaped convict.
____ 5. The prisoners planned their escape.
____ 6. The man escaped on July 22.

____ 7. The incident troubled Dan.
____ 8. I think we're in trouble.
____ 9. Jill gave me a troubled look.

____ 10. The reward money was stolen.
____ 11. The winner was rewarded a trophy.
____ 12. The reward was fifty dollars.

____ 13. Gilda has a good suggestion.
____ 14. Mr. Price suggested we think it over.
____ 15. Put your idea in the suggestion box.

____ 16. Welcome our guests.
____ 17. Tim was given a warm welcome.
____ 18. Mother bought a new welcome mat.

____ 19. Frank changed his mind again.
____ 20. Everyone was ready for a change.
____ 21. My change purse has a hole in it.

____ 22. The scale is broken.
____ 23. Isaac did a scale drawing.
____ 24. Mark scaled the wall.

____ 25. Eric promised to bring the book.
____ 26. The deal sounds promising.
____ 27. I never break a promise.

____ 28. Call the police.
____ 29. The army policed the area carefully.
____ 30. I've never ridden in a police car.

____ 31. Storms frighten me.
____ 32. We slept in the storm cellar.
____ 33. It stormed again last night.

____ 34. Joan watered the flowers.
____ 35. The water buffalo lives there.
____ 36. The water was cool and refreshing.

____ 37. The captain commanded his troops to stop.
____ 38. The singer gave a command performance.
____ 39. He disobeyed your command.

____ 40. We surprised you.
____ 41. Kelly gave Sue a surprise party.
____ 42. This is a pleasant surprise!

____ 43. She headed the ship for home.
____ 44. Phil is the head officer.
____ 45. Move your head to the right.

____ 46. Ms. Young graded our tests.
____ 47. Vera always makes good grades.
____ 48. The teacher lost her grade book.

Comprehension Check

A Identify the part of speech.

1——nouns   2——adjectives   3——adverbs   4——verbs

_4_ 1. worked	___ 16. opinion	___ 31. language	___ 46. nervous
___ 2. signature	___ 17. prosperous	___ 32. usually	___ 47. understand
___ 3. excellent	___ 18. always	___ 33. explain	___ 48. foreign
___ 4. changed	___ 19. remember	___ 34. terrific	___ 49. frequently
___ 5. securely	___ 20. famous	___ 35. inside	___ 50. nuisance
___ 6. laughter	___ 21. apply	___ 36. straight	___ 51. education
___ 7. delicious	___ 22. skeleton	___ 37. evenly	___ 52. today
___ 8. tonight	___ 23. government	___ 38. cheerful	___ 53. cautiously
___ 9. carefully	___ 24. thirteen	___ 39. painted	___ 54. studying
___ 10. protect	___ 25. believes	___ 40. problem	___ 55. champion
___ 11. career	___ 26. tomorrow	___ 41. beautiful	___ 56. finally
___ 12. nowhere	___ 27. vacant	___ 42. early	___ 57. valuable
___ 13. beg	___ 28. mirror	___ 43. quickly	___ 58. eagerly
___ 14. enormous	___ 29. wise	___ 44. red	___ 59. decision
___ 15. often	___ 30. buy	___ 45. nightmare	___ 60. honest

B Use each word as (a) noun, a (b) verb, and an (c) adjective.

1. order   a. _____
   b. _____
   c. _____

2. reward   a. _____
   b. _____
   c. _____

3. grade   a. _____
   b. _____
   c. _____

4. change   a. _____
   b. _____
   c. _____

5. water   a. _____
   b. _____
   c. _____

C Complete these sentences.

1. The flying fish may move at ___ _35_ ___ miles an hour.
2. The fox is a member of the _____ family.
3. Frigate birds have _____ wingspreads.
4. Flowerball builders live in the _____.
5. The frigate bird is also called a _____ _____ bird.
6. The flying squirrel is a _____.
7. Flowerball builders are _____.
8. Flying fish live in the _____ Ocean.
9. A flying squirrel _____.
10. The best known fox is the _____ fox.

Test 13 cont'd ☞

Comprehension Check (continued)

Ⓓ **Match these words and their definitions. These words appeared in the reading selections from units 61-65.**

_e_ 1. chosen   ___ 7. curious   a. not believable   g. rear

___ 2. formed   ___ 8. hind   b. get away   h. almost beyond hope

___ 3. scoop   ___ 9. desperate   c. to dig out   i. well known for

___ 4. escape   ___ 10. noted   d. shaped   j. hardly ever

___ 5. incredible   ___ 11. badgers   e. selected   k. annoys

___ 6. rarely   ___ 12. spectacular   f. having a desire to learn   l. showy

Ⓔ **Underline the correct answers.**

1. What are the flowerball builders?   (a) <u>ants</u>   (b) birds

2. Where is the flowerball built?   (a) in a tree   (b) near water

3. Where is the home of the flying fish?   (a) Atlantic Ocean   (b) Gulf of Mexico

4. How fast can the flying fish fly?   (a) 35 m.p.h.   (b) 5 m.p.h.

5. What does "nocturnal" mean?   (a) of the night   (b) curious

6. What does the squirrel eat?   (a) meat   (b) nuts

7. Why does the fox live near bushes?   (a) to make a home   (b) to hide

8. What do foxes eat?   (a) coyotes   (b) mice

9. Where do frigate birds roost?   (a) in trees   (b) on the coast

10. What is the frigate bird's nickname?   (a) feathered airplane   (b) wingspreader

Choose one of the following topics and write a paragraph.

(1) In the tropics are beautiful flowers. What are some of your favorite flowers? Write about some uses of flowers.

(2) Foxes are raised for their furs. Should this be allowed? Why or why not?

_____

_____

_____

_____

_____

_____

_____

_____

_____

_____

Gars

Study the spelling and meaning of each word. These words are used in today's story. Connect each word with its definition.

1. destructive
2. greedy
3. motionless
4. overlapping
5. representative
6. value

a. selfishly
b. without movement
c. tearing apart
d. worth
e. typical example
f. one part over another

Read the story carefully and remember the details.

Fishermen dislike the gar because it is very destructive of other fish. Also it has no value as food.

There are many kinds of gars. Most representative of the group are the longnose gars. Like other gars the longnose gars are killer fish. Gars are as deadly as they look.

The gar's body is covered with heavy, overlapping plates. These plates protect the fish from every other fish which lives in its habitat.

The gar is strong, greedy, and destructive. It lurks motionless, waiting for its prey. When the prey swims by, the gar attacks with lightning speed. It slashes at the victim and grabs it with razor-edged teeth. The gar swallows the prey whole.

A. Underline the correct answers about today's story.

1. Fishermen consider the gar   (a) a friend   (b) valuable   (c) a threat.

2. As food the gar   (a) is delicious   (b) has no value   (c) is tasty.

3. What protects the gar?   (a) size   (b) teeth   (c) heavy plates

4. Which word describes the gar?   (a) helpful   (b) destructive   (c) unselfish

5. A gar looks   (a) deadly   (b) friendly   (c) harmless.

B. Reread the story and write the answers to these questions.

1. Which gar is most representative?

_____

_____

_____

2. Why is the gar disliked?

_____

_____

_____

3. How does the gar eat?

_____

_____

_____

4. What does "razor-edged" mean?

_____

_____

_____

Unit 66 cont'd

Parts of Speech

A. Underline the nouns.

1. <u>season</u>	6. laughter	11. there	16. and	21. trouble
2. telephone	7. possess	12. we	17. adventure	22. ours
3. beautiful	8. pocket	13. mountain	18. pilot	23. luggage
4. governor	9. am	14. student	19. without	24. visitor
5. evenly	10. gypsy	15. answer	20. soonest	25. tried

B. Underline the verbs.

1. <u>arrive</u>	6. racer	11. read	16. if	21. whisper
2. coward	7. return	12. careless	17. wait	22. musical
3. paints	8. dance	13. hesitate	18. forget	23. slap
4. snowed	9. beg	14. drag	19. their	24. or
5. into	10. the	15. family	20. will	25. write

C. Underline the adjectives.

1. <u>electric</u>	6. steal	11. famous	16. happily	21. neither
2. freedom	7. sleepy	12. quiet	17. shy	22. tough
3. powerful	8. before	13. its	18. usually	23. decision
4. brave	9. higher	14. strange	19. clever	24. front
5. blew	10. elephants	15. easily	20. funny	25. fits

D. Underline the adverbs.

1. <u>tomorrow</u>	6. ugly	11. never	16. filed	21. frequently
2. now	7. here	12. captain	17. there	22. choice
3. spelling	8. waiting	13. clouds	18. today	23. always
4. me	9. useless	14. suddenly	19. nowhere	24. earth
5. easily	10. dreamily	15. often	20. blue	25. somewhere

E. Underline the word which completes each sentence.

1. Mrs. Fielder sat (between, among) Karen and Ralph.
2. A nomad (wonders, wanders) about in search of food.
3. Albert's family (emigrated, immigrated) here from East Germany.
4. Money and friends are both necessary, but the (later, latter) is best.
5. After that delicious meal, we were too full for (dessert, desert).

The Giant Panda

Study the spelling and meaning of each word. These words are used in today's story. Connect each word with its definition.

1. existed
2. indicated
3. recently
4. remote
5. reports
6. secluded

a. by itself
b. accounts
c. pointed out
d. lived
e. lately
f. far away

Read the story carefully and remember the details.

The giant panda lived in such a secluded habitat that until recently no one even knew it existed. The giant panda's home is high in the remote mountains of Asia.

The giant panda looks like a huge black and white teddy bear. Actually, the panda is not a bear but a member of the raccoon family. It is shy and keeps to itself.

Not much is known about the giant panda's habits. The panda lives in the bamboo forests. It feeds entirely on bamboo shoots. All reports indicate that the giant panda leads an easy life. The baby panda often makes a fine pet, but the adult is not so agreeable.

The giant panda looks clumsy, yet it gets around quite well in its thick jungle home. The giant panda is difficult to capture.

A. Underline the correct answers about today's story.

1. The giant panda is a member of the   (a) bear family   (b) cat family   (c) raccoon family.
2. Where does the panda live?   (a) Australia   (b) Asia   (c) Africa
3. What do pandas eat?   (a) bamboo   (b) grass   (c) insects
4. Which word describes the giant panda?   (a) outgoing   (b) shy   (c) aggressive
5. A habitat is a   (a) home   (b) habit   (c) piece of clothing.

B. Reread the story and write the answers to these questions.

1. What kind of animal does the giant panda resemble?

_____
_____
_____

2. Describe the animal's personality.

_____
_____
_____

3. Why has the panda only recently been discovered?

_____
_____
_____

4. What color or colors is the panda?

_____
_____
_____

Unit 67 cont'd ☞

Prepositions

A preposition connects a word group to the rest of the sentence.

Other prepositions are as follows:

above	by
across	concerning
against	during
along	except
among	for
around	from
before	in
behind	inside
beside	into
besides	near
between	off
beyond	

 Fill in the blanks. Then complete the puzzle.

Down

1. _o v e r_ above in place or position

2. _ _ to a higher place

3. _ _ _ _ _ _ _ from one end to the other

4. _ _ _ _ _ from a higher to a lower place in a river

5. _ _ _ _ forth from; away; not in or at a position

6. _ _ _ _ _ _ place lower than another

8. _ _ above or supported by

11. _ _ _ _ _ close to in space, time, condition, or relation

13. _ _ _ _ _ below the surface of

15. _ _ _ _ _ _ something near or close to; not far from

17. _ _ _ _ _ in the company of; in the same direction of; toward

Across

1. _ _ _ _ _ _ _ beyond the limits of; not inside

7. _ _ _ _ _ _ He stood _ _ _ _ _ the rung of the ladder.

9. _ _ made from; containing

10. _ _ in, on, by, or near

12. _ _ _ _ _ _ from a past time until now; at any time between

14. _ _ _ _ _ up to the time of

16. _ _ _ _ _ farther on than; later than; no longer capable of

18. _ _ _ _ _ resembling something or each other

20. _ _ _ _ _ _ going or coming in the rear of; behind

21. _ _ _ _ _ _ _ covered by; in a lower place; below

The Golden Eagle   Unit 68

Study the spelling and meaning of each word. These words are used in today's story. Connect each word with its definition.

1. breeding   a. far away
2. common   b. ordinary
3. inhabit   c. live in
4. magnificient   d. mating; reproducing
5. remote   e. splendid
6. restricted   f. limited

Read the story carefully and remember the details.

Large and powerful, the golden eagle was once trained for use by kings in hunting foxes and other mammals. Today it is still trained by falconers, but its use is no longer restricted to kings.

In the wild the golden eagle is a magnificent bird of prey. It is an excellent hunter, feeding on squirrels, prairie dogs, rodents, other birds, and snakes. It lives all year within its breeding range.

The golden eagle's nest is built on a high cliff or sometimes in a tall tree. The nest is large, sometimes as wide as five feet and equally as tall.

The golden eagle is not a common bird. It is found in the open country and deserts of the western United States. The bird may also inhabit remote mountain areas.

A. Underline the correct answers about today's story.

1. The use of eagles in falconry was
   restricted to   (a) kings   (b) nobility   (c) commoners.
2. The golden eagle is excellent   (a) hunter   (b) fisherman   (c) nest builder.
3. The eagle's nest is usually built   (a) in a tree   (b) on a cliff   (c) on low ground.
4. Golden eagles are usually found in   (a) cities   (b) remote areas   (c) cold climates.
5. Which word describes the golden eagle?   (a) weak   (b) small   (c) powerful

B. Reread the story and write the answers to these questions.

1. Name an early use of the golden eagle.

_____
_____
_____

2. Name two things the golden eagle eats.

_____
_____
_____

3. What part of the United States are golden eagles found?

_____
_____
_____

4. What is a "falconer"?

_____
_____
_____

Interjections

Interjections are often used to show strong surprise or strong feelings. An interjection is independent of the other words in a sentence. It should be followed by a comma or an exclamation point. If an interjection shows strong feeling, it is followed by an exclamation point. The first word following a strong interjection begins with a capital letter.

 Fill in the blanks. Then complete the puzzle.

Down

2. _r_ _a_ _t_ _s_ scornful impatience or disbelief

4. _ _ _ _ mild surprise or agreement or just to fill in

5. _ _ _ _ _ _ _ _ used as a mild oath or exclamation

6. _ _ great surprise

8. _ _ _ _ surprise, dismay, or relief

9. _ _ _ _ _ _ _ _ _ exclamation of surprise

11. _ _ _ _ exclamation of contempt

13. _ _ _ _ admiration, delight, fear, or other emotion or sensation

16. _ _ _ _ an exclamation or mild oath

17. _ _ used before a person's name when beginning to speak

18. _ _ used emphatically to say you can't or won't

Across

1. _ _ _ _ _ _ shout of joy or approval

3. _ _ _ exclamation of scorn, contempt, or impatience

7. _ _ _ _ _ sorrow, grief, regret, pity, dread, or concern

10. _ _ _ _ _ expressing sudden pain

12. _ _ _ expressing disgust, horror, or strong distaste

13. _ _ used before a person's name when beginning to speak

14. _ _ exclamation of surprise, joy, or scornful laughter

15. _ _ _ exclamation of surprise, joy, or dismay

16. _ _ _ _ having high quality

16. _ _ _ _ _ _ _ _ _ exclamation of surprise or alarm

19. _ _ _ admiration, delight, fear, or other emotion or sensation

20. _ _ used before a person's name when beginning to speak

21. _ _ _ _ _ exclamation of wonder, pleasure, joy, or the like

22. _ _ _ _ _ _ shout of joy or approval

23. _ _ _ _ _ _ shout of joy

166

Grass Houses

Unit 69

Study the spelling and meaning of each word. These words are used in today's story. Connect each word with its definition.

1. placed
2. privacy
3. safety
4. stilts
5. thatched
6. woven

a. being apart
b. covered with straw
c. put
d. to interlace threads
e. freedom from danger
f. tall poles

Read the story carefully and remember the details.

Grass houses can be built almost anywhere. Some are built on the ground. When there are many trees in an area, the grass house is sometimes placed on stilts.

The walls of the house are of woven grasses. The roof is thatched with leaves. Grass houses on stilts have a ladder to allow the owners to go up or down. At night the ladder is pulled up for safety and privacy.

Some grass houses even have fireplaces where the families cook their meals. The fireplaces are lined with clay or metal to keep the fire from spreading. Smoke escapes through holes in the roofs. Some grass houses even have running water.

A. Underline the correct answers about today's story.

1. Near wooded areas grass houses are   (a) forbidden   (b) rare   (c) on stilts.

2. The walls of the house are   (a) dried leaves   (b) grass   (c) rocks.

3. The roof is made of   (a) sticks   (b) leaves   (c) roots.

4. Entry to a house on stilts is by   (a) ladder   (b) rope   (c) nearby tree.

5. The fireplaces are lined with   (a) mud   (b) wood   (c) clay.

B. Reread the story and write the answers to these questions.

1. Why are the ladders taken in at night?

_____

_____

_____

2. Where do some families cook their meals?

_____

_____

_____

3. What two things line the fireplaces?

_____

_____

_____

4. Why do fireplaces have this lining?

_____

_____

_____

Unit 69 cont'd ☞

Making Compound Words

A compound word is made up of two or more words and written as one word.

 Draw a line connecting two words to make each compound word. Then write each new word.

1. bumble	burst	**bumblebee**
2. day	bee	_____
3. down	house	_____
4. cloud	hill	_____
5. court	break	_____
6. else	cake	_____
7. earth	bridge	_____
8. fruit	where	_____
9. grape	quake	_____
10. draw	fruit	_____
11. mean	while	_____
12. switch	land	_____
13. over	board	_____
14. pine	sight	_____
15. main	apple	_____
16. through	right	_____
17. up	basket	_____
18. type	out	_____
19. waste	writer	_____
20. what	ever	_____
21. snow	boat	_____
22. sea	storm	_____
23. bird	house	_____
24. speed	shore	_____
25. camp	fire	_____
26. up	brain	_____
27. piggy	song	_____
28. fire	cracker	_____
29. scatter	back	_____
30. sing	hill	_____

31. ship	puncher	_____
32. grass	shape	_____
33. cow	melon	_____
34. flash	hopper	_____
35. water	light	_____
36. text	book	_____
37. race	brush	_____
38. blood	box	_____
39. tooth	horse	_____
40. mail	hound	_____
41. wish	room	_____
42. week	set	_____
43. drive	way	_____
44. sun	bone	_____
45. store	end	_____
46. tooth	flower	_____
47. news	line	_____
48. sun	stick	_____
49. dead	ache	_____
50. yard	paper	_____
51. horse	ache	_____
52. head	noon	_____
53. after	fly	_____
54. side	print	_____
55. foot	walk	_____
56. car	ship	_____
57. hall	road	_____
58. rail	way	_____
59. steam	stop	_____
60. short	wash	_____

The Grasshopper Mouse

Study the spelling and meaning of each word. These words are used in today's story. Connect each word with its definition.

1. ambushes
2. beneficial
3. cannibalistic
4. devouring
5. earned
6. quest

    a. hunt or search
    b. deserved
    c. eats its own kind
    d. attacks by surprise
    e. eating; consuming
    f. helpful

Read the story carefully and remember the details.

Among rodents the grasshopper mouse has earned an unfavorable reputation. It is a killer, devouring many other species of mice. The grasshopper mouse is even cannibalistic; it stops at nothing in its quest for food.

Because of its short legs and heavy build, the grasshopper mouse is not a good runner. It ambushes its prey.

The grasshopper mouse lives only in North America. It is a grassland animal of warm, even hot, climates. The grasshopper mouse does not hibernate but stays active the year round.

The mouse's home is a den underneath the ground. The grasshopper mouse has keen senses of sight, sound, and smell. It is nocturnal. Aside from its bloody reputation, the grasshopper mouse is beneficial to people because it controls the rodent population.

A. **Underline the correct answers about today's story.**

1. The grasshopper mouse's reputation is   (a) favorable   (b) unfavorable   (c) kind.
2. "Cannibalistic" means the mouse eats   (a) plants   (b) meat   (c) it's own kind.
3. The grasshopper mouse lives in   (a) hot climates   (b) cold climates   (c) wet climates.
4. The grasshopper mouse is active   (a) in summer   (b) in winter   (c) year round.
5. People consider the grasshopper mouse   (a) beneficial   (b) a pest   (c) useless.

B. **Reread the story and write the answers to these questions.**

1. What does the grasshopper mouse eat?

_____

_____

_____

2. How does it catch its prey?

_____

_____

3. Why does it catch its food this way?

_____

_____

_____

4. What does "quest" mean?

_____

_____

_____

     Unit 70 cont'd ☞

Compound Words

A. Write the two words that make up each compound.

1. homework	_home_	_work_
2. sidewalk		
3. everybody		
4. mailbox		
5. catfish		
6. sunset		
7. birthday		
8. gentleman		
9. cookbook		
10. downtown		
11. quicksand		
12. toothache		
13. understand		
14. sunburn		
15. chalkboard		
16. himself		
17. sunflower		
18. sunshine		
19. airplane		
20. buttermilk		

21. classroom		
22. newspaper		
23. password		
24. schoolhouse		
25. everything		
26. watermelon		
27. chairperson		
28. outside		
29. seashore		
30. sometimes		
31. lighthouse		
32. crossword		
33. whenever		
34. daytime		
35. battleship		
36. yardstick		
37. bathroom		
38. salesclerk		
39. driveway		
40. vineyard		

B. Underline the compound words.

1. <u>snowball</u>	11. into	21. company	31. useful
2. interesting	12. replace	22. raincoat	32. mystery
3. highway	13. bookstore	23. fireplace	33. forever
4. remember	14. wishbone	24. weekend	34. stoplight
5. playground	15. sentence	25. between	35. travel
6. standing	16. birthday	26. hallway	36. broomstick
7. myself	17. upstairs	27. whoever	37. different
8. reason	18. younger	28. straight	38. football
9. footprint	19. grapevine	29. nothing	39. language
10. open	20. program	30. anyone	40. lesson

Comprehension Check

Ⓐ Identify the part of speech of each underlined word.

_____adjective_____ 1. Adam is a very clever young man.

_____ 2. Yuk! Did you see the color of Collier's new jacket?

_____ 3. Mr. Danforth hesitated before entering the classroom.

_____ 4. Tomorrow George will apply for the job at the office.

_____ 5. Kenneth carried our luggage to the bus.

_____ 6. The movie is about adventure on the high seas.

_____ 7. I haven't seen Murray since last November.

_____ 8. Lois and Kathy hiked up the mountain path.

_____ 9. The dinner at the Smiths tasted delicious.

_____ 10. Ouch! You're standing on my foot.

_____ 11. Florence always makes A's in language classes.

_____ 12. Put these books on the shelf beside the statue.

_____ 13. The Johnsons returned from their vacation yesterday.

_____ 14. Do you know the answer to these questions?

_____ 15. Someone told Ms. Casey about our plans to skip.

Ⓑ Which words make up each compound word?

1. scatterbrain _____scatter_____ _____brain_____
2. typewriter _____ _____
3. newspaper _____ _____
4. mailbox _____ _____
5. grasshopper _____ _____
6. everything _____ _____
7. football _____ _____
8. earthquake _____ _____
9. whenever _____ _____
10. deadline _____ _____

11. sunflower _____ _____
12. driveway _____ _____
13. headache _____ _____
14. railroad _____ _____
15. flashlight _____ _____
16. pineapple _____ _____
17. toothpaste _____ _____
18. cupcake _____ _____
19. meanwhile _____ _____
20. snowstorm _____ _____

Ⓒ Change each word to a compound word.

1. book _____bookstore_____
2. way _____
3. print _____
4. air _____
5. thing _____
6. day _____
7. room _____
8. land _____

Ⓓ Complete these sentences.

1. The grasshopper mouse stops at nothing in its quest for _____food_____ .

2. The golden eagle is a bird of _____ .

3. Fishermen _____ the gar.

4. Gars have no value as _____ .

5. Grass houses are often built on _____ .

6. The panda is a member of the _____ family.

7. The golden eagle lives in the _____ .

8. The grasshopper mouse lives only in _____ .

Test 14 cont'd ☞

Comprehension Check (continued)

(E) Match these words and their definitions. These words appeared in the reading selections from units 66-70.

_l_ 1. overlapping   ____ 7. remote

____ 2. ambushes   ____ 8. stilts

____ 3. cannibalistic   ____ 9. motionless

____ 4. quest   ____ 10. inhabit

____ 5. representative   ____ 11. secluded

____ 6. safety   ____ 12. restricted

a. attacks by surprise   g. without movement

b. by itself   h. far away

c. limited   i. typical example

d. tall poles   j. freedom from danger

e. eats its own kind   k. live in

f. hunt or search   l. one part over another

(F) Underline the correct answers.

1. Describe a gar.   (a) beneficial   (b) <u>destructive</u>
2. How do fishermen feel about gars?   (a) like them   (b) dislike them
3. Where does the giant panda live?   (a) Asia   (b) Africa
4. What do giant pandas eat?   (a) bamboo shoots   (b) insects
5. What kind of bird is the golden eagle?   (a) bird of prey   (b) aquatic bird
6. Describe a golden eagle.   (a) powerful   (b) large
7. Where can grass houses be built?   (a) almost anywhere   (b) only in tropics
8. Are grass homes common in the United States?   (a) yes   (b) no
9. Where do grasshopper mice live?   (a) South America   (b) North America
10. When is a grasshopper mouse active?   (a) at night   (b) during the day

Choose one of the following topics and write a paragraph.

(1) Describe a grass house. Would you like to live in one? Why or why not?

(2) Why are gars disliked by fishermen? Do you think their reputation is earned?

_____

_____

_____

_____

_____

_____

_____

_____

_____

_____

The Great Prairie Chicken Unit 71

Study the spelling and meaning of each word. These words are used in today's story. Connect each word with its definition.

1. beautiful	a. caught; snared
2. destroyed	b. biggest
3. greatest	c. lovely; pretty
4. remaining	d. ruined
5. sport	e. left over
6. trapped	f. fun; play

Read the story carefully and remember the details.

Once millions of prairie chickens roamed the Great Plains. The Indians trapped them for food. Then the white settlers came. They also killed the birds for food and sport. The greatest threat to the praire chickens came when settlers began plowing the grasslands of the plains. These grasslands were the prairie chickens' homes. The loss of these lands destroyed the birds' nests, food, and means of protection.

Today there are few remaining prairie chickens. They are still referred to as the fowls of the plains. They are strong fliers. When the birds take to the air, there are loud cackles and a burst of wings. Before it is too late, the prairie chickens must be protected. They are beautiful reminders of the old West.

A. Underline the correct answers about today's story.

1. The prairie chicken was hunted mostly for	(a) food	(b) feathers	(c) sport.
2. The greatest threat to the bird was the	(a) Indian	(b) white settler	(c) plowing of land.
3. The bird's home was the	(a) open prairie	(b) forests	(c) mountains.
4. As fliers, the birds are	(a) weak	(b) strong	(c) clumsy.
5. The bird is often referred to as the	(a) fowl of the West	(b) fowl of the plains	(c) last of the fowl.

B. Reread the story and write the answers to these questions.

1. Why were prairie chickens hunted?

_____

_____

_____

2. Who hunted prairie chickens?

_____

_____

_____

3. What did the loss of the land mean to the chicken?

_____

_____

_____

4. What is another name of the chicken?

_____

_____

_____

Unit 71 cont'd ☛

Writing Compound Words

A. Combine each set of words to make one big word.

1. foot + ball   *football*   21. side + walk _____
2. some + thing _____   22. near + by _____
3. home + work _____   23. hill + side _____
4. to + night _____   24. door + bell _____
5. mail + man _____   25. may + be _____
6. cow + boy _____   26. break + fast _____
7. base + ball _____   27. story + book _____
8. in + side _____   28. an + other _____
9. work + book _____   29. sand + box _____
10. some + where _____   30. never + more _____
11. no + thing _____   31. any + thing _____
12. up + on _____   32. sun + set _____
13. tooth + brush _____   33. rain + coat _____
14. for + ever _____   34. home + sick _____
15. play + ground _____   35. look + out _____
16. fire + place _____   36. yard + stick _____
17. under + stand _____   37. after + noon _____
18. week + end _____   38. butter + milk _____
19. bed + room _____   39. who + ever _____
20. birth + day _____   40. some + times _____

B. What two little words make up each compound word.

1. highway   *high*   *way*   11. outside _____ _____
2. bathroom _____ _____   12. everything _____ _____
3. sunlight _____ _____   13. however _____ _____
4. meatball _____ _____   14. tablecloth _____ _____
5. sandpaper _____ _____   15. roadside _____ _____
6. downtown _____ _____   16. boardwalk _____ _____
7. wishbone _____ _____   17. snowflake _____ _____
8. whatever _____ _____   18. password _____ _____
9. into _____ _____   19. fruitcake _____ _____
10. milkman _____ _____   20. seawater _____ _____

The Great White Shark

Study the spelling and meaning of each word. These words are used in today's story. Connect each word with its definition.

1. appears
2. dangerous
3. feared
4. instinctive
5. mystery
6. prevalent

a. something not understood
b. widespread
c. dreaded
d. likely to injure
e. comes into sight
f. done naturally

Read the story carefully and remember the details.

The great white shark is more commonly known as "man-eater." A giant of a fish, the shark is feared by all.

Most of the great white shark's habits are a mystery to scientists. It appears in many seas. It is more prevalent and more dangerous in the warmer seas.

The body of the white shark is gray and black on the top and white underneath. As it swims, its dorsal (back) fin sticks out of the water.

The white shark seems to have an instinctive urge to kill. It gulps the food down without chewing. It even eats its own kind.

A. Underline the correct answers about today's story.

1. Where does the shark live?   (a) sea   (b) rivers   (c) fresh water
2. What do sharks eat?   (a) meat   (b) plants   (c) sponges
3. "Dorsal" means   (a) "side"   (b) "back"   (c) "front."
4. Which word describes the white shark?   (a) friendly   (b) feared   (c) harmless
5. The shark's habits are   (a) a mystery   (b) unknown   (c) silly.

B. Reread the story and write the answers to these questions.

1. How is the great white shark commonly known?

_____
_____
_____

2. Where is the shark more dangerous?

_____
_____
_____

3. What does the shark's dorsal fin do as it swims?

_____
_____
_____

4. What color(s) is the fish?

_____
_____
_____

   Unit 72 cont'd

More Compound Words

A. Which two words make up each compound word?

1. airport _____air_____ _____port_____
2. downtown _____ _____
3. fingerprint _____ _____
4. strawberry _____ _____
5. suitcase _____ _____
6. playmate _____ _____
7. become _____ _____
8. nearby _____ _____
9. without _____ _____
10. rowboat _____ _____
11. classroom _____ _____
12. buttermilk _____ _____
13. crossword _____ _____
14. goldfish _____ _____
15. woodland _____ _____
16. houseboat _____ _____
17. daylight _____ _____
18. toothpick _____ _____
19. fireplace _____ _____
20. nevermore _____ _____

21. slowpoke _____ _____
22. upstairs _____ _____
23. grapevine _____ _____
24. sidewalk _____ _____
25. homesick _____ _____
26. landslide _____ _____
27. chalkboard _____ _____
28. deadline _____ _____
29. highway _____ _____
30. yardstick _____ _____
31. wishbone _____ _____
32. sunset _____ _____
33. driveway _____ _____
34. fairground _____ _____
35. reindeer _____ _____
36. hardware _____ _____
37. birthday _____ _____
38. seaweed _____ _____
39. meanwhile _____ _____
40. flashlight _____ _____

B. Write the plural of each word.

1. toothbrush _____toothbrushes_____
2. strawberry _____
3. airport _____
4. birthday _____
5. warehouse _____
6. sidewalk _____
7. grapevine _____
8. highway _____
9. doorbell _____
10. storybook _____

11. firefly _____
12. classroom _____
13. baseball _____
14. horseshoe _____
15. housewife _____
16. fireplace _____
17. battleship _____
18. cupcake _____
19. songbird _____
20. handcuff _____

C. Write a sentence using each plural compound word in part B.

176

Greenland

Study the spelling and meaning of each word. These words are used in today's story. Connect each word with its definition.

1. always
2. available
3. broad
4. consist
5. island
6. slanting

a. ready for use
b. land surrounded by water
c. all the time
d. is made up of
e. at an angle
f. wide

Read the story carefully and remember the details.

Greenland is a large island that is always covered with ice and snow. There are no trees and no grass.

The people of Greenland are called Eskimos. They have black, straight hair; broad faces; and slanting eyes.

In the winter, Eskimos live in igloos. They travel with sleds pulled by dogs. Their main foods consists of seals and fish. The Eskimos eat raw blubber from the seals to keep warm.

In the summer, Eskimos live in tents. These tents are made from sealskins. They use boats called kayaks.

The weather in Greenland is cold. However, the people of the land have learned to live happy lives using the materials available to them.

A. **Underline the correct answers about today's story.**

1. Greenland is	(a) an island	(b) a mountain	(c) a harbor.
2. The people of Greenland are	(a) Indians	(b) Eskimos	(c) farmers.
3. In winter, Eskimos live in	(a) caves	(b) igloos	(c) tunnels.
4. In summer Eskimos live in	(a) grass huts	(b) houses	(c) tents.
5. To keep warm, Eskimos	(a) eat blubber	(b) build fires	(c) stay inside.

B. **Reread the story and write the answers to these questions.**

1. What does the story say is not found in Greenland?

3. Describe the hair of someone from Greenland.

2. What type of boat is used in Greenland?

4. How do the people of Greenland travel?

Unit 73 cont'd ☞

Compounds

A. Underline the compound words.

1. <u>storeroom</u>	11. textbook	21. population	31. geography
2. milkman	12. mischievous	22. weekend	32. surrounding
3. flashlight	13. blindfold	23. volunteer	33. yardstick
4. universe	14. crossroads	24. otherwise	34. worship
5. strawberry	15. hardware	25. reindeer	35. driveway
6. beehive	16. instrument	26. unusually	36. chocolate
7. interstate	17. pavement	27. suitcase	37. whirlpool
8. envelope	18. sawmill	28. dictionary	38. fingerprint
9. dishwasher	19. government	29. slowpoke	39. retire
10. vocabulary	20. orchestra	30. tomorrow	40. meanwhile

B. Write the plural of each compound word.

1. highway	*highways*	11. rosebush	_____
2. footprint	_____	12. basketball	_____
3. crossroad	_____	13. bloodhound	_____
4. toothache	_____	14. gentleman	_____
5. mailbox	_____	15. yourself	_____
6. reindeer	_____	16. housewife	_____
7. warehouse	_____	17. sunflower	_____
8. newspaper	_____	18. horseshoe	_____
9. toothpick	_____	19. blueberry	_____
10. fairground	_____	20. saucepan	_____

C. Complete each sentence with a compound word.

1. Dad is reading the ____*newspaper*____.
2. The _____ is tomorrow.
3. My mother is the _____.
4. The car is blocking the _____.
5. Put the plates in the _____.
6. I'll pack my _____.
7. Come _____ my office.
8. This will be your math _____.
9. He works in a _____ store.
10. Meet me at the _____.
11. These are the thief's _____.
12. Santa Claus has eight _____.
13. My _____ is June 15th.
14. Wait for me in the _____.
15. The _____ are ripe.
16. Write these words on the _____.
17. The party is this _____.
18. Do you like _____?
19. Don't forget your _____.
20. The _____ was empty.

Hamsters

Study the spelling and meaning of each word. These words are used in today's story. Connect each word with its definition.

1. active   a. entertaining playfully
2. affection   b. love
3. alone   c. lively
4. amusing   d. separated from others
5. attention   e. careful observation
6. chubby   f. round and plump

Read the story carefully and remember the details.

Many people keep hamsters as pets. These soft, chubby little animals require little attention and make amusing and affectionate friends.

In the wild, hamsters live in underground tunnels. In the summer their homes are about two feet underground. Their winter homes may be twice as deep. The homes are large and contain storage places for their winter supply of good.

Hamsters are nocturnal animals, meaning they are active at night. They carry their supplies in cheek pouches. Hamsters eat vegetables, fruit, insects, small animals, and grain.

Both in the wild and in captivity, hamsters are neat housekeepers. Hamsters prefer to live alone. After mating, the female drives the male away.

A. Underline the correct answers about today's story.

1. Which word describes the hamster?   (a) unfriendly   (b) dangerous   (c) affectionate
2. Wild hamsters live in   (a) trees   (b) tunnels   (c) rivers.
3. Hamsters carry supplies   (a) in pouches   (b) on their backs   (c) with front feet.
4. As housekeepers, hamsters are   (a) messy   (b) neat   (c) unclean.
5. Hamsters prefer to live   (a) alone   (b) in pairs   (c) in large groups.

B. Reread the story and write the answers to these questions.

1. What do most people do with hamsters?

_____

_____

_____

2. How do wild hamsters' summer and winter homes compare?

_____

_____

_____

3. When are hamsters active?

_____

_____

_____

4. What does the female do to the male after mating?

_____

_____

_____

Recognizing Compound Words

A compound word consists of two words which are written as one.

EXAMPLE: side + walk = sidewalk

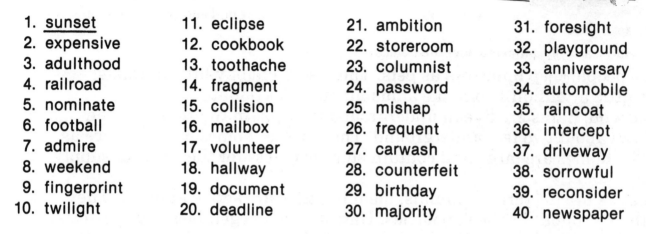

A. Underline the compound words.

1. <u>sunset</u>
2. expensive
3. adulthood
4. railroad
5. nominate
6. football
7. admire
8. weekend
9. fingerprint
10. twilight

11. eclipse
12. cookbook
13. toothache
14. fragment
15. collision
16. mailbox
17. volunteer
18. hallway
19. document
20. deadline

21. ambition
22. storeroom
23. columnist
24. password
25. mishap
26. frequent
27. carwash
28. counterfeit
29. birthday
30. majority

31. foresight
32. playground
33. anniversary
34. automobile
35. raincoat
36. intercept
37. driveway
38. sorrowful
39. reconsider
40. newspaper

B. Write the compound word from part A which matches each definition.

_____birthday_____

_____

_____

_____

_____

_____

_____

_____

_____

_____

_____

_____

_____

_____

_____

_____

_____

_____

1. the day of one's birth or its anniversary
2. a space set aside for recreation
3. a public print that circulates the news
4. a box into which private mail is delivered
5. a room in which supplies are stored
6. the descent of the sun below the horizon
7. a passage giving entrance to a building
8. a coat intended to be worn in rainy weather
9. the days of Saturday and Sunday
10. a word identifying one as entitled to pass
11. a road of metal rails for the passage of a train
12. pain in a tooth
13. an impression of the skin surface of a finger
14. a place where one may clean a car
15. a game played between two teams
16. a road providing access to a building or house
17. the time limit by which a thing must be completed
18. a book containing recipes

The Hawk

Study the spelling and meaning of each word. These words are used in today's story. Connect each word with its definition.

1. harmful
2. keen
3. prefers
4. prey
5. relative
6. seizes

a. captures; holds
b. causing harm
c. desire over something else
d. sharp and quick
e. related by blood
f. victim; animal hunted for food

Read the story carefully and remember the details.

Hawk is a name commonly given to a bird that seizes its prey. It is a relative of eagles and vultures.

The hawk has a hooked bill. Its claws are powerful. They are able to carry the prey to the nest to eat.

The hawk hunts by sight. It has keen eyesight. The hawk's eyes are about eight times as powerful as human eyes. A hawk can spot a rabbit in a field from hundreds of feet in the air.

The hawk prefers to live in wooded areas. Some farmers dislike the hawk because it is sometimes destructive to poultry. However, the hawk is useful in the killing of harmful rodents. It can be trained to hunt with man.

A. **Underline the correct answers about today's story.**

1. The hawk's claws are	(a) weak	(b) powerful	(c) helpless.
2. A hawk hunts by	(a) listening	(b) sight	(c) smell.
3. Hawks prefer to live	(a) near water	(b) on the desert	(c) in wooded areas.
4. Hawks are useful in killing	(a) rodents	(b) poultry	(c) insects.
5. Which animal has the best eyesight?	(a) rabbit	(b) man	(c) hawk

B. **Reread the story and write the answers to these questions.**

1. Name two birds that are relatives of the hawk.

_____

_____

_____

2. How does the bird hold its prey?

_____

_____

_____

3. Why might the hawk be disliked?

_____

_____

_____

4. Why might the hawk be liked?

_____

_____

_____

Unit 75 cont'd ☛

Base Words

A base word is the form of a word to which prefixes or suffixes are attached.

 Write the base word of each word.

1. adventures   *adventure*
2. allowed   _____
3. captains   _____
4. collection   _____
5. countries   _____
6. fearless   _____
7. honestly   _____
8. ideas   _____
9. keys   _____
10. laughing   _____
11. leaves   _____
12. matches   _____
13. owner   _____
14. promises   _____
15. raining   _____
16. rushes   _____
17. safely   _____
18. sleeping   _____
19. shouted   _____
20. speaking   _____
21. tickets   _____
22. suddenly   _____
23. useful   _____
24. vines   _____
25. thicker   _____
26. loser   _____
27. voices   _____
28. youngest   _____
29. kicked   _____
30. windows   _____
31. rebuild   _____
32. newest   _____
33. wiser   _____

34. sent   _____
35. opening   _____
36. helper   _____
37. skies   _____
38. western   _____
39. highest   _____
40. eating   _____
41. knew   _____
42. easier   _____
43. sunny   _____
44. racing   _____
45. shorter   _____
46. added   _____
47. looks   _____
48. hoped   _____
49. winning   _____
50. wrote   _____
51. ended   _____
52. began   _____
53. traded   _____
54. papers   _____
55. happiness   _____
56. reader   _____
57. eyes   _____
58. sadness   _____
59. visitor   _____
60. listened   _____
61. sitting   _____
62. broken   _____
63. watches   _____
64. carried   _____
65. numbers   _____
66. snowed   _____
67. liked   _____

68. lessons   _____
69. singing   _____
70. dancer   _____
71. women   _____
72. follows   _____
73. misses   _____
74. used   _____
75. brighter   _____
76. mixed   _____
77. days   _____
78. friendly   _____
79. flowers   _____
80. making   _____
81. yours   _____
82. largest   _____
83. hopeless   _____
84. taller   _____
85. needs   _____
86. waited   _____
87. arrows   _____
88. spelling   _____
89. meant   _____
90. fishing   _____
91. children   _____
92. sides   _____
93. boxes   _____
94. kindly   _____
95. covered   _____
96. stories   _____
97. smiles   _____
98. letters   _____
99. walked   _____
100. theirs   _____

Comprehension Check

A) Underline the compound words.

1. <u>goldfish</u>	11. windmill	21. childhood
2. chocolate	12. basketball	22. suitcase
3. headache	13. roadways	23. newspaper
4. warehouse	14. blueberry	24. uncontrolled
5. fragment	15. myself	25. windowpane
6. blackberry	16. housecoat	26. airplane
7. bookmark	17. hairbrush	27. ambition
8. cotton	18. reading	28. happiness
9. weekend	19. birthplace	29. watermelon
10. outside	20. playground	30. instrument

B) Connect the words which could make compound words. Write the new words.

1. cross	road	_crossroad_	11. rose	wind	
2. car	ground	_____	12. whirl	bushes	_____
3. under	book	_____	13. never	side	_____
4. cook	shine	_____	14. in	poke	_____
5. sun	wash	_____	15. slow	more	_____
6. blind	pan	_____	16. over	bone	_____
7. sauce	picks	_____	17. text	print	_____
8. gentle	fold	_____	18. hand	cuffs	_____
9. tooth	man	_____	19. thumb	book	_____
10. hall	way	_____	20. wish	look	_____

C) Write the plural of each word.

1. highway   _highways_
2. sidewalk   _____
3. sandbox   _____
4. firefly   _____
5. tablecloth   _____
6. snowflake   _____
7. deadline   _____
8. strawberry   _____
9. flashlight   _____
10. reindeer   _____
11. storybook   _____
12. dishwasher   _____

D) Complete these sentences.

1. Hamsters are _nocturnal_ animals.
2. Greenland is an _____ .
3. Prairie chickens were killed for food and _____ .
4. People often keep hamsters as _____ .
5. The great white shark is _____ by all.
6. The hawk hunts by _____ .
7. Prairie chickens lived on the _____ .
8. Greenland is always covered with _____ .
9. Hamsters prefer to live _____ .
10. The hawk is a bird of _____ .
11. Great white sharks are more common in _____ seas.
12. The weather in Greenland is _____ .

Test 15 cont'd ☞

Comprehension Check (continued)

(E) Match these words and their definitions. These words appeared in the reading selections from units 71-75.

<u>c</u> 1. mystery   _____ 7. slanting

_____ 2. keen   _____ 8. dangerous

_____ 3. harmful   _____ 9. sport

_____ 4. instinctive   _____ 10. available

_____ 5. destroyed   _____ 11. alone

_____ 6. relative   _____ 12. chubby

a. ready for use

b. at an angle

c. something not understood

d. fun; play

e. related by blood

f. round and plump

g. sharp and quick

h. likely to injure

i. causing harm

j. done naturally

k. ruined

l. separated from others

(F) Underline the correct answers.

		(a)	(b)
1.	Where do prairie chickens live?	(a) <u>West</u>	(b) South
2.	How did Indians use prairie chickens?	(a) food	(b) worship
3.	What is another name for the great white shark?	(a) "giant one"	(b) "man-eater"
4.	Where is a dorsal fin?	(a) on a back	(b) on a head
5.	Who are the people of Greenland?	(a) Ice Men	(b) Eskimos
6.	What is an Eskimo's boat called?	(a) igloo	(b) kayak
7.	How do hamsters prefer to live?	(a) alone	(b) in groups
8.	When are hamsters active?	(a) during the day	(b) at night
9.	How does a hawk hunt?	(a) by sight	(b) by sound
10.	Describe a hawk.	(a) weak	(b) powerful

Choose one of the following topics and write a paragraph.

(1) Describe life in Greenland. Would you like to live there? Why or why not?

(2) Describe a hamster's habits.

_____

_____

_____

_____

_____

_____

_____

_____

_____

Holland

Study the spelling and meaning of each word. These words are used in today's story. Connect each word with its definition.

1. canals
2. dikes
3. excess
4. famous
5. produce
6. protect

a. more than needed
b. keep from harm
c. high banks
d. drainage ditches
e. create; make
f. very well known

Read the story carefully and remember the details.

Holland is a lowland country because its land is lower than the ocean nearby. To protect the Dutch people from the water, high banks or dikes have been built. Many ditches have also been dug. These ditches, known as canals, help to drain the land. Most of the Dutch people live along the canals where they fish and enjoy passing boats. These canals are used in much the same way as American roads are used.

One of Holland's most famous features is the windmill. Windmills are used to pump water from the land up over the dikes and into the canals. Some windmills are used by farmers to grind grain. Many windmills are driven by electric pumps rather than by wind power.

Holland produces some dairy products. Many Dutch farmers raise cows that produce an excess of milk. This excess is used in making cheese.

A. Underline the correct answers about today's story.

1. People in Holland are called	(a) Dutch	(b) Hollands	(c) Germans.
2. What holds back ocean water?	(a) windmills	(b) dikes	(c) canals
3. How are today's windmills powered?	(a) wind	(b) electricity	(c) hand
4. What kind of products do the Dutch produce?	(a) cotton	(b) vegetables	(c) dairy
5. Dairy products are used to make	(a) cheese	(b) flour	(c) cereals.

B. Reread the story and write the answers to these questions.

1. Why is Holland called a lowland country?

_____

_____

_____

2. Name a use for canals.

_____

_____

_____

3. Name two uses of windmills.

_____

_____

_____

4. Name a product made in Holland.

_____

_____

_____

Unit 76 cont'd ☞

Identifying Base Words

A. Write the base word for each given word.

EXAMPLE: *reading* <u>*read*</u>

1. adding _____
2. used _____
3. books _____
4. classes _____
5. wishing _____
6. friendly _____
7. walked _____
8. fishes _____
9. streets _____
10. redo _____
11. baker _____
12. children _____
13. healthy _____
14. colder _____
15. sits _____

16. oranges _____
17. running _____
18. sandy _____
19. warmer _____
20. towns _____
21. ruler _____
22. buses _____
23. heard _____
24. building _____
25. going _____
26. words _____
27. writes _____
28. hearing _____
29. noises _____
30. looked _____

31. raining _____
32. chairs _____
33. played _____
34. seen _____
35. days _____
36. wider _____
37. eating _____
38. windows _____
39. sunny _____
40. called _____

B. Write two words using each base word.

EXAMPLE: *help*   *helper*   *helping*

1. want
_____ _____

2. talk
_____ _____

3. dream
_____ _____

4. start
_____ _____

5. snow
_____ _____

6. match
_____ _____

7. jump
_____ _____

8. quick
_____ _____

9. cook
_____ _____

10. drive
_____ _____

11. teach
_____ _____

12. ask
_____ _____

13. wait
_____ _____

14. meet
_____ _____

15. turn
_____ _____

16. plant
_____ _____

17. stay
_____ _____

18. need
_____ _____

19. pull
_____ _____

20. lead
_____ _____

The House Wren

Study the spelling and meaning of each word. These words are used in today's story. Connect each word with its definition.

1. boundless
2. characteristic
3. moment
4. never
5. routine
6. seldom

a. instant
b. feature
c. without limit
d. usual way of doing a task
e. not ever
f. rarely

Read the story carefully and remember the details.

The house wren is a little brown bird with boundless energy. It is seldom quiet, even for a moment.

An unusual characteristic of the house wren is its routine in setting up housekeeping. First, the male wren builds numerous nests. He leaves all of these nests unfinished. The nests are built in the most unlikely places — tin cans, mailboxes, old shoes.

Then, the female comes by to look over the nests. She chooses one to her liking and begins to remodel it to her own satisfaction. Her young receive the best of care.

Throughout the nesting period the male and female house wren never stop quarreling. They seem to enjoy the constant noise.

A. Underline the correct answers about today's story.

1. Which word describes the house wren?   (a) lazy   (b) quiet   (c) energetic
2. The male builds nests   (a) in trees   (b) on the ground   (c) in unusual places.
3. When the female chooses a nest, she   (a) destroys it   (b) remodels it   (c) doesn't change it.
4. As parents the house wrens are   (a) excellent   (b) unskilled   (c) lazy.
5. The male and female house wren are   (a) peaceful mates   (b) enemies   (c) always quarreling.

B. Reread the story and write the answers to these questions.

1. What color is the wren?

_____

_____

_____

2. How often is the wren quiet?

_____

_____

_____

3. What do wrens seem to enjoy?

_____

_____

_____

4. What do the male and female wren do while nesting?

_____

_____

_____

Unit 77 cont'd ☞

Base Words and Derived Words

A. Write the base word of each word.

1. trains _____*train*_____
2. showed _____
3. proudly _____
4. bought _____
5. schools _____
6. windy _____
7. cleaner _____
8. miles _____
9. gladly _____
10. watches _____
11. visiting _____
12. bottles _____
13. camping _____
14. drove _____
15. fixed _____
16. later _____
17. owner _____
18. teacher _____
19. softly _____
20. wheels _____

21. youngest _____
22. branches _____
23. invited _____
24. colder _____
25. clues _____
26. wolves _____
27. ending _____
28. expected _____
29. wrote _____
30. baskets _____
31. painting _____
32. dresses _____
33. laughing _____
34. glasses _____
35. suddenly _____
36. voices _____
37. women _____
38. muddy _____
39. building _____
40. thought _____

41. songs _____
42. paid _____
43. used _____
44. gardening _____
45. drank _____
46. slept _____
47. looked _____
48. walking _____
49. smaller _____
50. rides _____
51. ponies _____
52. keys _____
53. highest _____
54. spelling _____
55. numbers _____
56. played _____
57. ringing _____
58. stronger _____
59. slowly _____
60. sleeping _____

B. Listed are base words and derived words. Underline the derived words.

1. <u>lower</u>
2. people
3. noise
4. your
5. child
6. trusted
7. reading
8. wait
9. fence
10. farmer

11. speak
12. writes
13. tallest
14. chair
15. leader
16. bicycle
17. carry
18. missed
19. room
20. clown

21. sister
22. leaves
23. keeping
24. talks
25. turtles
26. short
27. voices
28. find
29. wishes
30. mice

31. stories
32. house
33. penny
34. gave
35. street
36. invited
37. buy
38. big
39. works
40. car

Houses on the Water

Study the spelling and meaning of each word. These words are used in today's story. Connect each word with its definition.

1. although
2. believe
3. buy
4. comforts
5. during
6. strange

a. unusual; odd
b. in the course of
c. purchase
d. think as truth
e. things that make life easy
f. in spite of the fact that

Read the story carefully and remember the details.

Can you believe that there are people today who have never set foot on land? Thousands of Chinese live on riverboats, and some never leave them during their lifetimes.

Each boat has a cabin for passengers. The family lives in the back of the boat. The boat is a complete home where the family lives, works, and plays. To keep young children from falling into the water, the mother ties ropes around their waists.

Some boats are stores. Some sell food or clothing. Others sell medicine or housewares. Families can buy everything they need from their boats.

Although living on the water may sound strange to most of us, the Chinese don't seem to mind. They have all the comforts of a home on land.

A. **Underline the correct answers about today's story.**

1. Thousands of Chinese have never | (a) seen water | (b) seen land | (c) set foot on land.
2. These Chinese live on | (a) the desert | (b) boats | (c) islands.
3. To keep children on the boat, mothers use | (a) ropes | (b) fences | (c) nets.
4. Home on the boat is | (a) uncomfortable | (b) difficult | (c) comfortable.
5. Where do the Chinese buy their supplies? | (a) mainland | (b) store boat | (c) city

B. **Reread the story and write the answers to these questions.**

1. What part of the boat does the family inhabit?

_____

_____

_____

2. What does the family do on the boat?

_____

_____

_____

3. What is sold on some boats?

_____

_____

_____

4. Where do the people on boats buy what they need?

_____

_____

_____

Unit 78 cont'd ☞

Using Base Words and Derived Words

A. Write the base word of each word.

1. uneasy _easy_
2. anxiously _____
3. winner _____
4. dangerous _____
5. wisest _____
6. powerful _____
7. territories _____
8. missing _____
9. women _____
10. worried _____

11. remodel _____
12. artist _____
13. dusty _____
14. unusual _____
15. quietly _____
16. selected _____
17. goodness _____
18. offices _____
19. seen _____
20. undo _____

21. appearance _____
22. roots _____
23. bought _____
24. review _____
25. follower _____
26. distrust _____
27. failure _____
28. votes _____
29. reading _____
30. sleepy _____

B. Underline the derived words.

1. <u>thankful</u>
2. picture
3. enjoy
4. guards
5. rough
6. samples
7. honestly
8. bad
9. judge
10. shoes

11. ghosts
12. come
13. back
14. successful
15. helpless
16. government
17. column
18. careless
19. ask
20. match

21. fish
22. lucky
23. speechless
24. disappear
25. worth
26. untouched
27. speeding
28. trouble
29. guide
30. surrounding

31. eat
32. heaviest
33. repeated
34. small
35. undecided
36. doubt
37. follower
38. roughly
39. win
40. touch

C. Write two derived words for each base word.

1. sign _signed_ _signature_
2. usual _____ _____
3. secret _____ _____
4. invite _____ _____
5. promise _____ _____
6. low _____ _____
7. easy _____ _____

8. power _____ _____
9. write _____ _____
10. taste _____ _____
11. finish _____ _____
12. do _____ _____
13. view _____ _____
14. work _____ _____

The Hyrax

Study the spelling and meaning of each word. These words are used in today's story. Connect each word with its definition.

1. consists   a. skin; fur
2. diet   b. is made up of
3. distant   c. not close
4. excellent   d. what one eats
5. pelt   e. more than one
6. plural   f. very good

Read the story carefully and remember the details.

The hyrax is a small animal which lives in Africa, Syria, and Arabia. Although it is small, it is believed to be a distant relative of the elephant and rhinoceros.

The hyrax usually lives in large communities. Its home is built in rocky places of high elevation. It may even live in trees.

The animal is mainly nocturnal. During the day the hyrax lies in the shade. The hyrax always rests near a hole to which it can run in time of danger.

The hyrax's diet consists of leaves and young shoots. The hyrax is an excellent climber.

The animal was once hunted for its pelt, but now there are laws to protect it. The plural of "hyrax" is "hyraces."

A. **Underline the correct answers about today's story.**

1. The hyrax is distantly related to the   (a) rabbit   (b) giraffe   (c) elephant.
2. A hyrax's home is usually built   (a) underground   (b) underwater   (c) in rocky places.
3. The hyrax always rests near   (a) water   (b) a hole   (c) a tree.
4. A pelt is a   (a) fur   (b) tooth   (c) claw.
5. The plural of "hyrax" is   (a) "hyraxs"   (b) "hyraxes"   (c) "hyraces."

B. **Reread the story and write the answers to these questions.**

1. Where does the hyrax live?

_____

_____

_____

2. What does the hyrax eat?

_____

_____

_____

3. Why was the hyrax hunted?

_____

_____

_____

4. What protects the hyrax?

_____

_____

_____

Unit 79 cont'd ☞

Prefixes Signal Verbs

A. All the verbs in this exercise were found by the addition of a permanent verb prefix to a root word. Write the prefixes and the roots for each verb in the proper spaces. Follow the example.

	Prefix	Root
EXAMPLE: *rewrite*	re	write
1. encircle	_____	_____
2. enact	_____	_____
3. enable	_____	_____
4. behold	_____	_____
5. begrudge	_____	_____
6. belabor	_____	_____
7. redecorate	_____	_____
8. rebound	_____	_____
9. rebuild	_____	_____
10. reappear	_____	_____
11. rework	_____	_____
12. refreeze	_____	_____
13. remix	_____	_____
14. rediscover	_____	_____
15. undress	_____	_____
16. untie	_____	_____
17. unzip	_____	_____
18. withdraw	_____	_____
19. withhold	_____	_____
20. withstand	_____	_____

B. Mark an "X" on the line next to each sentence that has a verb with a prefix.

__x__ 1. Lee withdraws her money from the bank.
_____ 2. Mom put the phone on the receiver.
_____ 3. A rebozo is a long scarf worn by Spanish women.
_____ 4. The company recalled all 1973 cars.
_____ 5. That baby has a lot of energy.
_____ 6. Mother mailed the letter.
_____ 7. I remade my bed.
_____ 8. The race car driver sighed in relief after the race.

The Incas

Study the spelling and meaning of each word. These words are used in today's story. Connect each word with its definition.

1. began   a. took
2. captured   b. started
3. connected   c. mighty
4. conquer   d. control; govern
5. great   e. gain by force
6. rule   f. joined together

Read the story carefully and remember the details.

The Incas of Peru began as a small tribe. They were an intelligent people who knew how to conquer and rule. They built a great empire.

The head Inca was a dictator. According to the law, all land belonged to him. The head Inca gave each family a plot of land to cultivate.

Although there were no horses or wagons, the Incas built roads which connected every part of the empire. The roads were used by runners that carried messages.

When the Spaniard Francisco Pizarro came to the land of the Incas, he was treated as a guest. Pizarro tricked the Incas and captured their ruler. The head Inca was killed and Pizarro took over. Without their leader the Incas were helpless, and the empire was destroyed.

A. Underline the correct answers about today's story.

1. The Incas were ruled by a	(a) dictator	(b) king	(c) president.
2. Who owned the land?	(a) the people	(b) priests	(c) the head Inca
3. Who used the roads?	(a) horses	(b) runners	(c) wagons
4. Who tricked the Incas?	(a) Columbus	(b) King George	(c) Pizarro
5. Without the head Inca the people were	(a) free	(b) helpless	(c) happy.

B. Reread the story and write the answers to these questions.

1. What did the Incas build?

_____

_____

_____

2. What did the Incas know?

_____

_____

_____

3. How did the Inca tribe begin?

_____

_____

_____

4. What did each family receive from the head Inca?

_____

_____

_____

Prefixes

A. Write the prefix of each word in the blank.

1. disappear __dis__
2. recover _____
3. indoors _____
4. forehead _____
5. absent _____
6. diagonal _____
7. uncertain _____
8. telephone _____
9. introduce _____
10. interstate _____
11. superman _____
12. mistake _____
13. nonstop _____
14. dishonest _____
15. imperfect _____
16. uninvited _____
17. recall _____
18. exclude _____
19. prefix _____
20. unfriendly _____

21. outdoors _____
22. misplace _____
23. preview _____
24. undo _____
25. subway _____
26. repay _____
27. untie _____
28. include _____
29. unexpected _____
30. discontinue _____
31. intrastate _____
32. return _____
33. repeat _____
34. paragraph _____
35. unchanged _____
36. prevent _____
37. television _____
38. remove _____
39. unusual _____
40. bicycle _____

41. unicycle _____
42. exchange _____
43. renew _____
44. disapprove _____
45. forewarn _____
46. mislead _____
47. upgrade _____
48. rearrange _____
49. undone _____
50. dislike _____
51. postpone _____
52. outdo _____
53. transport _____
54. pretest _____
55. discover _____
56. nonsense _____
57. incorrect _____
58. recount _____
59. superstar _____
60. semicircle _____

B. Add a prefix to each word.

1. __pre__ view
2. ____ side
3. ____ equal
4. ____ build
5. ____ courage
6. ____ safe
7. ____ break
8. ____ write
9. ____ use
10. ____ prove

11. ____ place
12. ____ look
13. ____ cover
14. ____ plore
15. ____ likely
16. ____ ample
17. ____ fair
18. ____ aware
19. ____ dress
20. ____ written

21. ____ trust
22. ____ do
23. ____ finished
24. ____ work
25. ____ real
26. ____ told
27. ____ tire
28. ____ agree
29. ____ clude
30. ____ decided

31. ____ cycle
32. ____ marine
33. ____ healthy
34. ____ gram
35. ____ nounce
36. ____ covery
37. ____ crease
38. ____ easy
39. ____ tract
40. ____ load

Comprehension Check

(A) Write the base words.

1. teacher	_teach_	11. reworded	_____	21. raining	_____
2. smiled	_____	12. boundless	_____	22. sunny	_____
3. enclose	_____	13. quietly	_____	23. exchange	_____
4. returned	_____	14. setting	_____	24. hopefully	_____
5. younger	_____	15. never	_____	25. children	_____
6. wolves	_____	16. unfinished	_____	26. useless	_____
7. shortly	_____	17. momentary	_____	27. quickly	_____
8. missing	_____	18. careful	_____	28. untied	_____
9. clowns	_____	19. windy	_____	29. asks	_____
10. speaker	_____	20. cleanest	_____	30. rewritten	_____

(B) Underline the derived words.

1. <u>wishful</u>	11. tell	21. farmers	31. work
2. exclude	12. famous	22. pressed	32. listener
3. stories	13. vision	23. door	33. forehead
4. honest	14. noisy	24. subway	34. telephone
5. smashing	15. smaller	25. state	35. sport
6. cycle	16. endless	26. weekly	36. unusually
7. reviewed	17. yours	27. undone	37. agree
8. counts	18. fix	28. reading	38. prove
9. real	19. bicycle	29. place	39. interstate
10. penniless	20. semicircle	30. booklet	40. superstar

(C) Identify the prefixes.

1. untie	_un_	6. enable	_____	11. postpone	_____
2. prevent	_____	7. discover	_____	12. subtract	_____
3. mislead	_____	8. behold	_____	13. transport	_____
4. withdraw	_____	9. upgrade	_____	14. unused	_____
5. relocate	_____	10. nonsmoker	_____	15. increase	_____

(D) Complete these sentences.

1. _Pizarro_ conquered the Incas.
2. The hyrax is an excellent _____ .
3. The Incas built a great _____ .
4. The people of Holland are called _____ .
5. The house wren is a little _____ bird.
6. Incas lived in _____ .
7. The land in Holland is lower than the _____ .
8. Male and female wrens always _____ .
9. Some Chinese live on _____ .
10. The plural of "hyrax" is " _____ ."

Test 16 cont'd ☞

Comprehension Check (continued)

(E) Match these words and their definitions. These words appeared in the reading selections from units 76-80.

_d_ 1. distant   ____ 7. during   a. is made up of   g. very well known

____ 2. consists   ____ 8. famous   b. more than needed   h. think as true

____ 3. protect   ____ 9. boundless   c. what one eats   i. keep from harm

____ 4. never   ____ 10. excess   d. not close   j. control; govern

____ 5. rule   ____ 11. believe   e. in the course of   k. without limit

____ 6. connected   ____ 12. diet   f. not ever   l. joined together

(F) Underline the correct answers.

			(a)		(b)	
1.	Who are the people of Holland?		(a)	<u>Dutch</u>	(b)	Hollands
2.	In Holland, which is lower?		(a)	sea level	(b)	land level
3.	Who begins the nest building?		(a)	male wren	(b)	female wren
4.	What kind of parents are wrens?		(a)	excellent	(b)	lazy
5.	What are rooms on boats called?		(a)	ports	(b)	cabins
6.	Where do Chinese boat people live?		(a)	on land	(b)	on their boats
7.	To what animal is the hyrax related?		(a)	elephant	(b)	mouse
8.	How does the hyrax live?		(a)	alone	(b)	in groups
9.	Where did the Incas live?		(a)	Mexico	(b)	Peru
10.	Who destroyed the Inca empire?		(a)	Spanish	(b)	French

Choose one of the following topics and write a paragraph.

(1) Describe the life of Chinese boat people. Would you like to live on a boat? Why or why not?

(2) Describe the Inca empire before Pizarro destroyed it.

_____

_____

_____

_____

_____

_____

_____

_____

_____

_____

An Indian Village

Study the spelling and meaning of each word. These words are used in today's story. Connect each word with its definition.

1. almost
2. customs
3. protect
4. slopes
5. steeply
6. usually

a. slants
b. in a steep way
c. nearly but not quite
d. established usages or ways
e. shield from danger
f. most often

Read the story carefully and remember the details.

The people of India have black hair. Their dark skins protect them from the sun. They are called Indians. The people of India follow many customs which are very old.

Many Indians live in a bamboo frame house that is plastered with thick mud. The mud is baked by the sun. The roof of the house is made of rice straw. The roof slopes steeply so that the heavy rains run off quickly. This type house usually has two rooms. There are no windows.

On hot summer nights the people sleep on the porch. During the day they are busy outside. The house is used only on cooler nights.

Rice is eaten with almost every meal. Many Indians use a large leaf as a plate. They eat with their fingers.

A. Underline the correct answers about today's story.

1. People of India have   (a) dark skin   (b) light skin   (c) red skin.
2. Many live in a house made of   (a) grass   (b) stones   (c) mud.
3. Roofs slope steeply to keep off   (a) rain   (b) birds   (c) intruders.
4. What is eaten at most meals?   (a) corn   (b) rice   (c) cheese
5. What do some Indians use for plates?   (a) flat rocks   (b) leaves   (c) wood

B. Reread the story and write the answers to these questions.

1. What color is an Indian's hair?

_____

_____

_____

2. What material makes up the roof of an Indian's house?

_____

_____

_____

3. How many windows are in an Indian's house?

_____

_____

_____

4. Where do Indians sleep on hot summer nights?

_____

_____

_____

         Unit 81 cont'd 🐾

Suffixes

A. Write the suffix of each word in the blank.

1. rudeness _ness_
2. colorless _____
3. shameful _____
4. friendly _____
5. worthy _____
6. clearing _____
7. roughest _____
8. frighten _____
9. childish _____
10. bashful _____
11. booklet _____
12. lovable _____
13. younger _____
14. darkness _____
15. dentist _____
16. worthless _____

17. childhood _____
18. inward _____
19. blinded _____
20. narrower _____
21. happiness _____
22. guards _____
23. penniless _____
24. lawyer _____
25. careless _____
26. thicker _____
27. quietly _____
28. easiest _____
29. hopeless _____
30. joyful _____
31. owner _____
32. protection _____

33. lonely _____
34. foolish _____
35. dangerous _____
36. neighbors _____
37. building _____
38. insecticide _____
39. fearless _____
40. suddenly _____
41. expected _____
42. kindness _____
43. action _____
44. cowardly _____
45. peaceful _____
46. greediness _____
47. counting _____
48. lucky _____

B. Add a suffix to each word to make a new word.

1. Add "ness" to "sad." _sadness_
2. Add "ly" to "different." _____
3. Add "ment" to "govern." _____
4. Add "er" to "new." _____
5. Add "ing" to "surround." _____
6. Add "hood" to "adult." _____
7. Add "ward" to "home." _____
8. Add "less" to "use." _____
9. Add "y" to "greed." _____
10. Add "ly" to "honest." _____
11. Add "ing" to "laugh." _____
12. Add "s" to "license." _____

13. Add "ful" to "forget." _____
14. Add "er" to "farm." _____
15. Add "y" to "trick." _____
16. Add "s" to "monkey." _____
17. Add "ing" to "stand." _____
18. Add "es" to "match." _____
19. Add "ment" to "state." _____
20. Add "ed" to "follow." _____
21. Add "ish" to "green." _____
22. Add "ly" to "correct." _____
23. Add "ing" to "sleep." _____
24. Add "es" to "branch." _____

The Jaguar   Unit 82

Study the spelling and meaning of each word. These words are used in today's story. Connect each word with its definition.

1. camouflage ——————— a. disguise
2. depends   b. marked with spots
3. excellent   c. moist
4. humid   d. unusually good
5. provides   e. relies on
6. spotted   f. furnishes

Read the story carefully and remember the details.

The largest cat in the Western Hemisphere is the jaguar. Heavily muscled, the jaguar is very powerful.

The jaguar lives in heavy forest areas. Its spotted coat provides an excellent camouflage. The jaguar's homeland is hot and humid. The animal frequently bathes in streams and rivers to cool off or rid itself of pesty insects. It swims well and fast.

The jaguar does not travel any great distances. Much of its hunting is done in the trees. The animal depends on eyesight both for locating its prey and protecting itself. Although the jaguar has no natural enemies, it must be alert for animals which would be dangerous if given the advantage. Mankind, of course, is an enemy of the jaguar.

A. **Underline the correct answers about today's story.**

1. The jaguar is a	(a) dog	(b) cat	(c) car.
2. The animal depends mainly on its sense of	(a) smell	(b) sight	(c) hearing.
3. To cool off, the jaguar	(a) fans itself	(b) rolls in grass	(c) takes a swim.
4. Usually the jaguar hunts from	(a) trees	(b) the ground	(a) a ledge.
5. Which word describes the jaguar?	(a) weak	(b) harmless	(c) powerful

B. **Reread the story and write the answers to these questions.**

1. Where does the jaguar live?

_____

_____

_____

2. What purpose is served by the cat's spotted coat?

_____

_____

_____

3. How many natural enemies does the jaguar have?

_____

_____

_____

4. For what reasons does the cat depend upon its eyesight?

_____

_____

_____

                                    Unit 82 cont'd ☞

Suffixes Point to Nouns

Column 1 lists words that were formed by adding the suffixes in column 2. Draw a line from each word in column 1 to its suffix in column 2.

1	2
1. prominence	A. acy
2. supremacy	B. age
3. bakery	C. al
4. assistant	D. ance
5. actor	E. ence
6. worker	F. ant
7. direction	G. ard
8. survival	H. dom
9. breakage	I. er
10. drunkard	J. or
11. performance	K. ery
12. failure	L. hood
13. happiness	M. ure
14. kingdom	N. ion
15. brotherhood	O. ty
16. hardship	P. ism
17. management	Q. ment
18. cruelty	R. ness
19. health	S. ship
20. patriotism	T. th

Japanese Homes

Study the spelling and meaning of each word. These words are used in today's story. Connect each word with its definition.

1. adjust
2. earthquake
3. materials
4. shaken
5. waterproof
6. withstand

a. parts
b. trembled
c. to become suited
d. shaking of the ground
e. that which does not admit water
f. to resist

Read the story carefully and remember the details.

Japan is a country that is often shaken by earthquakes. The people of Japan find that homes made of light materials withstand the quakes better than heavy ones. Thus, they began making their homes from paper.

The frame of the house is made of wood. The walls are thick pieces of strong and waterproof paper. The inside walls are moving panels. Rooms can be made larger or smaller.

The floors are covered with straw mats. The Japanese have a custom of removing their shoes when they enter the house.

The Japanese sleep on soft pads on the floor. Many use blocks of wood instead of pillows. The Japanese have learned to adjust to the earthquakes which sometimes shake their homes.

A. Underline the correct answers about today's story.

1. Japan is often hit by   (a) earthquakes   (b) hurricanes   (c) heavy rains.
2. Japanese homes are made of   (a) grass   (b) brick   (c) paper.
3. The inside walls are   (a) brick   (b) curtains   (c) moving panels.
4. When Japanese enter a house, they   (a) put on a cap   (b) remove shoes   (c) bow their heads.
5. The floors are covered with   (a) rugs   (b) thick pads   (c) straw mats.

B. Reread the story and write the answers to these questions.

1. Why do the Japanese build their homes of light materials?

_____
_____
_____

2. What comprises the frame of the house?

_____
_____
_____

3. What covers the floors of their houses?

_____
_____
_____

4. What do the Japanese use instead of pillows?

_____
_____
_____

Unit 83 cont'd

"Doer" Suffixes

Suffixes are added to the ends of words.

The suffixes "er," "or," "ist," "eer," "ant," and "ess" are often called "doer" suffixes. They usually mean "one who does something."

For example, one who buys something is a buyer.

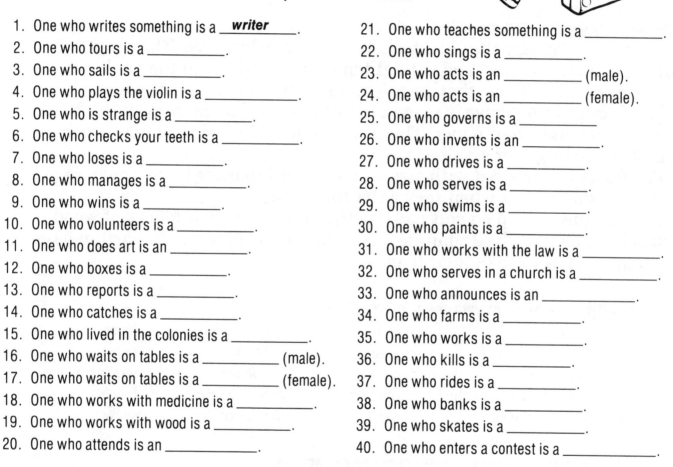

A. Complete each sentence with a word plus a "doer" suffix.

1. One who writes something is a __writer__.
2. One who tours is a _____.
3. One who sails is a _____.
4. One who plays the violin is a _____.
5. One who is strange is a _____.
6. One who checks your teeth is a _____.
7. One who loses is a _____.
8. One who manages is a _____.
9. One who wins is a _____.
10. One who volunteers is a _____.
11. One who does art is an _____.
12. One who boxes is a _____.
13. One who reports is a _____.
14. One who catches is a _____.
15. One who lived in the colonies is a _____.
16. One who waits on tables is a _____ (male).
17. One who waits on tables is a _____ (female).
18. One who works with medicine is a _____.
19. One who works with wood is a _____.
20. One who attends is an _____.

21. One who teaches something is a _____.
22. One who sings is a _____.
23. One who acts is an _____ (male).
24. One who acts is an _____ (female).
25. One who governs is a _____.
26. One who invents is an _____.
27. One who drives is a _____.
28. One who serves is a _____.
29. One who swims is a _____.
30. One who paints is a _____.
31. One who works with the law is a _____.
32. One who serves in a church is a _____.
33. One who announces is an _____.
34. One who farms is a _____.
35. One who works is a _____.
36. One who kills is a _____.
37. One who rides is a _____.
38. One who banks is a _____.
39. One who skates is a _____.
40. One who enters a contest is a _____.

B. Complete each sentence with a word plus its "doer" suffix.

1. The __lawyer__ defended his client.
2. The _____ is the head of a city.
3. The _____ received the most votes.
4. The _____ taught at the university.
5. The _____ sketched my profile.
6. The store lost its best _____.

7. A _____ works in the senate.
8. The _____ dismissed the class.
9. Benedict Arnold was a _____.
10. An _____ works on a train.
11. The _____ struck out.
12. The _____ loaned me the money.

202

Javelinas

Study the spelling and meaning of each word. These words are used in today's story. Connect each word with its definition.

1. capable   a. particularly
2. especially   b. to remain alive
3. prefers   c. able
4. severely   d. likes better
5. survive   e. extremely
6. unpredictable   f. not able to foretell

Read the story carefully and remember the details.

The javelina is often called the collared peccary. It is found in Arizona, Texas, and New Mexico. The javelina is a desert animal. It could not survive in severely low temperatures.

The javelina eats both plants and animals. It is especially fond of the prickly pear and other cacti. The cacti not only provide food but also water.

The javelina prefers to travel in groups. Its poor eyesight is offset by its keen hearing and excellent sense of smell. It does not attack people unless it is cornered or frightened. The animal is quite capable of protecting itself.

Strangely enough, javelinas are popular as pets. Many ranchers use them as watchdogs. Although they are playful and seemingly tame when young, javelinas are totally unpredictable when they are older.

A. Underline the correct answers about today's story.

1. The javelina only survives in   (a) hot temperatures   (b) wet climates   (c) cold temperatures.
2. The javelina gets water from   (a) plants   (b) rivers   (c) underground springs.
3. The javelina has a poor sense of   (a) smell   (b) hearing   (c) sight.
4. As a fighter, the javelina is   (a) helpless   (b) inadequate   (c) capable.
5. Ranchers use javelinas as   (a) food   (b) watchdogs   (c) beasts of burden.

B. Reread the story and write the answers to these questions.

1. What does the javelina eat?

_____

_____

_____

2. How does the javelina travel?

_____

_____

_____

3. When does the animal attack people?

_____

_____

_____

4. How are the javelinas described?

_____

_____

_____

Unit 84 cont'd ☞

Suffixes Signal Adjectives

 Combine the suffixes with the root words, and write the resulting adjectives on the lines. Then use each new word in a sentence.

suffix	root word	adjective
1. -ed	worry	*worried*
2. -ing	dance	
3. -ful	beauty	
4. -able	catch	
5. -ible	digest	
6. -al	music	
7. -ent	intelligence	
8. -ant	hesitance	
9. -ory	satisfy	
10. -ly	friend	
11. -ish	boy	
12. -y	smoke	
13. -en	wood	
14. -ive	disrupt	
15. -ous	danger	

The Kangaroo Rat

Study the spelling and meaning of each word. These words are used in today's story. Connect each word with its definition.

1. elaborate   a. jumps
2. inhabits   b. highly complicated
3. leaps   c. support
4. prop   d. lives in or on
5. rodent   e. mammal
6. serves   f. functions

Read the story carefully and remember the details.

The kangaroo rat looks and acts much like the kangaroo. It is a tiny animal that belongs to the rodent family.

The kangaroo rat leaps like a kangaroo. Its tail serves as a prop when it is resting. The tail is longer than the rat's body. Its front legs are very small.

The home of the kangaroo rat is an elaborate tunnel. There are dozens of entrances to the tunnel so that the rat can escape its enemies. A nocturnal animal, the kangaroo rat comes out at night to find seeds. The seeds are collected and stored for the cooler months. A kangaroo rat will fight over its food. Like the kangaroo, the rat fights by kicking with its hind feet.

The kangaroo rat inhabits dry and sandy areas. Very little water is required for the kangaroo rat's survival.

A. Underline the correct answers about today's story.

1. The kangaroo rat is a   (a) bird   (b) rodent   (c) small kangaroo.
2. The tail is used as a   (a) prop   (b) weapon   (c) extra leg.
3. The rat's home is a   (a) tunnel   (b) tree   (c) cave.
4. The rat's food is   (a) insects   (b) seeds   (c) meat.
5. The rat fights by   (a) biting   (b) clawing   (c) kicking.

B. Reread the story and write the answers to these questions.

1. What animal does the kangaroo rat resemble?

_____

_____

_____

2. Describe the animal's tail.

_____

_____

_____

3. Why does the rat's home have so many entrances?

_____

_____

_____

4. What type of climate does the rat inhabit?

_____

_____

_____

Unit 85 cont'd

Suffixes Signal Verbs

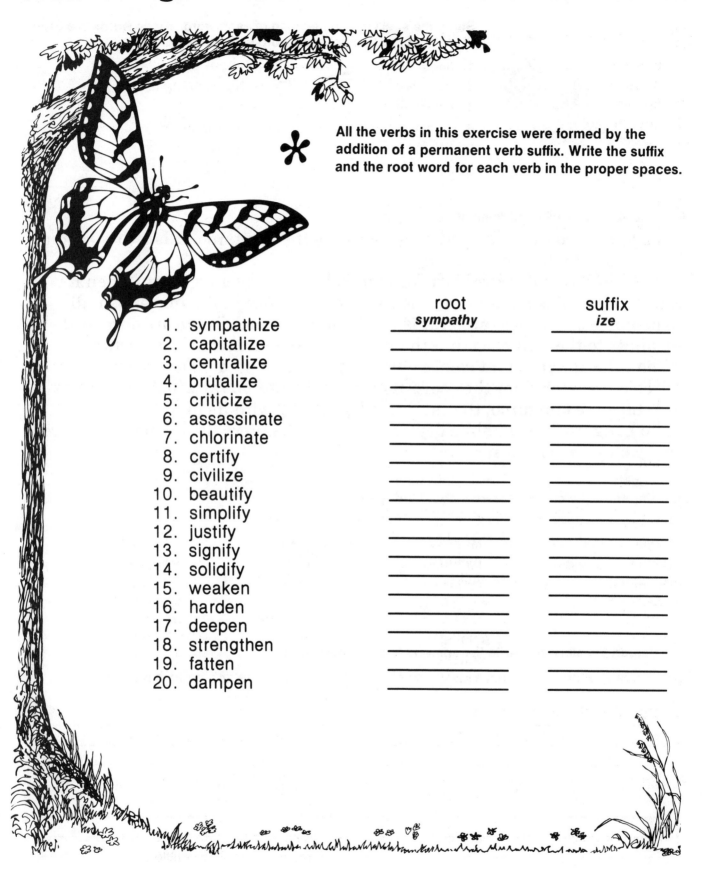

All the verbs in this exercise were formed by the addition of a permanent verb suffix. Write the suffix and the root word for each verb in the proper spaces.

1. sympathize
2. capitalize
3. centralize
4. brutalize
5. criticize
6. assassinate
7. chlorinate
8. certify
9. civilize
10. beautify
11. simplify
12. justify
13. signify
14. solidify
15. weaken
16. harden
17. deepen
18. strengthen
19. fatten
20. dampen

root	suffix
sympathy	*ize*

Comprehension Check

A Identify the suffix of each word.

1.	quickly	_ly_	11.	insecticide	_____	21.	reaction	_____
2.	hopeful	_____	12.	backward	_____	22.	truthful	_____
3.	childish	_____	13.	statement	_____	23.	lucky	_____
4.	cowardly	_____	14.	sadness	_____	24.	kingdom	_____
5.	famous	_____	15.	dentist	_____	25.	contestant	_____
6.	lovable	_____	16.	roughly	_____	26.	cruelty	_____
7.	laughing	_____	17.	needy	_____	27.	protection	_____
8.	sooner	_____	18.	steeply	_____	28.	shaken	_____
9.	seated	_____	19.	artist	_____	29.	stranger	_____
10.	treats	_____	20.	dependable	_____	30.	Japanese	_____

B Add a suffix to each word and write a new word.

1.	free	_freedom_	11.	mother	_____	21.	move	_____
2.	music	_____	12.	call	_____	22.	tour	_____
3.	green	_____	13.	usual	_____	23.	friend	_____
4.	out	_____	14.	large	_____	24.	smoke	_____
5.	direct	_____	15.	sail	_____	25.	beauty	_____
6.	bake	_____	16.	dance	_____	26.	wise	_____
7.	profess	_____	17.	danger	_____	27.	think	_____
8.	teach	_____	18.	fat	_____	28.	box	_____
9.	act	_____	19.	in	_____	29.	book	_____
10.	wealth	_____	20.	sudden	_____	30.	day	_____

C Underline the words which contain suffixes.

1. longer	9. identify	17. families	25. favorite
2. final	10. smiling	18. hunted	26. speedy
3. criticize	11. mall	19. homely	27. nice
4. believable	12. smoky	20. bursts	28. clenches
5. bluish	13. traitor	21. homicide	29. pockets
6. wolf	14. smaller	22. way	30. ranch
7. shortest	15. waltzes	23. knights	31. wonderful
8. independence	16. change	24. meal	32. basically

D Complete these sentences.

1. The kangaroo rat uses its ___tail___ as a prop.

2. The javelina is a _____ animal.

3. Indians eat _____ with almost every meal.

4. Homes in Japan are often made of _____ .

5. The jaguar usually hunts in the _____ .

6. People of India are called _____ .

7. The jaguar has a _____ coat.

8. _____ javelinas are unpredictable.

9. Japan is often shaken by _____ .

10. Kangaroo rats require little _____ .

Test 17 cont'd ☞

Comprehension Check (continued)

(E) Match these words and their definitions. These words appeared in the reading selections from units 81-85.

_j_ 1. almost   ____ 7. withstand

____ 2. protect   ____ 8. especially

____ 3. slopes   ____ 9. prefers

____ 4. camouflage   ____ 10. elaborate

____ 5. provides   ____ 11. prop

____ 6. shaken   ____ 12. serves

a. functions   g. particularly

b. support   h. slants

c. shield from danger   i. to resist

d. disguise   j. nearly

e. likes better   k. trembled

f. furnishes   l. highly complicated

(F) Underline the correct answers.

1. Describe the people of India.   (a) <u>dark skinned</u>   (b) reddish skinned
2. Why do the roofs in India slope?   (a) to keep off rain   (b) to keep out intruders
3. How does a jaguar cool itself?   (a) takes a swim   (b) rolls in grass
4. Which word describes a jaguar?   (a) powerful   (b) harmless
5. What often hits Japan?   (a) hurricanes   (b) earthquakes
6. Why are Japanese houses made of light materials?   (a) withstand the quakes better   (b) withstand the hurricanes better
7. Where does the javelina get water?   (a) underground springs   (b) plants
8. How do ranchers use javelinas?   (a) watchdogs   (b) beasts of burden
9. What do kangaroo rats eat?   (a) insects   (b) seeds
10. Describe a kangaroo rat's tail.   (a) very long   (b) very short

Choose one of the following topics and write a paragraph.

(1) People of other lands often have different cultures than we. What country would you most like to visit? Why? What would you do there?

(2) The jaguar is often considered a beautiful animal. What is your favorite animal? Why?

_____

_____

_____

_____

_____

_____

_____

_____

_____

_____

The Kit Fox

Study the spelling and meaning of each word. These words are used in today's story. Connect each word with its definition.

1. extinction	a. to brave
2. habit	b. not often
3. indication	c. usual way of doing things
4. rarely	d. taking place quickly
5. sudden	e. dying out
6. venture	f. sign

Read the story carefully and remember the details.

The kit fox is smaller than any of the other foxes. Its name refers to its size. The kit fox is rarely seen and not much is known about its habits.

The kit fox can run faster than the other foxes. Its sudden bursts of speed has earned it the name of swift fox.

By daylight the kit fox stays underground in its burrow. At night it ventures out to search for food. Its favorite food is rodents. Unless the kit fox is very hungry, it carries its catch home to eat.

The kit fox seldom wanders far from its burrow. At the slightest indication of danger, the kit fox runs for refuge in its burrow. Unlike other members of the fox family, the kit fox is not very cunning.

The kit fox was once feared in danger of extinction because it was hunted for its fur. Laws now protect the animal.

A. Underline the correct answers about today's story.

1. Compared to other foxes, the kit
   fox is   (a) greater   (b) larger   (c) smaller.
2. This fox gets its name from its   (a) size   (b) home   (c) habits.
3. Another name for kit fox is   (a) slow fox   (b) swift fox   (c) running fox.
4. When danger is near, the kit fox   (a) stands its ground   (b) runs away   (c) hides in a burrow.
5. Unlike other foxes, the kit fox is   (a) more clever   (b) less cunning   (c) more cunning.

B. Reread the story and write the answers to these questions.

1. Where can the kit fox be found during the day?

_____

_____

_____

2. When does the kit fox hunt for food?

_____

_____

3. What is the animal's favorite food?

_____

_____

4. Why was the kit fox once in danger of extinction?

_____

_____

Unit 86 cont'd ☞

Verb Endings

The suffixes "s," "ed," and "ing" are common verb endings.
The ending "s" is used for third person, singular.
The ending "ed" is a common past tense suffix.
The ending "ing" is used to show progressive tense.

A. Add "s," "ed," and "ing" to each verb.

EXAMPLES: a. use   _uses_   _used_   _using_
          b. camp   _camps_   _camped_   _camping_

1. smile _____ _____ _____
2. wait _____ _____ _____
3. cover _____ _____ _____
4. play _____ _____ _____
5. walk _____ _____ _____
6. help _____ _____ _____
7. cough _____ _____ _____
8. repeat _____ _____ _____

B. Complete each sentence by writing the verb plus its correct suffix.

EXAMPLES: (provide)   a. Jake _provided_ the supplies.
            (rain)   b. It always _rains_ on Mondays.
            (talk)   c. I was _talking_ to Mr. Owens.

(live) 1. Paul _____ in Nebraska.
(listen) 2. She is _____ to the radio.
(surround) 3. They _____ the house.
(save) 4. Don _____ stamps.
(taste) 5. The soup _____ terrible.
(select) 6. The class _____ a leader.

(borrow) 7. Jan _____ the money.
(jump) 8. The frog _____ on my shoe.
(touch) 9. Kim _____ the pan.
(invite) 10. I am _____ everyone.
(clean) 11. Betty _____ her room.
(forfeit) 12. We are _____ the game.

The suffixes "ize," "ify," "ate," and "en" are also verb endings.

C. Make a verb from each word by adding the suffix. Write the new verb.

EXAMPLES: a. sympathy + ize   _sympathize_
          b. beauty + ify   _beautify_

1. criticism + ize _____
2. fat + en _____
3. strength + en _____
4. deep + en _____
5. civil + ize _____
6. length + en _____

7. weak + en _____
8. assassin + ate _____
9. just + ify _____
10. appreciation + ate _____
11. damp + en _____
12. identical + fy _____

Klipspringer

Study the spelling and meaning of each word. These words are used in today's story. Connect each word with its definition.

1. ability   a. a peculiarity
2. brittle   b. power to do
3. characteristic   c. risk
4. danger   d. easily broken
5. sure-footed   e. changed from one language to another
6. translated   f. not likely to stumble

Read the story carefully and remember the details.

The klipspringer is a small African antelope. When translated, its name means "rock jumper." The name fits the animal perfectly. The klipspringer lives on bare rocky places.

The klipspringer has an amazing ability for jumping from one rock to another. It is the most sure-footed of all mountain animals, even the mountain goat. The klipspringer has landed on places too narrow for much smaller animals.

Another characteristic of the klipspringer is its coat of brittle hairs. When caught, the hairs break away in the predator's mouth, thus giving the klipspringer a second chance to escape. New growth replaces the lost hair.

Because the klipspringer can only live in restricted areas, it is in danger of extinction. It is seldom found far from rocks.

A. **Underline the correct answers about today's story.**

1. "Klipspringer" means   (a) "tiny jumper"   (b) "antelope"   (c) "rock jumper."
2. Where does the klipspringer live?   (a) Australia   (b) Africa   (c) Arctic
3. The hair of the klipspringer's coat is   (a) brittle   (b) shaggy   (c) strong.
4. Which word describes the klipspringer?   (a) sure-footed   (b) clumsy   (c) awkward
5. The klipspringer always lives near   (a) water   (b) rocks   (c) the desert.

B. **Reread the story and write the answers to these questions.**

1. Why does the klipspringer's name fit it so well?

_____

_____

_____

2. What happens when the animal is caught by a predator?

_____

_____

_____

3. Why is it important that the animal's hair break off?

_____

_____

_____

4. What threatens the klipspringer?

_____

_____

_____

Unit 87 cont'd ☞

Adding "-ed" and "-ing"

A. Add "-ed" to each word.

1. chase   _chased_
2. chop
3. ask
4. voice
5. deny
6. step
7. include
8. watch
9. love
10. supply
11. agree
12. decide
13. use
14. carry
15. try
16. create
17. result
18. fix
19. change
20. study

21. move
22. dip
23. answer
24. hurry
25. obey
26. rule
27. share
28. believe
29. finish
30. control
31. spy
32. owe
33. help
34. return
35. capture
36. squeeze
37. marry
38. arrive
39. ship
40. invent

41. delay
42. locate
43. hike
44. replace
45. bury
46. excuse
47. promote
48. supply
49. deserve
50. worry
51. open
52. reply
53. end
54. hesitate
55. puzzle
56. smile
57. spin
58. admire
59. look
60. state

B. Add "-ing" to each word.

1. open   _opening_
2. hurry
3. locate
4. walk
5. include
6. begin
7. help
8. race
9. change
10. earn
11. invite
12. buy
13. show

14. chase
15. spy
16. talk
17. arrive
18. chop
19. watch
20. share
21. whip
22. ride
23. use
24. eat
25. promote
26. write

27. decide
28. state
29. study
30. look
31. smile
32. finish
33. squeeze
34. send
35. wait
36. replace
37. listen
38. hike
39. step

Koalas

Study the spelling and meaning of each word. These words are used in today's story. Connect each word with its definition.

1. ample
2. diminishes
3. furnish
4. immediately
5. peaceful
6. seldom

a. lessens
b. at once
c. serene
d. plentiful
e. supply
f. not often

Read the story carefully and remember the details.

When one thinks of Australia, two animals immediately come to mind. One is the kangaroo. The other is the koala.

The koala is a cuddly, bearlike animal. Its home is the eucalyptus tree. In fact, it seldom comes out of the tree. When the food supply diminishes, the koala is forced to change homes. The move is done quickly.

The koala eats the leaves of the eucalyptus tree. The tree produces new leaves the year round. Even in winter the koala has an ample food supply.

The leaves also furnish the animal's water supply. The moisture in the leaves is all that the koala requires. The koala is a peaceful animal that is content to sleep all day and eat all night.

A. Underline the correct answers about today's story.

1. The koala is native to   (a) Australia   (b) Africa   (c) Europe.
2. The koala's home is   (a) in water   (b) a tree   (c) on the ground.
3. Which tree is the koala's home?   (a) eucalyptus   (b) pine   (c) willow
4. Water is taken from   (a) nearby streams   (b) leaves   (c) bark.
5. Which word describes the koala?   (a) untrustworthy   (b) dangerous   (c) peaceful

B. Reread the story and write the answers to these questions.

1. What other animal, besides the koala, makes Australia its home?

_____

_____

_____

2. What animal does the koala resemble?

_____

_____

_____

3. What does the koala eat?

_____

_____

_____

4. What does the koala do when its food supply diminishes?

_____

_____

_____

Unit 88 cont'd

Adding Suffixes to Verbs

A. Complete each sentence by adding "-ing" to the verb in parentheses.

(cut)   1. Kim is _cutting_ the rope.

(worry)   2. He is _____ about the test.

(move)   3. They are _____ to Texas.

(run)   4. The dog is _____ away.

(sit)   5. She was _____ on the porch.

(use)   6. Lynn is _____ mine.

(change)   7. Theo is _____ clothes.

(vote)   8. Are you _____ for me?

(shop)   9. She is _____ for a gift.

(spy)   10. They were _____ on us.

(take)   11. It is _____ too long.

(get)   12. I'm _____ bored.

(study)   13. We have been _____.

(practice)   14. Have you been _____?

(win)   15. We're _____!

(make)   16. Jay was _____ a mess.

(try)   17. He is _____ to reach you.

(arrive)   18. They are _____ today.

(cause)   19. It is _____ problems.

(dig)   20. Lewis was _____ a ditch.

(pave)   21. They were _____ our street.

(smile)   22. Mr. Reynolds was _____.

(bury)   23. My dog is _____ his bone.

(write)   24. Are you _____ a note?

B. Complete each sentence by adding "-ed" to the verb in parentheses.

(try)   1. Ralph _tried_ to call you.

(rub)   2. She _____ her eyes.

(worry)   3. Mom _____ about us.

(provide)   4. Ned _____ the drinks.

(save)   5. I have _____ my money.

(beg)   6. He _____ me to help him.

(escape)   7. The prisoner _____.

(receive)   8. Joyce _____ an invitation.

(trim)   9. The shirt was _____ in blue.

(cry)   10. The child _____.

(study)   11. We _____ for the test.

(drop)   12. I _____ my pencil.

(close)   13. Sam _____ the window.

(divide)   14. Ann _____ the pie.

(carry)   15. Chris _____ the box upstairs.

(chop)   16. I _____ wood.

(name)   17. It was _____ Bertha.

(rob)   18. He _____ a bank.

(prepare)   19. Dad _____ our dinner.

(trap)   20. We _____ the bear.

(believe)   21. I _____ you!

(hurry)   22. Sharon _____ home.

(taste)   23. Alice _____ the soup.

(wrap)   24. I _____ the present.

The Kodiak Bear

Study the spelling and meaning of each word. These words are used in today's story. Connect each word with its definition.

1. captivity
2. guards
3. offspring
4. powerful
5. protective
6. startled

a. keeps from harm
b. strong
c. sheltering
d. confinement
e. taken by surprise
f. the young of animals

Read the story carefully and remember the details.

The Kodiak bear is also called the Alaskan brown bear. It is an extremely large brown bear which may weigh up to 1,600 pounds. When standing on its hind legs, the Kodiak bear is about nine feet tall.

The bear is found along the Alaskan coast. There it finds its favorite food, salmon. The bear catches the fish with its powerful jaws.

The mother Kodiak is very protective of her cubs. She guards them carefully from the male Kodiak who has been known to eat even his own offspring.

In winter the bears seek refuge in a hillside cave or a burrow. They live off of the fat which they gain during the summer.

Usually the Kodiak avoids people. It will attack when wounded or startled. The Kodiak does well in captivity.

A. Underline the correct answers about today's story.

1. The Kodiak bear is extremely   (a) large   (b) dangerous   (c) helpless.
2. The bear's favorite food is   (a) plants   (b) rodents   (c) salmon.
3. Mother Kodiaks are very   (a) lazy   (b) protective   (c) bad parents.
4. In winter the bears live off   (a) stored fat   (b) plants   (c) insects.
5. When startled, the Kodiak   (a) runs away   (b) attacks   (c) climbs a tree.

B. Reread the story and write the answers to these questions.

1. How much can the Kodiak weigh?

_____
_____
_____

2. When on its hind legs, how tall is the Kodiak?

_____
_____
_____

3. Where is the Kodiak bear found?

_____
_____
_____

4. Where does the bear seek refuge in winter?

_____
_____
_____

    Unit 89 cont'd ☞

Doubling Final Consonants

When a word ends in a short vowel followed by a consonant, double the consonant before adding a suffix which begins with a vowel.

EXAMPLE: chop + ed = chopped

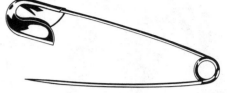

A. Add the suffix "ed" to each word.

1. plan _____planned_____
2. beg _____
3. pop _____
4. trip _____
5. rip _____

6. stop _____
7. hop _____
8. grab _____
9. pin _____
10. drop _____

11. plot _____
12. slip _____
13. map _____
14. fit _____
15. cap _____

B. Add the suffix "ing" to each word.

1. stir _____stirring_____
2. cut _____
3. stop _____
4. shut _____
5. plan _____

6. spin _____
7. run _____
8. get _____
9. win _____
10. sit _____

11. put _____
12. dig _____
13. quit _____
14. beg _____
15. let _____

C. Complete each sentence by writing the word in the parentheses plus a suffix.

(permit)   1. No one was ____permitted____ to speak during the film.

(occur)   2. The accident _____ at seven o'clock.

(prefer)   3. My mother _____ the green one.

(scan)   4. I _____ the story hurriedly.

(commit)   5. Betsy had never _____ a crime.

(regret)   6. I am _____ what I said to you yesterday.

(submit)   7. The paper was _____ by an anonymous writer.

(refer)   8. Are you _____ to the article on page six?

(wrap)   9. The package was _____ in orange paper.

(trim)   10. We _____ the tree with popcorn and berries.

(stir)   11. Jason was _____ the soup with a wooden spoon.

(admit)   12. The man has _____ to stealing the money.

The Lapps

Study the spelling and meaning of each word. These words are used in today's story. Connect each word with its definition.

1. heritage
2. katas
3. portable
4. simply
5. sturdy
6. wander

a. in a plain way
b. Lapp word for tents
c. ancestry
d. hardy
e. roam
f. moveable

Read the story carefully and remember the details.

The Lapps are people that wander freely over northern Norway, Sweden, Russia, and Finland. In Swedish the word "Lapp" means "nomad."

The Lapps follow herds of reindeer. They are small, sturdy people who are proud of their heritage. No one knows exactly where they came from.

When the herds stop, camp is made. The Lapps live in portable tents, called "katas." Inside the doorway the Lapps lay a log. The log is a sign that visitors are welcome and that they may enter without being invited. The visitors are welcome only in the front part of the home. The back of the tent is for the family only. The Lapps are a close family. They live simply and happily with nature.

A. Underline the correct answers about today's story.

1. In Swedish "Lapp" means   (a) "nomad"   (b) "happy"   (c) "cold."
2. Lapps follow the   (a) sun   (b) moon   (c) reindeer.
3. Where do Lapps come from?   (a) China   (b) the North Pole   (c) No one knows.
4. What welcome sign do Lapps give to visitors?   (a) a fire   (b) a log   (c) a light
5. The back of the tent is for the   (a) family   (b) supplies   (c) visitors.

B. Reread the story and write the answers to these questions.

1. Name two countries where the Lapps wander.

_____

_____

_____

2. What is the home of the Lapps?

_____

_____

_____

3. What is the name of the Lapps' home?

_____

_____

_____

4. In what part of the tent are visitors welcome?

_____

_____

_____

Unit 90 cont'd ☞

The Final "y"

To add a suffix to a word ending in a final "y," remember the following:

(1) If there is a vowel before the final "y," keep the "y."

(2) If there is a consonant before the final "y," change the "y" to "i," unless the suffix begins with an "i."

EXAMPLES: a. *say + ing = saying*
             b. *multiply + ing = multiplying*
             c. *multiply + ed = multiplied*

A. Add each word and suffix, and write the new word.

1. easy + ly = _____*easily*_____
2. happy + ness = _____
3. cry + ing = _____
4. notify + ed = _____
5. empty + ed = _____
6. primary + ly = _____
7. play + ing = _____
8. lazy + ness = _____
9. greedy + ly = _____
10. factory + es = _____
11. stay + ed = _____
12. hobby + ist = _____
13. carry + ing = _____
14. harmony + ous = _____
15. victory + ous = _____
16. dictionary + es = _____
17. rely + ed = _____
18. memory + es = _____
19. heavy + er = _____
20. voluntary + ly = _____
21. library + an = _____
22. worry + ed = _____
23. necessary + ly = _____
24. hurry + ing = _____

B. Complete each sentence with a word(s) from part A.

1. The _____*librarian*_____ will help you find the books you want.
2. The members were _____ about the meeting.
3. All the _____ closed down for the holidays.
4. George is _____ the tuba in the marching band.
5. Benjamin and Rita _____ at the bus station and waited.
6. These _____ will help you answer the questions.
7. Kelly has many _____ about living in South America.
8. This box is _____ than the one you are _____.
9. Sam is _____ about tomorrow's math exam.
10. The dog _____ ate all the food I gave him.

Comprehension Check

(A) Add "s," "ed," and "ing" to each verb.

1. help	*helps*	*helped*	*helping*
2. talk			
3. use			
4. select			
5. stop			
6. invite			
7. repeat			
8. worry			
9. clean			
10. wait			

(B) Which of these words would double the final letter to add "ed"?

1. <u>hop</u>	11. knock
2. hum	12. trade
3. web	13. pad
4. edit	14. trip
5. stop	15. pass
6. wash	16. rob
7. gag	17. sing
8. pull	18. grab
9. blab	19. occur
10. throb	20. wag

(C) Underline the verbs which end in suffixes.

1. <u>sees</u>	11. chooses
2. wishing	12. marked
3. rocked	13. tripping
4. names	14. reaches
5. leaned	15. pushing
6. widened	16. redo
7. loving	17. used
8. frozen	18. brushes
9. answer	19. unlocked
10. stands	20. swimming

(D) Which words would change "y" to "i" before adding "ing"?

1. dry	6. stay	11. fly	16. hurry
2. play	7. pay	12. carry	17. worry
3. try	8. pray	13. prey	18. say
4. bray	9. scurry	14. fray	19. fry
5. pry	10. marry	15. lay	20. bury

(E) Complete these sentences.

1. The Kodiak bear may weigh __*1,600*__ pounds.
2. Koalas live in _____ .
3. The kit fox is rarely _____ .
4. A klipspringer lives near _____ .
5. The Kodiak bear stands about _____ feet tall.
6. The kit fox gets its name from its _____ .
7. During the day koalas _____ .
8. In Swedish "Lapp" means " _____ ."
9. Lapps follow herds of _____ .
10. A klipspringer's name means " _____ _____ ."

219

Test 18 cont'd ☞

Comprehension Check (continued)

(F) Match these words and their definitions. These words appeared in the reading selections from units 86-90.

_b_ 1. rarely   ____ 7. immediately   a. at once   g. keeps from harm

____ 2. venture   ____ 8. diminishes   b. not often   h. power to do

____ 3. indication   ____ 9. powerful   c. lessens   i. risk

____ 4. ability   ____ 10. guards   d. to brave   j. ancestry

____ 5. brittle   ____ 11. heritage   e. strong   k. easily broken

____ 6. danger   ____ 12. simply   f. sign   l. in a plain way

(G) Underline the correct answers.

		(a)	(b)
1.	Compare the kit fox to other foxes.	<u>smaller</u>	larger
2.	How does the kit fox get its name?	its size	its home
3.	Where does the klipspringer live?	Australia	Africa
4.	Which word describes the klipspringer?	sure-footed	awkward
5.	What is a koala's home?	tree	pond
6.	Describe a koala.	peaceful	untrustworthy
7.	Describe a Kodiak bear.	extremely large	helpless
8.	How much can a Kodiak weigh?	500 pounds	1,600 pounds
9.	What is a kanta?	tent	wanderer
10.	Where do Lapps come from?	No one knows.	China

Choose one of the following topics and write a paragraph.

(1) Koalas come from Australia. What do you know about this country? Would you like to visit Australia? Why or why not?

(2) Kodiak bears come from Alaska. What do you know about this state? Would you like to visit this state? Why or why not?

_____

_____

_____

_____

_____

_____

_____

_____

Lemmings

Study the spelling and meaning of each word. These words are used in today's story. Connect each word with its definition.

1. arctic —————————— a. the region of the North Pole
2. common   b. making larger
3. expanding   c. gnawing mammal
4. migration   d. moving from one place to another
5. rodent   e. region surrounding the Arctic Circle
6. subarctic   f. ordinary

Read the story carefully and remember the details.

The lemming is the most common rodent in the arctic and subarctic regions. It is a burrowing animal which is always expanding its networks of tunnels.

Lemmings are best known for periodic migrations to the sea. The journey is begun when lemming cities become overpopulated. Usually an old male begins the journey. Other lemmings follow. As they move along, the group becomes steadily larger.

The migration takes the lemmings over mountains and across lakes and rivers. Many lemmings are killed along the way either by hardships or by predators. When the surviving lemmings reach the sea, they do not hesitate to jump in. They swim until they are exhausted and drown. Such migrations occur about every three years.

A. Underline the correct answers about today's story.

1. The lemming lives in   (a) the mountains   (b) the desert   (c) arctic regions.
2. Lemmings are best known
   for their   (a) tunnels   (b) migrations   (c) temper.
3. Migrations begin when cities are   (a) overpopulated   (b) destroyed   (c) invaded.
4. The migration is ended when
   the lemmings   (a) find a new home   (b) reach water   (c) drown in the sea.
5. Migrations occur about every   (a) two years   (b) three years   (c) ten years.

B. Reread the story and write the answers to these questions.

1. Who leads the migration?

   _____
   _____
   _____

2. What happens as the migration moves along?

   _____
   _____
   _____

3. What happens to some of the lemmings during the migration?

   _____
   _____
   _____

4. What type of mammal is the lemming?

   _____
   _____
   _____

The Final "e"

To add a suffix to a word ending in the final silent "e,"
remember the following:

(1) *If the suffix begins with a vowel, drop the "e."*

excite + ed = excited

(2) *If the suffix begins with a consonant, keep the "e."*

amuse + ment = amusement

A. Add each word and suffix, and write the new word.

1. require + ment = _____requirement_____
2. lecture + er = _____
3. hope + less = _____
4. hesitate + ed = _____
5. choose + ing = _____
6. polite + ly = _____
7. celebrate + ion = _____
8. care + ful = _____
9. unite + ed = _____
10. hibernate + ing = _____
11. fortunate + ly = _____
12. wise + dom = _____
13. excite + ment = _____
14. brave + er = _____
15. nice + ly = _____
16. operate + or = _____
17. erase + ed = _____
18. pave + ment = _____
19. taste + ful = _____
20. eliminate + ion = _____
21. secure + ly = _____
22. approximate + ly = _____
23. vote + er = _____
24. migrate + ed = _____

B. Complete each sentence with a word from part A.

1. Mr. Collier _____erased_____ the chalkboard and dismissed the class.
2. I asked the telephone _____ for Windy's number.
3. All of the windows and doors were fastened _____.
4. Nancy _____ before answering Dr. North's question.
5. Each _____ has the responsibility of casting his vote.
6. Mark was _____ not to mention the accident.
7. The victory _____ lasted four days.
8. Louis is a _____ man than Walter.
9. The birds have already _____ to the north.
10. The situation seemed _____ until you came along.
11. Steven _____ excused himself from the table.
12. The students _____ to protest the strict curfew.

Libraries

Study the spelling and meaning of each word. These words are used in today's story. Connect each word with its definition.

1. collected ———————— a. gathered
2. concept   b. idea
3. displayed   c. put out to be seen
4. frequently   d. prized
5. invention   e. something created
6. treasured   f. often

Read the story carefully and remember the details.

Most of us frequently visit the library and borrow books. How many of us stop to think how the concept of loaning books began?

Twenty-five hundred years ago people wrote on clay tablets. The tablets were very heavy. A king collected these tablets and displayed them in the first library in Nineveh.

Then papyrus was invented. Papyrus sheets were rolled on a stick and stored in jars or cupboards. Papyrus was expensive so there were few libraries. These libraries belong to the rich.

Parchment took the place of papyrus. Monks copied books by hand onto the parchment. The monks treasured the books and took good care of them.

The invention of the printing press made books available to the public. With more books came more libraries. Now almost every town has a public library.

A. **Underline the correct answers about today's story.**

1. Libraries   (a) loan books   (b) sell books   (c) make books.
2. The library in Nineveh had books made of   (a) rock   (b) wood   (c) clay.
3. Books made of papyrus were   (a) too heavy   (b) too fragile   (c) too expensive.
4. Who copied books onto parchment?   (a) teachers   (b) monks   (c) poor people
5. Which invention increased the number
   of libraries?   (a) ink   (b) paper   (c) printing press

B. **Reread the story and write the answers to these questions.**

1. Why do most people visit the library?

_____

_____

_____

2. Where was the first library?

_____

_____

_____

3. After papyrus was invented, who had libraries?

_____

_____

_____

4. Today, where can you find a public library?

_____

_____

_____

Unit 92 cont'd ☞

Prefixes and Suffixes

 Add the prefix and/or suffix to each base word.
Write the new word in the blank to complete the sentence.

1. column + ist
   She is a newspaper ___columnist___.
2. stand + under
   Do you _____ the assignment?
3. assemble + ed + pre
   The bike was _____.
4. operate + co
   Will they _____?
5. change + ed
   Our plans have _____.
6. foreign + er + s
   These people are _____.
7. frequent + ly
   It happens _____.
8. marine + sub
   The _____ is yellow.
9. noun + pro + s
   Those words are _____.
10. place + ed + mis
    I have _____ my keys.
11. set + re
    Ken _____ the alarm.
12. connect + ed + dis
    The phone was _____.
13. child + hood
    I had a happy _____.
14. like + able
    Pete is a _____ fellow.
15. reason + un + able
    Your request is _____.
16. suggest + ion
    Drop your _____ in the box.

17. way + sub
    We will ride the _____.
18. patient + im
    Must you be so _____?
19. appoint + dis + ed
    Are you _____?
20. law + out
    Jesse James was an _____.
21. threat + en
    That doesn't _____ me.
22. swim + ing
    I enjoy _____.
23. inform + ation
    This _____ is incorrect.
24. luck + un + y
    She is _____ at cards.
25. danger + ous
    The adventure sounds _____.
26. break + able
    The contents of this box are _____.
27. cover + dis + ed
    Columbus _____ America.
28. happy + un
    You look very _____.
29. change + ex + ed
    I _____ the hat.
30. rest + less
    The natives are _____.
31. faith + ful
    The dog is a _____ animal.
32. sleep + a
    The children are _____.

A Living Fossil

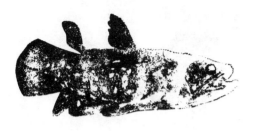

Study the spelling and meaning of each word. These words are used in today's story. Connect each word with its definition.

1. differs
2. evidence
3. existence
4. impression
5. prehistoric
6. prove

a. establish
b. before recorded history
c. varies
d. proof
e. imprint
f. the condition of being

Read the story carefully and remember the details.

Fossils are the only evidence we have about the prehistoric past. A fossil may be a preserved bone, skeleton, shell, or scale. It may only be an impression of a leaf or footprint.

Long ago there lived a fish called the coelacanth (see - la - kanth). This fish was one of the first creatures to have a backbone. Many fossils had been found to prove its existence, but scientists believed that the coelacanth was extinct.

Then in 1938 a fisherman in South Africa caught a coelacanth. Scientists were amazed. They put up rewards for more specimens, but fourteen years passed before another coelacanth was caught.

Today's coelacanth looks exactly like its ancestor, except it is bigger. It differs from other fish in that its fins are like paddles. It is a living fossil.

A. Underline the correct answers about today's story.

1. Fossils are evidence of the   (a) prehistoric past   (b) present   (c) future.
2. The coelacanth was a   (a) dinosaur   (b) snake   (c) fish.
3. The coelacanth was one of the first to have   (a) teeth   (b) a backbone   (c) feet.
4. The coelacanth's fins are like   (a) paddles   (b) wings   (c) claws.
5. Today's coelacanth is   (a) smaller   (b) larger   (c) shorter.

B. Reread the story and write the answers to these questions.

1. Give four examples of fossils.

_____

_____

_____

2. What did scientists believe about the coelacanth?

_____

_____

_____

3. What unique occurrence happened in 1938?

_____

_____

_____

4. How does the coelacanth differ from other fish?

_____

_____

_____

     Unit 93 cont'd

Using Synonyms

Synonyms are words that have similar meanings.

EXAMPLES: a. *halt*   *stop*
            b. *hike*   *walk*
            c. *rude*   *impolite*

A. Draw a line to connect each set of synonyms.

1. marvelous	stay	11. enormous	tell
2. labor	wonderful	12. recount	wander
3. bewilder	confuse	13. locate	find
4. remain	work	14. roam	obey
5. secure	hint	15. separate	gigantic
6. section	part	16. follow	sleepy
7. always	blunder	17. stupid	apart
8. clue	forever	18. journey	limb
9. mistake	safe	19. branch	trip
10. carry	transport	20. drowsy	dumb

B. Complete each sentence with a synonym of the word in the parentheses.

(delay)   1. We must ____*postpone*____ the game until Thursday.

(paused)   2. John _____ before entering the room.

(nuisance)   3. Kim's dog Alfie is a _____.

(glimpse)   4. I got a quick _____ at the President.

(important)   5. This letter contains a _____ clue.

(remember)   6. I don't _____ the man's name.

(greeted)   7. Ed stood at the door and _____ his guests.

(disappeared) 8. The ghost _____ before our eyes.

(smart)   9. Tina is an _____ girl.

(show)   10. We saw a _____ about World War II.

(perfect)   11. The diamond is _____.

(fake)   12. This money is _____.

(shy)   13. Jim was too _____ to ask her.

(pretend)   14. _____ you are on a deserted island.

(lost)   15. I have _____ my watch.

226

Lobsters

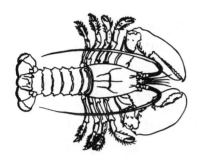

Study the spelling and meaning of each word. These words are used in today's story. Connect each word with its definition.

1. maturity	a. chiefly
2. mostly	b. reforms
3. regenerates	c. rarely
4. seashore	d. state of being fully grown
5. seldom	e. near the edge of the sea
6. shallow	f. not deep

Read the story carefully and remember the details.

Most people think lobsters are red, yet lobsters turn bright red only after they are cooked. In their seashore homes, lobsters are mostly green.

The lobster is covered with a thick, hard shell. This shell protects it from its enemies.

The lobster has five pairs of legs. Four pairs are used for walking. The fifth pair is used in getting food. The fifth pair has large claws at the end. One claw is larger. It is used to crush food. The smaller claw catches the food and holds it. If a claw is lost, the lobster regenerates a new one.

In the summer the lobsters stay in the shallow water near the coast. In winter they move out to deep water. The lobsters seldom reach full maturity because fishermen catch them for food.

A. Underline the correct answers about today's story.

1. In the sea, lobsters are mostly	(a) brown	(b) red	(c) green.
2. The lobster is protected by	(a) claws	(b) a stinger	(c) a shell.
3. The large claw is used for	(a) crushing	(b) holding	(c) catching.
4. In summer the lobster lives	(a) in deep water	(b) in shallow water	(c) out of water.
5. The lobster is valuable for its	(a) meat	(b) shell	(c) claws.

B. Reread the story and write the answers to these questions.

1. When does the lobster turn red?

_____

_____

_____

2. How many pairs of legs does the lobster have?

_____

_____

_____

3. What happens when a claw is lost?

_____

_____

_____

4. Where do lobsters go in the winter?

_____

_____

_____

Unit 94 cont'd ☞

Synonyms

 Underline the synonyms for each given word.

1. **academy**
   <u>school</u> <u>college</u> home business
2. **call**
   shout whisper listen cry yell
3. **possess**
   own sell have keep use
4. **accept**
   give take receive supply furnish
5. **book**
   novel dictionary album writer
6. **fat**
   skinny plump chubby thin
7. **elect**
   refuse choose select reject
8. **jump**
   hop leap bound stop sit
9. **command**
   order obey follow direct instruct
10. **valuable**
    precious worthless useless worthy
11. **disappear**
    vanish arrive come depart
12. **vacant**
    full empty unoccupied complete
13. **hint**
    clue suggestion reminder all
14. **remain**
    stay go leave survive linger
15. **necessary**
    unnecessary needed required
16. **doubt**
    disbelieve distrust trust suspect
17. **enormous**
    tiny huge small large
18. **among**
    away with included in separate
19. **smart**
    intelligent stupid dumb knowing
20. **battle**
    war fight argument peace
21. **easy**
    difficult simple hard effortless
22. **journey**
    trip tour work voyage
23. **dangerous**
    safe hazardous unsafe harmless
24. **error**
    truth mistake wrong right
25. **discover**
    lose find realize forget locate
26. **lucky**
    fortunate unlucky promising
27. **honest**
    dishonest sincere trustworthy
28. **job**
    occupation business pleasure work
29. **glad**
    unhappy content joyful discontent
30. **young**
    old aged youthful juvenile
31. **zero**
    none nothing many numerous
32. **write**
    sign copy erase print
33. **afraid**
    fearless scared frightened

The Magpie

Study the spelling and meaning of each word. These words are used in today's story. Connect each word with its definition.

1. magical ————————	a. supernatural
2. messy	b. abilities
3. object	c. like a thief
4. powers	d. untidy
5. suspected	e. thing; item
6. thievish	f. presumed

Read the story carefully and remember the details.

The magpie is a smaller cousin of the crow. It is best known for its noisy chattering and thievish habits.

The magpie will pick up any bright object and carry it off to the nest. The nest is huge, sometimes the size of a barrel. It is built in a tree. The nest is very messy, full of objects which the magpie has collected.

Long ago Europeans suspected the magpie of having magical powers. They connected the bird with witchcraft. The Europeans were so strong in their belief that they spit three times over their shoulders when they saw a magpie. By spitting, they hoped to prevent bad luck.

Of course, magpies aren't really able to perform magic. They are just noisy, messy birds.

A. Underline the correct answers about today's story.

1. Which word describes a magpie? (a) big (b) quiet (c) noisy
2. Which word does not describe its nest? (a) messy (b) huge (c) orderly
3. Europeans suspected the magpie of (a) magical powers (b) good deeds (c) stealing.
4. To ward off evil, the Europeans (a) carried feathers (b) wore charms (c) spit three times.
5. Magpies like to collect (a) silver (b) shiny objects (c) blue objects.

B. Reread the story and write the answers to these questions.

1. What bird is related to the magpie?

_____

_____

_____

2. How large can the nest of a magpie be?

_____

_____

_____

3. What does a magpie keep in his nest?

_____

_____

_____

4. Where are magpie's nests located?

_____

_____

_____

Unit 95 cont'd ☞

Identifying Synonyms

Synonyms are words with similar meanings.

A. Underline the synonym of each word.

1. begin . . . . <u>start</u>   complete
2. clue. . . . . solution   hint
3. came . . . . arrived   leave
4. choose. . . . . . elect   receive
5. simple . . . . . . difficult   easy
6. enough . . . . . plenty   needing
7. quiet. . . . . noisy   silent
8. cry. . . . . weep   laugh
9. fast . . . . speedy   slow
10. yard . . . . forest   lawn
11. small . . . . . . enormous   little
12. error . . . . answer   mistake
13. pretty . . . . plain   beautiful
14. close . . . . shut   open
15. fix . . . . destroy   repair

16. wrong. . . . . . . correct   incorrect
17. voyage . . . . . . walk   trip
18. see . . . . look   listen
19. market . . . . . farm   store
20. present . . . . . here   absent
21. walk . . . . hike   rest
22. create. . . . . . . buy   make
23. cover . . . . hide   show
24. result . . . . reason   end
25. snack . . . . meal   sleep
26. several. . . . . . few   many
27. evil . . . . bad   good
28. child. . . . . adult   baby
29. healthy. . . . . . well   sick
30. intelligent. . . smart   stupid

B. In each blank write a synonym of the underlined word.

1. a. I brought you a <u>present</u>.
   b. I brought you a ____*gift*____.
2. a. What is the <u>cost</u> of the car?
   b. What is the _____ of the car?
3. a. The <u>woman</u> bought a book.
   b. The _____ bought a book.
4. a. Your answers are <u>right</u>.
   b. Your answers are _____.
5. a. The test was <u>simple</u>.
   b. The test was _____.
6. a. The wind feels <u>cool</u>.
   b. The wind feels _____.
7. a. The boy was <u>hurt</u>.
   b. The boy was _____.
8. a. His room was <u>clean</u>.
   b. His room was _____.
9. a. My report is <u>finished</u>.
   b. My report is _____.
10. a. I will <u>keep</u> your share.
    b. I will _____ your share.

11. a. Sing a <u>song</u>.
    b. Sing a _____.
12. a. That's a <u>good</u> idea.
    b. That's an _____ idea.
13. a. We <u>ate</u> our dinner.
    b. We _____ our dinner.
14. a. Kim <u>talked</u> to the owner.
    b. Kim _____ to the owner.
15. a. He drives an <u>old</u> car.
    b. He drives a _____ car.
16. a. I <u>followed</u> my orders.
    b. I _____ my orders.
17. a. Come here <u>now</u>.
    b. Come here _____.
18. a. She was very <u>unkind</u>.
    b. She was very _____.
19. a. I <u>like</u> him.
    b. I _____ him.
20. a. Ben likes his <u>work</u>.
    b. Ben likes his _____.

Comprehension Check

(A) Add each word and suffix and write the new word.

1. shine + ing _____shining_____
2. care + less _____
3. late + est _____
4. snake + like _____
5. large + er _____

6. safe + ly _____
7. erase + er _____
8. skate + ing _____
9. store + ed _____
10. chose + en _____

11. write + er _____
12. migrate + ing _____
13. amuse + ment _____
14. drive + ing _____
15. example + s _____

(B) Write "p" if the word contains a prefix. Write "s" if it contains a suffix. Write "b" if it contains both.

__s__ 1. counts
____ 2. preview
____ 3. recalled
____ 4. prefix
____ 5. unfinished
____ 6. nests
____ 7. backward
____ 8. disliked
____ 9. unfriendly
____ 10. sweetly

____ 11. untold
____ 12. careful
____ 13. needlessly
____ 14. improper
____ 15. woven
____ 16. suddenly
____ 17. ahistorical
____ 18. turkeys
____ 19. tried
____ 20. linking

____ 21. rewording
____ 22. taller
____ 23. exit
____ 24. enclose
____ 25. reminded
____ 26. easily
____ 27. arts
____ 28. colorful
____ 29. unsuitable
____ 30. agreement

____ 31. submarine
____ 32. absentee
____ 33. useful
____ 34. lowest
____ 35. talking
____ 36. exchange
____ 37. incomplete
____ 38. woody
____ 39. sooner
____ 40. evenly

(C) Write a synonym for each word.

1. evidence _____proof_____
2. answer _____
3. collects _____
4. robber _____
5. close _____
6. below _____
7. get _____
8. troubles _____
9. suspected _____
10. messy _____

11. imprint _____
12. bigger _____
13. drowsy _____
14. different _____
15. recall _____
16. remain _____
17. discover _____
18. disappeared _____
19. seldom _____
20. silent _____

(D) Complete these sentences.

1. Lemmings are best known for _____migrations_____ .
2. Magpies are _____ birds.
3. The coelacanth is a _____ fossil.
4. Long ago books were written on _____ .
5. Lobsters turn _____ when cooked.
6. Libraries loan _____ .

7. A lemming is a _____ .
8. Fossils provide evidence of the _____ .
9. Lobsters are used for _____ .
10. Long ago magpies were associated with _____ .

Test 19 cont'd ☞

Comprehension Check (continued)

(E) Match these words and their definitions. These words appeared in the reading selections from units 91-95.

_a_ 1. common	___ 7. differs	a.	ordinary	g.	idea
___ 2. rodent	___ 8. evidence	b.	varies	h.	rarely
___ 3. collected	___ 9. mostly	c.	gnawing mammal	i.	supernatural
___ 4. concept	___ 10. seldom	d.	proof	j.	often
___ 5. frequently	___ 11. magical	e.	gathered	k.	presumed
___ 6. treasured	___ 12. suspected	f.	chiefly	l.	prized

(F) Underline the correct answers.

1.	Where do lemmings live?	(a) <u>arctic regions</u>	(b)	Africa
2.	Why do migrations happen?	(a) overpopulation	(b)	temper
3.	Why do most people visit libraries?	(a) borrow books	(b)	learn to read
4.	What is papyrus?	(a) paper	(b)	hardcover book
5.	Give an example of a fossil.	(a) shells	(b)	teeth
6.	What was believed about the coelacanth?	(a) extinct	(b)	dangerous
7.	What color are lobsters in the ocean?	(a) green	(b)	brown
8.	How are lobsters protected?	(a) stingers	(b)	shells
9.	Which word describes a magpie?	(a) noisy	(b)	quiet
10.	What do magpies collect?	(a) blue objects	(b)	shiny objects

Choose one of the following topics and write a paragraph.

(1) Magpies were once thought to have magical powers. What other animals are seen this way? Do you believe these superstitions? Why or why not?

(2) What is your favorite part of a library? Write about a library you have visited.

_____

_____

_____

_____

_____

_____

_____

_____

_____

_____

Man's First Home

Study the spelling and meaning of each word. These words are used in today's story. Connect each word with its definition.

1. discovered ———————— a. found
2. groups   b. supplied
3. huddled   c. crowded together
4. provided   d. numbers of individuals
5. searching   e. thing that protects
6. shelter   f. looking

Read the story carefully and remember the details.

Long ago there were no houses on the earth. People roamed around the land searching for food. At night many sought the shelter of the trees. Some huddled in groups on the ground. People were not protected from the weather.

It is not known when people first began to live in caves, their first real homes. Although the caves were damp and cold, they provided people with some protection from the rains and winds.

When fire was discovered, the caves became homes. The fire provided light. It also provided heat. People began to stay longer in one place. Each night they returned home to their caves. The caves provided protection from the weather and from wild animals.

A. Underline the correct answers about today's story.

1. People roamed the land searching for   (a) food   (b) shelter   (c) water.
2. The first caves protected man from   (a) the sun   (b) the weather   (c) enemies.
3. What made caves into homes?   (a) light   (b) running water   (c) fire
4. Fires provided   (a) weapons   (b) heat   (c) power.
5. Man's first home was a   (a) cave   (b) tent   (c) hut.

B. Reread the story and write the answers to these questions.

1. What sheltered people before there were any real homes?

_____

_____

_____

2. What two things did fire provide?

_____

_____

_____

3. Besides the weather, what protection did caves provide?

_____

_____

_____

4. Where did early groups huddle?

_____

_____

_____

Unit 96 cont'd ☞

Antonyms

A. Write an antonym for each word.

1. hot ___cold___
2. tall _____
3. dry _____
4. little _____
5. in _____
6. up _____
7. left _____
8. good _____
9. far _____
10. pretty _____

11. yes _____
12. soft _____
13. lose _____
14. happy _____
15. before _____
16. add _____
17. all _____
18. give _____
19. push _____
20. dark _____

21. come _____
22. dirty _____
23. high _____
24. over _____
25. new _____
26. fat _____
27. sell _____
28. few _____
29. sharp _____
30. easy _____

31. open _____
32. first _____
33. above _____
34. on _____
35. fast _____
36. late _____
37. less _____
38. narrow _____
39. stop _____
40. front _____

B. Complete each sentence by writing an antonym of the word in parentheses.

(**top**) 1. The price is on the ___bottom___.

(**never**) 2. I _____ do my homework.

(**end**) 3. She missed the _____.

(**smile**) 4. Don't _____ so much.

(**full**) 5. My glass is _____.

(**sour**) 6. The grapes are _____.

(**remember**) 7. Did you _____ it?

(**true**) 8. The statement is _____.

(**summer**) 9. They fly south for the _____.

(**friend**) 10. He is the _____.

(**asleep**) 11. Is your father _____?

(**with**) 12. Don't come _____ Roy.

(**old**) 13. I want a _____ car.

(**useful**) 14. This pen is _____.

(**polite**) 15. Don't be _____.

(**guessed**) 16. Dad _____ the truth.

(**short**) 17. We need a _____ rope.

(**absent**) 18. How many are _____?

(**right**) 19. These answers are _____.

(**alike**) 20. These are _____.

(**arrive**) 21. We will _____ on the 20th.

(**give**) 22. Did you _____ an invitation?

(**noisily**) 23. Everyone left _____.

(**ask**) 24. Nick will _____ the question.

(**start**) 25. _____ your dinner.

(**forward**) 26. Step _____.

(**lead**) 27. _____ me.

(**good-bye**) 28. Say _____.

(**enjoy**) 29. I _____ work.

(**brave**) 30. John is _____.

The Maned Wolf **Unit 97**

Study the spelling and meaning of each word. These words are used in today's story. Connect each word with its definition.

1. advance
2. except
3. native
4. shrunk
5. shy
6. wary

a. very cautious
b. bashful; timid
c. forward movement
d. born in a particular place
e. became smaller
f. leaving out

Read the story carefully and remember the details.

The maned wolf is often called a "fox on stilts." The animal looks very much like a fox, but it has extremely long legs.

The maned wolf is native to South America. It is a creature of the plains. Shy and wary, the maned wolf lives in remote areas. Except at mating time, the maned wolf lives alone.

At night the animal becomes active. It hunts guinea pigs, birds, lizards, and frogs. The maned wolf also eats fruits and even sugar cane.

Little is known about the maned wolf's habits. It prefers to stay away from people, its major enemies. The advance of civilization has shrunk the animal's habitat. The maned wolf is still rarely seen.

A. Underline the correct answers about today's story.

1. The maned wolf resembles a   (a) fox   (b) lion   (c) domestic dog.
2. The maned wolf is native to   (a) Africa   (b) Australia   (c) South America.
3. The maned wolf lives   (a) alone   (b) in pairs   (c) in packs.
4. The animal is active   (a) at night   (b) at dawn   (c) in the daytime.
5. The maned wolf's chief enemy is   (a) a bird of prey   (b) people   (c) weather.

B. Reread the story and write the answers to these questions.

1. How does the wolf react to people?

_____

_____

_____

2. When is the wolf not alone?

_____

_____

_____

3. What does the wolf hunt?

_____

_____

_____

4. What has civilization done to the wolf?

_____

_____

_____

Unit 97 cont'd 🖝

Using Antonyms

A. Complete each sentence by writing the antonym of the word in parentheses.

(present)   1. Bob was _**absent**_ today.

(safe)   2. It's _____ to go on.

(all)   3. _____ of us wanted to go.

(answer)   4. What was your _____?

(quiet)   5. It's so _____ in here.

(thick)   6. I'd like a _____ slice.

(wrong)   7. He was _____.

(open)   8. Please _____ the door.

(escaped)   9. Two prisoners were _____.

(greedy)   10. That was a _____ offer.

(weak)   11. He isn't _____ enough.

(careful)   12. Don't be _____.

(tiny)   13. The dinosaur was _____.

(unknown)   14. He is a _____ actor.

(day)   15. It rained last _____.

(unpleasant)   16. It was a _____ evening.

(backward)   17. Come _____.

(lead)   18. She will _____ us.

(gain)   19. I can't _____.

(cry)   20. Don't _____ at me.

(possible)   21. It seems _____.

(cooked)   22. The meat was _____.

(give)   23. You will _____ a copy.

(remember)   24. Don't _____ to call.

(stupid)   25. That was a _____ move.

(dishonest)   26. I want an _____ answer.

(useful)   27. It's _____.

(wide)   28. That is a _____ bridge.

(passed)   29. I _____ the math test.

(unlock)   30. _____ the door.

B. Match the antonyms.

_q_   1. borrow

___   2. purchase

___   3. heavy

___   4. fat

___   5. fearless

___   6. valuable

___   7. difficult

___   8. lucky

___   9. disappear

___   10. uncover

___   11. slowly

___   12. yours

___   13. sweet

___   14. true

___   15. normal

___   16. sorrow

___   17. now

___   18. frozen

___   19. clear

___   20. straight

a. sour

b. afraid

c. easy

d. later

e. mine

f. abnormal

g. light

h. appear

i. skinny

j. foggy

k. melted

l. worthless

m. sell

n. quickly

o. crooked

p. happiness

q. lend

r. cover

s. false

t. unlucky

Mars

Study the spelling and meaning of each word. These words are used in today's story. Connect each word with its definition.

1. agree
2. argument
3. guesses
4. other
5. probably
6. scientists

a. more than likely
b. ones who study facts
c. ones left
d. to be alike or similar
e. opinions with little evidence
f. debate

Read the story carefully and remember the details.

We know more about the planet Mars than any other planet in our solar system. Mars looks like a reddish star. Much of its surface is a dull red. Mars is a smaller planet than the earth.

Most scientists agree that Mars does have an atmosphere. There is probably little oxygen on Mars. There may be some water. There is less gravity on Mars. What weighs 100 pounds on the earth would weigh 40 pounds on Mars.

The days on Mars are about the same length as those on earth. The years on Mars are 687 days each.

There is much argument about what Mars is really like. Many scientists know how to make good guesses. No one knows for sure.

A. Underline the correct answers about today's story.

1. Mars is a   (a) star   (b) planet   (c) country.
2. Compared to the earth, Mars is   (a) smaller   (b) larger   (c) the same size.
3. On Mars, objects   (a) are bigger   (b) are heavier   (c) weigh less.
4. Compared to the earth, a year on Mars is   (a) the same   (b) longer   (c) shorter.
5. What color is Mars?   (a) red   (b) yellow   (c) black

B. Reread the story and write the answers to these questions.

1. Besides earth, what planet do we know the most about?

_____

_____

_____

2. Is Mars larger or smaller than earth?

_____

_____

_____

3. How long is a year on Mars?

_____

_____

_____

4. How much would something weigh on Mars that weighed 100 pounds on earth?

_____

_____

_____

Unit 98 cont'd ☛

Synonyms and Antonyms

Synonyms are words with similar meanings. Antonyms are words with opposite meanings.

A. Write a synonym for each word.

1. postpone __*delay*__
2. liberty _____
3. remedy _____
4. battle _____
5. fret _____

6. bashful _____
7. misplace _____
8. similar _____
9. notice _____
10. evidence _____

11. distrust _____
12. find _____
13. youth _____
14. brutal _____
15. comfortable _____

B. Write an antonym for each word.

1. follower __*leader*__
2. agree _____
3. complete _____
4. borrow _____
5. able _____

6. defeat _____
7. equal _____
8. future _____
9. chaos _____
10. different _____

11. always _____
12. innocent _____
13. shrink _____
14. enter _____
15. smile _____

C. Write "1" if the set of words is synonyms. Write "2" if the set of words is antonyms.

__1__ 1. obstinate   stubborn
_____ 2. problem   solution
_____ 3. importance   value
_____ 4. tomorrow   yesterday
_____ 5. recall   remember
_____ 6. addition   subtraction
_____ 7. combine   join
_____ 8. amusement   entertainment
_____ 9. organized   disorganized

_____ 10. counterfeit   real
_____ 11. blunder   mistake
_____ 12. expensive   cheap
_____ 13. create   destroy
_____ 14. cautious   careful
_____ 15. penalty   punishment
_____ 16. thirst   quench
_____ 17. united   together
_____ 18. forgive   pardon

Martens

Study the spelling and meaning of each word. These words are used in today's story. Connect each word with its definition.

1. catches   a. sturdy
2. favorite   b. desires over something else
3. prefers   c. most preferred
4. rugged   d. coldest season
5. travel   e. traps
6. winter   f. go from one place to another

Read the story carefully and remember the details.

Like other members of the weasel family, the marten is a small animal with a long body and short legs.

The marten is a rugged forest animal. It likes to travel in the treetops. There it catches its favorite prey, the red squirrel. The red squirrel makes up only a small part of the marten's diet. Also included are other small rodents, birds, and bird eggs. The marten prefers to catch wild prey.

The marten hunts day and night. It is active the year round. It does not hibernate or migrate in the winter. It does, however, stick more closely to the ground during the winter months.

The marten dislikes water and rarely catches its food from a stream. It does like to sunbathe. The animal is rarely seen.

A. Underline the correct answers about today's story.

1. Where does the marten live?	(a) forest	(b) desert	(c) mountains
2. What is its favorite prey?	(a) birds	(b) frogs	(c) red squirrels
3. When is the marten active?	(a) winter	(b) year round	(c) summer
4. In winter the marten	(a) hibernates	(b) migrates	(c) stays closer to the ground.
5. The marten dislikes	(a) water	(b) the sun	(c) the cold.

B. Reread the story and write the answers to these questions.

1. Describe the marten's appearance.

_____

_____

_____

2. Where does the marten travel?

_____

_____

_____

3. What does the marten not do during the winter?

_____

_____

_____

4. How often is the marten seen?

_____

_____

_____

Unit 99 cont'd ☛

Distinguishing Between Antonyms and Synonyms

Antonyms are words with opposite meanings.

EXAMPLES: a. win   lose
           b. over   under

Synonyms are words with similar meanings.

EXAMPLES: a. sack   bag
           b. invite   ask

A. Write an antonym for each word.

1. friend ___enemy___
2. victor _____
3. birth _____
4. offer _____
5. inner _____

6. short _____
7. borrow _____
8. pretty _____
9. soft _____
10. funny _____

11. even _____
12. real _____
13. finish _____
14. gain _____
15. love _____

B. Write a synonym for each word.

1. build ___construct___
2. agenda _____
3. foolish _____
4. enough _____
5. found _____

6. suggestion _____
7. place _____
8. nearly _____
9. hurt _____
10. jump _____

11. rival _____
12. paint _____
13. pledge _____
14. fast _____
15. organization _____

C. Write "a" for antonyms and "s" for synonyms.

___a___ 1. vacant   occupied
_____ 2. own   possess
_____ 3. visible   invisible
_____ 4. happiness   pleasure
_____ 5. familiar   unknown
_____ 6. wisdom   knowledge
_____ 7. needless   necessary
_____ 8. nobody   everybody
_____ 9. history   past
_____ 10. fragment   part
_____ 11. presently   today
_____ 12. worn   new

_____ 13. precise   exact
_____ 14. inform   tell
_____ 15. shy   bold
_____ 16. foreign   unknown
_____ 17. surprising expected
_____ 18. pardon   excuse
_____ 19. steady   shakey
_____ 20. welcome   unwanted
_____ 21. outline   plan
_____ 22. ruin   destroy
_____ 23. male   man
_____ 24. useful   useless

The Mayas

Study the spelling and meaning of each word. These words are used in today's story. Connect each word with its definition.

1. civilized ————————— a. refined
2. devised   b. significant
3. guided   c. worked out
4. important   d. learned about
5. religion   e. service and worship of something
6. studied   f. led

Read the story carefully and remember the details.

Long ago the Mayas inhabited the land in the Caribbean. They were a highly civilized people. Most were farmers.

To these people religion was very important. The priests ruled the people. Priests were intelligent. They guided the people wisely.

One of the greatest developments of the Mayas was a system to keep track of time. The priests studied the movements of the sun, moon, stars, and planets. From these movements the priests devised a very accurate calendar.

For some unknown reason the Mayan civilization came to an abrupt end. Most of the people abandoned their great cities. The few who stayed soon forgot their heritage. No one really knows what happened.

A. Underline the correct answers about today's story.

1. Most of the Mayas were   (a) warriors   (b) farmers   (c) fishermen.
2. What did the Mayas consider important? (a) religion   (b) family   (c) money
3. Who ruled the people?   (a) the priests (b) gods   (c) medicine men
4. The priests devised an accurate (a) ruler   (b) calendar   (c) watch.
5. What caused the empire to end?   (a) disease   (b) war   (c) No one knows.

B. Reread the story and write the answers to these questions.

1. Where did the Mayas live?

_____

_____

2. What finally happened to the empire?

_____

_____

_____

3. What was one of their greatest developments?

_____

_____

_____

4. What did the priests study?

_____

_____

Unit 100 cont'd ☞

Homonyms

✳ Underline the correct sentences.

EXAMPLE: **a. _Letters are written on stationery._**
             b. _Letters are written on stationary._

1. a. Did you here anything?
   b. Did you hear anything?
2. a. What is the some of 2 + 2?
   b. What is the sum of 2 + 2?
3. a. She is heir to the throne.
   b. She is air to the throne.
4. a. I need two volunteers.
   b. I need to volunteers.
5. a. The store is having a sail.
   b. The store is having a sale.
6. a. You have big feat.
   b. You have big feet.
7. a. Draw a straight line.
   b. Draw a strait line.
8. a. I will earn the money.
   b. I will urn the money.
9. a. Wait in the haul.
   b. Wait in the hall.
10. a. They're arriving at noon.
    b. There arriving at noon.
11. a. The letter is for me.
    b. The letter is four me.
12. a. My ant is a truck driver.
    b. My aunt is a truck driver.
13. a. We have bin looking for you.
    b. We have been looking for you.
14. a. The birds flew away.
    b. The birds flue away.
15. a. They will fight a dual.
    b. They will fight a duel.
16. a. What did you buy?
    b. What did you bye?
17. a. We will wear our uniforms.
    b. We will ware our uniforms.

18. a. What's for desert?
    b. What's for dessert?
19. a. Mrs. Coggins is our principal.
    b. Mrs. Coggins is our principle.
20. a. We had stake for dinner.
    b. We had steak for dinner.
21. a. I bought a pair of shoes.
    b. I bought a pare of shoes.
22. a. My dog has flees.
    b. My dog has fleas.
23. a. I stepped in a whole.
    b. I stepped in a hole.
24. a. A female deer is a doe.
    b. A female deer is a dough.
25. a. What root did you take?
    b. What route did you take?
26. a. The plain landed safely.
    b. The plane landed safely.
27. a. I had a grate time.
    b. I had a great time.
28. a. The bear chased us.
    b. The bare chased us.
29. a. Steve was too weak.
    b. Steve was too week.
30. a. I will slay the dragon.
    b. I will sleigh the dragon.
31. a. Do you need anything?
    b. Do you knead anything?
32. a. Comb your hair.
    b. Comb your hare.
33. a. He's in the forth grade.
    b. He's in the fourth grade.

Comprehension Check

Ⓐ Connect the antonyms.

1. enter	false	11. none	finish	21. backward	left
2. true	then	12. start	all	22. enjoy	know
3. fat	up	13. without	ugly	23. rude	forward
4. down	thin	14. pretty	with	24. guess	dislike
5. now	exit	15. winter	summer	25. right	polite
6. arrive	narrow	16. clean	after	26. give	receive
7. slowly	leave	17. strong	weak	27. noisy	close
8. front	add	18. few	many	28. absent	quiet
9. wide	back	19. early	dirty	29. open	present
10. subtract	quickly	20. before	late	30. night	day

Ⓑ Write an antonym for each word.

1. rich	_poor_	6. push	_____	11. future	_____
2. even	_____	7. cry	_____	12. always	_____
3. below	_____	8. friend	_____	13. bright	_____
4. new	_____	9. win	_____	14. frown	_____
5. truth	_____	10. inner	_____	15. shallow	_____

Ⓒ Underline the sets which are antonyms.

1. yes . . . no
2. borrow . . . loan
3. scare . . . frighten
4. first . . . last
5. nervous . . . calm

6. accept . . . take
7. victor . . . loser
8. nothing . . . everything
9. beginning . . . end
10. watch . . . observe

11. exact . . . precise
12. known . . . unknown
13. invite . . . ask
14. dangerous . . . safe
15. fragment . . . whole

Ⓓ Write a homonym for each word.

1. fourth	_forth_	6. dessert	_____	11. urn	_____
2. bin	_____	7. four	_____	12. weak	_____
3. dough	_____	8. ware	_____	13. sale	_____
4. pear	_____	9. sum	_____	14. stake	_____
5. aunt	_____	10. hear	_____	15. route	_____

Ⓔ Complete these sentences.

1. The maned wolf is called a "fox on _stilts_ ."
2. Mars is the red _____ .
3. People's first real homes were _____ .
4. Most Mayans were _____ .

5. _____ provided homes with light and heat.
6. The maned wolf is rarely _____ .
7. Mars is _____ than the earth.
8. Martens are members of the _____ family.

Test 20 cont'd ☞

Comprehension Check (continued)

(F) Match these words and their definitions. These words appeared in the reading selections from units 96-100.

_f_ 1. discovered	___ 7. favorite	a. noteworthy	g. led
___ 2. provided	___ 8. prefers	b. likely	h. made smaller
___ 3. shrunk	___ 9. guided	c. on guard; cautious	i. desires over something else
___ 4. wary	___ 10. important	d. debate	j. belief
___ 5. argument	___ 11. religion	e. furnished	k. most preferred
___ 6. probably	___ 12. studied	f. found	l. learned about

(G) Underline the correct answers.

1. What did caves provide?	(a) <u>protection</u>	(b) food
2. What made caves into homes?	(a) fire	(b) water
3. What does the maned wolf resemble?	(a) dog	(b) fox
4. Where did the maned wolf originate?	(a) Canada	(b) South America
5. Compare Mars to earth.	(a) smaller	(b) larger
6. How long is a year on Mars?	(a) 687 days	(b) 366 days
7. Where does the marten live?	(a) forest	(b) mountains
8. What is the marten's favorite prey?	(a) red squirrels	(b) cats
9. What did the Mayas consider important?	(a) family	(b) religion
10. What caused the Mayan empire to end?	(a) war	(b) No one knows.

Choose one of the following topics and write a paragraph.

(1) Caves were once a type of home. How many types of homes can you describe? Which do you prefer? Why?

(2) Earth is but one planet in the solar system. If you could live on another planet, which would you choose? Why?

_____
_____
_____
_____
_____
_____
_____
_____
_____
_____

The Mink

Study the spelling and meaning of each word. These words are used in today's story. Connect each word with its definition.

1. attack
2. considered
3. expensive
4. fighter
5. valuable
6. worst

a. thought to be
b. one that fights
c. of considerable worth
d. most harmful
e. set upon with force
f. costly

Read the story carefully and remember the details.

The mink is an active little animal that is a member of the weasel family. Although it is usually nocturnal, the mink is active both day and night. The mink is at home both in the forest and in the water. Its home is called a den.

The mink eats small game, birds, and fish. It is a fierce and deadly fighter. The mink will attack animals that are larger than itself.

People are the mink's worst enemy. The mink's fur is very valuable. It is used for making ladies' fur coats. Most of the fur now used in making coats comes from minks which are raised on mink ranches. A mink coat is very expensive and considered a luxury.

A. Underline the correct answers about today's story.

1. To which family does the
   mink belong?   (a) dog   (b) cat   (c) weasel
2. The mink is most active   (a) during the day (b) in the morning (c) at night.
3. Who is the mink's worst enemy?   (a) people   (b) lion   (c) snake
4. Which word describes a mink?   (a) weak   (b) fierce   (c) friendly
5. A mink coat is a   (a) requirement   (b) luxury   (c) necessity.

B. Reread the story and write the answers to these questions.

1. What two places is the mink at home?

   _____

   _____

   _____

2. What is a mink's home called?

   _____

   _____

3. Where are minks raised?

   _____

   _____

   _____

4. Who will the mink attack?

   _____

   _____

   _____

Unit 101 cont'd ☞

Using Homonyms

Homonyms are words that sound alike.

 Complete each sentence by writing the correct homonym in the blank.

1. weak — week
   a. The illness made him ___weak___.
   b. Seven days make one ___week___.

2. write — right
   a. _____ your answer on the back.
   b. Hold out your _____ hand.

3. hear — here
   a. Did you _____ anything?
   b. Come _____.

4. see — sea
   a. The _____ is calm.
   b. I can _____ you.

5. ate — eight
   a. She has _____ brothers.
   b. Rick _____ my pear.

6. weight — wait
   a. What is your correct _____?
   b. _____ for me outside.

7. sale — sail
   a. The store is having a _____.
   b. The ship will _____ tomorrow.

8. flour — flower
   a. The red _____ is a rose.
   b. May I borrow some _____?

9. road — rode
   a. The _____ was repaired.
   b. Jack _____ my horse.

10. pail — pale
    a. You look _____.
    b. He carried the _____ of water.

11. meet — meat
    a. The _____ is still frozen.
    b. Did you _____ my mother?

12. cent — sent
    a. A penny is one _____.
    b. I _____ him a card.

13. would — wood
    a. _____ you talk to her?
    b. I will cut the _____.

14. knows — nose
    a. Sharon _____ about the plan.
    b. Your _____ is red.

15. for — four
    a. Alex has _____ bicycles.
    b. This letter is _____ you.

16. won — one
    a. Andy _____ the game.
    b. Give her _____ of your pictures.

17. beats — beets
    a. I like _____.
    b. Fran always _____ me home.

18. mail — male
    a. Was there any _____?
    b. There is only one _____ member.

19. plain — plane
    a. The _____ landed safely.
    b. It was wrapped in a _____ box.

20. sum — some
    a. I need _____ money.
    b. The _____ is ten.

21. haul — hall
    a. I'll wait in the _____.
    b. Ben will _____ the supplies.

22. know — no
    a. Don't you _____ me?
    b. My answer is _____.

23. so — sew
    a. I can't _____.
    b. Don't eat _____ fast.

24. red — read
    a. Nancy _____ my story.
    b. I bought a _____ car.

The Mockingbird

Study the spelling and meaning of each word. These words are used in today's story. Connect each word with its definition.

1. afraid
2. against
3. habit
4. imitate
5. intruder
6. receives

a. usual behavior
b. trespasser
c. as defense from
d. gets
e. showing fear
f. copy

Read the story carefully and remember the details.

The mockingbird has one of the best singing voices in the bird world. The bird receives its name from its habit of mimicking the songs of other birds. It can imitate other songbirds, chickens, turkeys, cats, dogs, and even odd noises.

The mockingbird's own song is beautiful. It is a woodland bird. The mockingbird can become a fierce fighter. It will defend its nest against any intruder. It has even been known to attack people who have gotten too close.

The mockingbird, however, is usually friendly with people. Some have built their nests close to houses. They are not afraid of people.

A. Underline the correct answers about today's story.

1. The mockingbird is known for its | (a) nesting habits | (b) fighting | (c) imitations.
2. The bird's own song is | (a) plain | (b) beautiful | (c) ordinary.
3. Where do mockingbirds usually live? | (a) cities | (b) woods | (c) cages
4. Toward humans mockingbirds are | (a) friendly | (b) dangerous | (c) enemies.
5. An intruder is | (a) a neighbor | (b) a friend | (c) an unwelcome visitor.

B. Reread the story and write the answers to these questions.

1. Name two things a mockingbird can mimic.

_____

_____

_____

2. How do mockingbird's feel about people?

_____

_____

3. Where have some mockingbirds built their nests?

_____

_____

_____

4. Who does the mockingbird protect its nest against?

_____

_____

_____

Unit 102 cont'd ☞

Choosing the Correct Homonym

 Complete each sentence with the correct homonym.

1. aloud . . . allowed
   a. Read the poem ___*aloud*___.
   b. We were not ___*allowed*___ to talk.

2. course . . . coarse
   a. This material feels _____.
   b. What _____ do you plan to take?

3. thrown . . . throne
   a. The king sat on his _____.
   b. He was _____ into the pool.

4. root . . . route
   a. Don't touch the _____ of the plant.
   b. What _____ should we take home?

5. urn . . . earn
   a. You broke the _____.
   b. I will _____ the money.

6. sail . . . sale
   a. The store is having a _____.
   b. The ship will _____ tomorrow.

7. flee . . . flea
   a. He tried to _____.
   b. I saw a _____.

8. minor . . . miner
   a. He is a coal _____.
   b. The repairs were _____.

9. dough . . . doe
   a. A _____ is a female deer.
   b. I watched the _____ rise.

10. wave . . . waive
    a. _____ good-bye.
    b. He will _____ the charges.

11. eye . . . aye
    a. If you agree, say _____.
    b. She has a black _____.

12. their . . . there
    a. They have _____ own cars.
    b. They live over _____.

13. affect . . . effect
    a. It will not _____ your grade.
    b. What _____ did that have?

14. principle . . . principal
    a. Mr. Barton is our _____.
    b. It's against his _____.

15. capitol . . . capital
    a. What is the _____ of Texas?
    b. The Senate meets at the _____.

16. colonel . . . kernel
    a. He is a retired _____.
    b. This is a _____ of corn.

17. stationery . . . stationary
    a. The letter was written on blue _____.
    b. These objects are _____.

18. isle . . . aisle
    a. Walk down the _____ slowly.
    b. We visited the _____ of Wight.

19. duel . . . dual
    a. They will fight a _____.
    b. The car had _____ exhausts.

20. council . . . counsel
    a. Do you need legal _____?
    b. The _____ met today.

21. kill . . . kiln
    a. Did you _____ the spider?
    b. Put the pottery in the _____.

22. sleigh . . . slay
    a. We are going on a _____ ride.
    b. The prince will _____ the dragon.

23. rain . . . reign
    a. It will _____ tomorrow.
    b. She will _____ over the ceremonies.

24. need . . . knead
    a. I watched her _____ the dough.
    b. Do you _____ any help?

25. been . . . bin
    a. I have _____ working.
    b. Put this in the red _____.

The Monarch Butterfly

Study the spelling and meaning of each word. These words are used in today's story. Connect each word with its definition.

1. hatch
2. migrates
3. shapes
4. surround
5. unlike
6. wherein

a. forms
b. close on all sides
c. produce from eggs
d. different
e. in which
f. moves from one place to another

Read the story carefully and remember the details.

Butterflies come in many shapes, sizes, and colors. The king of the butterflies is the monarch butterfly. It is not the biggest butterfly, but it is certainly one of the most beautiful. The wings are dark orange with black stripes.

Unlike other butterflies, the monarch migrates south for the winter. It flies in flocks. In spring the monarch returns north. The monarch butterfly travels hundreds of miles.

The female monarch lays her eggs on milkweed leaves. The eggs hatch into caterpillars which feed on the milkweed leaves. The caterpillars attach themselves to the underside of the leaves. They surround themselves with a shell wherein they turn into butterflies. The shells break and out come the beautiful butterflies. Their wings are wet. The butterflies unfold their wings and dry them in the sun. Then they fly away.

A. Underline the correct answers about today's story.

1. The monarch butterfly is the	(a) biggest	(b) king	(c) most beautiful.
2. In winter the monarch	(a) dies	(b) lays eggs	(c) flies south.
3. The female lays her eggs	(a) on the water	(b) on the ground	(c) on milkweed leaves.
4. The eggs hatch into	(a) caterpillars	(b) butterflies	(c) flies.
5. Unlike other butterflies, the monarch	(a) migrates	(b) eats meat	(c) swims.

B. Reread the story and write the answers to these questions.

1. What color is the monarch butterfly?

_____
_____
_____

2. What does the monarch do in the spring?

_____
_____
_____

3. What do caterpillars do?

_____
_____
_____

4. What surrounds a caterpillar?

_____
_____
_____

Unit 103 cont'd 👉

Using "A" and "An"

A. Write "a" or "an" before each word.

EXAMPLES: __a__ secret   __an__ excuse

1. ____ television
2. ____ afternoon
3. ____ question
4. ____ onion
5. ____ joke
6. ____ movie
7. ____ cabin
8. ____ outline
9. ____ ocean
10. ____ shoe
11. ____ city
12. ____ adventure
13. ____ chair
14. ____ friend
15. ____ umbrella

16. ____ accident
17. ____ uncle
18. ____ post office
19. ____ mistake
20. ____ owl
21. ____ holiday
22. ____ key
23. ____ education
24. ____ business
25. ____ fact
26. ____ ostrich
27. ____ battle
28. ____ office
29. ____ potato
30. ____ echo

31. ____ newspaper
32. ____ vacation
33. ____ adult
34. ____ exercise
35. ____ ghost
36. ____ example
37. ____ reason
38. ____ opinion
39. ____ minute
40. ____ airport
41. ____ career
42. ____ daughter
43. ____ piano
44. ____ crowd
45. ____ person

46. ____ castle
47. ____ enemy
48. ____ reward
49. ____ elm tree
50. ____ surprise
51. ____ blanket
52. ____ idea
53. ____ chance
54. ____ eagle
55. ____ monster
56. ____ egg
57. ____ answer
58. ____ radio
59. ____ elephant
60. ____ sentence

B. Underline the sentences which have used "a" and "an" correctly.

EXAMPLES: *I own an airplane.*   *I own a airplane.*

1. May I have a cookie?
2. She is a important person.
3. Do you have a question?
4. You made an excellent choice.
5. Betty is reading an book.
6. I hear a echo.
7. We bought an old car.
8. Wait an minute.
9. I made a mistake.
10. Lynn was eating a orange.
11. A ostrich chased me!
12. I have a test today.
13. That was an interesting story.
14. You will need an umbrella.
15. Here is a ink pen.
16. An dog bit me.
17. It was a surprise.
18. I saw an elephant.
19. Tell me an secret.
20. Everyone needs an education.

Money

Study the spelling and meaning of each word. These words are used in today's story. Connect each word with its definition.

1. adopted —————— a. accepted
2. bartered   b. traded by exchange
3. objects   c. things owned
4. possessions   d. exchanged
5. traded   e. things
6. valuable   f. having worth

Read the story carefully and remember the details.

Long ago there was no money. It was not needed. If someone had something you wanted, you traded one of your possessions for it.

This trading was called bartering. Most often people traded animals such as cows, pigs, sheep, and goats. Sometimes people traded grain or corn. Salt was also valuable in trade. Even shells and tools were used.

Eventually people began to use metals as money. The metals had to be weighed to determine their value. To make things easier, the metals were marked for their value. They were called coins.

The use of coins soon was adopted by most countries in the world. Some places, however, still bartered. They used strange objects for trade. For example, a tribe in Africa considered the hair from an elephant's tail as very valuable. It was often used in trade.

A. **Underline the correct answers about today's story.**

1. Bartering is	(a) trading	(b) borrowing	(c) loaning.
2. Before metals were used, they had to be	(a) melted	(b) polished	(c) weighed.
3. Marked metals were called	(a) bills	(b) coins	(c) jewels.
4. A tribe in Africa used	(a) teeth	(b) trees	(c) elephant's hair.
5. Which items were used for trade?	(a) cows	(b) salt	(c) shells

B. **Reread the story and write the answers to these questions.**

1. What was not in existence long ago?

_____

_____

_____

2. What did you do if someone had something you wanted?

_____

_____

_____

3. How was the determining of the value of money made easier?

_____

_____

_____

4. Did all countries use money?

_____

_____

_____

Unit 104 cont'd ☞

"A" or "An"

Both "a" and "an" are indefinite articles.

"A" is used before words which begin with consonant sounds.

"An" is used before words which begin with vowel sounds.

A. Write "a" or "an" in each blank to complete each sentence.

EXAMPLES: a. *Jake is a stubborn boy.*

b. *He bought an expensive gift.*

1. Karen has _____ toothache.
2. I've never ridden in _____ elevator.
3. She wore _____ diamond necklace.
4. _____ letter came for you today.
5. He is _____ opera singer.
6. Hand me _____ dictionary.
7. We have _____ visitor.
8. I found _____ empty box.
9. Wes received _____ invitation.
10. That was _____ easy test.
11. He was eating _____ chocolate bar.
12. May I have _____ extra pencil?
13. Draw _____ square.
14. We went to _____ costume party.
15. You are _____ mischievous brat!
16. It was _____ unusual request.
17. I've always wanted _____ horse.
18. We must find _____ solution.
19. Six is _____ even number.
20. This is _____ very heavy box.
21. Bring me _____ newspaper.
22. The monkey was eating _____ apple.
23. We stayed in _____ hotel.
24. _____ officer went with us.
25. I forgot to wear _____ hat.

26. We visited _____ amusement park.
27. My aunt is _____ lawyer.
28. Louis has _____ bad temper.
29. That is _____ artificial flower.
30. I need _____ leather belt.
31. Do you have _____ problem?
32. George works in _____ museum.
33. He became _____ famous artist.
34. Can you play _____ instrument?
35. Bob is _____ wizard at math.
36. The man will make _____ fortune.
37. Let's eat _____ sandwich.
38. Do I have _____ choice?
39. It was _____ ridiculous story.
40. Have you seen _____ eclipse?
41. Roy is taking _____ afternoon nap.
42. The kitten is _____ year old.
43. I need _____ new notebook.
44. Do you have _____ suggestion?
45. The shirt has _____ torn pocket.
46. The dentist had to pull _____ tooth.
47. The bird is building _____ nest.
48. The woman told _____ old story.
49. I rode on _____ elephant.
50. Suddenly there was _____ explosion.

B. Write ten sentences using "a" and ten sentences using "an."

The Mongoose

Study the spelling and meaning of each word. These words are used in today's story. Connect each word with its definition.

1. captivity	a. how one is seen
2. famous	b. confinement
3. forbidden	c. well known
4. introduced	d. bothers or annoys
5. reputation	e. brought to
6. teases	f. not allowed

Read the story carefully and remember the details.

The mongoose has a famous reputation as a snake killer. It is native to Africa and southern Asia, but it has been introduced into many areas to help with the snake population.

The mongoose is a fierce and fearless fighter. It teases the snake so that the snake will strike out. Then the mongoose leaps on the snake's back and sinks its teeth into the victim's head. The mongoose also eats rats, birds, and insects.

In captivity the mongoose is often kept as a pet. In India it is kept in the house as a rat and snake killer. The mongoose seems to like being near people. When tamed, it is gentle and friendly.

In spite of its reputation, the mongoose is forbidden in the United States. After it kills all of the snakes, the mongoose begins to decrease the rabbit and chicken population.

A. Underline the correct answers about today's story.

1. The mongoose is famous for	(a) its speed	(b) its friendliness	(c) snake killing.
2. As a fighter, the mongoose is	(a) fearless	(b) helpless	(c) unskilled.
3. As a pet, the mongoose is	(a) wild	(b) gentle	(c) unpredictable.
4. In the United States the mongoose is	(a) forbidden	(b) welcome	(c) gladly received.
5. The mongoose also kills	(a) rats	(b) fish	(c) large animals.

B. Reread the story and write the answers to these questions.

1. Where does the mongoose live?

_____

_____

_____

2. How does the mongoose first handle the snake?

_____

_____

_____

3. In what country is the mongoose kept inside?

_____

_____

_____

4. Why do those people keep the mongoose inside?

_____

_____

_____

Unit 105 cont'd ☛

Recognizing Word Groups

A noun names a person, place, or thing.
A noun may be common or proper. A
noun may be singular or plural.
A pronoun is a noun substitute. It may
be singular or plural.
A verb shows action or state of being. It
may be written in present, past, or future tense.
An adjective tells which one, what kind, or how many.
An adverb tells when, where, why, or how.

 Underline the word in each group which does not fit in with the others in the group. What kind of words make up the group?

1. chocolate
   <u>frequently</u>
   strawberry
   vanilla
   nouns
   _____

2. chase
   quit
   select
   general
   _____

3. mine
   she
   voice
   you
   _____

4. kindness
   business
   lonely
   nonsense
   _____

5. safely
   always
   modern
   often
   _____

6. penny
   ran
   holiday
   machine
   _____

7. vacation
   journey
   is
   accident
   _____

8. quietly
   now
   today
   blue
   _____

9. curly
   dessert
   interesting
   favorite
   _____

10. it
    yourself
    like
    ours
    _____

11. tomorrow
    quickly
    evenly
    beautiful
    _____

12. cute
    newspaper
    angry
    magical
    _____

13. are
    zoo
    wisdom
    promise
    _____

14. ordered
    discover
    practice
    ghost
    _____

15. understand
    truth
    market
    surprise
    _____

16. they
    I
    people
    we
    _____

17. our
    protect
    buy
    defend
    _____

18. suddenly
    usually
    broken
    never
    _____

19. laughed
    raw
    crowded
    vacant
    _____

20. sleep
    cried
    wonderful
    talked
    _____

Comprehension Check

(A) Match the homonyms.

_b_	1. flower	____	11. plain	a. plane	k. right
____	2. there	____	12. write	b. flour	l. earn
____	3. urn	____	13. rode	c. flee	m. weight
____	4. flea	____	14. male	d. seen	n. some
____	5. throne	____	15. wait	e. would	o. capital
____	6. aloud	____	16. eight	f. road	p. allowed
____	7. wood	____	17. scene	g. kernel	q. rain
____	8. colonel	____	18. knows	h. course	r. their
____	9. reign	____	19. sum	i. nose	s. mail
____	10. capitol	____	20. coarse	j. thrown	t. ate

(B) Write "a" or "an" before each word.

1. _an_ ox	6. ____ beacon	11. ____ reason	16. ____ weasel
2. ____ forest	7. ____ storm	12. ____ egg	17. ____ exam
3. ____ butterfly	8. ____ enemy	13. ____ coin	18. ____ nest
4. ____ dream	9. ____ vacation	14. ____ word	19. ____ hour
5. ____ animal	10. ____ imitation	15. ____ luxury	20. ____ class

(C) Identify each word group.

nouns	pronouns	verbs	adjectives	adverbs
1. people	3. migrates	5. mink		7. friendly
homes	attaches	mockingbird		fierce
things	breaks	mongoose		beautiful
stories	flies	monkey		sweet
____ _nouns_ ____	____	____		____
2. I	4. there	6. valuable		8. drives
you	now	heavy		walks
they	silently	famous		runs
our	always	fearless		sleeps
____	____	____		____

(D) Complete these sentences.

1. Monarchs ____ _migrate_ ____ south for the winter.
2. The mongoose is a _____ killer.
3. The mockingbird's song is _____ .
4. In India a mongoose is often a _____ .

5. A mink's _____ is very valuable.
6. _____ is trading.
7. Coins are usually made of _____ .
8. The king of butterflies is the _____ butterfly.

Test 21 cont'd ☛

Comprehension Check (continued)

(E) **Match these words and their definitions. These words appeared in the reading selections from units 101-105.**

_c_ 1. expensive   ___ 7. objects   a. not allowed   g. imprisonment

___ 2. valuable   ___ 8. possessions   b. different   h. of considerable worth

___ 3. intruder   ___ 9. traded   c. costly   i. unwanted guest

___ 4. receives   ___ 10. captivity   d. forms   j. owned things

___ 5. shapes   ___ 11. famous   e. gets   k. well-known

___ 6. unlike   ___ 12. forbidden   f. things   l. given in exchange

(F) **Underline the correct answers.**

1. When is the mink active?   (a) <u>at night</u>   (b) during the day

2. Who is the mink's worst enemy?   (a) snake   (b) people

3. Where do mockingbirds usually live?   (a) woods   (b) cities

4. Describe the mockingbird's own song?   (a) beautiful   (b) plain

5. Where do monarch butterflies lay eggs?   (a) on the water   (b) on milkweed leaves

6. What color is the monarch butterfly?   (a) orange and black   (b) red and green

7. What were marked metals called?   (a) jewels   (b) coins

8. What is bartering?   (a) borrowing   (b) trading

9. Describe a mongoose as a pet.   (a) dangerous   (b) gentle

10. Where does the mongoose live?   (a) India   (b) United States

Choose one of the following topics and write a paragraph.

(1) The mongoose is forbidden in many countries. Explain why? Is this fair?

(2) Do you think it is humane to raise animals for their fur? Explain your answer.

_____

_____

_____

_____

_____

_____

_____

_____

_____

The Moose

Study the spelling and meaning of each word. These words are used in today's story. Connect each word with its definition.

1. awkward ————————— a. clumsy
2. oddly   b. strong; robust
3. proportioned   c. showy; magnificent
4. rugged   d. strangely
5. splendid   e. arranged in a balanced way
6. thrives   f. grows strong and healthy

Read the story carefully and remember the details.

Of all the animals, the moose is one of the most awkward-looking and oddly proportioned of all mammals. Even so, the moose boasts a splendid set of antlers.

The moose is a game animal. It thrives in cold weather, kept warm by its thick fur. The moose is a rugged animal. Its home is in Canada.

Moose travel very little. They usually live near ponds or swamps. Moose are very fond of pond lilies. The animals even dip under the water to nibble on water vegetation. Although large and ungainly, moose are good swimmers.

Except during the mating season, moose are not dangerous. They usually disappear before anyone gets too close.

A. Underline the correct answers about today's story.

1. Which word describes
   the moose?   (a) weak   (b) graceful   (c) rugged

2. The moose thrives   (a) in cold weather   (b) in hot weather   (c) in dry weather.

3. The moose lives   (a) in the mountains   (b) in the snow   (c) near water.

4. When anyone gets
   close, the moose   (a) attacks   (b) runs away   (c) becomes dangerous.

5. What food is a favorite
   of the moose?   (a) pond lilies   (b) grass   (c) twigs

B. Reread the story and write the answers to these questions.

1. Which country is the home of the moose?   3. How much do moose travel?

   _____   _____

   _____   _____

   _____   _____

2. How does the moose stay warm?   4. When are moose dangerous?

   _____   _____

   _____   _____

   _____   _____

Unit 106 cont'd ☞

Contractions

A. Underline the contractions which have been written correctly.

1. I'am
2. <u>isn't</u>
3. can'not
4. don't
5. she's
6. are'nt
7. I'll
8. that'is
9. aren't
10. isnt

11. you're
12. wasn't
13. didnt
14. who'is
15. wel'l
16. that's
17. it's
18. shes
19. he's
20. it'is

21. we'are
22. they're
23. Iv'e
24. we'll
25. wouldn't
26. wasno't
27. won't
28. haven't
29. you'll
30. dont

31. we're
32. theyr'e
33. hasn't
34. you'will
35. didn't
36. whats
37. who's
38. he'is
39. weren't
40. can't

B. What two words make up each of the following contractions?

1. I'm   _____I am_____
2. we're _____
3. don't _____
4. isn't _____
5. he's _____
6. can't _____
7. we'll _____
8. hasn't _____
9. shouldn't _____
10. we've _____

11. couldn't _____
12. aren't _____
13. she's _____
14. who's _____
15. wasn't _____
16. I've _____
17. didn't _____
18. you'll _____
19. he'd _____
20. they're _____

21. it's _____
22. I'll _____
23. that's _____
24. haven't _____
25. what's _____
26. weren't _____
27. she'd _____
28. wouldn't _____
29. you've _____
30. there's _____

C. Write the contraction for each group of words.

1. I am   _____I'm_____
2. you will _____
3. can not _____
4. he had _____
5. we are _____
6. is not _____
7. they have _____
8. did not _____
9. we will _____
10. have not _____

11. you are _____
12. she will _____
13. are not _____
14. I have _____
15. has not _____
16. she is _____
17. who is _____
18. were not _____
19. they are _____
20. could not _____

21. was not _____
22. he is _____
23. I will _____
24. do not _____
25. she had _____
26. you have _____
27. that is _____
28. should not _____
29. what is _____
30. there is _____

Mountain Goats

Study the spelling and meaning of each word. These words are used in today's story. Connect each word with its definition.

1. adapted ———————————— a. suited
2. altitudes   b. the elevations of something
3. excellent   c. unusually good
4. existence   d. living or being alone
5. peaceful   e. not fighting
6. solitary   f. life; the condition of being

Read the story carefully and remember the details.

The mountain goat is not really a goat. It is a member of the antelope family.

The mountain goat makes its home in the Rocky Mountains of the northern states. It lives in such cold weather and high altitudes that few animals ever share its home. The mountain goat, however, is well adapted to its rugged mountain home. The mountain goat seems content with its solitary existence. It has a warm fur coat of long, shaggy white hair. The fur keeps the goat warm in the extremely cold weather.

The mountain goat has short legs. It is an excellent climber.

Usually the mountain goat is a peaceful animal. However, when attacked, the goat puts up an excellent fight. Its horns, though small, are powerful weapons.

A. Underline the correct answers about today's story.

1. Where does the mountain goat live?   (a) Rockies   (b) Andes   (c) Alps
2. To keep warm, the animal   (a) runs   (b) eats a lot   (c) has a fur coat.
3. The mountain goat is really   (a) a goat   (b) a sheep   (c) an antelope.
4. Usually the mountain goat is   (a) dangerous   (b) peaceful   (c) quarrelsome.
5. When attacked, the mountain goat   (a) runs away   (b) fights   (c) is helpless.

B. Reread the story and write the answers to these questions.

1. What does the mountain goat do when attacked?

   _____
   _____
   _____

2. What color is the mountain goat?

   _____
   _____
   _____

3. Describe the animal's mountain home.

   _____
   _____
   _____

4. How does the mountain goat use its horns?

   _____
   _____
   _____

Unit 107 cont'd ☞

Using Contractions

A. Match the contractions with the words for which they stand.

_h_	1. can't	___	16. you'll	a. you will	p. there is
___	2. I'll	___	17. don't	b. he is	q. what is
___	3. that's	___	18. there's	c. has not	r. I have
___	4. you're	___	19. shouldn't	d. are not	s. would not
___	5. isn't	___	20. I'm	e. she is	t. could not
___	6. hasn't	___	21. didn't	f. they had	u. will not
___	7. she's	___	22. you've	g. do not	v. have not
___	8. what's	___	23. we're	h. can not	w. is not
___	9. couldn't	___	24. wouldn't	i. I am	x. should not
___	10. wasn't	___	25. haven't	j. was not	y. did not
___	11. she'd	___	26. he's	k. I will	z. you are
___	12. we'll	___	27. weren't	l. we are	A. they are
___	13. won't	___	28. they're	m. that is	B. she had
___	14. they'd	___	29. aren't	n. were not	C. you have
___	15. I've	___	30. it's	o. we will	D. it is

B. Complete each sentence with a contraction.

1. ___I'll___ wait for you at home.
2. He _____ called yet.
3. You _____ come in here!
4. Karen _____ feeling well.
5. _____ not sure.
6. _____ late for school again.
7. _____ your name?
8. _____ in the office.
9. We _____ told anything.
10. _____ you come in?
11. _____ told you everything.
12. _____ taken the wrong turn.
13. Kim _____ want to go.
14. I _____ like that.
15. _____ nothing in here.
16. You _____ have done that.
17. _____ in the same class.
18. Why _____ you in school?
19. _____ be in the kitchen.
20. _____ too late.

21. _____ not true!
22. _____ my uncle.
23. I _____ like spinach.
24. _____ be sorry.
25. _____ already gone home.
26. I _____ help myself.
27. The door _____ locked.
28. _____ come again tomorrow.
29. It _____ have helped.
30. They _____ heard the news.
31. _____ our new leader.
32. It _____ your fault.
33. _____ bring the punch.
34. _____ talk to me!
35. It _____ work.
36. _____ my friends.
37. _____ you do anything?
38. Kate _____ remember.
39. _____ nothing to do.
40. _____ wrong?

260

Musk Oxen

Study the spelling and meaning of each word. These words are used in today's story. Connect each word with its definition.

1. center   a. commonly
2. defend   b. protect from harm
3. named   c. move eagerly
4. rush   d. middle
5. sometimes   e. now and them
6. usually   f. called

Read the story carefully and remember the details.

Musk oxen are called the cattle of the Arctic. They are found only in Arctic America and Greenland.

Musk oxen have thick bodies with short legs. They are protected from the cold by their coats of long dark hair. The hair grows so long that it sometimes drags the ground.

The oxen were named for their strong musky odor. They usually live together in bands. Buds, twigs, and grasses are their main foods.

To defend themselves, musk oxen rush into a circle. They stand with their tails together in the center. Their horns are good weapons.

The oxen were hunted by Eskimos for meat and clothing until the animals were near extinction. They are now protected by laws.

A. Underline the correct answers about today's story.

1. Where do musk oxen live?   (a) Arctic   (b) Africa   (c) China
2. What protects the oxen from the cold?   (a) thick bodies   (b) fur   (c) skin
3. The oxen were named for their   (a) sizes   (b) habits   (c) odor.
4. What is the ox's weapon?   (a) legs   (b) odor   (c) horns
5. Who hunted the oxen?   (a) Eskimos   (b) Indians   (c) white settlers

B. Reread the story and write the answers to these questions.

1. What are musk oxen called?

_____

_____

_____

2. What are the main foods of the oxen?

_____

_____

_____

3. How do the oxen defend themselves?

_____

_____

_____

4. Why were the oxen hunted?

_____

_____

_____

From "Cam" to "Test"

Top border: C A M P A I R O D E N | J

Right border (top to bottom): O Y O R E S T I C K N E W A S

Left border (top to bottom): T S E T O R

Bottom border (left to right): W O L L E Y E K N O M R E T | T

1. _c_ _a_ _m_ noncircular wheel mounted on a shaft
2. _ _ _ _ _ a group of tents where people live for a time
3. _ _ I _ _ a boy; you are a girl.
4. _ _ _ (slang) a high-fidelity amplifier set
5. _ _ (informal) father, papa
6. _ _ _ _ a set of two
7. _ _ _ mixture of gases that surround the earth
8. _ _ _ _ stick used to beat or punish
9. _ _ _ _ _ sat on a horse and made it go
10. _ _ _ _ a poem intended to be sung
11. _ _ _ _ a wild animal's home
12. _ _ _ _ _ _ take pleasure in
13. _ _ _ _ a glad feeling, glad behavior
14. _ _ _ _ _ of long ago, of times past
15. _ _ _ mineral containing enough metal to make mining profitable
16. _ _ _ _ _ sleep, a state of quiet and ease
17. _ _ _ _ _ _ a long thin piece of wood
18. _ _ _ _ _ tiny eight-legged animal related to a spider
19. _ _ _ _ _ had the facts
20. _ _ _ _ never having been before
21. _ _ _ _ He _____ here but he left.
22. _ _ _ _ _ _ to make poor use of
23. _ _ As black _ _ _ coal
24. _ _ _ _ _ _ common plant having daisylike flowers
25. _ _ _ _ _ one of the long periods in which school is divided
26. _ _ _ _ _ man in monastery living a life of prayer and worship
27. _ _ _ _ _ _ _ _ an animal most like man
28. _ _ above and supported by
29. _ _ _ instrument for fastening or unfastening a lock
30. _ _ _ _ _ cry out with a strong, loud sound
31. _ _ _ _ _ _ _ the color of gold or ripe lemons
32. _ _ _ _ the letter "L" spelled
33. _ _ _ _ not high or tall, near the ground
34. _ _ _ _ _ _ made letters with a pencil
35. _ _ _ _ decay, to become rotten
36. _ _ _ _ _ a set mechanical way of doing things
37. _ _ _ _ _ an examination

The Mussel

Study the spelling and meaning of each word. These words are used in today's story. Connect each word with its definition.

1. catch————————a. seize
2. fasten   b. of the sea
3. hinged   c. attached by a joint
4. marine   d. remains
5. stays   e. attach
6. wharves   f. docks for ships

Read the story carefully and remember the details.

On all shores of the world is found the mussel. The mussel is a marine animal that lives inside its shell. The mussel's shell is a bivalve, that is, the shell is made of two shells hinged at the top.

The mussel builds its home on the rocks. It fastens itself to the rock and usually stays on the same rock all its life. Some mussels fasten themselves to piers, mudbanks, or wharves. A few have even fastened themselves to other mussels.

The incoming tide brings the mussel its food. It simply opens its mouth to catch tiny sea animals and plants.

The mussel's main enemies are people and the starfish. Both use the mussel for food. People also use mussel shells for making buttons.

A. Underline the correct answers about today's story.

1. Where does the mussel live?   (a) in a shell   (b) beneath rocks   (c) among seaweed
2. A bivalve is made up of   (a) two shells   (b) three shells   (c) one shell.
3. Most mussels attach to   (a) piers   (b) rocks   (c) other mussels.
4. How does the mussel get its food?   (a) from the sand   (b) with the tide   (c) from the rock
5. Besides people, who is the mussel's enemy?   (a) shark   (b) octopus   (c) starfish

B. Reread the story and write the answers to these questions.

1. Which shores of the world are home to the mussel?

_____
_____
_____

2. What kind of animal is the mussel?

_____
_____

3. What do mussels eat?

_____
_____
_____

4. What unusual use do people have for mussels?

_____
_____
_____

Unit 109 cont'd ☞

Capital Letters

A. Which of the following words begin with capital letters? Underline them.

1. <u>November</u>	11. play	21. Mars	31. sister
2. family	12. Terry	22. Atlantic Ocean	32. Sunday
3. New York	13. pet	23. dinner	33. Peter Pan
4. hungry	14. Father	24. Honda	34. fun
5. paper	15. dance	25. water	35. Easter
6. Dr. Johnson	16. language	26. October	36. Superman
7. Monday	17. home	27. candy	37. homework
8. bug	18. chair	28. Charlie	38. class
9. General Electric	19. MacDonalds	29. Texas	39. Mrs. Lester
10. game	20. Mr. Cameron	30. cake	40. English

B. Underline the words which should be capitalized.

1. <u>wednesday</u>	11. uncle	21. country	31. america
2. month	12. mrs. wilson	22. people	32. week
3. ozark mountains	13. christmas	23. nancy	33. kelly
4. valley	14. school	24. mexico	34. police
5. cracker jacks	15. ohio river	25. aunt becky	35. april
6. movie	16. friend	26. music	36. river
7. moon	17. pepsi	27. day	37. everything
8. spiderman	18. arithmetic	28. ms. reynolds	38. fran
9. newspaper	19. pacific ocean	29. television	39. tuesday
10. dr. sans	20. doctor	30. california	40. sky

C. Underline the words in each sentence which should be capitalized.

1. <u>his</u> name is <u>daniel</u>.	11. i live in michigan.
2. let's watch the ''wizard of oz.''	12. paul owns a volkswagen.
3. ms. allison is my neighbor.	13. we drink dr. pepper.
4. she is visiting the united states.	14. mr. keller sells houses.
5. have you met jean?	15. here comes mrs. green.
6. janet is my cousin.	16. do you want a pepsi?
7. they live in arizona.	17. tomorrow is saturday.
8. where is warren avenue?	18. the winner is karen.
9. you know the answer.	19. my birthday is in september.
10. he has a pet tiger.	20. bob and i are friends.

Myths

Study the spelling and meaning of each word. These words are used in today's story. Connect each word with its definition.

1. argue
2. explanation
3. problem
4. puzzle
5. repeat
6. solved

a. question proposed for solution
b. confuse
c. to say again
d. dispute; debate
e. that which makes understood
f. cleared up

Read the story carefully and remember the details.

All over the world people have always wanted an explanation for things which puzzle them. The Greeks and Romans solved the problem by inventing gods and goddesses. These gods and goddesses lived on Mount Olympus. Each one ruled a different thing. The gods and goddesses had feelings like humans. Their stories are called myths.

To explain the mystery of the echo, the Greeks and Romans told a story about a beautiful nymph named Echo. Echo loved to argue. Once she argued with the goddess Juno and won. Juno was so angry that she punished Echo. From then on Echo could only repeat the words of others. Echo fell in love with the handsome Narcissus, but he did not return her love. Echo was heartbroken. She hid in a cave. In time she grew thinner and thinner until only her voice remained. Her voice still answers anyone who calls to her.

A. **Underline the correct answers about today's story.**

1. Greeks and Romans invented gods
   to explain   (a) the unknown   (b) the weather   (c) their feelings.
2. Where did the gods and goddesses live?   (a) Greece   (b) Rome   (c) Mount Olympus
3. Echo was punished because she   (a) argued   (b) smiled   (c) hid.
4. Where did Echo hide?   (a) under water   (b) in a cave   (c) in a cloud
5. "To echo" means   (a) "to repeat"   (b) "to cry"   (c) "to keep silent."

B. **Reread the story and write the answers to these questions.**

1. What was invented to explain puzzling things?

   _____

   _____

   _____

2. What do we call stories about gods
   and goddesses?

   _____

   _____

   _____

3. What did Echo love to do?

   _____

   _____

   _____

4. What does Echo's voice do?

   _____

   _____

   _____

Unit 110 cont'd ☞

Capitalization

A. Underline the words which should always be spelled with capital letters.

1. dr. morrison
2. organization
3. english
4. question
5. new york
6. school
7. river
8. pepsi
9. sentence
10. washington
11. rocky mountains
12. parrot
13. combination
14. i
15. central park
16. mixture
17. language
18. french
19. detroit zoo
20. mississippi river
21. doctor
22. wheaties
23. karen
24. answer
25. christmas
26. country
27. michael
28. dutch
29. people
30. america
31. newspaper
32. king
33. homework
34. lake ryan
35. miss winston
36. classmate
37. catholic
38. queen anne
39. capt. nelson
40. landscape
41. hawaii
42. donald duck
43. plumber
44. atlantic ocean
45. citizen
46. spanish
47. conjunction
48. alice
49. south america
50. company

B. Underline the words which should be capitalized.

1. do you speak german?
2. the window is broken.
3. we visited the overton park.
4. i am going to california.
5. anne is talking to you.
6. have you met conrad?
7. the show begins tomorrow.
8. these students have volunteered.
9. you know the answer.
10. my aunt is a judge.
11. the lady bought a magazine.
12. my cousin lives in boston.
13. kathy made us an apple pie.
14. did you eat lunch?
15. what did you tell mrs. stephens?
16. where do you live?
17. the building was built in 1907.
18. today is wednesday.
19. our vacation begins next week.
20. have you ever been to canada?
21. mr. and mrs. martin are here.
22. it's jack's birthday.
23. the house needs repainting.
24. look at these pictures.
25. i saw him at school.
26. tomorrow is thanksgiving.
27. dr. weston came from australia.
28. the people here speak chinese.
29. kim and i live next door.
30. may i introduce donovan?

Comprehension Check

(A) Write the contractions.

1. she has _____she's_____
2. you have _____
3. have not _____
4. will not _____
5. who is _____
6. were not _____
7. that is _____
8. can not _____
9. is not _____
10. we are _____

11. of the clock _____
12. where is _____
13. you were _____
14. I am _____
15. they will _____
16. should not _____
17. it is _____
18. did not _____
19. there is _____
20. are not _____

(B) Use a contraction to complete each sentence.

1. I _____don't_____ like spinach or cauliflower.
2. The meeting is at seven _____ .
3. _____ someone listen to me!
4. Sally _____ coming with us.
5. _____ too tired to eat.

6. _____ you want to go with us?
7. _____ already tried that.
8. Dennis _____ ever on time.
9. They _____ remember the code.
10. Les and Andy _____ paid their dues.

(C) Underline the words which should be capitalized.

1. united states
2. brandon
3. history
4. main street
5. mark twain

6. annette
7. french
8. uncles
9. thanksgiving
10. wednesday

11. aunt lucy
12. tomorrow
13. dr. hillary
14. new york city
15. answer

16. neighbor
17. romans
18. mickey mouse
19. st. louis zoo
20. birthday

(D) Write a specific name for each of these words.

1. a river _____Ohio River_____
2. a city _____
3. a month _____
4. a drink _____
5. a country _____

6. an ocean _____
7. a lake _____
8. a state _____
9. a candy _____
10. a day _____

11. a man's name _____
12. a language _____
13. a holiday _____
14. a woman's name _____
15. a mountain range _____

(E) Complete these sentences.

1. Musk oxen are the _____cattle_____ of the Arctic.
2. A bivalve has _____ shells.
3. The mountain goat _____ really a goat.
4. Gods and goddesses lived on _____ .

5. The mountain goat is an excellent _____ .
6. The plural of "moose" is " _____ ."
7. _____ was a nymph who loved to argue.
8. Mussels are found all over the _____ .

267

Test 22 cont'd ☞

Comprehension Check (continued)

(F) Match these words and their definitions. These words appeared in the reading selections from units 106-110.

_g_ 1. splendid   ___ 7. usually

___ 2. ungainly   ___ 8. fasten

___ 3. excellent   ___ 9. marine

___ 4. existence   ___ 10. argue

___ 5. solitary   ___ 11. problem

___ 6. sometimes   ___ 12. puzzle

a. living or being alone

b. unusually good

c. clumsy

d. commonly

e. attach

f. question proposed for solution

g. showy; magnificent

h. life

i. now and then

j. of the sea

k. dispute; debate

l. confuse

(G) Underline the correct answers.

#	Question	(a)	(b)
1.	Which country is the home of the moose?	(a) <u>Canada</u>	(b) Germany
2.	Describe the moose.	(a) rugged	(b) graceful
3.	Where does the mountain goat live?	(a) Andes	(b) Rockies
4.	What does the mountain goat do when attacked?	(a) fights	(b) runs
5.	How were musk oxen named?	(a) odor	(b) habits
6.	Who hunted the musk oxen?	(a) Indians	(b) Eskimos
7.	What is the mussel's home?	(a) shell	(b) ocean
8.	How does the mussel get its food?	(a) with the tide	(b) from the sand
9.	Where did gods and goddesses live?	(a) Greece	(b) Mount Olympus
10.	Why was Echo punished?	(a) she fled	(b) she argued

Choose one of the following topics and write a paragraph.

(1) Just like many animals, people often attack when threatened. Why might this not be the best idea? How can talking about differences help?

(2) A myth is a story that is supposed to explain something. Pick something and make up a myth to explain how or why it happens.

_____

_____

_____

_____

_____

_____

_____

_____

_____

The Navajos

Study the spelling and meaning of each word. These words are used in today's story. Connect each word with its definition.

1. gathering
2. heritage
3. hogan
4. reservation
5. roamed
6. unoccupied

a. wandered about
b. collecting
c. birthright
d. Navajo home
e. land set aside for specific use
f. unfilled

Read the story carefully and remember the details.

Today the Navajo Indians live on a reservation in the southwest United States. Many years ago these people roamed the land which was then unoccupied by white settlers. They lived by gathering wild fruits and hunting wild game.

Although their lives have changed considerably because of the white settlers, the Navajos still hold on to the proud heritage of their ancestors. They believe in the land. The earth is known as "Changing Woman." In the winter she is old. She wears a robe of snow. In the spring she is young again.

The Navajos' homes are called hogans. The home has no windows. There is only one door which must always face the east to meet the spirit of the rising sun. The Navajos are proud people, proud of their history, and proud of their land.

A. Underline the correct answers about today's story.

1. Today the Navajos live   (a) in cities   (b) on a mountain   (c) on a reservation.
2. "Changing Woman" is the   (a) sun   (b) earth   (c) moon.
3. The earth is young in the   (a) winter   (b) fall   (c) spring.
4. A hogan is a   (a) home   (b) custom   (c) spirit.
5. To meet the rising sun, the door faces   (a) east   (b) west   (c) north.

B. Reread the story and write the answers to these questions.

1. How did the Navajo live?

_____

_____

_____

2. Where are the Navajos' reservations?

_____

_____

_____

3. Who changed the Navajos' life?

_____

_____

_____

4. What does the Indians' home not have?

_____

_____

_____

Unit 111 cont'd

Writing Numbers

A hyphen is used in compound names of numbers from twenty-one through ninety-nine.

A. Write the number name for each number.

1 - _one_
2 - _____
3 - _____
4 - _____
5 - _____
6 - _____
7 - _____
8 - _____
9 - _____
10 - _____
11 - _____
12 - _____
13 - _____
14 - _____
15 - _____

16 - _____
17 - _____
18 - _____
19 - _____
20 - _____
21 - _____
22 - _____
23 - _____
24 - _____
25 - _____
26 - _____
27 - _____
28 - _____
29 - _____
30 - _____

31 - _____
32 - _____
33 - _____
34 - _____
35 - _____
36 - _____
37 - _____
38 - _____
39 - _____
40 - _____
41 - _____
42 - _____
43 - _____
44 - _____
45 - _____

46 - _____
47 - _____
48 - _____
49 - _____
50 - _____
51 - _____
52 - _____
53 - _____
54 - _____
55 - _____
56 - _____
57 - _____
58 - _____
59 - _____
60 - _____

Ordinal numbers are names like "first," "second," or "third." To write some ordinal numbers, simply add "th" to the regular number names. Here are some exceptions:

1. five — fifth
2. eight — eighth
3. nine — ninth
4. number names that end in "y" but change the "y" to "i" and add "eth" (twenty — twentieth)
5. twelve — twelfth

B. Write the ordinal number name for each number.

1 - _first_
2 - _____
3 - _____
4 - _____
5 - _____
6 - _____
7 - _____
8 - _____
9 - _____
10 - _____

11 - _____
12 - _____
13 - _____
14 - _____
15 - _____
16 - _____
17 - _____
18 - _____
19 - _____
20 - _____

30 - _____
31 - _____
40 - _____
42 - _____
50 - _____
53 - _____
60 - _____
64 - _____
70 - _____
75 - _____

The Ocelot

Study the spelling and meaning of each word. These words are used in today's story. Connect each word with its definition.

1. fearless
2. hunting
3. most
4. often
5. pattern
6. peaceful

a. seeking
b. the majority of
c. design
d. frequently
e. without fear
f. serene

Read the story carefully and remember the details.

The ocelot is often called the tiger cat or the leopard cat. It has a spotted coat whose right side does not match the left. No two coats of ocelots have the same pattern.

In the wild the ocelot lives in the forest. The ocelot makes its home in a cave or a hollow tree. It eats small mammals, birds, and reptiles. Most of its hunting is done at night. Although the ocelot is a good climber, it usually hunts on the ground. It may, however, attack from the trees.

The ocelot is a fearless animal, but it is usually peaceful. When attacked, however, the ocelot becomes vicious.

Many people have ocelots as pets. When taken as cubs, ocelots are easily tamed.

A. **Underline the correct answers about today's story.**

1. To which family does the ocelot belong?   (a) dog   (b) cat   (c) bird
2. Where do ocelots live?   (a) forests   (b) mountains   (c) deserts
3. Ocelots usually hunt   (a) at dawn   (b) at night   (c) at sundown.
4. When attacked, the ocelot is   (a) helpless   (b) vicious   (c) defenseless.
5. The ocelot is often used as   (a) food   (b) a watchdog   (c) a pet.

B. **Reread the story and write the answers to these questions.**

1. Give two other names for the ocelot.

_____

_____

_____

2. Where do ocelots make their home?

_____

_____

3. What do ocelots eat?

_____

_____

_____

4. From where might the ocelot attack?

_____

_____

_____

Unit 112 cont'd ☛

Abbreviations

A. Match the abbreviations with the words for which they stand.

_x_	1. Capt.	___	21. Amer.	a. November	u. married lady
___	2. a.m.	___	22. Mrs.	b. Thursday	v. highway
___	3. p.m.	___	23. sing.	c. quart	w. September
___	4. yd.	___	24. pl.	d. August	x. Captain
___	5. ft.	___	25. Mon.	e. singular	y. Tuesday
___	6. in.	___	26. Tues.	f. morning	z. centimeter
___	7. cm	___	27. Wed.	g. October	A. Friday
___	8. qt.	___	28. Thurs.	h. Monday	B. year
___	9. l	___	29. Fri.	i. weeks	C. December
___	10. oz.	___	30. Sat.	j. January	D. number
___	11. lb.	___	31. Sun.	k. United States	E. plural
___	12. wks.	___	32. Jan.	l. Saturday	F. evening
___	13. yr.	___	33. Feb.	m. foot	G. February
___	14. hwy.	___	34. Mar.	n. March	H. pound
___	15. ave.	___	35. Apr.	o. mister	I. April
___	16. co.	___	36. Aug.	p. inch	J. English
___	17. no.	___	37. Sept.	q. ounce	K. yard
___	18. U.S.	___	38. Oct.	r. company	L. Sunday
___	19. Eng.	___	39. Nov.	s. Wednesday	M. avenue
___	20. Mr.	___	40. Dec.	t. liter	N. American

B. Write an abbreviation in each blank.

1. We live in the __U.S.__
2. _____ Rogers is my neighbor.
3. It is now 6:30 _____.
4. Who is _____ Wilson?
5. Take Route _____ 12.
6. Have you been to Washington, _____?
7. _____ Fisher is our principal.
8. We will leave at 4:30 _____.
9. My father is _____ Conrad.
10. _____ Davis is here.
11. Her teacher is _____ Adams.
12. The meeting is at 7:15 _____.
13. _____ Peters called him.
14. Where is _____ Thomas?
15. My brother is in the _____ Army.
16. He owns the Wilshire _____.
17. _____ Richards is waiting.
18. She left at 2:45 _____.
19. Do you know _____ and _____ King?
20. School begins at 8:15 _____.

The Otter

Study the spelling and meaning of each word. These words are used in today's story. Connect each word with its definition.

1. disposition
2. flexible
3. gentle
4. marvelous
5. pastime
6. sleek

a. smooth, well-groomed look
b. terrific
c. bendable
d. hobby
e. personality
f. kindly and patient

Read the story carefully and remember the details.

The otter is a sleek animal which is well-suited to its life in the water. It has webbed feet and a flexible body. The otter is a marvelous swimmer and an excellent diver.

One of the most playful animals, the otter's favorite pastime is sliding down slippery mudbanks or snowy slopes. It has a gentle disposition. The otter can make a good pet.

The otter is a member of the weasel family. It has no trouble staying warm in the winter. Underneath its thick fur is a layer of fat. It even stays warm in the cold, icy water.

The otter has short legs which make land travel difficult. It usually travels by water where it moves about gracefully.

A. **Underline the correct answers about today's story.**

1. The otter spends most of its time on   (a) land   (b) sand   (c) water.
2. The otter's pastime is sliding on   (a) mountains   (b) grass   (c) mudbanks.
3. To which family does the otter belong?   (a) dog   (b) weasel   (c) cat
4. On land the otter is   (a) adept   (b) graceful   (c) awkward.
5. As a pet, the otter is   (a) gentle   (b) ill-tempered   (c) dangerous.

B. **Reread the story and write the answers to these questions.**

1. Name two things the otter does well.

_____

_____

_____

2. What keeps the animal warm?

_____

_____

3. Why is land travel difficult?

_____

_____

_____

4. How does it move in water?

_____

_____

_____

Unit 113 cont'd

Writing Abbreviations and Numbers

A. Match the abbreviations with the words they abbreviate.

_u_ 1. Sun.	___ 21. st.	a. in care of	u. Sunday
___ 2. Mon.	___ 22. ave.	b. November	v. Captain
___ 3. Tues.	___ 23. etc.	c. dozen	w. apartment
___ 4. Wed.	___ 24. vs.	d. Monday	x. liter
___ 5. Thurs.	___ 25. Capt.	e. anonymous	y. Saturday
___ 6. Fri.	___ 26. M.D.	f. millimeter	z. quart
___ 7. Sat.	___ 27. Lt.	g. January	A. doctor of medicine
___ 8. Jan.	___ 28. no.	h. mountain	B. March
___ 9. Feb.	___ 29. mm	i. Tuesday	C. October
___ 10. Mar.	___ 30. in.	j. weekly	D. Wednesday
___ 11. Apr.	___ 31. ft.	k. highway	E. feet
___ 12. Aug.	___ 32. lb.	l. centimeter	F. Lieutenant
___ 13. Sept.	___ 33. doz.	m. versus	G. afternoon
___ 14. Oct.	___ 34. l	n. February	H. street
___ 15. Nov.	___ 35. cm	o. September	I. number
___ 16. Dec.	___ 36. qt.	p. inch	J. Thursday
___ 17. a.m.	___ 37. anon.	q. Friday	K. pound
___ 18. p.m.	___ 38. mt.	r. avenue	L. and so forth
___ 19. c/o	___ 39. apt.	s. morning	M. April
___ 20. hwy.	___ 40. wkly.	t. August	N. December

B. Write out each number.

EXAMPLES: 3 — _____three_____   21 — _____twenty-one_____

1 — _____	11 — _____	21 — _____
2 — _____	12 — _____	22 — _____
3 — _____	13 — _____	23 — _____
4 — _____	14 — _____	24 — _____
5 — _____	15 — _____	25 — _____
6 — _____	16 — _____	26 — _____
7 — _____	17 — _____	27 — _____
8 — _____	18 — _____	28 — _____
9 — _____	19 — _____	29 — _____
10 — _____	20 — _____	30 — _____

Oysters

Study the spelling and meaning of each word. These words are used in today's story. Connect each word with its definition.

1. allowing   a. foe
2. another   b. permitting
3. bores   c. moves smoothly
4. diet   d. food one eats
5. enemy   e. one more
6. flows   f. drills

Read the story carefully and remember the details.

Oysters are sea animals that live in shells. The shells are fastened together at one end by hinges, thus allowing the oysters to open and close their homes.

Most of the time oysters keep their shells open so that water flows through. Oysters get oxygen from the water. They also get their diet of tiny marine plants from the flowing water.

Oysters have many enemies. One enemy is the oyster drill, a small animal that bores holes in the oysters' shells and sucks out the oysters. Another enemy is the starfish. People eat oysters, although those oysters are usually raised on farms.

The insides of oyster shells are used to make buttons and other ornaments. Sometimes pearls are found there. Most pearls, however, are found in pearl oysters; they are seldom found in the kind of oysters we eat.

A. **Underline the correct answers about today's story.**

1. Oysters usually keep their shells   (a) open   (b) closed   (c) buried in sand.
2. From the water oysters get   (a) food   (b) oxygen   (c) carbon dioxide.
3. Oysters eat   (a) starfish   (b) oyster drills   (c) marine plants.
4. Oysters we eat are usually found   (a) in rivers   (b) on oyster farms (c) in ponds.
5. Which jewel is found in oysters?   (a) emerald   (b) diamond   (c) pearl

B. **Reread the story and write the answers to these questions.**

1. Name the enemies of the oyster.

_____

_____

_____

2. Where do oysters live?

_____

_____

_____

3. What is made from the insides of oysters?

_____

_____

_____

4. Why do oysters keep their shells open?

_____

_____

_____

Unit 114 cont'd ☞

Words That Rhyme

 Connect the words that rhyme.

1. beg	rocket
2. round	ground
3. name	egg
4. sign	fine
5. pocket	game

6. mile	clue
7. wind	smile
8. clear	pinned
9. true	had
10. glad	fear

11. reason	season
12. grade	muddy
13. clean	trade
14. never	seen
15. study	ever

16. silly	late
17. great	enter
18. smoke	chilly
19. winter	receive
20. believe	folk

21. build	toast
22. coast	row
23. corn	filled
24. drive	hive
25. grow	horn

26. pride	burn
27. learn	hide
28. meet	pain
29. rain	call
30. reach	feet
31. small	land
32. stand	teach

33. there	child
34. wild	pair
35. stone	you
36. wheel	race
37. place	phone
38. do	feel

39. habit	rabbit
40. cozy	think
41. leave	rosy
42. wink	rust
43. trust	eve

44. rough	bunny
45. funny	calf
46. trick	tough
47. for	kick
48. laugh	pour

49. sleep	long
50. strong	keep
51. three	guard
52. hard	catch
53. match	free

54. night	rock
55. berry	see
56. clock	light
57. knee	make
58. take	merry

59. will	soon
60. near	took
61. book	pill
62. moon	ring
63. thing	let
64. not	tear
65. mad	sad
66. wet	pot

67. each	house
68. could	would
69. knit	so
70. know	hen
71. mouse	hit
72. pen	peach

73. lost	honey
74. must	loud
75. nose	cost
76. money	goes
77. cloud	gust

78. bread	lead
79. drink	team
80. shoe	link
81. cream	too
82. what	lot

83. bear	bean
84. smell	care
85. green	gain
86. plane	bell
87. fat	rat

88. give	life
89. save	bow
90. knife	live
91. low	cow
92. now	cave

93. river	liver
94. love	date
95. hay	dove
96. thick	hike
97. bike	way
98. more	floor
99. man	sick
100. wait	ran

Pearls

Study the spelling and meaning of each word. These words are used in today's story. Connect each word with its definition.

1. accident
2. becomes
3. foreign
4. irritated
5. perfectly
6. tiny

a. not belonging naturally
b. not planned
c. without flaws
d. very small
e. gets to be
f. bothered

Read the story carefully and remember the details.

The pearl is a tiny gem which is found in an oyster. How does the pearl get inside the oyster?

Actually, the making of a pearl is an accident. Something gets inside the oyster shell. It may be a tiny worm or a grain of sand. The foreign object irritates the oyster. To protect itself, the oyster makes a covering around the worm or sand. The covering keeps the oyster from being irritated.

The covering is smooth and beautiful. The covering is in layers. The more layers formed around a foreign object, the bigger the pearl becomes.

Pearls are seldom found in those oysters which we eat. Pearl oysters are found in warmer seas. The most valuable pearls are those which are perfectly round.

A. Underline the correct answers about today's story.

1. Pearls are commonly found in (a) oysters (b) lobsters (c) clams.
2. The oyster makes a pearl (a) for food (b) for protection (c) for its home.
3. The pearl's size depends on the (a) size of the sand (b) size of the worm (c) number of layers.
4. Pearl oysters are found in (a) warm seas (b) cold seas (c) deep water.
5. The most valuable pearls are (a) the smallest (b) the biggest (c) perfectly round.

B. Reread the story and write the answers to these questions.

1. Is the making of a pearl intentional?

_____

_____

_____

2. Describe the pearl's covering.

_____

_____

_____

3. Why are some pearls larger than others?

_____

_____

_____

4. How many pearls are found in oysters we eat?

_____

_____

_____

 Unit 115 cont'd ☞

Identifying Words That Rhyme

Underline the words that rhyme with the first word in each row.
Then write your own rhyming word in the blank.

1.	wrong	sing	ring	<u>long</u>	<u>song</u>	hang	<u>pong</u>	*gong*
2.	bowl	coal	bell	roll	gold	hole	soul	
3.	crowd	bowed	rowed	aloud	rude	allowed		
4.	danger	hanger	manger	singer	ringer	stranger		
5.	knock	flock	dock	boat	mock	sock	tuck	
6.	laugh	calf	last	raft	self	left	graph	
7.	match	patch	church	hatch	much	batch		
8.	right	quiet	knight	light	height	eight		
9.	raw	draw	row	law	paw	meow		
10.	own	grown	been	loan	train	moan		
11.	straight	string	date	ate	rate	leave		
12.	dues	news	does	lose	loose	sues		
13.	reach	roach	peach	most	teach	beach		
14.	through	you	three	knew	threw	knees		
15.	although	so	throw	hoe	through	toe		
16.	later	better	mother	traitor	waiter	water		
17.	weigh	say	wait	way	day	do	pay	
18.	plant	point	pant	rent	can't	blank		
19.	dress	yes	nest	mess	miss	test	east	
20.	oil	sell	toil	foil	soil	build		
21.	flower	lower	fewer	flour	lighter	power		
22.	eye	lie	ever	try	sigh	ace	it	
23.	round	hound	find	found	pond	pound		
24.	price	west	ice	yeast	us	nice		
25.	that	at	pocket	fat	rat	rate	sat	
26.	free	my	tree	me	sea	meet	tea	
27.	track	pack	truck	jack	ache	mack	make	
28.	pick	like	lick	bike	cot	chick	sick	
29.	book	good	flood	took	food	hook	crook	
30.	witch	light	itch	kite	hitch	sit	pitch	
31.	pore	done	core	corn	soar	roar	morn	
32.	clear	bear	dear	hear	air	near	hair	
33.	able	cable	bull	fable	fill	ape	label	

Comprehension Check

Ⓐ Write the number names.

1 — *one*   6 — _____   0 — _____   51 — _____

2 — _____   7 — _____   21 — _____   57 — _____

3 — _____   8 — _____   30 — _____   58 — _____

4 — _____   9 — _____   36 — _____   60 — _____

5 — _____   10 — _____   40 — _____   63 — _____

Ⓑ Write the abbreviation for each word.

1. morning _____*a.m.*_____
2. highway _____
3. Thursday _____
4. apartment _____
5. December _____
6. pound _____
7. centimeter _____
8. dozen _____
9. foot _____
10. February _____
11. Saturday _____
12. weekly _____

13. November _____
14. avenue _____
15. captain _____
16. American _____
17. quart _____
18. liter _____
19. afternoon _____
20. ounce _____
21. mountain _____
22. August _____
23. millimeter _____
24. street _____

25. in care of _____
26. versus _____
27. and so forth _____
28. singular _____
29. Wednesday _____
30. and others _____
31. Monday _____
32. inches _____
33. Christmas _____
34. October _____
35. married lady _____
36. lieutenant _____

Ⓒ Write a word that rhymes with each word.

1. each _____*beach*_____
2. rough _____
3. cake _____
4. will _____
5. cold _____
6. feet _____
7. money _____
8. see _____

9. cozy _____
10. breeze _____
11. burn _____
12. cave _____
13. think _____
14. smile _____
15. ground _____
16. name _____

17. rain _____
18. mouse _____
19. river _____
20. cream _____
21. never _____
22. drive _____
23. toast _____
24. grade _____

Ⓓ Complete these sentences.

1. Today Navajos live on ____*reservations*____ .
2. Pearls are found in _____ .
3. The otter makes its home near _____ .
4. Ocelots have _____ coats.
5. Oysters live in _____ .

6. "Changing Woman" is Navajo for " _____ ."
7. Otters are described as _____ .
8. Ocelots belong to the _____ family.
9. Oysters eat _____ .
10. Pearl oysters are found in _____ seas.

Comprehension Check (continued)

Ⓔ **Match these words and their definitions. These words appeared in the reading selections from units 111-115.**

_k_ 1. gathering	___ 7. flexible	a. bothered	g. permitting
___ 2. hogan	___ 8. marvelous	b. fabulous	h. bendable
___ 3. fearless	___ 9. allowing	c. the majority of	i. drills
___ 4. most	___ 10. bores	d. Navajo home	j. frequently
___ 5. often	___ 11. irritated	e. without fear	k. collecting
___ 6. peaceful	___ 12. tiny	f. very small	l. serene

Ⓕ **Underline the correct answers.**

1.	What is "Changing Woman"?	(a)	fall	(b)	<u>earth</u>
2.	When is the earth young to the Navajos?	(a)	summer	(b)	spring
3.	What is an ocelot?	(a)	bird	(b)	cat
4.	How is the ocelot used?	(a)	as a pet	(b)	to train cats
5.	Describe an otter on land.	(a)	awkward	(b)	graceful
6.	Describe an otter in water.	(a)	graceful	(b)	helpless
7.	What do oysters eat?	(a)	starfish	(b)	marine plants
8.	What might be found in an oyster?	(a)	pearl	(b)	emerald
9.	How are pearls made?	(a)	intentionally	(b)	accidentally
10.	Describe a pearl's covering?	(a)	solid	(b)	layered

Choose one of the following topics and write a paragraph.

(1) Do you agree or disagree with the Navajos' outlook on life? Explain your answer.

(2) An otter makes an unusual pet. What other unusual animals might be kept as pets? Would you like an unusual pet? If so, tell why.

_____

_____

_____

_____

_____

_____

_____

_____

_____

The Peregrine Falcon   Unit 116

Study the spelling and meaning of each word. These words are used in today's story. Connect each word with its definition.

1. benumbed   a. enclosed on all sides
2. blow   b. sees
3. entirely   c. completely
4. incredible   d. made numb
5. sights   e. strike
6. surrounded   f. hard to believe

Read the story carefully and remember the details.

The most common bird used by falconers is the peregrine falcon. It is fast, and its range is almost worldwide.

The peregrine falcon feeds almost entirely on birds. Watching this bird hunt makes it easy to see why the falcon is called the supreme hunter.

The peregrine falcon begins the hunt by circling high in the sky. It flies so high that it can scarcely be seen from the ground. The falcon has keen eyesight. When it sights its prey, the falcon dives down at an incredible speed and hits the prey with stunning force. Even large prey are benumbed by the blow. The falcon kills its prey by breaking the neck with its sharp beak.

In the wild the peregrine falcon lives in open country surrounded by cliffs where it builds its makeshift nest. Most states protect the peregrine falcon by law.

A. Underline the correct answers about today's story.

1. The falcon is known for its   (a) flying   (b) hunting   (c) killing.
2. The falcon hunts by   (a) sight   (b) smell   (c) hearing.
3. A falcon kills its prey by   (a) choking   (b) biting   (c) breaking its neck.
4. A hunter who uses falcons is   (a) a falconer (b) a hawker   (c) a falconry.
5. The peregrine is found   (a) in hot climates (b) in cold climates (c) almost worldwide.

B. Reread the story and write the answers to these questions.

1. Which bird is most commonly used by falconers?

_____
_____
_____

2. Where does the falcon begin its hunt?

_____
_____
_____

3. What is a falcon's range?

_____
_____
_____

4. Where do wild falcons live?

_____
_____
_____

Unit 116 cont'd 👉

Writing Rhyme

Words rhyme when their sounds correspond.

EXAMPLES: a. *hold*   *gold*   d. *wait*   *late*
            b. *dare*   *scare*   e. *table*   *label*
            c. *ride*   *side*   f. *follow* *hollow*

 Complete each short verse with a word which rhymes with the last word in the first line.

1. The sly, old fox
   hid in a ___**box**___.

2. The cat
   sat on my _____.

3. The brown and white dog
   jumped over a _____.

4. My mother
   spanked my _____.

5. The happy little boy
   played with a _____.

6. The big plane
   flew through the _____.

7. A fish
   doesn't live in a _____.

8. The hungry mouse
   moved out of the _____.

9. Young Paul
   likes to play _____.

10. A red rose
    doesn't look like a _____.

11. A turtle
    can't wear a _____.

12. That silly fly
    got stuck in the _____.

13. Honey
    reminds me of _____.

14. These bears
    like to eat _____.

15. The bread
    tasted like _____.

16. The queen
    didn't want to be _____.

17. The room
    was swept with a _____.

18. A rocket
    won't fit in a _____.

19. They never fail
    to deliver the _____.

20. Snow and ice
    are not very _____.

21. The judge
    makes good _____.

22. It was too hot to run
    in the heat of the _____.

23. The egg
    broke on my _____.

24. The fawn
    fell asleep on the _____.

25. My thumb
    looks like a _____.

26. The snake
    crawled into the _____.

27. In a car
    you can go_____.

28. The letter
    made me feel _____.

29. Fishes are free
    when they swim in the _____.

30. When I go to school,
    I follow the _____.

31. The king
    wore a gold _____.

32. Sally's play
    lasted all _____.

33. I turned on the light,
    but it was too _____.

The Pika   Unit 117

Study the spelling and meaning of each word. These words are used in today's story. Connect each word with its definition.

1. crosswise   a. scatters
2. dawn   b. selective
3. particular   c. runs quickly
4. safe   d. free from harm
5. scurries   e. across
6. spreads   f. sunrise

Read the story carefully and remember the details.

The pika's home is in the Rocky Mountains. The pika is a furry little animal whose home is a burrow in the ground.

The pika begins its day at dawn. It scurries about heading for the nearest grass patch. The pika cuts all the grass it can carry crosswise in its mouth. Then it carries the grass to its home. At home the pika spreads the grass out to dry in the sun. It goes back for more grass until the day is done.

The pika is very particular about caring for its grass. When it begins to rain, the pika rushes about collecting its grass and putting it under a safe, dry place. Dried grass is stored in the pika's home. The pika feeds on the grass during the cold winter months.

A. Underline the correct answers about today's story.

1. Where is the pika's home?   (a) Rockies   (b) desert   (c) water
2. The pika's home is a   (a) tree   (b) burrow   (c) hollow log.
3. The pika collects   (a) rocks   (b) grass   (c) sticks.
4. Which word describes the pika?   (a) dangerous   (b) lazy   (c) hard-working
5. The grass is used   (a) for food   (b) for protection (c) for nesting.

B. Reread the story and write the answers to these questions.

1. When does the pika's day begin?

_____

_____

_____

2. What does the animal feed on in the winter?

_____

_____

_____

3. How much grass does the pika cut?

_____

_____

_____

4. What does the pika do when it rains?

_____

_____

_____

Unit 117 cont'd ☞

Arranging Words into Sentences

A sentence is a group of words that expresses a complete thought. Words in a sentence must come in a definite order so that the meaning is clear.

 Arrange each set of words into a sentence.

EXAMPLES: **a.** *is favorite green color my*

<u>Green is my favorite color.</u>

       b. *don't ghosts I in believe*

<u>I don't believe in ghosts.</u>

1. finally speech over his was
   _____

2. understand I the couldn't man
   _____

3. hour make sixty an minutes
   _____

4. never at she laughs jokes my
   _____

5. delivers John after newspapers school
   _____

6. umbrella I in car left my the
   _____

7. Lynn history lesson studying is her
   _____

8. contest won the Chris essay
   _____

9. ordered bowl soup Joe a of chicken
   _____

10. your I advice need
    _____

11. did we our together homework
    _____

12. usually at home Mr. lunch eats Redd
    _____

13. meeting next Monday the is night
    _____

14. bird nest built the a our in tree
    _____

15. not purple match and do green
    _____

16. bike flat my tire has a
    _____

17. important is an education
    _____

18. went her to Cheryl visit aunt
    _____

19. piano I'm lessons taking
    _____

20. egg I the dropped the on floor
    _____

21. trouble I you think in are
    _____

22. weighs the box pounds four
    _____

23. want job I a airport the at
    _____

24. honest dependable is and Ben
    _____

25. knock door was there a the on
    _____

26. rain it will tomorrow
    _____

27. Patty keep secret a cannot
    _____

28. movie everyone the enjoyed
    _____

29. noon the melted snow by
    _____

30. list here is of a members the
    _____

31. Ed another cake wants of piece
    _____

32. family a week spent the Mexico in
    _____

The Piranhas

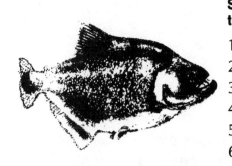

Study the spelling and meaning of each word. These words are used in today's story. Connect each word with its definition.

1. detection ——————— a. discovery
2. directions   b. meant to harm
3. rove   c. courses
4. slightest   d. three sided
5. triangular   e. most unimportant
6. vicious   f. wander

Read the story carefully and remember the details.

In the rivers of South America live the most dreaded fish, the piranhas. Some are no longer than a man's hand. Others may reach a length of two feet. Piranhas have earned a reputation of being the most vicious of all the world's fish.

Piranhas rove through the water, ready to attack anything that comes their way. They travel in large schools. At the slightest detection of blood, piranhas go crazy. They begin snapping in all directions, even at their own kind.

The piranhas have powerful jaw muscles. Their teeth are triangular and very sharp. The piranhas' bites are so strong that they can bite off a human finger in one snap.

In South America the piranhas are valued as food. Great care, however, must be taken in catching these dangerous little fish.

A. Underline the correct answers about today's story.

1. Piranhas live in   (a) lakes   (b) rivers   (c) oceans.
2. Piranhas have a reputation of being   (a) friendly   (b) poisonous   (c) vicious.
3. Piranhas attack   (a) anything   (b) other fish   (c) humans.
4. The piranha's jaw muscles are   (a) powerless   (b) weak   (c) powerful.
5. Piranhas are valued for their   (a) meat   (b) teeth   (c) fins.

B. Reread the story and write the answers to these questions.

1. In what country do piranhas live?

       _____

       _____

       _____

2. What drives piranhas crazy?

       _____

       _____

       _____

3. How large are piranhas?

       _____

       _____

       _____

4. What shape are their teeth?

       _____

       _____

       _____

Unit 118 cont'd

Changing Word Order

Word order is very important to a sentence's meaning. If you change the word order, you change the meaning.

Notice how word order affects the meaning of this sentence.
    My uncle plays the tuba.   *The tuba plays my uncle.*

Even though we did not use any additional words or leave out any words, we have a completely different meaning in the second sentence. Now let's change the word order in this sentence: Wilma read a poem by Keats. Keats read a poem by Wilma. Although the second sentence makes more sense than the one used in the first example, we still have a completely different meaning.

 Change the word order in each sentence, and write the new sentence on the blank.

1. The cat tried to catch the goldfish.
   The goldfish tried to catch the cat.

2. The frog turned into a handsome prince.

3. The father scolded his son.

4. Roger owes Harry $1,000.

5. Kim borrowed a book from Terry.

6. Wes copied from Thurmond.

7. The monkey chased the lion up a tree.

8. Isaac bought the puppy a collar.

9. The animal bit Rudy on the nose.

10. Arnie was frightened by the ghost.

11. The collie barked at the stranger.

12. Kelly loaned Paula her book.

13. Nancy purchased the car from Mr. Delzt.

14. Rob threw Louis into the lake.

15. Sylvia voted for Debbie.

16. Sam plays the piano better than Chris.

17. The barn is behind the house.

18. The mother carried the baby upstairs.

19. Sterling Heights is a surburb of Detroit.

20. Liz is older than Aunt Sally.

21. The judge ordered Dean to be quiet.

22. The pole hit a car.

23. I found the money under the rug.

24. Ginger smiled at William.

25. Vicki saw Francis take the money.

26. The witch became a beautiful princess.

Plants That Eat Insects

Study the spelling and meaning of each word. These words are used in today's story. Connect each word with its definition.

1. attracts   a. certain
2. secretes   b. not deep
3. shallow   c. gives off
4. shaped   d. formed
5. such   e. so; to that degree
6. sure   f. makes come closer

Read the story carefully and remember the details.

Have you ever heard of plants that eat insects? There are many plants that do just that. No one is really sure how the plants eat the insects, but many insects lose their lives to these plants.

One such plant is the pitcher plant. The plant has a large leaf that is shaped like a cup. Around the top of the cup are many hairs. The plant secretes a sweet liquid. This liquid attracts the insects. When the insects crawl inside the cup to find the sweet liquid, the hairs prevent them from crawling out. The insects drown in the liquid.

Another such plant is called the bladderwort. It is a floating plant usually found in shallow water.

Still another is the Venus's-flytrap. Its favorite food is the fly; but like the other insect-eating plants, the Venus's-flytrap devours whatever insect falls into its trap.

A. Underline the correct answers about today's story.

1. Some plants eat   (a) dirt   (b) paper   (c) insects.
2. What draws insects to the pitcher plant?   (a) flowers   (b) sweet liquid   (c) color
3. What prevents the insects from escaping? (a) hairs   (b) thorns   (c) sticky liquid
4. How do the insects die?   (a) drown   (b) choke   (c) smother
5. "To devour" means   (a) "to trap"   (b) "to eat"   (c) "to catch."

B. Reread the story and write the answers to these questions.

1. Name three plants that eat insects.

_____

_____

_____

2. Where do bladderworts live?

_____

_____

_____

3. What does the pitcher plant secrete?

_____

_____

_____

4. What does Venus's-flytrap do if something other than a fly falls into its trap?

_____

_____

_____

Unit 119 cont'd ☞

From "Joke" to "Leg"

J O K E E P A T O L D R

1. _j o k e_ something said or done to make one laugh
2. _ _ _ _ _ to have for a long time, forever
3. _ _ (informal) papa, father
4. _ _ _ _ to tap lightly
5. _ _ in, on, by, near, in the direction of
6. _ _ in the direction of
7. _ _ _ _ _ was given the account of orally
8. _ _ _ _ not young
9. _ _ _ _ _ percussion instrument, makes sound when beaten
10. _ _ _ liquor made from sugar cane or molasses
11. _ _ _ _ _ winged insect that flies mostly at night
12. _ _ _ _ _ _ _ woman that has given birth to a child
13. _ _ _ _ _ _ not this one but the _____
14. _ _ _ _ a word that shows a certain one
15. _ _ the male spoken about
16. _ _ _ _ female spoken about, objective case
17. _ _ _ _ _ group of cattle
18. _ _ _ _ _ going a long way down from the top
19. _ _ _ _ _ to braid, plait
20. _ _ _ _ _ _ food is served on
21. _ _ _ _ _ happening after the usual time
22. _ _ _ _ chewed and swallowed
23. _ _ _ _ common drink made from dried leaves
24. _ _ _ _ _ to pull apart by force
25. _ _ _ organ for hearing
26. _ _ _ _ between shoulder and hand
27. _ _ _ _ _ the military forces of a nation
28. _ _ belonging to me
29. _ _ _ _ a turn from a straight course
30. _ _ _ _ _ open mouth because of being sleepy
31. _ _ _ _ _ one of the hairs forming the beard on a head of oats
32. _ _ _ word used to say you can't or won't
33. _ _ _ _ _ twelve o'clock in the daytime
34. _ _ _ above and supported by
35. _ _ _ _ dry seed with a hard shell and good to eat
36. _ _ _ _ _ higher than the average
37. _ _ _ _ every one of
38. _ _ _ _ limb a person stands on

Right column (top to bottom): R U M O T H E R D E E P L A T E A

Left column (bottom, top to bottom): G E L

Bottom row: L L A T U N O O N W A Y M R

The Portuguese Man-of-War

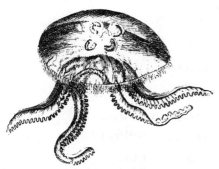

Study the spelling and meaning of each word. These words are used in today's story. Connect each word with its definition.

1. appropriately   a. part
2. close   b. without sound
3. deliberately   c. near
4. portion   d. properly
5. silently   e. quickly
6. swiftly   f. on purpose

Read the story carefully and remember the details.

The Portuguese man-of-war is more appropriately named "a floating battleship." It is one of the most dangerous creatures of the sea.

The man-of-war is a member of the large jellyfish family. It is commonly found in the warmer seas and seldom travels alone. Usually very large numbers of men-of-war live together. They move silently and swiftly through the water.

The Portuguese man-of-war has a top portion which is really a bag of gas. This portion propels the animal through the water. Underneath the bag are countless numbers of streamers. Some of these streamers contain poisonous darts which the man-of-war shoots at its prey. These streamers may reach a length of fifty feet.

The man-of-war shoots at anything which is close to it. It does not deliberately shoot swimmers, but many such cases are reported each year.

A. **Underline the correct answers about today's story.**

1. The man-of-war is   (a) friendly   (b) harmless   (c) very dangerous.
2. The man-of-war is a   (a) jellyfish   (b) shark   (c) whale.
3. The man-of-war moves about (a) slowly   (b) noisily   (c) swiftly.
4. The man-of-war attacks prey by (a) biting   (b) choking   (c) shooting poison.
5. The man-of-war shoots   (a) only at small fish (b) anything near it (c) at bright objects.

B. **Reread the story and write the answers to these questions.**

1. What does the man-of-war shoot?

_____

_____

_____

2. How loud is the man-of war?

_____

_____

_____

3. Give another name for the man-of-war.

_____

_____

_____

4. How long are its streamers?

_____

_____

_____

Unit 120 cont'd ☛

Alphabetical Order I

 Underline the words which would come first in alphabetical order.

1.	zoo	<u>young</u>	34.	book	bank	67.	enter	end
2.	great	heaven	35.	rock	road	68.	winter	wishes
3.	easy	east	36.	small	smell	69.	busy	enough
4.	sell	save	37.	bottom	bottle	70.	active	action
5.	heavy	hide	38.	bake	care	71.	clue	clay
6.	go	going	39.	reach	some	72.	box	body
7.	visit	write	40.	later	latter	73.	sheet	sheep
8.	habit	ground	41.	climb	corner	74.	wind	win
9.	echo	down	42.	repair	report	75.	but	butter
10.	send	sent	43.	some	soap	76.	test	come
11.	little	letter	44.	silly	time	77.	branch	brave
12.	quite	plant	45.	cozy	cow	78.	owl	nice
13.	can	candle	46.	much	neat	79.	grow	gray
14.	soft	sold	47.	place	please	80.	finally	find
15.	very	voyage	48.	rest	tell	81.	smile	sitting
16.	extra	expect	49.	drive	dig	82.	breeze	break
17.	ask	bite	50.	storm	stone	83.	poem	size
18.	may	mud	51.	like	ice	84.	mild	mile
19.	arrow	art	52.	know	lead	85.	have	hate
20.	arrive	carry	53.	read	reach	86.	never	now
21.	driver	drive	54.	tree	to	87.	part	park
22.	fresh	enjoy	55.	well	wall	88.	news	more
23.	voice	up	56.	able	fry	89.	extra	fullest
24.	world	word	57.	music	lake	90.	clear	clean
25.	pay	open	58.	ride	rice	91.	guess	jam
26.	trust	try	59.	late	love	92.	gate	game
27.	quiet	race	60.	meet	meat	93.	would	wood
28.	shoe	show	61.	fire	first	94.	often	friend
29.	sign	runner	62.	dance	dove	95.	base	basket
30.	true	truck	63.	nice	over	96.	cave	build
31.	trade	until	64.	quick	quiet	97.	into	inside
32.	pearl	pear	65.	lose	lost	98.	day	desk
33.	earth	earn	66.	coat	coast	99.	money	monkey

Comprehension Check

(A) Write a word that rhymes with each word.

1. much _____touch_____
2. cross _____
3. near _____
4. rush _____
5. lazy _____
6. power _____
7. winter _____
8. fish _____
9. sweet _____
10. just _____
11. right _____
12. care _____
13. reach _____
14. thing _____
15. plants _____

(B) Arrange each set of words into sentences.

1. stores the a pika for winter grass
   _____A pika stores grass for the winter._____

2. silently the moves man-of-war
   _____

3. a a bird falcon is
   _____

4. in Mountains the pikas Rocky live
   _____

5. flies eat Venus's-flytraps
   _____

6. by is the law falcon protected
   _____

7. have piranhas teeth sharp
   _____

8. the sky flies in falcon high the
   _____

9. moves falcon the fast
   _____

10. grass crosswise pikas carry
    _____

11. keen the falcon eyesight has
    _____

12. fish piranha a a is dreaded
    _____

13. a the in burrow lives pika
    _____

14. piranhas food are as valued
    _____

15. man-of-war in the a lives group
    _____

16. little furry a is the animal pika
    _____

(C) Arrange each list in alphabetical order.

1. ocean _____beach_____
2. desert _____
3. mountain _____
4. beach _____
5. land _____
6. river _____
7. school _____
8. group _____
9. pairs _____
10. crowd _____
11. alone _____
12. member _____
13. insect _____
14. rodent _____
15. mammal _____
16. fish _____
17. plant _____
18. bird _____

(D) Complete these sentences.

1. Piranhas live in _____South_____ America.
2. The pika feeds on _____ .
3. The man-of-war is _____ .
4. The peregrine falcon lives in _____ country.
5. A bladderwort is a _____ plant.
6. The peregrine falcon is a supreme _____ .
7. The man-of-war is a _____ .
8. The pika begins its day at _____ .
9. Piranhas travel in large _____ .
10. The pitcher plant _____ its victims.

Test 24 cont'd ☞

Comprehension Check (continued)

Ⓔ Match these words and their definitions. These words appeared in the reading selections from units 116-120.

_c_ 1. blow   ____ 7. triangular   a. part   g. formed

____ 2. entirely   ____ 8. shallow   b. apart from others   h. three-sided

____ 3. dawn   ____ 9. shaped   c. strike   i. merest

____ 4. particular   ____ 10. sure   d. completely   j. not deep

____ 5. safe   ____ 11. close   e. early morning light   k. near

____ 6. slightest   ____ 12. portion   f. free from harm   l. certain

Ⓕ Underline the correct answers.

1.	How does the falcon hunt?	(a)	by sight	(b)	by sound
2.	Who hunts with falcons?	(a)	falconry	(b)	falconer
3.	Where is the pika's home?	(a)	Andes	(b)	Rockies
4.	What is the pika's home?	(a)	burrow	(b)	hollow tree
5.	Where do piranhas live?	(a)	lakes	(b)	rivers
6.	What do piranhas attack?	(a)	meat only	(b)	anything
7.	What do some plants eat?	(a)	paper	(b)	insects
8.	What does "devour" mean?	(a)	"to eat"	(b)	"to catch"
9.	What is the man-of-war?	(a)	jellyfish	(b)	shark
10.	How loud is the man-of-war?	(a)	very noisy	(b)	silent

Choose one of the following topics and write a paragraph.

(1) How did piranhas acquire their reputation?

(2) Do you think animals should be used to hunt? Why or why not?

_____

_____

_____

_____

_____

_____

_____

_____

_____

_____

The Praying Mantis

Study the spelling and meaning of each word. These words are used in today's story. Connect each word with its definition.

1. camouflages
2. clasped
3. lightning speed
4. motionless
5. patient
6. resembles

a. held together
b. looks similar to
c. without movement
d. not minding to wait
e. amazing quickness
f. disguises

Read the story carefully and remember the details.

The praying mantis is a slow-moving insect. Its green color camouflages the insect against its surrounding of green leaves. The praying mantis is the only insect that can turn its head and look from side to side.

The praying mantis eats nothing but raw meat. It waits motionless and patient. Its arms are lifted. The position resembles the clamped hands of a person praying. Thus the mantis receives the name praying mantis.

When an insect flies past, the mantis strikes with lightning speed. The insect is helpless under the mantis's strong hold.

The praying mantis will attack almost any other insect. It has an enormous appetite for its size and has been known to turn cannibal.

A. Underline the correct answers about today's story.

1. A camouflage is a	(a) disguise	(b) color	(c) hiding place.
2. What color is the praying mantis?	(a) brown	(b) green	(c) yellow
3. What does the mantis eat?	(a) leaves	(b) meat	(c) wood
4. One who eats his own kind is a	(a) cannibal	(b) devil	(c) vampire.
5. Which word does not describe a mantis?	(a) patient	(b) strong	(c) helpless

B. Reread the story and write the answers to these questions.

1. What is the insect's usual surroundings?

_____

_____

_____

2. What can the praying mantis do that other insects cannot do?

_____

_____

_____

3. Where does its name come from?

_____

_____

_____

4. How does the insect sometimes get food?

_____

_____

_____

   Unit 121 cont'd ☛

Alphabetical Order II

Write each group of words in alphabetical order.

1. ants _____answer_____
2. answer _____ants_____

3. invite _____
4. intake _____
5. inward _____
6. inside _____
7. into _____

8. beach _____
9. beat _____
10. bear _____
11. bean _____
12. beating _____

13. easy _____
14. each _____
15. eagle _____
16. east _____
17. eat _____

18. normal _____
19. not _____
20. no _____
21. nose _____
22. north _____

23. eleven _____
24. enemy _____
25. egg _____
26. end _____
27. either _____

28. quit _____
29. quick _____
30. quite _____
31. quiz _____
32. quiet _____

33. lady _____
34. lane _____
35. lake _____

36. grain _____
37. grass _____
38. grade _____
39. grow _____
40. grape _____

41. scene _____
42. scar _____
43. scarf _____
44. scale _____
45. scare _____

46. doctor _____
47. done _____
48. doll _____
49. dog _____
50. dollar _____

51. journey _____
52. just _____
53. join _____
54. joke _____
55. job _____

56. hold _____
57. home _____
58. honest _____
59. holiday _____
60. hole _____

61. talk _____
62. tall _____
63. tale _____
64. take _____
65. taii _____

66. change _____
67. charge _____
68. chance _____

69. above _____
70. about _____
71. absent _____
72. aardvark _____
73. accident _____

74. real _____
75. reading _____
76. ready _____
77. read _____
78. reader _____

79. milk _____
80. mind _____
81. mine _____
82. mile _____
83. mink _____

84. fire _____
85. fill _____
86. five _____
87. find _____
88. fight _____

89. zoo _____
90. zest _____
91. zone _____
92. zebra _____
93. zero _____

94. often _____
95. office _____
96. off _____
97. of _____
98. offer _____

The Proboscis Monkey

Study the spelling and meaning of each word. These words are used in today's story. Connect each word with its definition.

1. acquires
2. bothersome
3. escape
4. native
5. periods
6. proboscis

a. born in a particular place
b. causing trouble
c. get free
d. time frames
e. receives; gets
f. nose

Read the story carefully and remember the details.

The proboscis monkey is the strangest-looking monkey in the world. The proboscis monkey is a native of Borneo. It acquires its name from the large nose of the adult male. The nose is about three inches long, often hanging below his chin. The nose is bothersome. The monkey sometimes has to push it aside in order to eat.

Like most monkeys the proboscis monkey is a tree dweller. Its home is always near a river bank. The proboscis monkey is a good swimmer. It often dives under water to hide or escape from its enemies.

The proboscis monkey travels in small groups. It is a vegetarian. A calm animal, the proboscis monkey often sits for long periods of time without moving.

A. Underline the correct answers about today's story.

1. The proboscis monkey is
   named for (a) its nose (b) its ears (c) its tail.
2. Where does the monkey live? (a) mountains (b) desert (c) trees
3. To escape from enemies, it (a) hides in burrows (b) climbs trees (c) dives under water.
4. A vegetarian eats only (a) meat (b) vegetables (c) fruit.
5. Which word describes
   the monkey? (a) nervous (b) calm (c) easily excited

B. Reread the story and write the answers to these questions.

1. Where is the monkey's home?

   _____
   _____
   _____

2. What does the monkey eat?

   _____
   _____
   _____

3. What does "proboscis" mean?

   _____
   _____
   _____

4. What is the monkey's home always near?

   _____
   _____
   _____

  Unit 122 cont'd

Alphabetical Order III

 Arrange each list of words in alphabetical order.

1. aardwolf   _aardvark_
2. above   _____
3. abandon   _____
4. about   _____
5. ability   _____
6. aardvark   _____
7. abolish   _____
8. abbreviate   _____
9. absent   _____
10. able   _____

1. demonstrate   _demand_
2. democratic   _____
3. department   _____
4. dentist   _____
5. demand   _____
6. deny   _____
7. den   _____
8. democracy   _____
9. depart   _____
10. demolish   _____

1. grade   _grab_
2. grammar   _____
3. grain   _____
4. gravel   _____
5. grab   _____
6. grasp   _____
7. gray   _____
8. grand   _____
9. gravy   _____
10. grace   _____
11. grass   _____
12. grant   _____
13. grave   _____
14. graceful   _____
15. grape   _____

1. smoke   _small_
2. snatch   _____
3. small   _____
4. smear   _____
5. smile   _____
6. snack   _____
7. smart   _____
8. smog   _____
9. snake   _____
10. smash   _____
11. sneak   _____
12. smooth   _____
13. smell   _____
14. snag   _____
15. smudge   _____

1. where   _wheel_
2. whey   _____
3. whether   _____
4. wheel   _____
5. whew   _____
6. when   _____

1. they   _the_
2. their   _____
3. them   _____
4. the   _____
5. there   _____
6. these   _____

The Pronghorn

Study the spelling and meaning of each word. These words are used in today's story. Connect each word with its definition.

1. alarmed
2. grazes
3. nervous
4. sagebrush
5. shrubs
6. slender

a. jumpy; uneasy
b. slim; thin
c. frightened
d. a low shrub
e. stemmed, woody plant
f. feeds on growing grass

Read the story carefully and remember the details.

At sixty miles an hour the pronghorn is one of America's fastest mammals. Its slender legs and powerful muscles also make it one of the most beautiful animals.

In summer the pronghorn grazes on grass and weeds. In the winter it eats sagebrush and shrubs.

The pronghorn is a nervous animal. When alarmed, the hair on a large white rump patch stands erect. This signal warns other members of the group that danger may be near. At the slightest movement the pronghorns speed away.

The enemies of the pronghorn are the coyote and the wolf. When the pronghorn cannot run away, it fights vigorously, using its hoofs as weapons. Once killed for meat and sport, the pronghorn now is protected by strict laws.

A. Underline the correct answers about today's story.

1. How fast can the pronghorn travel?   (a) 10 m.p.h.   (b) 60 m.p.h.   (c) 100 m.p.h.
2. Which word describes the pronghorn?   (a) awkward   (b) calm   (c) nervous
3. At the slightest movement the pronghorn   (a) faints   (b) attacks   (c) runs away.
4. What are the pronghorn's weapons?   (a) hoofs   (b) horns   (c) teeth
5. Pronghorns usually travel   (a) alone   (b) in pairs   (c) in groups.

B. Reread the story and write the answers to these questions.

1. What does the pronghorn eat in summer?

_____

_____

_____

2. What does it eat in winter?

_____

_____

_____

3. Name two enemies of the pronghorn.

_____

_____

_____

4. What happens when the pronghorn is alarmed?

_____

_____

_____

Unit 123 cont'd ☛

Using Guide Words

  If the words in the boxes were guide words in a dictionary, on which page would the following words appear?

21	
call	**cat**

_21_	1. caller	____	11. cave
____	2. cause	____	12. catcher
____	3. cell	____	13. change
____	4. chain	____	14. camp
____	5. can	____	15. charm
____	6. charge	____	16. card
____	7. chew	____	17. candle
____	8. Canada	____	18. certain
____	9. car	____	19. captain
____	10. chair	____	20. cherry

22	
catch	**chill**

____	21. cent	____	31. carry
____	22. came	____	32. chase
____	23. chart	____	33. camel
____	24. care	____	34. child
____	25. chance	____	35. cart
____	26. candy	____	36. check
____	27. cheese	____	37. chick
____	28. cape	____	38. cane
____	29. chicken	____	39. cheer
____	30. center	____	40. cap

46	
man	**may**

____	41. men	____	51. March
____	42. meal	____	52. melt
____	43. map	____	53. mark
____	44. melody	____	54. manly
____	45. met	____	55. mice
____	46. match	____	56. many
____	47. merry	____	57. milk
____	48. mean	____	58. market
____	49. medium	____	59. mast
____	50. math	____	60. measure

47	
me	**milk**

____	61. manner	____	71. medal
____	62. mess	____	72. mend
____	63. member	____	73. mash
____	64. matter	____	74. medicine
____	65. meet	____	75. Max
____	66. master	____	76. middle
____	67. metal	____	77. Mexico
____	68. meat	____	78. memory
____	69. mass	____	79. mat
____	70. melon	____	80. meeting

98	
race	**rat**

____	81. reason	____	86. raccoon
____	82. reach	____	87. ray
____	83. raft	____	88. rain
____	84. radio	____	89. remove
____	85. remain	____	90. ran

99	
raw	**repair**

____	91. red	____	96. range
____	92. rail	____	97. read
____	93. rake	____	98. receive
____	94. rang	____	99. rag
____	95. real	____	100. rent

Pueblos

Study the spelling and meaning of each word. These words are used in today's story. Connect each word with its definition.

1. abandon
2. constantly
3. intelligent
4. intruders
5. peaceful
6. simple

a. always occurring
b. serene
c. not complicated
d. desert; leave behind
e. showing knowledge
f. unwanted guests

Read the story carefully and remember the details.

Pueblos is the name given to a group of Indians who lived in the southwest United States long ago. They were a simple and yet intelligent people.

The Pueblos are best remembered for their large apartment dwellings which still lay in ruins in the Southwest. These apartments were built high in hillside caves. Some were so big that they sheltered entire cities. Entry to the cities was by ladders. Then the ladders were pulled up to keep out unwanted intruders.

The Pueblos were peaceful people. They were constantly bothered by their warlike neighbors who stole their food and possessions.

Pueblos were farmers. After a severe drought, the Pueblos were forced to abandon their homes. They scattered in all directions and soon intermingled with other Indian tribes. All that remained was the huge apartment houses in the cliffs.

A. Underline the correct answers about today's story.

1. Pueblos is the name given to   (a) land   (b) people   (c) mountains.
2. Pueblos are remembered for their   (a) farming   (b) pottery   (c) homes.
3. Entry to the city was by   (a) horseback   (b) ladder   (c) ship.
4. Pueblos were   (a) farmers   (b) warriors   (c) fishermen.
5. Pueblos abandoned their homes because of   (a) heavy rains   (b) war   (c) a drought.

B. Reread the story and write the answers to these questions.

1. What part of the United States did the people inhabit?

_____

_____

_____

2. Where were their homes built?

_____

_____

_____

3. Who or what bothered these people?

_____

_____

_____

4. What did the people do after they abandoned their homes?

_____

_____

_____

Unit 124 cont'd ☞

Guide Words

 Each box contains a set of guide words. On which page would each word appear?

accident	20	actress

_21_ 1. adventure   ____ 6. ace
____ 2. act   ____ 7. adjust
____ 3. address   ____ 8. active
____ 4. adopt   ____ 9. admit
____ 5. again   ____ 10. acquire

add	21	against

____ 11. after   ____ 16. actor
____ 12. admire   ____ 17. against
____ 13. acorn   ____ 18. acting
____ 14. action   ____ 19. acre
____ 15. advice   ____ 20. activity

do	35	dot

____ 21. done   ____ 26. dock
____ 22. double   ____ 27. dragon
____ 23. drip   ____ 28. dome
____ 24. dog   ____ 29. dove
____ 25. draw   ____ 30. doll

double	36	drive

____ 31. down   ____ 36. dress
____ 32. doctor   ____ 37. door
____ 33. drag   ____ 38. dot
____ 34. dream   ____ 39. dozen
____ 35. doodle   ____ 40. dolphin

fold	53	for

____ 41. forget   ____ 46. fold
____ 42. food   ____ 47. follow
____ 43. form   ____ 48. force
____ 44. fool   ____ 49. fond
____ 45. for   ____ 50. forgive

force	54	forward

____ 51. forehead   ____ 56. forward
____ 52. foot   ____ 57. forest
____ 53. fork   ____ 58. football
____ 54. folk   ____ 59. fort
____ 55. fortune   ____ 60. follower

lace	78	large

____ 61. land   ____ 66. ladder
____ 62. last   ____ 67. late
____ 63. lamp   ____ 68. lane
____ 64. lay   ____ 69. large
____ 65. lazy   ____ 70. lead

last	79	leave

____ 71. law   ____ 76. lap
____ 72. lady   ____ 77. leader
____ 73. leaf   ____ 78. lake
____ 74. laugh   ____ 79. lamb
____ 75. language   ____ 80. layer

table	96	tape

____ 81. team   ____ 86. teach
____ 82. tea   ____ 87. tap
____ 83. talker   ____ 88. tan
____ 84. tail   ____ 89. task
____ 85. target   ____ 90. tablet

tar	97	tease

____ 91. take   ____ 96. taxi
____ 92. taste   ____ 97. tale
____ 93. talk   ____ 98. tear
____ 94. tax   ____ 99. tank
____ 95. talent   ____ 100. teacher

The Red Cross

Study the spelling and meaning of each word. These words are used in today's story. Connect each word with its definition.

1. charitable
2. designed
3. disasters
4. largest
5. oldest
6. volunteer

a. planned
b. offer of one's own free will
c. most ancient
d. great misfortunes
e. giving to the needy
f. biggest

Read the story carefully and remember the details.

The Red Cross is the world's oldest and largest charitable organization. When it was first founded in 1864, the Red Cross was designed to help wounded soldiers. However, the Red Cross soon branched out to help civilians as well as soldiers.

The Red Cross is a voluntary organization. Its primary goal is to work for peace. It protects the sick and wounded members of the armed services. When natural disasters occur, the Red Cross helps the victims.

Anyone can volunteer his services to the Red Cross. The organization seeks to ease human suffering. It encourages health.

Since 1864 the Red Cross has been successful in achieving its goals. It proves that people of all races and beliefs can work together in peace.

A. Underline the correct answers about today's story.

1. The Red Cross is located   (a) worldwide   (b) in the U.S. only   (c) in Europe only.
2. The Red Cross works   (a) year round   (b) only in wartime   (c) only in peacetime.
3. The Red Cross first helped   (a) the needy   (b) the sick   (c) wounded soldiers.
4. The Red Cross is open to   (a) college graduates   (b) anyone   (c) soldiers.
5. The Red Cross is working for   (a) peace   (b) the army   (c) businesses.

B. Reread the story and write the answers to these questions.

1. When was the Red Cross founded?

_____

_____

_____

2. What type of organization is the Red Cross?

_____

_____

_____

3. What does the organization encourage?

_____

_____

_____

4. What is its primary goal?

_____

_____

_____

Unit 125 cont'd ☞

More Guide Words

In each box is a set of guide words. Underline on what page each word would appear in a dictionary.

93			
dark			**date**

1. deadline	before 93	on 93	on 94	<u>on 95</u>	after 95
2. dash	before 93	on 93	on 94	on 95	after 95
3. dare	before 93	on 93	on 94	on 95	after 95
4. dear	before 93	on 93	on 94	on 95	after 95
5. darkness	before 93	on 93	on 94	on 95	after 95
6. deadly	before 93	on 93	on 94	on 95	after 95
7. daughter	before 93	on 93	on 94	on 95	after 95
8. day	before 93	on 93	on 94	on 95	after 95
9. death	before 93	on 93	on 94	on 95	after 95
10. danger	before 93	on 93	on 94	on 95	after 95
11. dart	before 93	on 93	on 94	on 95	after 95
12. dawn	before 93	on 93	on 94	on 95	after 95
13. deaf	before 93	on 93	on 94	on 95	after 95

Guide words:
- **94**: daughter — daze
- **95**: dead — deal

156			
rear			**recall**

Guide words:
- **157**: receive — recess
- **158**: recite — record

14. reach	before 156	on 156	on 157	on 158	after 158
15. receiver	before 156	on 156	on 157	on 158	after 158
16. recount	before 156	on 156	on 157	on 158	after 158
17. rebel	before 156	on 156	on 157	on 158	after 158
18. recreation	before 156	on 156	on 157	on 158	after 158
19. react	before 156	on 156	on 157	on 158	after 158
20. recommend	before 156	on 156	on 157	on 158	after 158
21. reason	before 156	on 156	on 157	on 158	after 158
22. read	before 156	on 156	on 157	on 158	after 158
23. recent	before 156	on 156	on 157	on 158	after 158
24. recovery	before 156	on 156	on 157	on 158	after 158
25. recognize	before 156	on 156	on 157	on 158	after 158

Comprehension Check

(A) Arrange each set of words in alphabetical order.

1. program ___*direction*___
2. speed _____
3. volunteer _____
4. direction _____
5. organize _____

6. summer _____
7. winter _____
8. fall _____
9. spring _____
10. autumn _____

11. band _____
12. history _____
13. typing _____
14. algebra _____
15. science _____

16. gasoline _____
17. general _____
18. gum _____
19. going _____
20. giggle _____

21. travel _____
22. trade _____
23. train _____
24. trail _____
25. trace _____

26. enroll _____
27. east _____
28. escape _____
29. earth _____
30. extra _____

31. solution _____
32. space _____
33. sound _____
34. sports _____
35. soon _____
36. south _____
37. special _____
38. so _____
39. speech _____
40. spare _____

(B) On which page would each word appear?

sea	13	second		seed	14	sell		send	15	share

___*14*___ 1. seldom
____ 2. sense
____ 3. seat
____ 4. settle
____ 5. share
____ 6. select
____ 7. seed
____ 8. senior
____ 9. shadow
____ 10. self

____ 11. seven
____ 12. seas
____ 13. seize
____ 14. serve
____ 15. send-off
____ 16. seating
____ 17. shake
____ 18. seeding
____ 19. seeds
____ 20. seep

____ 21. shall
____ 22. second
____ 23. sensitive
____ 24. sea
____ 25. seem
____ 26. segment
____ 27. senile
____ 28. sell
____ 29. sender
____ 30. shallow

____ 31. shade
____ 32. selfish
____ 33. send
____ 34. sentry
____ 35. season
____ 36. seek
____ 37. shape
____ 38. selection
____ 39. shampoo
____ 40. seemingly

(C) Complete these sentences.

1. Pueblos are remembered for ___*dwellings*___ .
2. The pronghorn moves _____ .
3. The Red Cross is a _____ organization.
4. The praying mantis can turn its _____ .
5. The proboscis monkey gets its name from its _____ .

6. A praying mantis' color is _____ .
7. Pueblos were _____ .
8. Proboscis monkeys live in _____ .
9. The pronghorn is a _____ animal.
10. The Red Cross encourages _____ .

Test 25 cont'd ☞

Comprehension Check (continued)

(D) Match these words and their definitions. These words appeared in the reading selections from units 121-125.

_f_ 1. resembles   ____ 7. grazes   a. leave behind   g. get free

____ 2. intelligent   ____ 8. abandon   b. feeds on growing   h. amazing quickness

____ 3. nervous   ____ 9. escape   grass   i. giving to the needy

____ 4. disasters   ____ 10. native   c. showing knowledge   j. planned

____ 5. charitable   ____ 11. constantly   d. great misfortunes   k. jumpy; uneasy

____ 6. designed   ____ 12. lightning speed   e. always occurring   l. born in a

    f. looks similar to   particular place

(E) Underline the correct answers.

1. How does the praying mantis differ from other insects?   (a) can turn head   (b) can close eyes
2. What does the praying mantis eat?   (a) raw meat   (b) plants
3. Which proboscis monkey has the larger nose?   (a) male   (b) female
4. Which word describes the proboscis monkey?   (a) nervous   (b) calm
5. Which word describes the pronghorn?   (a) slow   (b) fast
6. What signal warns other pronghorns of danger?   (a) low growl   (b) hair on rump
7. Where did the Pueblos live?   (a) Southwest   (b) South
8. What are the Pueblos remembered for?   (a) homes   (b) farming
9. When was the Red Cross founded?   (a) 1864   (b) 1964
10. What is the Red Cross' primary goal?   (a) peace   (b) help soldiers

Choose one of the following topics and write a paragraph.

(1) What things does the Red Cross do?

(2) Why did the Pueblos leave their homes?

_____

_____

_____

_____

_____

_____

_____

_____

_____

_____

The Red-Tailed Hawk

Study the spelling and meaning of each word. These words are used in today's story. Connect each word with its definition.

1. keen
2. locates
3. renowned
4. seldom
5. superb
6. unjustly

a. famous
b. rarely; not often
c. unfairly
d. finds
e. of the highest quality
f. sharp and quick

Read the story carefully and remember the details.

The red-tailed hawk is unjustly called the chicken hawk. Although capable of catching a bird the size of a chicken, it seldom does so. The red-tailed hawk, like other hawks and birds of prey, is a superb hunter.

The hawk is renowned for its excellent eyesight. Its prey includes rodents and small animals. When hunting, the hawk perches on a tree near a field. With its keen eyes it locates its prey. Then it sweeps down with lightning speed and captures the animal.

The hawk is a large heavy bird, yet it is handsome and graceful. Its wingspan may reach five feet.

The red-tailed hawk's home is in the eastern United States. During the winter most hawks migrate to the tropics.

A. Underline the correct answers about today's story.

1. The reputation as a chicken hawk is   (a) not fair   (b) completely false   (c) completely true.
2. The hawk has excellent   (a) hearing   (b) sense of smell   (c) eyesight.
3. The hawk's prey is mainly   (a) snakes   (b) rodents   (c) fish.
4. Which word describes the hawk?   (a) tiny   (b) graceful   (c) ugly
5. The hawk is a superb   (a) hunter   (b) fisherman   (c) fighter.

B. Reread the story and write the answers to these questions.

1. Where does the red-tailed hawk perch when hunting?

_____

_____

_____

2. How large is the hawk's wingspan?

_____

_____

3. What kind of bird is the red-tailed hawk?

_____

_____

_____

4. Where do hawks migrate?

_____

_____

Unit 126 cont'd ☞

Counting Syllables I

A. Underline the one-syllable words.

1. <u>peace</u>	11. voice	21. foreign	31. smart
2. greed	12. urge	22. none	32. young
3. exam	13. unless	23. ghost	33. rejoice
4. truth	14. fright	24. wrong	34. usual
5. laugh	15. visual	25. leaf	35. lawn
6. final	16. shut	26. measure	36. squeeze
7. engage	17. bowl	27. triumph	37. ideal
8. cause	18. knob	28. knock	38. globe
9. kick	19. night	29. threat	39. battle
10. quite	20. device	30. grief	40. count

B. Underline the two-syllable words.

1. <u>fragile</u>	11. occupy	21. giant	31. nuisance
2. surprise	12. absent	22. nonsense	32. machine
3. remedy	13. movies	23. luxury	33. needy
4. modern	14. ignore	24. career	34. fierce
5. equip	15. pledge	25. explode	35. persuade
6. significant	16. journey	26. similar	36. ignorance
7. partner	17. legal	27. lonesome	37. minute
8. shrewd	18. forbidden	28. daughter	38. question
9. itself	19. quiet	29. bewilder	39. chatter
10. honest	20. anxious	30. motto	40. eternal

C. Underline the words which contain three or more syllables.

1. <u>ambition</u>	11. condemn	21. conquer	31. opinion
2. distinct	12. idea	22. favorite	32. ruin
3. happiness	13. tragic	23. impossible	33. piano
4. confused	14. exercise	24. separate	34. vacant
5. securely	15. identify	25. wisdom	35. decision
6. welcome	16. television	26. zone	36. hesitate
7. wonderful	17. vanish	27. outstanding	37. skeleton
8. plunder	18. penalty	28. bleach	38. yummy
9. flexible	19. combine	29. zigzag	39. value
10. xylophone	20. publisher	30. furious	40. interesting

The Ring-Necked Pheasant

Study the spelling and meaning of each word. These words are used in today's story. Connect each word with its definition.

1. adapted
2. concealing
3. described
4. native
5. near
6. outwitting

a. gave an account of
b. being smarter than
c. belonging naturally
d. made to fit
e. hiding from view
f. close

Read the story carefully and remember the details.

The ring-necked pheasant is not a native American bird. However, it has adapted remarkably well to this land and become one of America's most beautiful game birds. It is a popular bird with hunters. The pheasant gets its name from the white ring around its neck.

The pheasant is a strong flier, but it seems to be more at home on the ground. It is quite good at concealing itself in bushy undergrowth. When the enemy comes too near, however, the ringnecked pheasant bolts and takes to the air quickly. It has been described as bold and sly at outwitting its opponent.

In the winter the pheasants gather in small flocks. The pheasants stay wherever there is food. They build their nests in tall weeds at the edge of a field.

A. Underline the correct answers about today's story.

1. The pheasant is popular with   (a) farmers   (b) hunters   (c) children.
2. The pheasant is more at home   (a) in the air   (b) in the water   (c) on the ground.
3. Which word describes the pheasant?   (a) sly   (b) stupid   (c) unskilled
4. Where do pheasants build their nests?   (a) trees   (b) on water   (c) edge of a field
5. The pheasant gets its name from its   (a) call   (b) white ring   (c) long neck.

B. Reread the story and write the answers to these questions.

1. What does the pheasant do when the enemy is near?

_____

_____

_____

2. With whom is the pheasant popular?

_____

_____

_____

3. What kind of bird is the ring-necked pheasant?

_____

_____

_____

4. Where do pheasants stay?

_____

_____

_____

Unit 127 cont'd 👉

Counting Syllables II

A. Underline each word that has more than one syllable.

1. <u>office</u>
2. cause
3. suddenly
4. allow
5. finally
6. even
7. lawn
8. together
9. night
10. hospital
11. giant
12. gain
13. accident
14. safe
15. prize
16. possible
17. weigh
18. folks
19. terrible
20. anxious
21. juice
22. favorite
23. separate
24. license
25. career
26. quite
27. medium
28. history
29. magic
30. wisdom
31. telephone
32. voice
33. none
34. return
35. job
36. umbrella
37. ghost
38. piano
39. straight
40. mistake
41. comma
42. modern
43. strong
44. through
45. guess
46. exercise
47. own
48. television
49. holiday
50. key

B. How many syllables are in each word?

__2__ 1. although
____ 2. guest
____ 3. wonderful
____ 4. explain
____ 5. early
____ 6. match
____ 7. honest
____ 8. language
____ 9. information
____ 10. sleep
____ 11. reason
____ 12. reward
____ 13. tooth
____ 14. journey
____ 15. neighbor
____ 16. nonsense
____ 17. welcome
____ 18. bowl
____ 19. forever
____ 20. secret
____ 21. knock
____ 22. freedom
____ 23. tomato
____ 24. melt
____ 25. leaf
____ 26. machine
____ 27. peace
____ 28. protection
____ 29. wrong
____ 30. tunnel
____ 31. habit
____ 32. raw
____ 33. vacation
____ 34. laugh
____ 35. adventure
____ 36. bold
____ 37. famous
____ 38. thought
____ 39. zero
____ 40. important
____ 41. between
____ 42. shape
____ 43. unless
____ 44. rush
____ 45. person
____ 46. visit
____ 47. sentence
____ 48. remember
____ 49. itself
____ 50. pleasure

Rodents

Study the spelling and meaning of each word. These words are used in today's story. Connect each word with its definition.

1. adapted
2. chisels
3. destructive
4. except
5. include
6. valuable

a. other than
b. sharp-edged tools
c. of considerable worth
d. destroying
e. take in
f. fit

Read the story carefully and remember the details.

"Rodents" is the name given to a group of gnawing animals. Common rodents include squirrels, rabbits, chipmunks, beavers, and muskrats. Mice and rats have given rodents a bad name. Not all rodents are destructive. A few rodents are very valuable as fur bearers.

The rodents are well adapted to their roles as gnawing animals. Their jaws are made to move sideways as well as up and down. Their front teeth have edges that serve as chisels. Their back teeth are used to grind the food.

Rodents are found almost everywhere in the world except in the seas. They live on the ground, under the ground, in trees, and in the water.

A. Underline the correct answers about today's story.

1. Rodents are animals that   (a) gnaw   (b) burrow   (c) swim.
2. The front teeth work like   (a) grinders (b) chisels   (c) shovels.
3. Rodents are found almost everywhere except (a) seas (b) deserts (c) underground.
4. Which rodent is the most destructive? (a) mouse (b) chipmunk (c) beaver
5. Which animal is not a rodent?   (a) rabbit (b) muskrat (c) dog

B. Reread the story and write the answers to these questions.

1. Which two rodents have given them a bad name?

_____
_____
_____

2. What purpose is served by a rodent's back teeth?

_____
_____
_____

3. How are some rodents valuable?

_____
_____

4. Name two places rodents are found.

_____
_____
_____

Unit 128 cont'd ☞

Dividing Words into Syllables

 Divide each word into syllables if possible.

1. ago   _a go_
2. number
3. barn
4. water
5. yellow
6. flag
7. basket
8. correct
9. seven
10. sweet
11. cabin
12. follow
13. monkey
14. watch
15. name
16. summer
17. bicycle
18. reason
19. music
20. country
21. help
22. smoke
23. family
24. farmer
25. again
26. ground
27. puppy
28. clown
29. candy
30. room
31. bridge
32. newspaper
33. person
34. easy

35. island
36. money
37. obey
38. swimming
39. better
40. think
41. different
42. please
43. pony
44. football
45. always
46. vacation
47. airplane
48. now
49. often
50. almost
51. upon
52. over
53. color
54. ruler
55. soon
56. season
57. under
58. within
59. raincoat
60. window
61. question
62. sea
63. hearing
64. sometime
65. more
66. wishes
67. tomorrow

68. meaning
69. reading
70. teacher
71. pencil
72. lake
73. highway
74. here
75. into
76. waiting
77. the
78. sending
79. write
80. telling
81. me
82. sentence
83. without
84. sitting
85. week
86. yard
87. mirror
88. pancake
89. from
90. curtain
91. clock
92. cookie
93. picture
94. today
95. little
96. many
97. off
98. bird
99. river
100. apple

310

The Ruby-Throated Hummingbird Unit 129

Study the spelling and meaning of each word. These words are used in today's story. Connect each word with its definition.

1. complete
2. kinds
3. replace
4. reverse
5. travels
6. various

a. backward
b. total, absolute
c. take the place of
d. different
e. types
f. moves from place to place

Read the story carefully and remember the details.

The hummingbird family is made up of the smallest birds in the entire bird family. Among the various kinds of hummingbirds is the ruby-throated hummingbird. This bird measures only 3½ inches long and weighs a mere one-eighth of an ounce.

The ruby-throated hummingbird is the traveler of the family. During migration this bird travels some 2,000 miles from Central America to southern Canada.

The female has complete charge of building the nest and caring for the young. The nest is very tiny — no larger than a quarter.

The hummingbird is best noted for its ability to fly. It is able to travel up and down and sideways. It can even fly in reverse! No wonder the bird has a big appetite. It must replace all of that energy which was lost in constant flight.

A. **Underline the correct answers about today's story.**

1. Which word describes hummingbirds?	(a) pests	(b) small	(c) dangerous
2. Among hummingbirds, the ruby-throated is	(a) the traveler	(b) the smallest	(c) the largest.
3. The bird's nest is the size of	(a) an apple	(b) a dollar	(c) a quarter.
4. The bird is best noted for its ability to	(a) eat	(b) fly	(c) walk.
5. Who takes care of the young?	(a) male	(b) female	(c) both parents

B. **Reread the story and write the answers to these questions.**

1. Which bird is the smallest of the entire family?

_____
_____
_____

3. How much does the hummingbird weigh?

_____
_____
_____

2. Where does the hummingbird begin its migration?

_____
_____
_____

4. Where does the bird's migration end?

_____
_____
_____

Unit 129 cont'd

Syllables

A syllable is part of a word pronounced as a unit. Usually a syllable consists of a vowel or a vowel with one or more consonants.

 Divide each word into syllables if possible.

1. instrument *in stru ment*
2. afternoon _____
3. hundred _____
4. ache _____
5. journey _____
6. insect _____
7. thirst _____
8. banana _____
9. instead _____
10. view _____
11. although _____
12. magazine _____
13. sponge _____
14. wizard _____
15. leather _____
16. bucket _____
17. certain _____
18. tomorrow _____
19. knight _____
20. amusement _____
21. misplace _____
22. yesterday _____
23. secret _____
24. necklace _____
25. alive _____
26. chocolate _____
27. narrow _____
28. taste _____
29. universe _____
30. lively _____
31. stubborn _____
32. freedom _____
33. yacht _____
34. common _____

35. organize _____
36. shy _____
37. permission _____
38. costume _____
39. wonderful _____
40. ought _____
41. snack _____
42. distance _____
43. parachute _____
44. invent _____
45. dream _____
46. edge _____
47. pavement _____
48. without _____
49. entertain _____
50. sunset _____
51. person _____
52. pattern _____
53. furniture _____
54. empty _____
55. danger _____
56. courage _____
57. doubt _____
58. proof _____
59. anxious _____
60. rough _____
61. enough _____
62. relieve _____
63. advice _____
64. quick _____
65. regular _____
66. faithful _____
67. equal _____

68. agreement _____
69. sandwich _____
70. future _____
71. hesitate _____
72. concern _____
73. ghost _____
74. promise _____
75. spelling _____
76. scheme _____
77. disgrace _____
78. arrange _____
79. borrow _____
80. climate _____
81. extra _____
82. tongue _____
83. invitation _____
84. belong _____
85. weather _____
86. choice _____
87. middle _____
88. medicine _____
89. surround _____
90. unit _____
91. worth _____
92. volunteer _____
93. sofa _____
94. eating _____
95. yes _____
96. homework _____
97. cheat _____
98. report _____
99. catcher _____
100. music _____

The Sage Grouse

Study the spelling and meaning of each word. These words are used in today's story. Connect each word with its definition.

1. acquires
2. obstacles
3. overcome
4. pitifully
5. protect
6. tracts

a. pieces of land without exact boundaries
b. conquer
c. guard
d. causing pity
e. things in the way
f. gets as one's own

Read the story carefully and remember the details.

Next to the wild turkey the sage grouse is the largest game bird in America. The sage grouse usually lives where there are small streams and springs. Its home ground always includes large tracts of sagebrush. Thus the sage grouse acquires its name.

The sage grouse must overcome many obstacles. Hard rains and predators kill many young birds. Coyotes are the bird's worst enemy.

To protect the nest, the mother sage grouse puts on a very good act. When the enemy gets too near, the mother cries pitifully and limps away dragging a wing. When the coyote is lured away safely, the mother recovers and flies away.

The sage grouse is a strong bird which is able to withstand cold temperatures. It helps people by destroying many insects and grasshoppers.

A. Underline the correct answers about today's story.

1. How does the sage grouse get its name?   (a) sagebrush   (b) call   (c) eating habits
2. What is the bird's worst enemy?   (a) weather   (b) coyote   (c) snake
3. Who protects the nest?   (a) mother   (b) father   (c) both parents
4. To lure the enemy, the mother pretends   (a) to die   (b) to fight   (c) to be hurt.
5. To people the sage grouse is   (a) a menace   (b) helpful   (c) dangerous.

B. Reread the story and write the answers to these questions.

1. Which game bird is larger than the sage grouse?

_____
_____
_____

2. Name two things that kill young sage grouse birds.

_____
_____
_____

3. What can the bird withstand?

_____
_____
_____

4. How is the bird beneficial?

_____
_____
_____

Unit 130 cont'd ☞

Marking Stressed Syllables

Divide each word into syllables. Then place an accent mark (´) over the stressed syllable.

EXAMPLES: wisdom ___wis´dom___   remember ___re mem´ber___

1. reason _____
2. convince _____
3. alike _____
4. necklace _____
5. talent _____
6. worship _____
7. music _____
8. certain _____
9. relieve _____
10. distrust _____
11. stubborn _____
12. insect _____
13. awkward _____
14. select _____
15. voyage _____
16. surface _____
17. daily _____
18. freedom _____
19. persuade _____
20. weather _____
21. forgive _____
22. normal _____
23. repeat _____
24. income _____
25. thunder _____

26. pretend _____
27. author _____
28. advice _____
29. sandwich _____
30. punish _____
31. magnet _____
32. sofa _____
33. breakfast _____
34. shoulder _____
35. measure _____
36. heaven _____
37. provide _____
38. splendid _____
39. costume _____
40. slender _____
41. success _____
42. narrow _____
43. regard _____
44. believe _____
45. enough _____
46. visit _____
47. taxi _____
48. future _____
49. pleasure _____
50. suggest _____

51. promise _____
52. retire _____
53. belong _____
54. truthful _____
55. easy _____
56. remind _____
57. journey _____
58. over _____
59. shadow _____
60. warning _____
61. headache _____
62. echo _____
63. problem _____
64. lengthen _____
65. wishing _____
66. public _____
67. union _____
68. surround _____
69. distance _____
70. follow _____
71. sidewalk _____
72. sample _____
73. answer _____
74. wizard _____
75. nonsense _____

76. tomorrow _____
77. amusement _____
78. victory _____
79. furniture _____
80. library _____
81. happiness _____
82. territory _____
83. necessary _____
84. population _____

85. banana _____
86. magazine _____
87. organize _____
88. citizen _____
89. instrument _____
90. museum _____
91. parachute _____
92. elevator _____

93. government _____
94. mischievous _____
95. camera _____
96. invitation _____
97. medicine _____
98. direction _____
99. regular _____
100. chocolate _____

Comprehension Check

Ⓐ **Underline the words which can be divided at the end of a line.**

1. <u>wonderful</u>	11. identify	21. excellent
2. exercise	12. voice	22. prey
3. decision	13. lonesome	23. lightning
4. impossible	14. handsome	24. nonsense
5. migrate	15. gnaw	25. capture
6. securely	16. vocabulary	26. chocolate
7. breeze	17. became	27. opinion
8. remember	18. nuisance	28. ounce
9. adventure	19. outstanding	29. umbrella
10. straight	20. vacation	30. agreement

Ⓑ **How many syllables are in each word?**

_4_ 1. television	___ 11. obstacles	___ 21. eastern	___ 31. temperature
___ 2. hummingbird	___ 12. energy	___ 22. chipmunks	___ 32. ability
___ 3. important	___ 13. seldom	___ 23. fence	___ 33. rodent
___ 4. welcome	___ 14. wherever	___ 24. pheasant	___ 34. native
___ 5. opponent	___ 15. weather	___ 25. medium	___ 35. away
___ 6. speed	___ 16. field	___ 26. insects	___ 36. grasshopper
___ 7. various	___ 17. destructive	___ 27. hawk	___ 37. streams
___ 8. parachute	___ 18. strong	___ 28. acquires	___ 38. undergrowth
___ 9. grouse	___ 19. newspaper	___ 29. laugh	___ 39. migration
___ 10. homework	___ 20. appetite	___ 30. sagebrush	___ 40. enough

Ⓒ **Divide each word into syllables.**

1. sideways _side ways_	6. reverse _____	11. complete _____
2. common _____	7. almost _____	12. replace _____
3. unjustly _____	8. except _____	13. withstand _____
4. although _____	9. popular _____	14. protect _____
5. locate _____	10. safely _____	15. overcome _____

Ⓓ **Complete these sentences.**

1. Pheasants are ___ _game_ ___ birds.
2. Hummingbirds are the _____ birds.
3. The red-tailed hawk is a superb _____ .
4. Mice and rats are _____ .
5. The hummingbird is best known for its ability to _____ .

6. Rodents are _____ animals.
7. Pheasants are _____ fliers.
8. _____ are the grouse's worst enemies.
9. The sage grouse is a _____ bird.
10. The red-tailed hawk is unjustly called the _____ hawk.

Test 26 cont'd ☞

Comprehension Check (continued)

(E) Match these words and their definitions. These words appeared in the reading selections from units 126-130.

_i_ 1. reverse   ___ 7. keen   a. other than   g. gets as one's own

___ 2. valuable   ___ 8. superb   b. take in   h. things in the way

___ 3. except   ___ 9. described   c. of the highest quality   i. gave an account of

___ 4. concealing   ___ 10. replace   d. sharp and quick   j. backward

___ 5. include   ___ 11. acquires   e. of considerable worth   k. hiding from view

___ 6. obstacles   ___ 12. travels   f. take the place of   l. moves from place to place

(F) Underline the correct answers.

1. Where is the red-tailed hawk's home?   (a) eastern U.S.   (b) western U.S.
2. What kind of bird is the hawk?   (a) bird of prey   (b) songbird
3. What kind of bird is the pheasant?   (a) bird of prey   (b) game bird
4. Where does the ring-necked pheasant build its nest?   (a) on the ground   (b) in a tree
5. What are rodents known for?   (a) gnawing   (b) singing
6. Where do rodents not live?   (a) in trees   (b) in the sea
7. Which word describes a hummingbird?   (a) tiny   (b) enormous
8. How does the hummingbird differ from other birds?   (a) has big appetite   (b) can fly in reverse
9. What is the sage grouse's worst enemy?   (a) weather   (b) coyote
10. How do people view the sage grouse?   (a) destructive   (b) helpful

Choose one of the following topics and write a paragraph.

(1) Describe rodents.

(2) The hummingbird inspired the invention of the helicopter. Why do you think this is so?

_____

_____

_____

_____

_____

_____

_____

_____

_____

Sea Anemones

Study the spelling and meaning of each word. These words are used in today's story. Connect each word with its definition.

1. near
2. prey
3. reality
4. reflecting
5. remain
6. stunned

a. animal hunted for food
b. what is real
c. close by
d. stopped by a blow
e. giving an image
f. stay

Read the story carefully and remember the details.

Sea anemones are often referred to as the flowers of the sea. In reality, however, sea anemones are not flowers but deadly animals.

Some sea anemones are small. Others are large. Some live near the shore. Others live in the deepest part of the ocean. They are colorful creatures — reflecting all the colors of the rainbow.

Although sea anemones are able to move about slowly, they usually remain attached to one spot all their lives.

The petals lure the sea anemone's prey. When the prey swims by, the sea anemone shoots out a poisonous dart. The poison kills a smaller fish. A bigger fish is stunned long enough to allow the anemone's petals to pull it into its mouth.

Sea anemones can be dangerous to divers and swimmers. Their darts are shot into anything that comes close.

A. Underline the correct answers about today's story.

1. Sea anemones are	(a) flowers	(b) animals	(c) fish.
2. Sea anemones	(a) are always moving	(b) stay in one spot	(c) move in the winter.
3. What lures the prey?	(a) smell	(b) sweet taste	(c) colorful petals
4. The prey is trapped by	(a) clinging arms	(b) sharp spines	(c) a poisonous dart.
5. To swimmers, the anemones are	(a) dangerous	(b) harmless	(c) nontoxic.

B. Reread the story and write the answers to these questions.

1. What sizes are anemones?

_____

_____

_____

2. What is the sea anemone's weapon?

_____

_____

_____

3. What does this weapon do to larger fish?

_____

_____

_____

4. What might be shot by a sea anemone?

_____

_____

_____

Unit 131 cont'd

Stressed Syllables

Break each word into syllables. Then place an accent mark (**/**) over the stressed syllable.

EXAMPLES: a. program   pro´gram

b. forward   for´ward

1. airport	35. winter	68. backward
2. itself	36. sugar	69. awful
3. zebra	37. along	70. certain
4. easy	38. awkward	71. final
5. against	39. forget	72. hero
6. journey	40. able	73. happy
7. wagon	41. receive	74. combine
8. normal	42. secret	75. useless
9. became	43. eagle	76. freedom
10. market	44. escape	77. habit
11. yellow	45. woman	78. vacant
12. heavy	46. obey	79. movie
13. under	47. seldom	80. study
14. candy	48. except	81. hidden
15. machine	49. sorrow	82. visit
16. collect	50. include	83. color
17. captain	51. hungry	84. teacher
18. practice	52. extra	85. mother
19. garden	53. famous	86. enjoy
20. begin	54. surprise	87. seven
21. center	55. arrive	88. police
22. question	56. morning	89. leader
23. number	57. after	90. welcome
24. about	58. silent	91. zero
25. story	59. ticket	92. honest
26. nonsense	60. favor	93. wisdom
27. reason	61. tunnel	94. hurry
28. country	62. fellow	95. simple
29. danger	63. because	96. watching
30. person	64. children	97. hungry
31. cartoon	65. today	98. singing
32. summer	66. around	99. over
33. decide	67. unless	100. window
34. return		

Sea Snakes

Study the spelling and meaning of each word. These words are used in today's story. Connect each word with its definition.

1. afraid
2. escape
3. kinds
4. replenishing
5. submerged
6. usually

a. commonly
b. varieties; types
c. stayed under water
d. get away from
e. filling again
f. scared

Read the story carefully and remember the details.

There are many kinds of sea snakes. Many are poisonous. In general, sea snakes are very easygoing. They are usually afraid of humans and, unless cornered, will not attack. Sea snakes are found in the warm waters of the Pacific and Indian Oceans. Many people catch sea snakes for food.

Sea snakes breathe air and must come to the surface to do so. They can remain under water for half an hour before replenishing their supply of oxygen. However, when sea snakes are asleep, their bodily functions slow down; and they are able to stay submerged for long periods of time.

To escape from enemies, sea snakes dive to the bottom of the sea and hide in the darkness. Among their own kind they are very social.

A. Underline the correct answers about today's story.

1. Which word describes sea
   snakes in general?   (a) mean   (b) easygoing   (c) dangerous
2. To breathe, sea snakes   (a) surface   (b) go on land   (c) take oxygen from the water.
3. Where do sea snakes sleep? (a) on land   (b) near surface   (c) under water
4. To escape enemies,
   sea snakes   (a) hide   (b) bury in the sand (c) move to new homes.
5. Sea snakes are used as   (a) pets   (b) food   (c) bait.

B. Reread the story and write the answers to these questions.

1. When do sea snakes attack?

   _____

   _____

   _____

2. What happens to the snake's bodily functions when it is asleep?

   _____

   _____

   _____

3. Which two oceans are inhabited by sea snakes?

   _____

   _____

   _____

4. How long can sea snakes remain under water?

   _____

   _____

   _____

Unit 132 cont'd ☞

Respellings

A. Draw a line to connect each pronunciation key with the word it describes.

1. af′tər	box	21. flī	high	41. uv	water
2. bā′bē	after	22. hap′ē	fly	42. pen′ē	of
3. bûrd	baby	23. hī	joy	43. wô′tər	you
4. boks	bridge	24. joi	happy	44. rit	right
5. brij	bird	25. nok	knock	45. yoo	penny
6. en′ē	blue	26. kamp	upon	46. snō	small
7. bāk	bake	27. toun	front	47. strēt	snow
8. bloo	any	28. ə pon′	town	48. shoor	sure
9. bild	cat	29. men′ē	camp	49. smīl	smile
10. kat	build	30. frunt	many	50. smôl	street
11. doun	fix	31. āt	lumber	51. bet′ər	circle
12. duk	ear	32. ek′ō	eight	52. sûr′kəl	name
13. doo	down	33. luv	dry	53. kōld	cloud
14. ir	duck	34. lum′bər	echo	54. nām	better
15. fiks	do	35. drī	love	55. kloud	cold
16. rok	new	36. haf	work	56. flud	under
17. fō′tō	rock	37. wûrk	year	57. wûrd	flood
18. noo	make	38. wāt	use	58. un′dər	world
19. ōk	oak	39. yir	half	59. wûrld	word
20. māk	photo	40. yooz	wait	60. wīf	wife

B. Write the word described by each pronunciation key.

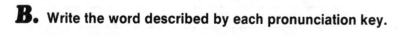

1. oul   _owl_
2. kwīt _____
3. bīt   _____
4. fēl   _____
5. lī′un _____

6. āj   _____
7. bilt _____
8. skī   _____
9. kool _____
10. nūz _____

11. ûrth _____
12. moov _____
13. ȧsk _____
14. pā   _____
15. tē   _____

16. blō _____
17. mīlz _____
18. hooz _____
19. bōrd _____
20. kāj _____

The Scorpion

Study the spelling and meaning of each word. These words are used in today's story. Connect each word with its definition.

1. bother
2. dawn
3. except
4. fatal
5. hide
6. usually

a. first light of morning
b. other than
c. commonly; ordinarily
d. deadly
e. disturb
f. to keep out of sight

Read the story carefully and remember the details.

The scorpion is famous for its sting. It will sting anything which tries to bother it.

In the tropics there is a scorpion whose sting can be fatal. The scorpion usually lives alone except during mating season. The female often kills the male after mating. Her young ride on her back until they are able to take care of themselves.

The scorpion is usually active at night. When dawn comes, the animal seeks a hiding place.

People in the tropics have learned to be careful in looking for scorpions. They shake their clothes in the morning before putting them on. Many have found scorpions trying to hide from the dawn's light.

A. **Underline the correct answers about today's story.**

1. The scorpion is famous for its   (a) bite   (b) sting   (c) habits.
2. The scorpion usually lives   (a) alone   (b) in pairs   (c) in groups.
3. The dangerous scorpion lives   (a) in the sea   (b) in the river   (c) in the tropics.
4. At dawn the scorpion   (a) looks for food   (b) hides   (c) becomes active.
5. "Fatal" means   (a) "deadly"   (b) "painful"   (c) "to make ill."

B. **Reread the story and write the answers to these questions.**

1. With whom does the scorpion usually live?

_____

_____

_____

2. What does the female scorpion often do after mating?

_____

_____

_____

3. What will the scorpion sting?

_____

_____

_____

4. When are scorpions active?

_____

_____

_____

321

Unit 133 cont'd ☞

Pronunciations

Write the word described by each pronunciation key.

1. lā′dē _lady_
2. mōōv
3. hap′ē
4. dôg
5. frunt
6. tā′bəl
7. kwik
8. ə buv′
9. grēn
10. ō′vər
11. win′do
12. wīz
13. stud′ē
14. sāf
15. kab′ən
16. boks
17. drēm
18. wôk
19. pāj
20. hav
21. lēf
22. sôlt
23. ə pon′
24. ēst
25. frōōt
26. haz
27. nōō
28. lok
29. strēt
30. un′dər
31. pen′səl
32. bild
33. fûrst

34. snō
35. drīv
36. grāt
37. flud
38. kul′ər
39. häf
40. hous
41. lō
42. ō′pən
43. ruf
44. shad′ō
45. vōt
46. mun′ē
47. ī′lənd
48. on′ist
49. blō
50. tung
51. vīn
52. pik
53. moun′tən
54. plēz
55. pub′lik
56. yir
57. zē′rō
58. pō′nē
59. brīt
60. sûrv
61. thôt
62. wûrk
63. wûrd
64. jûr′nē
65. bod′ē
66. skōr
67. yot

68. viz′it
69. bûrth′dā
70. rōō′lər
71. sīn
72. hap′ən
73. tī′nē
74. ī dē′ə
75. mung′kē
76. vûrb
77. pûr′sən
78. woolf
79. fō′tō
80. plen′tē
81. yōō
82. tôk
83. val′yōō
84. pok′it
85. yōōz
86. wô′tər
87. rông
88. hōm
89. kôl
90. prak′tis
91. stōr
92. tûr′kē
93. wag′ən
94. prīz
95. yung
96. wā
97. yel′ō
98. stik
99. bī′sik əl
100. kwī′ət

The Secretary Bird

Study the spelling and meaning of each word. These words are used in today's story. Connect each word with its definition.

1. excited
2. pins
3. proceeds
4. protect
5. swoops
6. valuable

a. goes on
b. of considerable worth
c. holds in one position
d. stirred up
e. to snatch with a sweeping movement
f. keep from harm

Read the story carefully and remember the details.

The secretary bird is native to South Africa. Its legs and neck are very long for its size. The bird has been referred to as a "vulture on stilts." It is usually three feet high.

The secretary bird is valuable to people because of its ability to kill snakes. The bird circles its victim. Then it swoops down quickly and pins the snake down with its powerful feet. The bird then beats the snake with its wings and feet until the victim is dead. It proceeds to swallow the snake headfirst.

The secretary bird gets its unusual name from the feathers on its head. When the bird becomes excited, the feathers stand up. They resemble pens stuck behind a secretary's ear. People protect the secretary bird.

A. Underline the correct answers about today's story.

1. Where does the bird live?   (a) South Africa   (b) Australia   (c) South America
2. The bird has been called a   (a) "killer stork" (b) "snake bird"   (c) "vulture on stilts."
3. The bird is valuable because it kills (a) fish   (b) snakes   (c) insects.
4. The bird's name comes from its   (a) habits   (b) feet   (c) head feathers.
5. To people, the bird is   (a) a pest   (b) valuable   (c) dangerous.

B. Reread the story and write the answers to these questions.

1. How tall are secretary birds?

_____

_____

_____

2. How does the bird eat a snake?

_____

_____

_____

3. When the bird is excited, what do its head feathers resemble?

_____

_____

_____

4. With what does the bird pin the snake?

_____

_____

_____

Unit 134 cont'd ☞

Choosing the Best Definition

 Choose the best definition of each word.

_a_ 1. exchange   (a) give and take   (b) to remake   (c) to throw away

____ 2. understand   (a) that which is true (b) to get the meaning of (c) study

____ 3. repeat   (a) to do again   (b) to do for the first time   (c) to do for the last time

____ 4. final   (a) beginning   (b) middle   (c) end

____ 5. weigh   (a) to measure the length of   (b) find out how heavy (c) to make larger

____ 6. hidden   (a) out of sight   (b) out in the open   (c) clearly seen

____ 7. advance   (a) move forward (b) move backward (c) stay the same

____ 8. perfume   (a) bad smell   (b) sweet smell   (c) strong odor

____ 9. unable   (a) capable   (b) able to do well   (c) not able

____ 10. worry   (a) feel uneasy about   (b) certain   (c) having a happy ending

____ 11. capture   (a) to allow to escape   (b) to make prisoner of (c) to volunteer

____ 12. easily   (a) with difficulty   (b) without trying hard (c) uncomfortably

____ 13. lonely   (a) in a group   (b) with someone (c) without company

____ 14. permit   (a) allow   (b) prevent   (c) answer

____ 15. depart   (a) to arrive on time   (b) to go away   (c) to come back

____ 16. grasp   (a) to take a firm hold   (b) to let go   (c) to lose

____ 17. expert   (a) one who knows nothing   (b) one who tries to help (c) one who has a special skill

____ 18. invent   (a) copy   (b) make something new   (c) destroy

____ 19. partner   (a) person who takes place of another   (b) one who shares   (c) someone who needs help

____ 20. regular   (a) usual   (b) unusual   (c) not often

____ 21. supply   (a) take from   (b) use   (c) furnish

____ 22. protect   (a) to keep from harm   (b) to hurt   (c) to endanger

____ 23. unite   (a) separate   (b) join together   (c) break apart

____ 24. worse   (a) less good   (b) better   (c) improving

____ 25. selfish   (a) caring about others (b) having no cares (c) caring too much for oneself

Shooting Stars

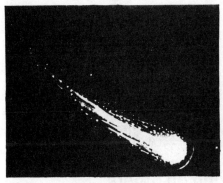

Study the spelling and meaning of each word. These words are used in today's story. Connect each word with its definition.

1. average   a. fulfilling all needs
2. craters   b. usual, normal
3. determined   c. idea, guess
4. satisfactory   d. called, named
5. termed   e. hollows
6. theory   f. defined

Read the story carefully and remember the details.

On an average night if a person watches the heavens, he will see about ten shooting stars per hour. Correctly termed, these shooting stars are called meteors. No satisfactory theory exists to account for the origin of a meteor.

A meteor is seen only when it enters the earth's atmosphere. The brightness of the meteor is determined by its speed; the fastest ones are the brightest. The brightest meteors are called fireballs.

Most meteors burn up before they reach the earth. A few do hit the earth. The fallen meteors are called meteorites. It is not known whether a person has ever been killed by a meteor, but there are many reports where people have been hit by meteors.

Very seldom do huge meteorites hit the earth. When they do, they cause explosions which make deep craters.

A. Underline the correct answers about today's story.

1. Meteors are   (a) big stars   (b) bright stars   (c) shooting stars.
2. Brightness is determined by   (a) speed   (b) size   (c) the distance from earth.
3. The fastest meteors are the   (a) smallest   (b) biggest   (c) brightest.
4. A meteorite is a   (a) bright meteor   (b) fallen meteor   (c) huge meteor.
5. Meteorites cause   (a) craters   (b) rain   (c) mountains.

B. Reread the story and write the answers to these questions.

1. How many shooting stars can you see on an average night?

     _____

     _____

     _____

3. When can a meteor be seen?

     _____

     _____

     _____

2. What are the brightest meteors called?

     _____

     _____

     _____

4. What happens to most meteors before they reach earth?

     _____

     _____

     _____

Unit 135 cont'd

Definitions

A definition is a phrase that defines or explains a word.

 Choose the best definitions.

_a_ 1. independent (a) free of rule or control (b) relying on others (c) helping others

____ 2. general (a) in particular (b) meaningless (c) concerning all

____ 3. acquainted (a) have knowledge of (b) know nothing about (c) to discover

____ 4. hollow (a) solid (b) not solid (c) see through

____ 5. organize (a) out of order (b) put in order (c) to order

____ 6. exhibit (a) hide (b) repair (c) display

____ 7. advance (a) move forward (b) move backward (c) stay in place

____ 8. refuse (a) agree (b) say no (c) say yes

____ 9. equal (a) not the same (b) of lesser value (c) of the same value

____ 10. unite (a) join together (b) break apart (c) to keep away

____ 11. secure (a) to feel unsafe (b) to feel safe (c) to doubt

____ 12. capture (a) to free from prison (b) to allow to escape (c) to make prisoner

____ 13. latest (a) most recent (b) happening in the future (c) now

____ 14. loose (a) not tight (b) tight (c) unable to find

____ 15. prevent (a) cause to happen (b) allow to happen (c) keep from happening

____ 16. tame (a) wild (b) gentle (c) dangerous

____ 17. escape (a) get free (b) make prisoner (c) get caught

____ 18. worry (a) to be content (b) feel anxious (c) carefree

____ 19. volunteer (a) to force someone (b) to do willingly (c) to do out of habit

____ 20. level (a) uneven (b) rough (c) flat

____ 21. instead (a) in place of (b) in front of (c) behind

____ 22. ordinary (a) occurs seldom (b) occasionally (c) common

____ 23. furnish (a) provide (b) take away (c) receive

____ 24. theory (a) know for a fact (b) evidence (c) guess

____ 25. surrender (a) to fight back (b) to give up (c) to conquer

Comprehension Check

(A) Underline the words in which the first syllables are stressed.

1. <u>seldom</u>
2. secret
3. extra
4. because
5. forward
6. famous
7. enjoy
8. teacher
9. wisdom
10. awful
11. airport
12. itself
13. zebra
14. journey
15. machine
16. normal
17. market
18. yellow
19. captain
20. collect
21. cartoon
22. program
23. question
24. hungry
25. begin
26. reason
27. eagle
28. country
29. about
30. vacant
31. nonsense
32. welcome
33. escape
34. hero
35. surprise
36. ticket
37. silent
38. backward
39. summer
40. police

(B) Write the word for each respelling.

1. ek′ ō _____echo_____
2. skī _____
3. nūz _____
4. lī′ ən _____
5. haz _____
6. fō′ tō _____
7. nām _____
8. pen′ ē _____
9. wāt _____
10. bet′ ər _____
11. hap′ ē _____
12. snō _____
13. frunt _____
14. kab′ ən _____
15. drēm _____

(C) Match each word with its definition.

_i_ 1. invent
___ 2. repeat
___ 3. hidden
___ 4. exchange
___ 5. grasp
___ 6. organize
___ 7. lonely
___ 8. refuse
___ 9. equal
___ 10. advance

a. out of sight
b. say no
c. without company
d. to do again
e. put in order
f. to take a firm hold
g. of the same value
h. give and take
i. move forward
j. make something new

(D) Complete these sentences.

1. Sea anemones are _____flowers_____ of the sea.
2. A scorpion is famous for its _____ .
3. Shooting stars are _____ .
4. The fastest meteors are the _____ .
5. Scorpions _____ during the day.
6. Sea anemones can move _____ .
7. Many sea snakes are _____ .
8. People _____ secretary birds.
9. Secretary birds kill _____ .
10. A meteor's brightness is determined by _____ .
11. Sea anemones are deadly _____ .
12. When cornered, sea snakes _____ .
13. Scorpions usually live _____ .
14. Meteors _____ hit the earth.
15. Sea snakes are found in _____ waters.
16. Secretary birds are called " _____ on stilts."

Test 27 cont'd ☞

Comprehension Check (continued)

(E) Match these words and their definitions. These words appeared in the reading selections from units 131-135.

_a_ 1. lure	____ 7. usually	a. attract	g. commonly
____ 2. prey	____ 8. dawn	b. stay	h. first light of morning
____ 3. kinds	____ 9. valuable	c. of considerable worth	i. named
____ 4. remain	____ 10. excited	d. agitated	j. disturb
____ 5. bother	____ 11. termed	e. types	k. deadly
____ 6. fatal	____ 12. theory	f. animal hunted for food	l. idea; guess

(F) Underline the correct answers.

1. What are sea anemones?   (a) animals   (b) plants
2. Why do swimmers avoid sea anemones?   (a) smell   (b) dangerous
3. Where do sea snakes breathe?   (a) on surface   (b) under water
4. How are sea snakes used?   (a) as pets   (b) as food
5. Why are scorpions famous?   (a) color   (b) sting
6. What do scorpions do at dawn?   (a) hide   (b) hunt
7. Where do secretary birds live?   (a) South Africa   (b) United States
8. How is the secretary bird regarded?   (a) valuable   (b) pest
9. What are meteors?   (a) big stars   (b) shooting stars
10. What do meteorites cause?   (a) craters   (b) fires

Choose one of the following topics and write a paragraph.

(1) Have you ever seen a meteor? A meteorite? If so, describe your experience.

(2) Why are sea anemones called the "flowers of the sea"? Describe the sea anemones' habits.

_____

_____

_____

_____

_____

_____

_____

_____

_____

_____

The Shrew

Study the spelling and meaning of each word. These words are used in today's story. Connect each word with its definition.

1. disagreeable
2. extremely
3. greedy
4. order
5. reputation
6. tremendous

a. very large; great
b. how one is seen by others
c. hard to get along with
d. to a great degree
e. in science, a group in-between family and class
f. wanting more than necessary

Read the story carefully and remember the details.

No one can get along with a shrew. Not even another shrew. This small animal has earned itself the reputation of being the most disagreeable member of the order of mammals.

Because the shrew is always running about, it uses up an enormous amount of energy. Thus the shrew has a tremendous appetite. Where food is concerned, the shrew is greedy and fierce. It will fight fiercely with another shrew for a single insect. The winner of such a fight gets the insect and eats the loser. As soon as the young are able to trap their own food, the mother shrew throws them out of the nest.

The shrew is extremely nervous. It moves about with quick, jerky movements. The shrew may be the smallest of the North American mammals, but it is also the fiercest. The shrew's victim doesn't stand a chance.

A. Underline the correct answers about today's story.

1. Who gets along well with a shrew?   (a) insects   (b) another shrew   (c) no one
2. Shrews often fight over   (a) food   (b) territory   (c) leadership.
3. When two shrews fight, the winner   (a) chases the loser   (b) eats the loser   (c) shares its food.
4. Which word does not describe the shrew?   (a) calm   (b) nervous   (c) fierce
5. The shrew has a reputation of being   (a) friendly   (b) shy   (c) disagreeable.

B. Reread the story and write the answers to these questions.

1. Describe the shrew's appetite.

_____
_____
_____

2. How does the shrew move?

_____
_____
_____

3. What does the mother shrew do when her young can trap food?

_____
_____
_____

4. Compare the size of the shrew to other North American mammals.

_____
_____
_____

Unit 136 cont'd ☞

Word Origins

 Each short story contains three (3) misspelled words. Underline them. Then write the correct spellings in the blanks.

A umbrella

The <u>wurd</u> "umbrella" coms from the Latin words "**umbra**" and "**ella**." "Umbra" means "shade," and "ella" means "little." The furst umbrella was used in the sun. Now the umbrella is used in the rain.

word
_____   _____

B July and August

The month of July was named in onor of Julius Caesar. The munth of August was named for Augustus Caesar. Both Julius and Augustus were Roman leeders.

_____   _____

C fool

The word "fool" comes from the Latin word "**follis**." In the begining "fool" ment "windbag." Latter the meaning changed to mean a "person who talks much, but says little."

_____   _____

D omnibus

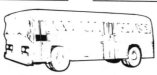

Our word "bus" is a shortined form of the word "omnibus." In Latin "omnibus" means "four all." "Bus" has become the most populer form of the word.

_____   _____

E neighbor

The word "neighbor" is made up of too Old English words, "**neah**" and "**gebur**." "Neah" means "neerby." "Gebur" means "farmer." The meaning now encludes anyone who lives nearby.

_____   _____

F automobile

Automobile is maid from two words, "auto" and "mobile." "Auto" comes from the Greek "**autos**," witch means "self." "Mobile" comes from the Latin "**mobilis**," which means "movabel."

_____   _____

G manufacture

Before factorys took over the production of goods, things were made by hand. The word "manufacture" comes from the Latin words "**manu**" and "**facture**." The orijinal meaning was "made by hand." The word now reffers to all production.

_____   _____

H sandwich

The sandwich was named for the Earl of Sandwich. When the Earl was bisy, he refused to stop for meels. He asked that bread and meat be brot to him, thus inventing the sandwich.

_____   _____   _____

Skates and Rays

Study the spelling and meaning of each word. These words are used in today's story. Connect each word with its definition.

1. ambush
2. characteristics
3. difficult
4. primary
5. resemble
6. somewhat

a. to some degree
b. main
c. look like
d. features
e. lay waiting to attack
f. hard

Read the story carefully and remember the details.

Skates and rays make up a group of marine animals which are found the world over. There are many kinds of skates and rays, but their primary characteristics are the same.

The bodies of skates or rays somewhat resemble large butterflies or sea bats. They swim in graceful, rippling movements. When they want to move quickly, they flap their wings like birds.

Skates and rays lie on the ocean floor, waiting to ambush unsuspecting prey. The animals are difficult to spot. They easily blend in with the surroundings. Some even throw sand over themselves to camouflage their bodies.

By day the skates and rays sleep. At night they hunt for food. They hug their victims with their wings and devour them with sharp teeth.

A. Underline the correct answers about today's story.

1. The bodies of skates and rays resemble (a) eels (b) birds (c) butterflies.
2. When swimming, the animals are (a) graceful (b) harmless (c) awkward.
3. On the ocean floor the animals are (a) easy targets (b) helpless (c) well camouflaged.
4. To camouflage themselves, some use (a) seaweed (b) sand (c) other fish.
5. During the day skates and rays (a) hunt for food (b) sleep (c) find hiding places.

B. Reread the story and write the answers to these questions.

1. Where are skates and rays found?

_____
_____
_____

2. Where do skates and rays wait for prey?

_____
_____
_____

3. What do these marine animals do to move quickly?

_____
_____
_____

4. What do skates and rays do at night?

_____
_____
_____

Unit 137 cont'd ☞

Writing the Names of the 50 States

 Twenty-five (25) of the fifty (50) states are misspelled. Cross out the misspelled names, and write them correctly in the blanks.

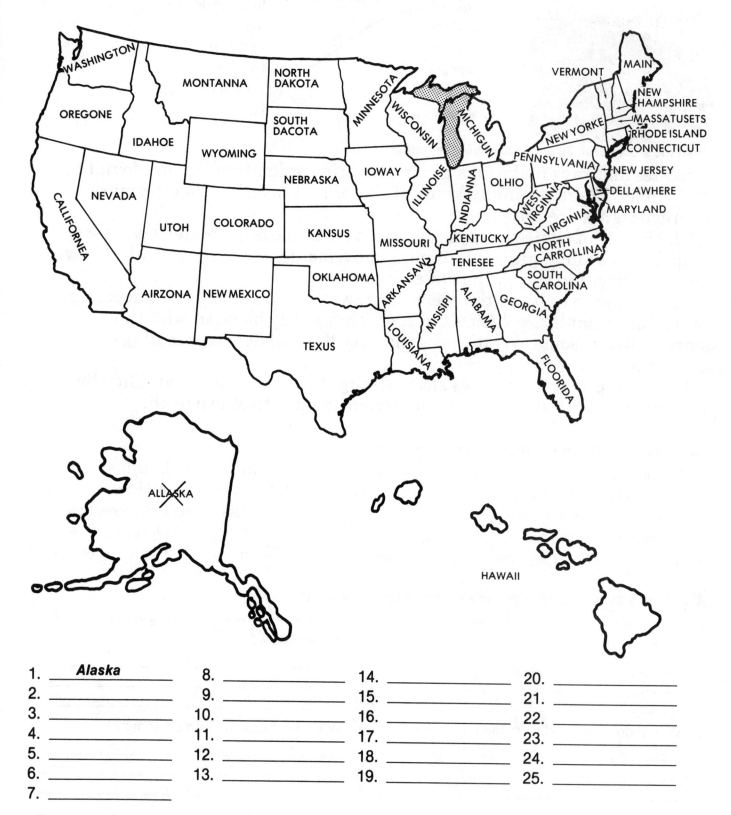

1. *Alaska*
2. _____
3. _____
4. _____
5. _____
6. _____
7. _____

8. _____
9. _____
10. _____
11. _____
12. _____
13. _____

14. _____
15. _____
16. _____
17. _____
18. _____
19. _____

20. _____
21. _____
22. _____
23. _____
24. _____
25. _____

Snails for Food

Study the spelling and meaning of each word. These words are used in today's story. Connect each word with its definition.

1. dampness   a. luxury foods
2. delicacies   b. furnish
3. destination   c. living in nature
4. gather   d. final point
5. provide   e. wet quality
6. wild   f. collect

Read the story carefully and remember the details.

Every year tons of snails are eaten. The most snails are eaten in France. To meet the demand, French farmers raise snails on snail farms.

In the spring after a rain, the farmers gather wild snails from the grasses where they feed. The snails are taken to fenced lanes. Here tall trees provide shade and dampness. The snails grow fatter.

In the fall the farmers gather the snails for market. Some snails are sent to the cannery. Others are shipped in special compartments designed so that the snails reach their destination alive. The moisture in the compartment is controlled so that the snails stay asleep. Too much moisture would cause them to wake up. The temperature is also controlled. When the temperature is too high, the snails become warm and hungry. Then the snails would begin to use up their stored fat. They would be too thin for the market.

People consider snail dishes as delicacies. Would you like to have snails for dinner?

A. Underline the correct answers about today's story.

1. Most snails are eaten in   (a) China   (b) France   (c) the United States.
2. Snails feed on   (a) roots   (b) grasses   (c) insects.
3. The snail crop is harvested in the   (a) spring   (b) summer   (c) fall.
4. Too much moisture would cause snails to   (a) wake up   (b) go to sleep   (c) die.
5. When the temperature is too warm, snails   (a) get hungry   (b) get too fat   (c) fall asleep.

B. Reread the story and write the answers to these questions.

1. When are snails gathered and taken to farms?

_____

_____

_____

2. Where are snails taken after harvest?

_____

_____

_____

3. How is the demand for snails met?

_____

_____

_____

4. What happens to snails that wake up?

_____

_____

_____

Writing the Days of the Week

October

sun	mon	tue	wed	thu	fri	sat
1	2	3	4	5	6	7
8	9	10	11	12	13	14
15	16	17	18	19	20	21
22	23	24	25	26	27	28
29	30	31				

 Answer each question by writing the correct day of the week in the blank. Use the calendar to find the answer.

1. What is the first day of the week? — _Sunday_
2. What is the second day of the week?
3. What is the third day of the week?
4. What is the fourth day of the week?
5. What is the fifth day of the week?
6. What is the sixth day of the week?
7. What is the seventh day of the week?
8. On what day is October 1st?
9. What day does **wed** stand for?
10. What day is the last day in October?
11. On what day is October 20th?
12. What is the day before Friday?
13. What is the day after Friday?
14. What two days make up the weekend?
15. On what day is Halloween, October 31st?
16. On what day is October 16th?
17. On what day do many people go to church?
18. On what day is October 9th?
19. What is the day before Sunday?
20. What is the day after Monday?
21. What day does the **fri** stand for?
22. On what day is October 15th?
23. On what day is October 4th?
24. On what day is October 5th?
25. On what day is October 28th?

Snakeheads

Study the spelling and meaning of each word. These words are used in today's story. Connect each word with its definition.

1. another
2. damage
3. favorite
4. moist
5. several
6. supply

a. something provided
b. most preferred
c. one more
d. destruction
e. many; quite a few
f. slightly wet

Read the story carefully and remember the details.

Did you know that there is a fish that can live out of the water? The snakehead can live out of water for several months if its skin is kept moist.

When a pond dries up, the snakehead burrows deep into the mud. It waits for rain.

The snakehead eats frogs, snakes, and insects. Its favorite food is fish. When the food supply runs out, the snakehead will get out of the water and search for food.

In the Orient a snakehead is used for food. It is caught in a net. Sometimes it is fished for with knives.

The snakehead can do serious damage to a pond. It eats all of the fish and moves on to another home.

A. **Underline the correct answers about today's story.**

1. To live out of water, the snakehead needs   (a) cold air   (b) moisture   (c) sunshine.
2. When a pond dries up, the snakehead   (a) dies   (b) moves on   (c) burrows in mud.
3. What is the snakehead's favorite food?   (a) snakes   (b) fish   (c) insects
4. Where are snakeheads found?   (a) Orient   (b) United States   (c) South America
5. Which word describes a snakehead?   (a) helpful   (b) harmful   (c) helpless

B. **Reread the story and write the answers to these questions.**

1. How long can the snakehead live out of water?

_____

_____

_____

2. Besides its favorite food, what might the snakehead eat?

_____

_____

3. What does the snakehead wait for when a pond dries up?

_____

_____

_____

4. What can the snakehead do to a pond?

_____

_____

_____

     Unit 139 cont'd ☞

Writing the Months of the Year

 Answer each question by writing the correct name of the month in the blank.

1. What is the first month of the year? _____ *January* _____
2. What is the last month of the year? _____
3. Which month follows January? _____
4. Which month follows April? _____
5. Which month follows July? _____
6. Which two months begin with the letter "M"? _____
7. Which two months begin with the letter "A"? _____
8. Which three months begin with the letter "J"? _____
9. Which month begins with the letter "S"? _____
10. Which month begins with the letter "D"? _____
11. Which month begins with the letter "O"? _____
12. Which month begins with the letter "F"? _____
13. Which month begins with the letter "N"? _____
14. Which month is abbreviated as "Sept."? _____
15. Which month is abbreviated as "Jan."? _____
16. Name each month which begins with a vowel. _____
17. Which month ends in "ch"? _____
18. Which month ends in "l"? _____
19. Which three months are one-syllable words? _____
20. In which month is New Year's Day? _____
21. In which month is Halloween? _____
22. In which month is Christmas? _____
23. In which month is Valentine's Day? _____
24. In which month is Thanksgiving? _____
25. How many months are in a year? _____

Snipe Hunting

Study the spelling and meaning of each word. These words are used in today's story. Connect each word with its definition.

1. inexperienced
2. newcomer
3. popular
4. practical joke
5. pretend
6. trick

a. act as if
b. without prior knowledge
c. fraud; deception
d. widely known
e. one who has arrived recently
f. trick played in fun

Read the story carefully and remember the details.

Have you ever been snipe hunting? Snipe hunting is a popular practical joke played at night.

A group of people get an inexperienced hunter or camper. The group takes the newcomer out in the woods where the snipes live. They have the newcomer stay in one place with a flashlight and a sack. The others pretend to drive the snipes toward the newcomer. The newcomer is to catch the snipes in the sack and wait for the others to return. The others, of course, never come back.

Some newcomers take longer than others to catch on to the trick. Don't be fooled too easily. There really is a bird called a snipe.

A. Underline the correct answers about today's story.

1. Snipe hunting usually occurs   (a) at night   (b) in the morning   (c) in the afternoon.
2. Snipes live in   (a) the woods   (b) the desert   (c) water.
3. The newcomer catches the snipe with   (a) a net   (b) a sack   (c) his hands.
4. Snipe hunting is a   (a) sport   (b) way of life   (c) joke.
5. A real snipe is a   (a) cat   (b) bird   (c) fish.

B. Reread the story and write the answers to these questions.

1. Who is the victim of snipe hunting?

_____

_____

2. What are the others supposedly doing?

_____

_____

3. What is the newcomer told to do?

_____

_____

4. How long does it take the others to return?

_____

_____

Unit 140 cont'd ☞

Finding the Hidden Word

* **Find the answer which is hidden in each set of letters. Underline it. Then rewrite it in the blank.**

EXAMPLE: *a red fruit*   g s a p p l e t i   _____apple_____

1. something that you read   p b o o k l i r z a   _____

2. an animal that barks   d i d o g k a n b q   _____

3. something that you ride to school   u z t l o b u s s c   _____

4. something that you pull   w a g o n w c d e e   _____

5. an animal that meows   e m z t o u c a t l   _____

6. something that you wear   c i w j c o a t c a   _____

7. a person who bakes bread   s e g h b a k e r m   _____

8. an insect that stings   r f p z o e s b e e   _____

9. something that you sit on   c c h a i r l n a u   _____

10. something that you drive   r e n j k c a r b s   _____

11. an animal that you ride   h r f h o r s e c q   _____

12. something that you eat   f o o d r e g m u u   _____

13. a place where you live   h n i n h o m e c s   _____

14. something that you write on   p b k p a p e r n m   _____

15. something that you write with   e z p e n c i l a h   _____

16. something that you see with   u w e x l j n e y e   _____

17. something that is wet   s n w a t e r u i b   _____

18. an animal that crawls   h s s n a k e l p g   _____

19. something that tells time   c l e j c l o c k b   _____

20. a person who goes to school   s t u d e n t d o h   _____

Comprehension Check

Test 28

A Write the days of the week.

1. _____Sunday_____
2. _____
3. _____
4. _____
5. _____
6. _____
7. _____

B Write the months of the year.

1. _____January_____
2. _____
3. _____
4. _____
5. _____
6. _____
7. _____
8. _____
9. _____
10. _____
11. _____
12. _____

C Identify the states.

__i__ 1. Michigan
____ 2. California
____ 3. Texas
____ 4. Florida
____ 5. Alaska
____ 6. Illinois
____ 7. New York
____ 8. Hawaii
____ 9. Missouri
____ 10. New Mexico
____ 11. Rhode Island
____ 12. Pennsylvania

a. a state which is the home to Disneyland
b. a state which is the farthest north
c. a state along the Mississippi River
d. a state whose motto is "Show Me"
e. a state which is the home to the Liberty Bell
f. a Southern state known for its beaches
g. a state which is home to New York City
h. a state known for its size and oil wells
i. a state which is surrounded by lakes on three sides
j. a state named after our southern neighbor
k. the smallest state
l. a state which consists of tropical islands

D Correct the spelling of each word.

1. wurd _____word_____
2. bisy _____
3. onor _____
4. brot _____
5. tyde _____
6. begining _____
7. munth _____
8. shortined _____
9. furst _____
10. populer _____
11. becum _____
12. neerby _____
13. movabel _____
14. orijinal _____
15. reffers _____

E Complete these sentences.

1. ____No one____ gets along with a shrew.
2. Snipe hunting is a _____ .
3. Snakeheads eat _____ .
4. Skates and rays are _____ swimmers.
5. Snails require _____ to live.
6. Snakeheads can live _____ water.
7. Skates and rays lie on the ocean _____ .
8. Shrews have _____ appetites.
9. The most snails are eaten in _____ .
10. A snipe is a _____ .

339

Test 28 cont'd ☞

Comprehension Check (continued)

(F) Match these words and their definitions. These words appeared in the reading selections from units 136-140.

_g_ 1. ambush	___ 7. resemble	a. act as if	g. lay waiting to attack
___ 2. pretend	___ 8. extremely	b. slightly wet	h. hard to get along with
___ 3. disagreeable	___ 9. another	c. living in nature	i. luxury foods
___ 4. moist	___ 10. popular	d. to a great degree	j. look like
___ 5. delicacies	___ 11. reputation	e. widely known	k. one more
___ 6. wild	___ 12. favorite	f. most preferred	l. how one is seen by others

(G) Underline the correct answers.

1. Which word describes a shrew?   (a) friendly   (b) <u>cruel</u>
2. How does a shrew compare to other mammals?   (a) smaller   (b) larger
3. Where do skates and rays wait for their prey?   (a) behind rocks   (b) ocean floor
4. How do skates and rays camouflage themselves?   (a) throw sand over themselves   (b) hide in seaweed
5. Who eats more snails?   (a) Americans   (b) French
6. What happens to snails when temperatures are warm?   (a) They sleep.   (b) They are hungry.
7. What is the snakehead's favorite food?   (a) frogs   (b) fish
8. How do people view snakeheads?   (a) beneficial   (b) destructive
9. What is a snipe?   (a) bird   (b) joke
10. Besides a sack, what does a snipe hunter carry?   (a) flashlight   (b) bells

Choose one of the following topics and write a paragraph.

(1) Snipe hunting is a practical joke. Describe a practical joke that you have either played on someone else or have had played on you.

(2) Snails are delicacies. Would you like to eat snails? Why or why not?

_____

_____

_____

_____

_____

_____

_____

The Snow Leopard

Study the spelling and meaning of each word. These words are used in today's story. Connect each word with its definition.

1. agile ——————————— a. able to move quickly
2. among   b. very; to much degree
3. camouflages   c. of the number
4. extinction   d. dying out
5. extremely   e. excellently
6. superbly   f. hides naturally

Read the story carefully and remember the details.

Among the highest ranges of the Himalaya Mountains where the winters are extremely cold lives one of the most beautiful of all the mountain dwellers. The inhabitant is the snow leopard.

The snow leopard is protected from the cold by its long and thick fur. The leopard's coat also camouflages it against the snowy rocks where it hunts.

The snow leopard rests during the day. At evening it becomes active and goes in search of wild sheep and goats and small rodents.

Unlike other leopards, the snow leopard is not a good climber. It is, however, superbly agile. In summer the snow leopard lives at a higher elevation than in winter. The snow leopard is in danger of extinction because its fur is valuable.

A. Underline the correct answers about today's story.

1. The snow leopard lives in the   (a) mountains   (b) jungles   (c) desert.
2. The snow leopard is active   (a) at noon   (b) at dawn   (c) at evening.
3. The snow leopard is at home in   (a) hot weather   (b) cold weather   (c) wet weather.
4. Which word describes the snow leopard?   (a) awkward   (b) ungainly   (c) agile
5. The snow leopard is valued for its   (a) meat   (b) fur   (c) teeth.

B. Reread the story and write the answers to these questions.

1. In what mountain range do snow leopards live?

_____

_____

_____

2. Why is the snow leopard in danger of extinction?

_____

_____

_____

3. What protects the snow leopard from the cold?

_____

_____

_____

4. When does the snow leopard rest?

_____

_____

_____

Unit 141 cont'd ☞

Just for Fun

A. Every animal makes its own distinct sound. For example, you would not say that a cow talks. A cow moos. Fill in the blanks using the words from the box.

barks	hisses	gobbles	sings
neighs	squeaks	roars	meows
clucks	buzzes	caws	quacks
crows	oinks	chirps	honks
brays	croaks	laughs	hoots

1. A cricket ___*chirps*___.
2. A rooster _____.
3. A dog _____.
4. A donkey _____.
5. A pig _____.
6. A goose _____.
7. A mouse _____.
8. A canary _____.
9. A frog _____.
10. A chicken _____.

11. An owl _____.
12. A duck _____.
13. A bee _____.
14. A cat _____.
15. A turkey _____.
16. A lion _____.
17. A crow _____.
18. A hyena _____.
19. A snake _____.
20. A horse _____.

B. Different words also tell us how something is said. For example, if you were to talk constantly about anything and everything, people would probably say you chatter. Fill in the blanks with the best words from the box.

shriek
repeat
ask
beg
lecture
recite
whisper
cry
laugh
scream
order
giggle
demand
sigh

1. If you spoke quietly, you would ___*whisper*___.
2. If you would say the same thing again, you would _____.
3. If you would say something from memory, you would _____.
4. If you were very sad, you would _____.
5. If you were telling someone to do something, you would _____.
6. If you would reprimand someone, you would _____.
7. If you were very happy, you would _____.
8. If you were to laugh nervously, you would _____.
9. If you were to plead with someone, you would _____.
10. If you were hurt, you might _____.
11. If you were frightened by something, you might _____.
12. If you were to insist on something, you would _____.
13. If you were very tired, you might _____.
14. If you were to question something, you would _____.

The Snowy Owl

Study the spelling and meaning of each word. These words are used in today's story. Connect each word with its definition.

1. consists
2. devours
3. diet
4. range
5. scarce
6. surroundings

a. territory
b. what one eats
c. environment
d. not easily found
e. is made up of
f. eats

Read the story carefully and remember the details.

The snowy owl is a large, heavy-built owl. It lives on the Arctic tundra and in swamps and open areas of the far north. Like the snow of its surroundings, the snowy owl is white. It is protected from the cold by its heavy coat of feathers. Even its feet are covered with down.

The snowy owl nests on the ground, for much of its range has no trees. The nest is lined with feathers and grass.

Unlike other owls, the snowy owl often hunts during the day. The owl is a bird of prey. Its main diet consists of lemmings, mice, and hares. The owl falls swiftly on its prey which it usually devours then and there. The snowy owl migrates south when food is scarce.

A. Underline the correct answers about today's story.

1. Where does the snowy owl live?   (a) desert   (b) warm areas   (c) far north
2. What color is the snowy owl?   (a) brown   (b) white   (c) yellow
3. Where does the owl nest?   (a) ground   (b) trees   (c) underground
4. Unlike other owls, the snowy owl   (a) eats seeds   (b) hunts at night   (c) hunts in the daytime.
5. The snowy owl migrates   (a) to breed   (b) in cold weather   (c) to search for food.

B. Reread the story and write the answers to these questions.

1. Describe the snowy owl's surroundings.

_____

_____

_____

2. What does the snowy owl do when food is scarce?

_____

_____

_____

3. Name two things in this animal's diet.

_____

_____

_____

4. Why does the snowy owl nest where it does?

_____

_____

_____

Unit 142 cont'd

Spelling Problems

A. vowels before "r"   Add the missing vowels.

1. n_a_rrow
2. ov__r
3. doct__r
4. coll__r
5. answ__r

6. auth__r
7. lumb__r
8. tract__r
9. elevat__r
10. feath__r

11. guit__r
12. sciss__rs
13. __rganize
14. w__rship
15. op__ra

16. regul__r
17. weath__r
18. vict__ry
19. und__r
20. th__rsty

21. mat__rial
22. p__rachute
23. __rder
24. f__rst
25. c__rry

B. silent "gh"   Underline the words in which the "gh" is silent.

1. sigh
2. trough
3. bough
4. ghost
5. high
6. through
7. although

8. gherkin
9. neighbor
10. laugh
11. weight
12. ought
13. ghoul

C. "gh" sounding like "f"   Underline the words in which the "gh" sounds like "f."

1. laughter
2. daughter
3. tough
4. sight
5. bought
6. laugh

7. midnight
8. rough
9. highway
10. weigh
11. thought
12. enough

D. "c" with "k" sound   Underline the words in which the "c" sounds like "k."

1. curtain
2. science
3. camera
4. copy
5. ice

6. officer
7. cocoa
8. contest
9. cement
10. police

11. musical
12. common
13. public
14. scene
15. principal

16. scissors
17. certain
18. clothes
19. courage
20. niece

21. citizen
22. climate
23. comb
24. court
25. score

E. "y" as a vowel   Underline each word in which the "y" functions as a vowel.

1. community
2. yacht
3. vineyard
4. healthy
5. dictionary

6. they
7. youth
8. empty
9. railway
10. library

11. yes
12. windy
13. beauty
14. lawyer
15. hay

16. territory
17. destroy
18. journey
19. yet
20. easily

21. chimney
22. cherry
23. hungry
24. year
25. necessary

The South American Forest   Unit 143

Study the spelling and meaning of each word. These words are used in today's story. Connect each word with its definition.

1. alert   a. all the time
2. always   b. watchful and ready
3. build   c. construct
4. explored   d. dense
5. thick   e. searched for discovery
6. travel   f. journey

Read the story carefully and remember the details.

South American forests are so thick that one can hardly see the sun for all the trees. The forests are very large. Not all of the land has been explored.

There is no winter in the forests. There is no summer. The trees are always green.

The people of the South American forests live near a river. They build homes with leaves and branches. Many people live together under the same roof. They sleep on the floor. Inside the large house are many fires. Each family has its own fire. The smoke from the fire helps to keep out flies and mosquitos.

There are no roads in the forests. Rivers are used for travel.

There are many dangers in the forests. The people of the forests must always be alert for trouble, but they are happy in their homes.

A. Underline the correct answers about today's story.

1. Which word does not describe the forest?   (a) thick   (b) dark   (c) small
2. One can hardly see the sun for the   (a) trees   (b) rocky cliffs (c) animals.
3. People of the forests live near   (a) fruit trees (b) a river   (c) mountains.
4. Each family has its own   (a) house   (b) fire   (c) land.
5. The roads of the forests are   (a) paved   (b) gravel   (c) rivers.

B. Reread the story and write the answers to these questions.

1. Where do people living in the forest sleep?

_____

_____

_____

2. What purpose is served by the smoke of the fire?

_____

_____

_____

3. What two seasons are not found in the forest?

_____

_____

_____

4. Describe the appearance of the trees.

_____

_____

_____

Misspelled Words I

Underline the correctly spelled word in each row.

EXAMPLE: (a) *faverite*   (b) *favrite*   (c) <u>*favorite*</u>   (d) *favarite*

1. (a) author	(b) awthor	(c) auther	(d) authar
2. (a) invitashun	(b) invitation	(c) envitation	(d) envatation
3. (a) jelous	(b) jellous	(c) jealus	(d) jealous
4. (a) problem	(b) problim	(c) problam	(d) problom
5. (a) sample	(b) sampel	(c) sampple	(d) sampil
6. (a) throte	(b) throat	(c) throwt	(d) throt
7. (a) unnite	(b) unitte	(c) unite	(d) unnight
8. (a) vissitor	(b) visiter	(c) visitar	(d) visitor
9. (a) yaht	(b) yact	(c) yacht	(d) yocht
10. (a) excillent	(b) excellint	(c) excilent	(d) excellent
11. (a) connduct	(b) conduct	(c) conduck	(d) conduc
12. (a) jaggad	(b) jaggid	(c) jagged	(d) jaggod
13. (a) diserve	(b) desirve	(c) deserv	(d) deserve
14. (a) publish	(b) pubblish	(c) publesh	(d) publich
15. (a) wizdom	(b) wisdum	(c) wisdom	(d) wisdem
16. (a) iggnore	(b) ignore	(c) egnore	(d) igknore
17. (a) cozy	(b) kozy	(c) cozey	(d) kozey
18. (a) voiage	(b) voyuge	(c) voyage	(d) voyege
19. (a) missplace	(b) misplase	(c) mistplace	(d) misplace
20. (a) enternal	(b) enternel	(c) internel	(d) internal
21. (a) interval	(b) inturval	(c) intarval	(d) intervel
22. (a) eksercise	(b) exercize	(c) exercise	(d) exurcise
23. (a) ekco	(b) echo	(c) ecko	(d) echoe
24. (a) surender	(b) surinder	(c) surrender	(d) surrinder
25. (a) diffikult	(b) dificult	(c) difficult	(d) diffacult
26. (a) valluable	(b) valuabul	(c) valueabel	(d) valuable
27. (a) allphabet	(b) alphabet	(c) alfabet	(d) alfabut
28. (a) tranzport	(b) transport	(c) trainsport	(d) transpurt
29. (a) decizion	(b) decision	(c) dicision	(d) desision
30. (a) comedian	(b) commedian	(c) comedien	(d) comediun
31. (a) klue	(b) clue	(c) cluwe	(d) clu
32. (a) instrument	(b) insterment	(c) enstrument	(d) insturment
33. (a) hundrid	(b) hundrad	(c) hundred	(d) hunddred
34. (a) musical	(b) musikal	(c) musicel	(d) mussical
35. (a) whitness	(b) witness	(c) witnuss	(d) wittness

The South Pole

Study the spelling and meaning of each word. These words are used in today's story. Connect each word with its definition.

1. barren
2. bitter
3. except
4. much
5. slant
6. sustain

a. great in quantity
b. unfruitful
c. leaving out
d. sharp, painful
e. to hold up
f. not straight up and down

Read the story carefully and remember the details.

The poles are the coldest places in the world. There the ice and snow and bitter winds sweep across the barren lands.

The South Pole is much colder than the North Pole. In fact, the South Pole, which is also called Antarctica, is the coldest place in the world. In winter the temperature drops to 125° below zero with winds up to 200 miles an hour.

There are no cities, trees, streams, grasses, or lakes to sustain life. No people have ever lived there except scientists and explorers. The South Pole is one of the loneliest places in the world. A few animals live there — penguins, whales, and fur seals.

The warmest days are in December and January. The coldest days are in June and July. The sun always hits the pole at a slant. The ice never melts.

No one owns the South Pole. It belongs to everyone for scientific study.

A. Underline the correct answers about today's story.

1. Where is the coldest place in the world?   (a) North Pole   (b) South Pole   (c) Iceland
2. The South Pole is also called   (a) Arctic   (b) Antarctica   (c) Alaska.
3. The people who live there are   (a) scientists   (b) Eskimos   (c) natives.
4. The warmest days are in   (a) June   (b) December   (c) August.
5. Which word does not describe Antarctica?   (a) barren   (b) lonely   (c) fertile

B. Reread the story and write the answers to these questions.

1. How cold is the South Pole?

_____

_____

_____

2. When are the coldest days?

_____

_____

3. How hard do the winds blow at the South Pole?

_____

_____

_____

4. What animals live at the South Pole?

_____

_____

_____

   Unit 144 cont'd ☛

Misspelled Words II

Underline the correctly spelled word in each row.

EXAMPLES: (a) operra   (b) oppera   (c) <u>opera</u>   (d) opara

                 (a) <u>whom</u>   (b) whum   (c) whoym   (d) whumn

	(a)	(b)	(c)	(d)
1.	liberty	libberty	liburty	libertey
2.	prepair	prepere	prepare	preapare
3.	sucess	success	suces	succes
4.	mishap	misshap	mishapp	mishep
5.	fiktion	fiction	ficshun	fictun
6.	fragil	frajile	frajil	fragile
7.	releeve	relieve	releave	releive
8.	unnusual	unuzual	unusual	unusuel
9.	private	privat	privete	privite
10.	fantastik	fantastek	fantastic	fantasstic
11.	sapreme	supreme	sipreme	supream
12.	lullaby	lulaby	lulliby	lullabye
13.	vokabulary	vocabulary	vocabilary	vocabulery
14.	guidance	guideance	guydance	guidence
15.	uneverse	univirse	univorse	universe
16.	spunge	sponje	sponge	sponnge
17.	immagination	imagination	emagination	imagonation
18.	violent	violant	violint	violunt
19.	centery	sentury	centeury	century
20.	frontier	fronteir	fruntier	frunteir
21.	mastar	mastir	master	mastor
22.	struggel	struggal	struggle	struggil
23.	yungster	youngster	yongster	youngstir
24.	gipsy	gipsey	gypsy	jypsy
25.	brilliant	briliant	brilient	briliunt
26.	subbmarine	submerine	submarine	submarrine
27.	baskitball	basketball	basketbal	baskutball
28.	detail	detale	detayl	detaile
29.	cumpare	compare	compaire	compaer
30.	sumthing	somethin	somthing	something
31.	progrim	progrem	progrom	program
32.	playground	plaground	playgrownd	playgroun
33.	bilding	billding	buildin	building

Spelunkers

Study the spelling and meaning of each word. These words are used in today's story. Connect each word with its definition.

1. amateur
2. explore
3. professionally
4. reliable
5. rule
6. spelunker

a. to search for discovery
b. one who explores caves
c. principle
d. nonprofessional
e. dependable
f. for pay

Read the story carefully and remember the details.

Are you an amateur spelunker? If you like to explore caves, then you are a spelunker. A person who studies caves professionally is also a spelunker.

Exploring caves is not a seasonal sport. The temperature inside a cave ranges from 52°F to 60°F the year round.

Anyone can become an amateur spelunker. Anyone who wants to explore a cave must be willing to squeeze through difficult passages. A spelunker should wear stout boots and a protective hat. The hat saves the head from falling rocks.

The first rule of cave exploring is never go alone. It is easy to get lost and often dangerous. There is always the possibility of falling into a pit or into water.

The second rule is to have a reliable light. It is best to take along extra batteries. The inside of a cave is completely dark.

A. Underline the correct answers about today's story.

1. A spelunker   (a) studies stars   (b) collects rocks   (c) explores caves.
2. In which season is it best to
   explore caves?   (a) winter   (b) summer   (c) year round
3. The first rule of cave exploring is   (a) never go alone   (b) wear warm clothes   (c) wear a hat.
4. It is important to take along   (a) food   (b) a good light   (c) extra clothes.
5. An "amateur" is a/an   (a) "professional"   (b) "nonprofessional"   (c) "expert."

B. Reread the story and write the answers to these questions.

1. Who can become an amateur?

_____

_____

_____

2. What must a spelunker be willing to do?

_____

_____

_____

3. What is the temperature range in caves?

_____

_____

_____

4. What should a spelunker wear?

_____

_____

_____

Unit 145 cont'd ☞

Misspelled Words III

 Each of the following words is misspelled. Rewrite each one correctly.

1. krazy _____crazy_____
2. caffeteria _____
3. invelope _____
4. liberary _____
5. maggazine _____
6. orkestra _____
7. popullation _____
8. sceane _____
9. tomorow _____
10. unuon _____
11. vollunteer _____
12. kaos _____
13. forsight _____
14. thery _____
15. oponent _____
16. riddiculus _____
17. criticise _____
18. flexibul _____
19. confuzed _____
20. significent _____
21. postpoan _____
22. remmedy _____
23. drouwsy _____
24. glanse _____
25. mayntayn _____
26. allready _____
27. egzist _____
28. classrum _____
29. pronownce _____
30. tabblit _____
31. nervus _____
32. matearial _____
33. iland _____

34. goverment _____
35. choccolate _____
36. insterment _____
37. kichen _____
38. neccessary _____
39. pairachute _____
40. reguler _____
41. scisors _____
42. thurst _____
43. unniverse _____
44. yesturday _____
45. remorese _____
46. hinceforth _____
47. autommatic _____
48. temptaton _____
49. freequent _____
50. expennsive _____
51. almanak _____
52. prospurous _____
53. combin _____
54. simplifi _____
55. glimps _____
56. champeon _____
57. interduction _____
58. chalenge _____
59. particuler _____
60. sistem _____
61. updayte _____
62. exampul _____
63. funktion _____
64. prepair _____
65. curteous _____
66. possition _____

67. amusment _____
68. dellicious _____
69. geografy _____
70. hankerchief _____
71. mischievious _____
72. purswade _____
73. sandwitch _____
74. spong _____
75. tungue _____
76. vocabullary _____
77. twilite _____
78. asociate _____
79. fragmint _____
80. newtral _____
81. aniversary _____
82. obstinnate _____
83. aginda _____
84. evaperate _____
85. acomplish _____
86. ambittion _____
87. obeadience _____
88. glamorus _____
89. rekwire _____
90. devilop _____
91. companun _____
92. populor _____
93. undirstan _____
94. expearment _____
95. langwage _____
96. begger _____
97. reccord _____
98. discontant _____
99. thundur _____

Comprehension Check

A **Connect the animals with the sounds they make.**

1. turkeys	quack	11. bees	meow
2. crickets	chirp	12. owls	hoot
3. people	talk	13. cats	buzz
4. ducks	gobble	14. lions	caw
5. roosters	crow	15. crows	roar
6. dogs	honk	16. snakes	laugh
7. pigs	bark	17. hyenas	hiss
8. geese	croak	18. horses	neigh
9. mice	oink	19. donkeys	cluck
10. frogs	squeak	20. chickens	bray

B **Underline the misspelled words.**

1. <u>missplace</u>	11. sumthing	21. surroundings	31. migrate
2. neccessary	12. extinct	22. envitation	32. inhabitent
3. mountains	13. cumpare	23. fantastik	33. operra
4. vistor	14. summir	24. snowey	34. insterment
5. protected	15. grownd	25. diet	35. mispell
6. wizdom	16. spelunker	26. evning	36. mosquito
7. echoe	17. bilding	27. scientist	37. progrem
8. describe	18. amung	28. sertainly	38. succes
9. interupt	19. submerine	29. unusuel	39. releave
10. extreme	20. complete	30. world	40. iland

C **Correct these misspelled words.**

1. forrests	*forests*	6. tomorow	_____	11. allready	_____
2. leppard	_____	7. undirstan	_____	12. thurst	_____
3. coverd	_____	8. prepair	_____	13. scisors	_____
4. becauze	_____	9. vollunteer	_____	14. kichen	_____
5. fethers	_____	10. populer	_____	15. nineth	_____

D **Complete these sentences.**

1. Snow leopards live in the ___*Himalayas*___ .
2. The poles are the _____ places.
3. Snowy owls rest on the _____ .
4. Spelunkers explore _____ .
5. The snow leopard prefers _____ weather.
6. The South Pole is _____ than the North Pole.
7. Snowy owls live in the _____ .
8. There are no _____ in South American forests.
9. The inside of a cave is completely _____ .
10. People of the South American forests live near _____ .

Test 29 cont'd ☞

Comprehension Check (continued)

E Match these words and their definitions. These words appeared in the reading selections from units 141-145.

_b_ 1. camouflages   ___ 7. sustain   a. to hold up   g. search to find

___ 2. agile   ___ 8. slant   b. hides naturally   h. not for pay

___ 3. protected   ___ 9. except   c. kept from harm   i. for pay

___ 4. unlike   ___ 10. explore   d. at an angle   j. different

___ 5. thick   ___ 11. amateur   e. able to move quickly   k. dense

___ 6. always   ___ 12. professional   f. without   l. all the time

F Underline the correct answers.

1. Why is the snow leopard valued?   (a) fur   (b) teeth
2. Where does the snow leopard live?   (a) mountains   (b) desert
3. Where does the snowy owl live?   (a) desert   (b) far north
4. Where does the owl nest?   (a) trees   (b) ground
5. Describe the South American forest.   (a) thick   (b) small
6. How does one travel the forest?   (a) on paved roads   (b) on rivers
7. Give another name for the South Pole.   (a) Arctic   (b) Antarctic
8. What is the warmest month at the South Pole?   (a) June   (b) December
9. What is a spelunker?   (a) one who collects   (b) one who explores caves
10. What is a cave's temperature range?   (a) 52°F to 60°F   (b) 0°F to 10°F

Choose one of the following topics and write a paragraph.

(1) Have you ever explored a cave? Describe your adventure. If you haven't explored one, would you like to? Why or why not?

(2) Would you like to live at the South Pole? Why or why not?

_____

_____

_____

_____

_____

_____

_____

_____

_____

_____

_____

Spider Monkeys

Study the spelling and meaning of each word. These words are used in today's story. Connect each word with its definition.

1. able
2. acquire
3. appearance
4. extra
5. loyal
6. only

a. merely
b. receive
c. capable
d. looks
e. additional
f. faithful

Read the story carefully and remember the details.

Spider monkeys are found in Central America and South America. They are only two feet long. Their tails are longer than their bodies. Their tails are often used like extra hands. Their arms are long. Spider monkeys acquire their name from their appearance.

Spider monkeys are able to walk upright like humans. They seldom come down to the ground, staying in their treetop homes. They even drink by hanging from low branches.

Spider monkeys live in small groups. They travel through the trees by leaping from branch to branch.

The monkeys are playful. They love to wrestle. Spider monkeys are loyal to their own kind. Spider monkeys are gentle, and some people even take them as pets.

A. Underline the correct answers about today's story.

1. Spider monkeys are native to
2. The tail is
3. Where do spider monkeys live?
4. Spider monkeys get their name from their
5. Which word describes the monkey?

(a) Europe	(b) Africa	(c) South America.
(a) useless	(b) short	(c) used like a hand.
(a) treetops	(b) ground	(c) underground
(a) habits	(b) home	(c) appearance.
(a) disloyal	(b) playful	(c) dangerous

B. Reread the story and write the answers to these questions.

1. Where do spider monkeys spend most of their time?

_____

_____

_____

2. How do they travel?

_____

_____

_____

3. How do they drink?

_____

_____

_____

4. To whom are spider monkeys loyal?

_____

_____

_____

Unit 146 cont'd

Misspelled Words IV

A. Each sentence contains one incorrectly spelled word. Underline the wrong spelling. Then write the correct spelling in the blank.

1. I have her new <u>adress</u>. *address*
2. He has allready gone. _____
3. It tastes awfull. _____
4. Do you beleive him? _____
5. My baskit is full. _____
6. Paul is bisy now. _____
7. My dog chases truks. _____
8. He drives hour bus. _____
9. The urth is round. _____
10. Where did you hyde it? _____
11. Take this one insted. _____
12. We have done nuthing. _____
13. She comes here oftin. _____
14. Opin the door. _____
15. I finished my reaport. _____
16. The hat is two small. _____
17. You are too yung. _____
18. Give me a klue. _____
19. Did you envite Mary? _____
20. What is the secret wurd? _____

21. Tomorow is Monday. _____
22. Finaly the show was over. _____
23. The air is kold. _____
24. Don't bee rude. _____
25. Does he wurk here? _____
26. I studyed for the test. _____
27. Witch one is mine? _____
28. Wat did you tell them? _____
29. I saw the smok. _____
30. The skool was closed today. _____
31. The stars are brit. _____
32. The leter is for you. _____
33. He guarded the sheeps. _____
34. Karen lost the muney. _____
35. Walt is absent agan. _____
36. Show her the foto. _____
37. Reed this sentence. _____
38. Are you hongry? _____
39. Did you injoy the film? _____
40. Rob is my freind. _____

B. Rewrite each word correctly.

1. sumer *summer*
2. absint _____
3. lisen _____
4. unkle _____
5. anser _____
6. butiful _____
7. klock _____
8. eech _____
9. tak _____
10. nuz _____

11. jist _____
12. babee _____
13. wintur _____
14. katch _____
15. reeson _____
16. miny _____
17. rize _____
18. fuw _____
19. helpt _____
20. klean _____

21. allright _____
22. fone _____
23. ruf _____
24. nite _____
25. musik _____
26. yu _____
27. pincil _____
28. durty _____
29. wurk _____
30. diffrent _____

The Stegosaurus

Study the spelling and meaning of each word. These words are used in today's story. Connect each word with its definition.

1. believe	a. protected
2. defended	b. taken as true
3. double	c. something unexplained
4. equipped	d. reason for
5. mystery	e. furnished with
6. purpose	f. two

Read the story carefully and remember the details.

About 150 million years ago the stegosaurus lived in North America. The animal was about twenty feet long with a tiny head and back legs twice as long as the front. Because its head was close to the ground, scientists believe that the stegosaurus lived on flat ground.

Up and down most of the animal's back was a double row of bony plates. These plates were covered with tough skin. Scientists don't know what the purpose of the plates was. On the tail of the animal were two enormous pairs of hornlike spikes with which the stegosaurus defended itself.

The stegosaurus has often been referred to as the "roofed dinosaur." Since it ate plants and was equipped to ward off meat-eating dinosaurs, the reason for its extinction is a mystery.

A. Underline the correct answers about today's story.

1. The stegosaurus lived   (a) in water   (b) in swamps   (c) on flat ground.
2. What were the plates on the back used for?   (a) defense   (b) balance   (c) No one knows.
3. The animal defended itself with its   (a) teeth   (b) tail   (c) claws.
4. What did the stegosaurus eat?   (a) plants   (b) meat   (c) fish
5. What is another name for stegosaurus?   (a) "plated dinosaur"   (b) "war club"   (c) "roofed dinosaur"

B. Reread the story and write the answers to these questions.

1. How many years ago did the stegosaurus live?

_____
_____
_____

2. Which continent was home to this animal?

_____
_____
_____

3. How long was the stegosaurus?

_____
_____
_____

4. Why is the stegosaurus now extinct?

_____
_____
_____

    Unit 147 cont'd ☞

Misspelled Words V

Each sentence contains a misspelled word. Underline it. Then write the correct spelling in the blank.

1. We are planning a <u>surprize</u> party.
   surprise

2. This is the corect answer.

3. The ball crashed threw the window.

4. We had a wunderful time.

5. He leaned aganst the tree.

6. Did someone nock on the door?

7. Did you eat brekfast?

8. I am not shure.

9. Sherry is a gues in our house.

10. Writ your name on the bottom line.

11. The box was hiden under the bed.

12. Dad's offic is upstairs.

13. These banenas are not ripe.

14. I come here offen.

15. Don steped on a snake.

16. Who is the othur person?

17. He alsways complains.

18. I want a carear in medicine.

19. You are always wellcome.

20. Dee will chooz the winner.

21. It was a terribul storm.

22. The kastle is haunted.

23. We need a duzen eggs.

24. My foks are from California.

25. What's for desert?

26. Our jurney began in August.

27. I sat in the middul.

28. That was a gost!

29. The potatos are cooked.

30. The skool was closed today.

31. That is the rong one.

32. Everything is alright.

The Stickleback

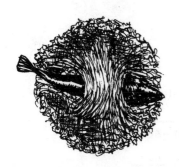

Study the spelling and meaning of each word. These words are used in today's story. Connect each word with its definition.

1. champion————————a. superior
2. collects   b. not typical
3. deposits   c. gathers
4. fierce   d. ferocious
5. prevent   e. keep from happening
6. unusual   f. places

Read the story carefully and remember the details.

The stickleback is a small but fierce fish whose name comes from the spines on its back. However, the most unusual thing about the stickleback is not its name or appearance. The stickleback is noted for its ability to build a nest.

The fish is often referred to as the champion nest builder. All of the credit should go to the male. The male stickleback collects twigs, stems, and leaves. With his mouth he makes a hollow structure with a single entrance. The nest is attached to reeds to prevent it from floating way.

The male forces the female inside the nest. There she deposits her eggs. Then she breaks through the back wall and swims away. The male guards the nest and cares for the young.

A. **Underline the correct answers about today's story.**

1. How does the stickleback
   get its name?   (a) habits   (b) nest   (c) spines
2. The stickleback is a champion   (a) swimmer   (b) fighter   (c) nest builder.
3. To keep the nest in place, it is   (a) attached to reeds   (b) weighed down   (c) built on rocks.
4. After laying the eggs,
   the female   (a) dies   (b) swims away   (c) destroys the nest.
5. Who cares for the young?   (a) female   (b) male   (c) both parents

B. **Reread the story and write the answers to these questions.**

1. Describe the size of the stickleback.

   _____

   _____

   _____

2. Who deserved the credit for building
   the nest?

   _____

   _____

   _____

3. What is the nest attached to?

   _____

   _____

   _____

4. How does the female escape the nest?

   _____

   _____

   _____

          Unit 148 cont'd 📌

Misspelled Words VI

Each sentence contains a misspelled word. Underline it. Then write it correctly.

1. The <u>furneture</u> was delivered today.
   furniture

2. What insterment do you play?

3. Go to the liberary.

4. I lost my hankerchief.

5. The cake was delishus.

6. What type of goverment do they have?

7. Our attendence is down again.

8. This one looks the healthyest.

9. He owns the vinyard.

10. Tomorrow is their anniversry.

11. There was too much moysture.

12. It was a wonderful discovry.

13. Make a punkin pie.

14. The company manufatures pipes.

15. The film was intresting.

16. How are they diffrent?

17. Tom is a mischievious boy.

18. These items are neccessary.

19. Did you perswede them?

20. I want another sandwitch.

21. What is the problim?

22. Adam plays the part of a wizzard.

23. Bring a pair of scisors.

24. These towils are dirty.

25. Yestirday was Thursday.

26. We cleaned the chimley.

27. I heard strange laufter.

28. The wolf lives in the willderness.

29. This is my favorute class.

30. Sam decoratid the room.

31. We drove seprate cars.

32. I like cold klimates.

Struthiomimus

Study the spelling and meaning of each word. These words are used in today's story. Connect each word with its definition.

1. against
2. habits
3. imitator
4. nevertheless
5. remarkable
6. resemblance

a. likeness
b. one who copies
c. ways of doing things
d. in spite of that
e. opposite to
f. striking

Read the story carefully and remember the details.

The name "struthiomimus" (stroo•thee•oh•my•muhs) means "ostrich imitator." In both looks and habits the struthiomimus did have a remarkable resemblance to the present-day ostrich. The struthiomimus, however, was a dinosaur. The struthiomimus lived in North America about 75 million years ago.

The struthiomimus was about eight feet tall. It had a tiny head and a long, thin neck. It walked on two birdlike back legs. Its front legs were small and held against its chest. The struthiomimus moved about with surprising speed. It protected itself by running.

Unlike other dinosaurs, the struthiomimus had no teeth. Nevertheless, it is believed that the animal was a meat-eater, feasting on worms, insects, and small lizards which the struthiomimus swallowed whole. Many scientists believe the animal also ate plants and eggs.

A. Underline the correct answers about today's story.

1. The struthiomimus resembled the	(a) turtle	(b) ostrich	(c) snake.
2. The struthiomimus was a	(a) bird	(b) dinosaur	(c) fish.
3. The struthiomimus protected itself by	(a) biting	(b) burrowing	(c) running.
4. Unlike other dinosaurs, the struthiomimus had	(a) claws	(b) teeth	(c) no teeth.
5. The animal's main diet was	(a) meat	(b) plants	(c) eggs.

B. Reread the story and write the answers to these questions.

1. What does "struthiomimus" mean?

_____

_____

_____

2. Where did this dinosaur live?

_____

_____

_____

3. How long ago did the struthiomimus live?

_____

_____

_____

4. How did this dinosaur eat its food?

_____

_____

_____

Unit 149 cont'd

Misspelled Words VII

 Each sentence contains a misspelled word. Underline it. Then write it correctly in the blank.

EXAMPLES: a. I <u>trid</u> to warn you!

tried

b. Freedom is too <u>presious</u> to lose.

precious

1. Al's familly lives in Mexico.
_____

2. I would rathur talk to Ms. Allison.
_____

3. Someone is trying to skare me.
_____

4. Jim thot you had gone home.
_____

5. Have you seen my new furneture?
_____

6. Everyone will laf at me.
_____

7. The sunnset was beautiful.
_____

8. Sally seldum talks in class.
_____

9. Did anyone invit George to the party?
_____

10. Can you repare the machine?
_____

11. We play football on the vakant lot.
_____

12. I won first prise!
_____

13. Bobby was sent to the principal's offic.
_____

14. All the snow had mellted by noon.
_____

15. Sue and Karen act like enemys.
_____

16. He is an outstandeng writer.
_____

17. The tiger is a feerce fighter.
_____

18. I need your advise.
_____

19. The skelleton is in the closet.
_____

20. The bom will explode at midnight.
_____

21. The police surounded the house.
_____

22. My dog went to obedince school.
_____

23. Does it come in a diffrent color?
_____

24. The whale is an enormus animal.
_____

25. The signeture has been forged.
_____

26. Do I have your permision?
_____

27. The prisoner was kept in the dungune.
_____

28. Robert is always so pollite.
_____

29. We have plinty of money.
_____

30. Everyone should have confidance.
_____

31. We had apple pie for desert.
_____

32. I want to become a comedion.
_____

The Sun Bear

Study the spelling and meaning of each word. These words are used in today's story. Connect each word with its definition.

1. climate
2. commonly
3. hibernate
4. sunbathes
5. unpredictable
6. variety

a. usually
b. sleep through winter
c. exposes to the sun
d. unable to foretell
e. average weather
f. of many kinds

Read the story carefully and remember the details.

The smallest of all the bears is the Malayan sun bear. It is commonly found in Asia. The sun bear is an excellent climber. It spends much of its time in the trees. During the day the sun bear sleeps and sunbathes in the trees. At night it hunts for food. The sun bear eats a variety of foods — fruit, insects, small animals, birds, termites, and honey.

Although the sun bear is small as compared to other bears, it is strong. Its claws are sharp and curved. Because of the warm climate in which it lives, the sun bear does not hibernate.

Young sun bears are extremely intelligent and make good pets. Older sun bears are unpredictable and can even be dangerous. In the wild the sun bears are very shy.

A. Underline the correct answers about today's story.

1. Compared to other bears, the sun bear is   (a) smaller   (b) bigger   (c) more ferocious.

2. Where does the sun bear spend most of its time?   (a) water   (b) trees   (c) shade

3. During the day the sun bear   (a) sleeps in the shade   (b) hunts for food   (c) sunbathes.

4. As pets, older sun bears are   (a) intelligent   (b) friendly   (c) unpredictable.

5. Which word describes the sun bear?   (a) shy   (b) aggressive   (c) bold

B. Reread the story and write the answers to these questions.

1. Where is the sun bear commonly found?

_____

_____

2. Name two things the sun bear eats.

_____

_____

3. What does the sun bear do at night?

_____

_____

4. What does the sun bear not do because of the warm climate?

_____

_____

Unit 150 cont'd ☞

From "Tab" to "One"

T A B L E T H E M U C H

U R N E V E R S E E D A R K I T

A E M A L L I T S W E N E T

E N O T

1. *t a b* small extension to a card
2. _ _ _ _ _ furniture on which food is served
3. _ _ _ _ _ _ small flat piece of medicine
4. _ _ _ _ having enough power
5. _ _ _ allow, permit
6. _ _ _ _____ door was open.
7. _ _ _ _ the persons talked about
8. _ _ the male spoken of
9. _ _ _ the border of a garment
10. _ _ _ _ a great amount
11. _ _ _ _ _ container used to make butter from milk
12. _ _ _ vase with a foot or pedestal
13. _ _ _ _ _ not ever
14. _ _ _ first woman
15. _ _ _ _ at any time
16. _ _ _ _ _ short division of a chapter in the Bible
17. _ _ _ to look at
18. _ _ _ _ part of a plant from which another plant grows
19. _ _ _ _ without light
20. _ _ _ boat in which Noah saved himself
21. _ _ _ any young furry animal
22. _ _ _ _ _ _ a young cat
23. _ _ _ six plus four
24. _ _ _ never having been before
25. _ _ _ _ something told that has just happened
26. _ _ _ _ _ without motion
27. _ _ _ _ before, up to the time of
28. _ _ _ not well, sick
29. _ _ _ _ not able to walk properly
30. _ _ I ____ present.
31. _ _ the person speaking
32. _ _ _ _ animal flesh
33. _ _ _ to chew and swallow
34. _ _ _ _ _ to make up, make amends
35. _ _ _ _ quality of sound
36. _ _ above and supported by
37. _ _ _ three minus two

Comprehension Check

Ⓐ Underline the misspelled words.

1. <u>adress</u>	11. spider	21. surprize	31. loyal
2. allready	12. offen	22. branch	32. extra
3. ground	13. dinosaur	23. aganst	33. unkle
4. mystery	14. othur	24. scientist	34. tomorow
5. beleive	15. alsways	25. dangerous	35. muney
6. nuthing	16. wellcome	26. jurney	36. extremely
7. animal	17. habits	27. finaly	37. hongry
8. wintur	18. duzen	28. female	38. leter
9. jist	19. musik	29. envite	39. enuf
10. reeson	20. excellent	30. common	40. champion

Ⓑ Correct the spelling of each word.

1. skare	_scare_	16. cafeteeria _____
2. diffrent	_____	17. furneture _____
3. skelleton	_____	18. liberary _____
4. suround	_____	19. signeture _____
5. enemys	_____	20. delishus _____
6. permision	_____	21. intresting _____
7. sunnset	_____	22. seprate _____
8. seldum	_____	23. problim _____
9. plinty	_____	24. healthyest _____
10. feerce	_____	25. chimley _____
11. familley	_____	26. vinyard _____
12. scisors	_____	27. discovry _____
13. wizzard	_____	28. yestirday _____
14. wunderful	_____	29. necesary _____
15. potatos	_____	30. goverment _____

Ⓒ Complete these sentences.

1. The stegosaurus is the ____*roofed*____ dinosaur.
2. The sun bear is the _____ bear.
3. The stegosaurus lived in _____ .
4. The struthiomimus was a _____ .
5. The stickleback is a _____ .
6. The sun bear lives in a _____ climate.
7. The stickleback is a champion _____ builder.
8. Spider monkeys have very long _____ .

9. Spider monkeys get their name from their _____ .
10. The stickleback is _____ .
11. Sun bears are very _____ .
12. Spider monkeys live in _____ .
13. The struthiomimus had no _____ .
14. The stegosaurus ate _____ .
15. "Struthiomimus" means " _____ imitator."
16. Sun bears live in _____ .

Test 30 cont'd ☞

Comprehension Check (continued)

(D) Match these words and their definitions. These words appeared in the reading selections from units 146-150.

_g_ 1. acquire	___ 7. imitator	a.	merely	g.	receive
___ 2. only	___ 8. resemblance	b.	one who copies	h.	likeness
___ 3. defended	___ 9. against	c.	average weather	i.	exposes to the sun
___ 4. mystery	___ 10. sunbathes	d.	protected	j.	unable to be explained
___ 5. fierce	___ 11. climate	e.	vicious	k.	places
___ 6. deposits	___ 12. unpredictable	f.	opposite to	l.	unable to foretell

(E) Underline the correct answers.

1. Where do spider monkeys live?   (a) <u>treetops</u>   (b) underground
2. What is the spider monkey's homeland?   (a) South America   (b) Asia
3. Which continent was home to the stegosaurus?   (a) Asia   (b) North America
4. What is another name for stegosaurus?   (a) roofed dinosaur   (b) war club
5. How does the stickleback get its name?   (a) habits   (b) spines
6. Who builds the nest of the stickleback?   (a) male   (b) female
7. What did the struthiomimus resemble?   (a) ostrich   (b) snake
8. What was the struthiomimus lacking?   (a) teeth   (b) claws
9. Name two things the sun bear eats.   (a) fruit and insects   (b) snakes and fish
10. What does the sun bear do during the day?   (a) sleeps in the shade   (b) sunbathes

Choose one of the following topics and write a paragraph.

(1) No one knows why dinosaurs became extinct. What possible reason can you offer for this phenomenon?

(2) Describe the nest-building habits of the stickleback.

_____

_____

_____

_____

_____

_____

_____

_____

In a Swiss Village

Study the spelling and meaning of each word. These words are used in today's story. Connect each word with its definition.

1. goatherd
2. member
3. retained
4. tradition
5. village
6. wage

a. one of a group
b. area less than a town
c. held back
d. one who tends sheep
e. unwritten practice
f. money earned

Read the story carefully and remember the details.

Every year many Swiss villages elect a young boy to serve as the village goatherd. Every morning the boy makes his rounds collecting all the goats in the village. His job is to drive the animals out to pasture.

The goatherd watches the goats all day. He is responsible for every member of the flock. The boy must make sure that every goat is returned safely to its owner in the evening.

For his work, the boy receives a small wage. His lunch is provided by the families who own the goats. Each day a different family supplies the meal.

The election of the goatherd is an old Swiss tradition. It is but one of the many customs retained by the Swiss.

A. **Underline the correct answers about today's story.**

1. A lad is a	(a) young boy	(b) young girl	(c) young person.
2. The goatherd takes the goats to	(a) market	(b) the river	(c) the pasture.
3. The goatherd is elected to serve	(a) one year	(b) five years	(c) all his life.
4. Wages are	(a) thanks	(b) money	(c) food.
5. Which word describes a goatherd?	(a) lazy	(b) responsible	(c) careless

B. **Reread the story and write the answers to these questions.**

1. What does the goatherd do all day?

_____

_____

_____

2. What must he do each evening?

_____

_____

_____

3. Who provides the goatherd's lunch?

_____

_____

_____

4. What is a "custom"?

_____

_____

_____

Unit 151 cont'd ☞

Following the Rules

Rule One

Use "i" before "e" except after "c." Underline the words which are exceptions to the rule.

1. <u>their</u>	6. eight	11. ceiling	16. believe	21. patient
2. friend	7. sufficient	12. being	17. experience	22. niece
3. leisure	8. skies	13. chief	18. either	23. foreign
4. cities	9. audience	14. heir	19. forfeit	24. weigh
5. counterfeit	10. sleigh	15. neighbor	20. reign	25. hygiene

Rule Two

When a word ends with a consonant and "y," change the "y" to "i" and add "es" to form the plural. Underline the words which follow the rule.

1. <u>territory</u>	6. pony	11. highway	16. company	21. turkey
2. attorney	7. alley	12. anniversary	17. toy	22. memory
3. duty	8. bluejay	13. story	18. penalty	23. birthday
4. mystery	9. luxury	14. holiday	19. delay	24. discovery
5. key	10. enemy	15. country	20. monkey	25. sky

Rule Three

The letters "ed" often sound like "t" at the end of a verb. Underline the words which follow the rule.

1. <u>passed</u>	6. needed	11. missed	16. watched	21. answered
2. changed	7. checked	12. invented	17. marched	22. furnished
3. matched	8. loved	13. pushed	18. wanted	23. filled
4. used	9. washed	14. hoped	19. added	24. laughed
5. wished	10. escaped	15. cared	20. milked	25. sounded

Rule Four

Many words contain letters which are written but not pronounced. These written letters are called silent letters. Underline the words which contain silent letters.

1. <u>write</u>	6. park	11. debt	16. word	21. walk
2. now	7. window	12. has	17. knee	22. ate
3. bridge	8. scissors	13. wrist	18. silent	23. pine
4. candy	9. know	14. knead	19. high	24. singer
5. comb	10. jump	15. blank	20. better	25. thumb

The Tasmanian Devil Unit 152

Study the spelling and meaning of each word. These words are used in today's story. Connect each word with its definition.

1. accurate
2. captivity
3. chunky
4. poultry
5. reputation
6. variety

a. of many kinds
b. confinement
c. correct
d. fowl raised for food
e. how one is looked at publicly
f. stocky

Read the story carefully and remember the details.

Because of its name, the Tasmanian Devil has a reputation for being mean and troublesome. Although its name is not entirely accurate, it is not entirely wrong either.

The Tasmanian Devil, a chunky little animal from the land of Tasmania, has powerful jaws. In the wild it can be a savage beast and is dangerous only to poultry, ground birds, lizards, and rodents. When angry or frightened, the animal makes a variety of strange sounds.

In captivity, however, the Tasmanian Devil loses its ugly spirit. If treated with kindness, the Tasmanian Devil can be an excellent pet.

A. Underline the correct answers about today's story.

1. Which word describes the Tasmanian Devil's reputation?   (a) mean   (b) gentle   (c) lovable
2. In the wild the Tasmanian Devil can be   (a) friendly   (b) savage   (c) affectionate.
3. In captivity the Tasmanian Devil is   (a) a pest   (b) dangerous   (c) a good pet.
4. When frightened, the Tasmanian Devil   (a) hides   (b) attacks   (c) makes sounds.
5. Where is the Tasmanian Devil's home?   (a) Africa   (b) Tasmania   (c) South America

B. Reread the story and write the answers to these questions.

1. What gave the Tasmanian Devil its reputation?

_____
_____
_____

2. Where is this animal from?

_____
_____
_____

3. What is necessary to keep this animal as a pet?

_____
_____
_____

4. What does the Tasmanian Devil lose in captivity?

_____
_____
_____

Unit 152 cont'd ☞

Recognizing Correctly Spelled Words I

 **Underline the correctly spelled words.
Then use each answer in a sentence.**

1. a) <u>disappear</u>   b) dissappear   c) disapear   *It will disappear like magic.*
2. a) similiar   b) simlar   c) similar   _____
3. a) counterfeit   b) counturfeit c) counterfiet   _____
4. a) business   b) bussiness   c) busines   _____
5. a) imposible   b) impossible   c) empossible   _____
6. a) freqent   b) frequnt   c) frequent   _____
7. a) depind   b) dipend   c) depend   _____
8. a) familiar   b) familar   c) fameliar   _____
9. a) demolush   b) demolish   c) dimolish   _____
10. a) examune   b) examin   c) examine   _____
11. a) patient   b) pateint   c) patchunt   _____
12. a) identufy   b) idintify   c) identify   _____
13. a) deside   b) decide   c) dicide   _____
14. a) obey   b) obay   c) obeay   _____
15. a) apearance   b) appearance   c) appearence   _____
16. a) disagree   b) dissagree   c) disagre   _____
17. a) ridiculus   b) ridiculous   c) ridiculis   _____
18. a) ocurred   b) occurred   c) occured   _____
19. a) kruel   b) cruel   c) crul   _____
20. a) ignore   b) ignor   c) egnore   _____
21. a) desurv   b) deserve   c) disurve   _____
22. a) substitute   b) substute   c) substitut   _____
23. a) furniture   b) ferniture   c) furneture   _____
24. a) lether   b) leathur   c) leather   _____
25. a) hundrid   b) hundred   c) hundrud   _____
26. a) skore   b) scor   c) score   _____
27. a) grocery   b) growsry   c) grochury   _____
28. a) parachute   b) parashoot   c) perachute   _____
29. a) spunge   b) sponge   c) spong   _____
30. a) other   b) othur   c) uther   _____
31. a) tuff   b) tugh   c) tough   _____
32. a) prepair   b) prepare   c) prepear   _____
33. a) kwikly   b) qwickly   c) quickly   _____

The Trap-Door Spider

Study the spelling and meaning of each word. These words are used in today's story. Connect each word with its definition.

1. derives
2. entrance
3. feast
4. genius
5. harmful
6. intruders

a. place one enters
b. unwanted visitors
c. comes from
d. extremely intelligent
e. hurtful
f. big meal

Read the story carefully and remember the details.

The trap-door spider is a genius at building a home. The home is equipped with a trap door, and thus the spider derives its name.

First, the spider digs a tunnel. The tunnel is lined with silk to prevent loose dirt from falling in. Then, the spider makes a door to fit the entrance to the tunnel. The door is made of several layers of silk. The door is fastened to one side of the tunnel. The outside of the door is covered with plants which grow near the nest. Sometimes the spider builds a side tunnel which leads off the main one in order to afford itself extra protection.

When the nest is finished, the spider stands just under the closed door. It listens for the movements of an approaching insect. When the insect is close, the spider lifts the door, grabs the insect, and carries it down to feast upon its catch. The door also protects the home from rain and harmful intruders.

A. Underline the correct answers about today's story.

1. The trap-door spider gets its name from its   (a) looks   (b) home   (c) habits.
2. The trap door is made of   (a) silk   (b) dirt   (c) leaves.
3. The home is made in   (a) hollow trees   (b) sand   (c) the ground.
4. A side tunnel is used for   (a) sleeping   (b) eating   (c) protection.
5. The spider eats   (a) insects   (b) plants   (c) worms.

B. Reread the story and write the answers to these questions.

1. What is the first step in the building of the home?

_____
_____
_____

2. Where does the spider wait for victims?

_____
_____
_____

3. Name a use of the trap door.

_____
_____
_____

4. What is the lining of the tunnel?

_____
_____

    Unit 153 cont'd

Recognizing Correctly Spelled Words II

 Underline each correctly spelled word.
Then write a sentence with it.

1. (a) banena	(b) banana	(c) benana	*Give the monkey a banana.*
2. (a) dauter	(b) daugter	(c) daughter	
3. (a) croud	(b) crowd	(c) krowd	
4. (a) careful	(b) carefull	(c) carefil	
5. (a) favorit	(b) favorite	(c) favurite	
6. (a) wunderful	(b) wonderful	(c) wondurful	
7. (a) remember	(b) remimber	(c) remembur	
8. (a) infurmation	(b) informatiun	(c) information	
9. (a) excellent	(b) excellint	(c) xcellent	
10. (a) nuwspaper	(b) newspaper	(c) newspapur	
11. (a) praktis	(b) practice	(c) practus	
12. (a) umbrella	(b) umbrilla	(c) umberella	
13. (a) inturesting	(b) interisting	(c) interesting	
14. (a) surprize	(b) surprise	(c) sirprise	
15. (a) sepurate	(b) seprate	(c) separate	
16. (a) adress	(b) address	(c) addres	
17. (a) school	(b) skool	(c) schol	
18. (a) windo	(b) whindow	(c) window	
19. (a) sandwich	(b) sandwhich	(c) sandwitch	
20. (a) radeo	(b) radio	(c) raydeo	
21. (a) offic	(b) ofice	(c) office	
22. (a) mystery	(b) mistery	(c) mystory	
23. (a) freedum	(b) freedim	(c) freedom	
24. (a) busyness	(b) business	(c) bisiness	
25. (a) dificult	(b) diffikult	(c) difficult	
26. (a) cabin	(b) kabin	(c) cabbin	
27. (a) laff	(b) laugh	(c) lagh	
28. (a) together	(b) togither	(c) togethur	
29. (a) tiket	(b) tickit	(c) ticket	
30. (a) possible	(b) possibul	(c) posible	
31. (a) straight	(b) strat	(c) straght	
32. (a) spind	(b) spend	(c) spende	
33. (a) rong	(b) wron	(c) wrong	

The Trumpeter Swan

Study the spelling and meaning of each word. These words are used in today's story. Connect each word with its definition.

1. demand
2. gracefulness
3. native
4. marshy
5. quills
6. waterfowl

a. natural resident
b. birds that live on water
c. desire
d. beauty of movement
e. hollow parts of feathers
f. low wet land

Read the story carefully and remember the details.

Like other swans the trumpeter swan is noted for its gracefulness. The trumpeter swan gets its name from its low-pitched sound. The sound is said to resemble the French horn.

In the past the trumpeter swan was killed for food. Its quills were used as pens. Its feathers were used to stuff pillows and featherbeds. The bird was in such demand that the trumpeter swan was soon in danger of extinction. Laws were passed to protect the bird.

Nowadays the trumpeter swan seems to be out of danger. It builds its large nest on marshy soil. The huge nest of grasses and water plants sometimes reaches five feet across. The trumpeter swan always nests near the water. It is the world's largest waterfowl. The trumpeter swan is native to North America.

A. Underline the correct answers about today's story.

1. Swans are noted for their   (a) size   (b) gracefulness   (c) noise.
2. The trumpeter swan is named for its   (a) sound   (b) large size   (c) habits.
3. Long ago the swan's quills were used   (a) as pens   (b) as needles   (c) as hat feathers.
4. The swan's nest is made of   (a) mud   (b) grasses   (c) sticks.
5. The swan always lives   (a) in open country   (b) in trees   (c) near water.

B. Reread the story and write the answers to these questions.

1. What does the trumpeter swan's sound resemble?

_____

_____

_____

2. What once threatened the bird?

_____

_____

_____

3. Why was the swan once killed?

_____

_____

_____

4. What was made of the swan's feathers?

_____

_____

_____

Unit 154 cont'd ☞

Vocabulary Study I

A. Complete each sentence with a word from the list.

1. available 2. business 3. champion 4. definition 5. diagnose 6. double 7. furniture 8. headache 9. mountain 10. necklace 11. organize 12. parents 13. recent 14. separate 15. sidewalk 16. speeds 17. unable 18. volunteer 19. yesterday 20. zone	1. My sister is a ___*volunteer*___ at the hospital. 2. The lady wore a beautiful diamond _____. 3. Don't ride your bicycle on the _____. 4. _____ was the first day of winter. 5. Paul was _____ to come to the meeting. 6. Rockets fly at tremendous _____. 7. _____ the pencils from the pens. 8. The _____ was very modern. 9. Sarah is our new tennis _____. 10. Wayne's _____ are flying to Paris. 11. I have a _____. 12. The doctor will _____ the illness. 13. At the top of the _____ was snow. 14. Look up the _____ in a dictionary. 15. More information is _____ at the library. 16. The gambler tried to _____ his money. 17. It is important to _____ your speech. 18. My uncle is in the real estate _____.

B. Match each definition with a word from the list.

___6___   1. twice as much
_____   2. pain in the head
_____   3. the day before today
_____   4. jewelry worn around the neck
_____   5. mother and father
_____   6. to put in order
_____   7. not able
_____   8. the meaning of
_____   9. lately
_____   10. to take apart
_____   11. a concrete walk on the side of a road
_____   12. sofa, chairs, tables
_____   13. person who does something without being asked
_____   14. land formation with tall peak
_____   15. another word for winner

C. Answer each question with a word from the list.

1. Which word begins with a prefix which means "not"? ___*unable*___
2. Which word begins with the schwa sound? _____
3. Which word ends with the "ā" sound? _____
4. Which words are one-syllable words? _____ _____
5. Which words begin with consonant blends? _____ _____
6. Which word rhymes with "trouble"? _____
7. In which word does the "ch" sound like a "k"? _____
8. Which word begins with a vowel plus "r"? _____

372

Mark Twain

Study the spelling and meaning of each word. These words are used in today's story. Connect each word with its definition.

1. direct
2. famous
3. lectures
4. memories
5. passage
6. popular

a. well liked
b. very well known
c. crossing; journey
d. talks
e. to the point
f. things remembered

Read the story carefully and remember the details.

Two famous stories, *Huckleberry Finn* and *Tom Sawyer,* were written by one of the best-known American writers, Samuel Clemens. He lived in the Mississippi River town of Hannibal, Missouri. When he was a boy, he dreamed of traveling on the river and of becoming a riverboat captain. Clemens used his boyhood memories of the river and river town to write his books.

When he began to write, Clemens adopted the pen name "Mark Twain." The term "mark twain" is a riverboat term which means the water is two fathoms, or 12 feet deep, which is deep enough for safe passage.

Twain became a successful and delightful writer with his simple, direct, and humorous style. He traveled abroad a great deal writing books and giving lectures. He was popular not only at home but also in Europe.

A. Underline the correct answers about today's story.

1. What was Samuel Clemens' pen name?	(a) Tom Sawyer	(b) Huck Finn	(c) Mark Twain
2. Which river did Twain write about?	(a) Mississippi	(b) Missouri	(c) Ohio
3. What does "mark twain" mean?	(a) riverboat	(b) two fathoms	(c) safe passage
4. Where did Twain grow up?	(a) Missouri	(b) Mississippi	(c) Europe
5. What boats did Twain write about?	(a) sailing ships	(b) clipper ships	(c) riverboats

B. Reread the story and write the answers to these questions.

1. Name the two famous stories by Mark Twain.
_____
_____
_____

3. What is Mark Twain's real name?
_____
_____
_____

2. Besides America, where else was Twain popular?
_____
_____

4. How deep is two fathoms?
_____
_____

Unit 155 cont'd

Vocabulary Study II

A. Complete each sentence with a word from the list.

1. audience
2. authentic
3. brilliant
4. climate
5. comedy
6. copy
7. distance
8. forgive
9. instead
10. investigate
11. legend
12. mischievous
13. necessary
14. orchestra
15. parachute
16. shoulder
17. sponge
18. tunnel
19. vocabulary
20. witness

1. Everyone in the ___audience___ applauded.
2. The _____ of Brazil is very hot.
3. The _____ played my favorite song.
4. May I have a _____ of your report?
5. Matthew is a _____ little boy.
6. The teacher told us the _____ of the gold box.
7. A _____ absorbs water.
8. The detective will _____ the murder.
9. We had to crawl through a long dark _____.
10. Ray jumped from the plane and pulled the _____ cord.
11. What is the _____ between here and Memphis?
12. Thomas chose Wally _____ of me.
13. Every day I try to increase my _____ by one word.
14. How can we be certain that this gun is _____?
15. Will you ever be able to _____ me?
16. There was only one _____ to the robbery.
17. The movie was a _____ about love.
18. It won't be _____ to call.

B. Match each definition with a word from the list.

__9__ 1. in place of
____ 2. used for jumping out of planes
____ 3. needed
____ 4. story with happy ending
____ 5. duplicate
____ 6. real
____ 7. space between two points
____ 8. people watching an event
____ 9. animal which lives in ocean
____ 10. person who sees something happen
____ 11. to look into
____ 12. to pardon
____ 13. weather
____ 14. a tale
____ 15. passageway, usually long and narrow

C. Answer each question with a word from the list.

1. Which word ends with a ''k'' sound?
   ___authentic___
2. Which word rhymes with ''funnel''?
   _____
3. Which word is a one-syllable word?
   _____
4. Which word ends with a ''v'' sound?
   _____
5. Which words begin with consonant blends?
   _____ _____
   _____ _____
6. In which words do the ''g's'' sound like ''j's''? _____ _____
7. Which words end with vowel sounds?
   _____ _____
   _____ _____
   _____

374

Comprehension Check

(A) Correct the spelling of each word.

1. sceince _science_
2. recieve _____
3. territorys _____
4. benana _____
5. riter _____
6. croud _____
7. liesure _____
8. carefull _____
9. laff _____
10. wiegh _____

11. similiar _____
12. favrite _____
13. sponje _____
14. adress _____
15. obay _____
16. egnore _____
17. ofice _____
18. desurv _____
19. emty _____
20. freedum _____

21. surprize _____
22. schol _____
23. tickit _____
24. doktor _____
25. othir _____
26. qwickly _____
27. windo _____
28. hundrid _____
29. thier _____
30. storys _____

(B) Match the words and their definitions.

_e_ 1. parents
____ 2. instead
____ 3. authentic
____ 4. organize
____ 5. legend

____ 6. double
____ 7. necessary
____ 8. headache
____ 9. separate
____ 10. forgive

a. needed
b. real
c. to put in order
d. to pardon
e. mother and father

f. twice as much
g. a tale
h. in place of
i. to take apart
j. pain in the head

(C) Complete each sentence with a word from part B.

1. _Separate_ _____ the blues from the reds.
2. Would you like to _____ your money?
3. Today I ordered fish _____ of ham.
4. It is not _____ to rewrite your paper.
5. The first thing you should do is _____ .
6. The loud noise gave me a _____ .
7. Both of my _____ are plumbers.
8. That story is an Indian _____ .

(D) Complete these sentences.

1. _Laws_ _____ protect the trumpeter swan.
2. Trumpeter swans nest near _____ .
3. "Mark twain" means " _____ fathoms."
4. Goatherds are common in _____ .
5. Goatherds tend to _____ .
6. A trumpeter swan sounds like a

   _____ .

7. Mark Twain is an _____ writer.
8. The swan is a _____ bird.
9. The Tasmanian Devil lives in _____ .
10. A goatherd is a _____ .
11. Twain wrote about the _____ River.
12. The trap-door spider is a genius _____ builder.

Comprehension Check (continued)

(E) Match these words and their definitions. These words appeared in the reading selections from units 151-155.

<u>c</u> 1. village   ____ 7. intruders   a. person who tends goats   g. hurtful

____ 2. tradition   ____ 8. demand   b. very well known   h. how one is seen

____ 3. reputation   ____ 9. waterfowl   c. very small town   i. correct; right

____ 4. accurate   ____ 10. famous   d. unwanted guests   j. birds of the water

____ 5. derive   ____ 11. direct   e. handed-down custom   k. obtain from a source

____ 6. harmful   ____ 12. goatherd   f. expressed desire   l. straight forward

(F) Underline the correct answers.

1. How long does a goatherd serve?   (a) <u>one year</u>   (b) all his life
2. Which word describes a goatherd?   (a) responsible   (b) lazy
3. Describe a Tasmanian Devil in the wild?   (a) savage beast   (b) friendly and affectionate
4. What does a Tasmanian Devil do when frightened?   (a) makes strange sounds   (b) attacks viciously
5. Where is the trap-door spider's home?   (a) in the sand   (b) in the ground
6. Why was the swan in danger of extinction?   (a) great demand   (b) illness
7. Name an old-time use for quills.   (a) pens   (b) hat feathers
8. Where do swans always live?   (a) near water   (b) in open country
9. What was Mark Twain's real name?   (a) Samuel Jones   (b) Samuel Clemens
10. How deep is a fathom?   (a) six feet   (b) twelve feet

Choose one of the following topics and write a paragraph.

(1) Mark Twain wrote about life on the river. What do you think about this type of life? Would you have liked to live on a riverboat?

(2) Describe the trap-door spider's home.

_____

_____

_____

_____

_____

_____

_____

_____

_____

The Vampire Bat

Study the spelling and meaning of each word. These words are used in today's story. Connect each word with its definition.

1. awaken————————————a. to rouse from sleep
2. diet   b. mild
3. emerges   c. comes into view
4. gentle   d. animal hunted for food
5. hollow   e. empty on the inside
6. prey   f. food one eats

Read the story carefully and remember the details.

Like other bats, the vampire bat is active at night. Its home is a cave or a hollow tree trunk. The vampire bat is native to Central America and South America. It sleeps by hanging upside down. It travels through the darkness by using its built-in radar system to let it know where objects are located.

What makes this bat different from other bats is its diet. The vampire bat lives on blood.

When the bat emerges from its home, it watches for prey. The prey may be a horse, a cow, a goat, or even a sleeping person. It lands gently on the victim, makes a bite, and laps up the blood. When full, the bat flies homeward.

The vampire bat is so gentle that it does not awaken its victim. Its bite does not kill humans or large animals.

A. Underline the correct answers about today's story.

1. Bats are active   (a) in early morning   (b) in daytime   (c) at night.
2. Vampire bats are different because of   (a) their diet   (b) habits   (c) environment.
3. What do vampire bats eat?   (a) fruit   (b) blood   (c) meat
4. The bat's bite is not deadly to   (a) birds   (b) large animals   (c) other bats.
5. The vampire bat is native to   (a) Europe   (b) India   (c) South America.

B. Reread the story and write the answers to these questions.

1. What is the animal's home?

_____

_____

_____

2. How does the animal travel at night?

_____

_____

_____

3. How does the bat sleep?

_____

_____

_____

4. Name a possible victim.

_____

_____

_____

Unit 156 cont'd ☞

Vocabulary Study III

A. Complete each sentence with a word from the list.

1. attention
2. circle
3. combine
4. confuse
5. dictionary
6. disappear
7. favorite
8. grocery
9. library
10. memory
11. nervous
12. problem
13. scheme
14. shadow
15. singular
16. suddenly
17. surface
18. tongue
19. victory
20. yacht

1. The doctor said, "Stick out your ___*tongue*___."
2. My brother works at the _____ store on weekends.
3. Sandpaper has a very rough _____.
4. I dream of sailing around the world on a _____.
5. Check the spelling in a _____.
6. The boy was afraid of his own _____.
7. The _____ closes at 6 o'clock.
8. The army celebrated its _____.
9. _____ it began to rain.
10. Pay _____.
11. Can you solve the math _____?
12. My _____ flavor of ice cream is strawberry.
13. John was too _____ to make a speech.
14. You are trying to _____ us.
15. Brad devised a _____ to get control of the plant.
16. The opposite of plural is _____.
17. _____ the sugar and the flour.
18. We sat in a _____ and told ghost stories.

B. Match each definition with a word from the list.

__20__ 1. a luxury ship
_____ 2. the one you like best
_____ 3. place where books are kept
_____ 4. to happen quickly
_____ 5. to put together
_____ 6. one
_____ 7. book
_____ 8. that which remembers
_____ 9. a plan
_____ 10. a round shape
_____ 11. upset
_____ 12. to vanish
_____ 13. success
_____ 14. top
_____ 15. to jumble

C. Answer each question with a word from the list.

1. In which word does the "ch" sound like a "k"? ___*scheme*___
2. Which word begins with an "s" sound but does not begin with an "s"? _____
3. Which words are one-syllable words?

   _____ _____ _____
4. Which word begins with a vowel?

   _____
5. Which words end with the "t" sound?

   _____ _____
6. Which word rhymes with "theme"?

   _____
7. Which word ends with the "əl" sound?

   _____
8. Which word begins with the prefix "dis"?

   _____

Venus's-Flytrap

Study the spelling and meaning of each word. These words are used in today's story. Connect each word with its definition.

1. crawl   a. actually is
2. exist   b. bites suddenly
3. finish   c. complete
4. ideal   d. device for catching animals
5. snaps   e. to move as a worm
6. trap   f. best

Read the story carefully and remember the details.

Have you ever seen a plant eat a fly? Such a plant does exist and is called Venus's-flytrap. It is a small plant that lives only in the swamplands of North America.

Each plant has a circle of small leaves at the end of which lies the trap. The trap is open and waiting. When something crawls over the trap, it snaps shut.

The ideal victim is the fly. It is just the right size. An ant would be too small; it could crawl out of the trap. A grasshopper would be too big; it would tear the leaves apart.

What happens to the fly that is caught in the trap? It is eaten. Juices inside the trap digest the fly. It takes about seven days for the plant to finish the fly. Then the plant opens again, ready for its next victim.

A. Underline the correct answers about today's story.

1. Venus's-flytrap is a/an   (a) plant   (b) animal   (c) machine.
2. The ideal victim is the   (a) fly   (b) ant   (c) grasshopper.
3. The grasshopper is too   (a) small   (b) big   (c) fast.
4. The trap is located   (a) under the leaf   (b) in the center   (c) at the end of the leaf.
5. A victim is a/an   (a) prey   (b) friend   (c) enemy.

B. Reread the story and write the answers to these questions.

1. On what continent does Venus's flytrap live?

_____

_____

_____

2. Why is the fly such a good victim?

_____

_____

_____

3. What happens when something crawls over the trap?

_____

_____

_____

4. Why is an ant not a good victim?

_____

_____

_____

     Unit 157 cont'd ☞

Vocabulary Study IV

A. Complete each sentence with a word from the list.

1. avoid	1. The prisoner tried to __escape__ again last night.
2. camera	2. Roberta is a _____ of Spain.
3. citizen	3. In her hat she wore a bright orange _____.
4. direction	4. My grandfather was a _____ old man.
5. dozen	5. Henry played a song on the _____.
6. escape	6. In which _____ did the woman go?
7. extra	7. The police began to _____ the building.
8. feather	8. Change each of these singular words to their _____ forms.
9. guitar	9. In a library you must try to be _____.
10. middle	10. Do you have an _____ pencil?
11. ought	11. Mother needs a _____ eggs.
12. plural	12. What was the game's final _____?
13. provide	13. Your _____ takes beautiful pictures.
14. quiet	14. Juan is a _____ to our country.
15. score	15. We will _____ you with the necessary supplies.
16. silence	16. In the _____ of the circle sat the puppy.
17. surround	17. Don't dry your hands on the blue _____.
18. towel	18. The driver tried to _____ hitting the truck.
19. visitor	
20. wise	

B. Match each definition with a word from the list.

__9__ 1. a musical instrument
____ 2. to supply
____ 3. to get away
____ 4. used for taking pictures
____ 5. more than enough
____ 6. twelve
____ 7. one who visits
____ 8. should have
____ 9. the center
____ 10. used for drying
____ 11. smart
____ 12. to encircle
____ 13. more than one
____ 14. resident of a country
____ 15. point of the compass

C. Answer each question with a word from the list.

1. Which word begins with the schwa sound?
   __avoid__
2. Which word ends with the ''z'' sound?
   _____
3. Which word begins with a ''k'' sound?
   _____
4. Which word ends with a ''p'' sound?
   _____
5. Which words end with the ''əl'' sound?
   _____ _____ _____
6. Which word rhymes with ''brought''?
   _____
7. Which words begin with consonant blends?
   _____ _____ _____
8. Which words contain diphthongs?
   _____ _____ _____

380

A Walking Leaf

Study the spelling and meaning of each word. These words are used in today's story. Connect each word with its definition.

1. camouflage
2. disguise
3. exactly
4. master
5. replica
6. unique

a. conceal by something
b. precisely
c. duplication
d. hiding naturally
e. skillful person
f. one of a kind

Read the story carefully and remember the details.

Have you ever seen a leaf walking? It's really not as silly as it may sound. The Ceylonese walking leaf looks exactly like a leaf.

The walking leaf is a master of disguise. It is an insect with a green body which is shaped and veined in the exact replica of a leaf. Even the legs are shaped like smaller leaves. The legs are flat and appear like leaves with ragged edges.

The walking leaf's disguise does not end with its looks. It even acts like a leaf. When the wind blows, the walking leaf wiggles back and forth. The movement imitates a leaf blowing in the wind.

Other than its unique camouflage, the walking leaf has no other protection from its enemies. With such a good disguise, there is little danger of attack.

A. Underline the correct answers about today's story.

1. What color is the walking leaf?   (a) brown   (b) green   (c) yellow
2. The insect's body looks like a   (a) stick   (b) leaf   (c) flower.
3. When the wind blows, the insect   (a) wiggles   (b) hides   (c) falls off.
4. Besides camouflage, the insect   (a) stings   (b) has a sharp bite   (c) has no protection.
5. Camouflage is a   (a) color   (b) disguise   (c) hiding place.

B. Reread the story and write the answers to these questions.

1. In addition to looking like a leaf, how is the insect like a leaf?

_____

_____

_____

2. Of what is the walking leaf a master?

_____

_____

_____

3. Why is there little danger of attack for the walking leaf?

_____

_____

_____

4. What is the insect imitating when it is wiggling?

_____

_____

_____

Unit 158 cont'd

Building Your Vocabulary

A. Match each definition with a word in the box.

a. airport	__e__ 1. to overcome by using force
b. betray	____ 2. at long last
c. blunder	____ 3. place where planes land and take off
d. chatter	____ 4. to shelter from harm
e. conquer	____ 5. not occurring very often
f. finally	____ 6. to pass the time in inactivity
g. hibernate	____ 7. that which is seen
h. hospital	____ 8. excellent
i. journey	____ 9. to be a traitor to; to prove faithless
j. nuisance	____ 10. to bring to mind
k. outstanding	____ 11. having great worth
l. protect	____ 12. place where sick and wounded are cared for
m. recall	____ 13. the bony framework of an animal
n. seldom	____ 14. to make less complex
o. simplify	____ 15. to talk rapidly about trivial matters
p. skeleton	____ 16. passage from one place to another
q. toward	____ 17. if it be not a fact that
r. unless	____ 18. something which annoys
s. valuable	____ 19. in the direction of
t. visual	____ 20. a stupid mistake

B. Complete each sentence with a word from the box.

1. The diamond is a ___valuable___ stone.
2. He was awarded a certificate for _____ achievement.
3. When Tom broke his arm, he stayed in the _____ for a week.
4. Andrew _____ finishes his homework.
5. _____ you call, we will leave without you.
6. We rushed to the _____ to catch our plane.
7. How could you make such a stupid _____!
8. I don't _____ the old man's name.
9. Lester's pet dog is becoming a _____.
10. He has plans to _____ the world.
11. The bull charged _____ the red cape.
12. An umbrella will _____ you from the rain.
13. Bears _____ during the cold winter months.
14. _____ we were able to see the lights of the boat.
15. Jill screamed when she saw the _____.

The Water Bug Unit 159

Study the spelling and meaning of each word. These words are used in today's story. Connect each word with its definition.

1. attach
2. bristles
3. captive
4. enable
5. hind
6. strong

a. make capable
b. short, stiff hair
c. back, rear
d. fasten
e. powerful
f. confined

Read the story carefully and remember the details.

The largest and most bloodthirsty of the water insects is the water bug. It has strong front legs that are used to hold its captive. The water bug does not eat its prey; it merely drinks the victim's juices.

The hind legs have hairlike bristles which enable the insect to swim quickly through the water. The speed is important when catching its dinner.

Female water bugs attach eggs to the backs of the males. The males swim around with the eggs until the eggs hatch and fall off into the water.

The water bug is sometimes called the electric light bug. It seems to be attracted to electric light.

A. **Underline the correct answers about today's story.**

1. Which word does not describe
   the bug?   (a) bloodthirsty   (b) large   (c) tiny
2. What do water bugs eat?   (a) plants   (b) juices   (c) fish eggs
3. The prey is caught with the bug's   (a) front legs   (b) hind legs   (c) mouth.
4. Which legs help the bug to swim?   (a) all of them   (b) front legs   (c) hind legs
5. Water bugs are attracted to   (a) darkness   (b) electric lights   (c) moving objects.

B. **Reread the story and write the answers to these questions.**

1. Which water insect is most bloodthirsty?

_____

_____

_____

2. What does the female do with her eggs?

_____

_____

3. What happens when the eggs hatch?

_____

_____

_____

4. What is another name for the water bug?

_____

_____

_____

Unit 159 cont'd ☞

Increasing Your Vocabulary

A. Match each definition with a word in the box.

a. ambition	_c_ 1. to gather together
b. awkward	____ 2. assurance given by one person to another
c. collect	____ 3. living, being, or going alone
d. convince	____ 4. conforming to fact or reality
e. enormous	____ 5. that which imparts excitement
f. guilty	____ 6. a conclusion or judgment
g. interval	____ 7. one who takes part with another
h. laugh	____ 8. of everyday occurrence; common
i. match	____ 9. ungraceful in bearing
j. opinion	____ 10. to persuade by argument
k. ordinary	____ 11. containing or holding nothing
l. partner	____ 12. to know again
m. promise	____ 13. extraordinary in size
n. recognize	____ 14. a period of slumber
o. shut	____ 15. to bring to a close
p. sleep	____ 16. time between two periods
q. solitary	____ 17. having violated a law or rule
r. truth	____ 18. eager desire for distinction
s. vacant	____ 19. similar or equal in appearance
t. zest	____ 20. to express amusement

B. Complete each sentence with a word from the box.

1. John's ____ambition____ is to become a professional boxer.
2. The jury found the woman _____ of murder.
3. Dan went to _____ at eight o'clock.
4. I could not _____ him that he was wrong.
5. Eve likes to _____ old coins and stamps.
6. Ned chose Wanda as his science _____.
7. We play baseball on the _____ lot.
8. The comedians made us _____.
9. Do you _____ me without my glasses?
10. What is your _____ on the crisis, Dr. Linden?
11. The dinosaur was an _____ animal.
12. I swear I am telling you the _____!
13. These colors _____ perfectly.
14. You must _____ to help us raise the money.
15. _____ the door and turn out the lights.

The White Pelican

Study the spelling and meaning of each word. These words are used in today's story. Connect each word with its definition.

1. awkward
2. impressive
3. inhabitant
4. prevent
5. refuges
6. social

a. one who lives in a place
b. protective retreats
c. clumsy
d. gets along with others
e. capable of making an impression on the mind
f. keep from happening

Read the story carefully and remember the details.

A common inhabitant of both coastal and inland waters is the white pelican. The pelican is a large, impressive bird. It has a long neck, short legs, and webbed feet. The most distinguishing feature of the pelican is its long bill and deep pouch.

On land the pelicans are awkward. In the air they are strong. When migrating, pelicans fly in a V-formation.

The pelican is a social bird. It even fishes in a group, when gathering fish and marine animals in its pouch.

Like many other birds the pelican is in danger of becoming extinct. To prevent this extinction, many refuges have been set up to protect the bird. Each spring these refuges are filled with crowds of pelicans. They leave to go south in the fall.

A. Underline the correct answers about today's story.

1. Which word describes the pelican? (a) unimpressive (b) small (c) impressive
2. The most distinguishing feature
   is the pelican's (a) feet (b) neck (c) pouch.
3. On land, the pelican is (a) awkward (b) graceful (c) helpless.
4. Pelicans always live near (a) rice fields (b) water (c) woods.
5. A refuge is a (a) safe place (b) prison (c) dangerous place.

B. Reread the story and write the answers to these questions.

1. Where can crowds of pelicans be found in spring?

3. Where do the pelicans carry fish?

2. How do pelicans fly when migrating?

4. When do pelicans go south?

Unit 160 cont'd ☞

Improving Your Word Power

A. Match each definition with a word in the box.

a. account	_**b**_ 1. opportunity; fate; luck
b. chance	____ 2. something which is done on a regular basis
c. deplete	____ 3. without noise; calm
d. dozen	____ 4. to take unawares; to come upon suddenly
e. habit	____ 5. to greet; to receive cordially
f. hurry	____ 6. a grouping of twelve
g. legal	____ 7. something given for merit
h. lonesome	____ 8. to act or move rapidly
i. modern	____ 9. distress felt because of loss or injury
j. paralyze	____ 10. that which is in agreement with the law
k. persuade	____ 11. pleasing; agreeable
l. pleasant	____ 12. to empty or partially empty
m. quiet	____ 13. of a nature to excite terror
n. reward	____ 14. lonely or secluded
o. shrewd	____ 15. to bring over to one's side
p. sorrow	____ 16. to come to know the meaning of
q. surprise	____ 17. pertaining to the present period
r. terrible	____ 18. to make powerless or inactive
s. understand	____ 19. having keen insight
t. welcome	____ 20. to give an explanation of

B. Complete each sentence with a word from the box.

1. I don't __*understand*__ how to work the math assignment.
2. We must _____ Annie to forgive Steven.
3. You will stand at the door and _____ the guests.
4. Dr. Morrison is a _____ business woman.
5. Before you come home, stop and pick up a _____ eggs.
6. They are planning a _____ birthday party for Kris.
7. I want to _____ home and tell my parents the news.
8. Let's give Chuck one more _____.
9. It is courteous to be _____ in a library.
10. Smoking is an unhealthy _____.
11. The furnishings in the house were _____.
12. A _____ is being offered for the return of the wallet.
13. George felt _____ at the death of the bird.
14. Give us your _____ of the accident.
15. Is it _____ to jaywalk?

Comprehension Check

(A) Match each word with its definition.

_c_	1. library	a. place where planes land and take off
___	2. skeleton	b. containing or holding nothing
___	3. camera	c. place where books are kept for loan
___	4. conquer	d. place where sick and wounded are cared for
___	5. surprise	e. something which is done on a regular basis
___	6. airport	f. to overcome by using force
___	7. citizen	g. the bony framework of an animal
___	8. promise	h. to take unawares; to come upon suddenly
___	9. direction	i. point of the compass
___	10. match	j. to pass the time in inactivity
___	11. vacant	k. that which is in agreement with the law
___	12. hospital	l. resident of a country
___	13. hibernate	m. thing used for taking pictures
___	14. legal	n. similar or equal in appearance
___	15. habit	o. assurance given by one person to another

(B) Complete each sentence with a word from part A.

1. In which ___*direction*___ did the boy run?
2. Be sure to take a _____ and film on your vacation.
3. I went to the _____ to check out a book by Hawthorne.
4. We are planning a _____ birthday party for Katherine.
5. Will you _____ not to go near the old silver mine?
6. The soldiers set out to _____ the enemy camp.
7. I am proud to be an American _____ .
8. Your left sock doesn't _____ your right sock.
9. I will meet you at the _____ at Gate 62.
10. The apartment upstairs is _____ again.
11. Bears _____ during the winter.
12. Biting your fingernails is a bad _____ .

(C) Complete these sentences.

1. The walking leaf is a master of ___*disguise*___ .
2. A distinguishing feature of the pelican is its _____ .
3. The Venus's-flytrap is a _____ .
4. The vampire bat is active at _____ .
5. The water bug swims _____ .
6. The pelican is in danger of _____ .
7. The pelican is a large _____ .
8. The walking leaf is an _____ .
9. The _____ is the ideal victim of the Venus's-flytrap.
10. The vampire bat sleeps _____ .
11. The water bug is attracted to _____ .
12. On land pelicans are _____ .
13. It takes _____ days for the Venus's-flytrap to digest a fly.
14. When the wind blows, the walking leaf _____ .

Test 32 cont'd ☛

Comprehension Check (continued)

D Match these words and their definitions. These words appeared in the reading selections from units 156-160.

_c_ 1. emerges   ___ 7. strong

___ 2. prey   ___ 8. captive

___ 3. finishes   ___ 9. enable

___ 4. crawl   ___ 10. inhabitant

___ 5. exactly   ___ 11. awkward

___ 6. replica   ___ 12. refuges

a. places to protect animals

b. move as a worm

c. comes into view

d. animal hunted for food

e. completes

f. a resident

g. clumsy

h. precisely

i. duplication

j. prisoner

k. powerful

l. to make able

E Underline the correct answers.

1. When are bats active?   (a) during the day   (b) <u>at night</u>

2. Where is the vampire bat's home?   (a) Transylvania   (b) South America

3. What is a Venus's flytrap?   (a) plant   (b) machine

4. What is a victim?   (a) prey   (b) enemy

5. What is camouflage?   (a) place to hide   (b) disguise

6. What protects the walking leaf besides camouflage? (a) no other protection   (b) sharp sting

7. What attracts water bugs?   (a) electric lights   (b) moving objects

8. What does a water bug eat?   (a) its victim's juices   (b) fish eggs

9. What do pelicans put in their pouches?   (a) fish and other marine animals   (b) metal and other shiny objects

10. What do pelicans live near?   (a) water   (b) woods

Choose one of the following topics and write a paragraph.

(1) Write a creative paragraph about a day in the life of a vampire bat.

(2) Write a creative paragraph about a day in the life of a Venus's flytrap.

_____

_____

_____

_____

_____

_____

_____

Wild Hogs

Study the spelling and meaning of each word. These words are used in today's story. Connect each word with its definition.

1. comfort
2. defense
3. domestic
4. muscular
5. provocation
6. slightest

a. having noticeable muscles
b. not foreign
c. means of protection
d. smallest
e. relief
f. excitement to anger

Read the story carefully and remember the details.

Wild hogs are native to Europe and Asia. Unlike their cousins, the domestic hogs, wild hogs are thin and muscular.

A wild hog is quick to anger. At the slightest provocation, it slashes away with its tusks. The tusks and the hog's speed are its only means of defense.

Wild hogs move about only as much as necessary to find food. They are active during the daylight hours. The hogs feed on anything they can find, but their main diet is vegetation.

To get comfort and relief from the heat and pesty insects, wild hogs frequently wallow in the mud. Wild hogs never hurry unless absolutely necessary. People hunt wild hogs for sport.

A. Underline the correct answers about today's story.

1. Wild hogs are	(a) fat	(b) thin	(c) obese.
2. At the slightest provocation the hog	(a) runs away	(b) buries in the mud	(c) slashes with its tusks.
3. Besides tusks the hog's defense is its	(a) speed	(b) tough hide	(c) strong feet.
4. Hogs move about to find	(a) shelter	(b) food	(c) mud holes.
5. People hunt the wild hog for	(a) food	(b) sport	(c) tusks.

B. Reread the story and write the answers to these questions.

1. What two areas are home to wild hogs?

_____

_____

_____

2. When are wild hogs active?

_____

_____

_____

3. How do wild hogs get relief from heat and pesty insects?

_____

_____

_____

4. When do wild hogs hurry?

_____

_____

_____

Unit 161 cont'd

Expanding Your Word Power

A. Write the word which best matches each definition.

order	1. way one thing follows another	a. advice
_____	2. change from solid to liquid	b. cellar
_____	3. reaping and gathering in grain	c. contest
_____	4. time for recreation or rest	d. destroy
_____	5. clear to the senses; plain	e. distinct
_____	6. underground room	f. favorite
_____	7. a large pot for cooking	g. harvest
_____	8. person who lives near another	h. increase
_____	9. reason for doing something	i. journey
_____	10. a trial of skill	j. kettle
_____	11. paid for breaking a rule	k. melt
_____	12. to make greater	l. neighbor
_____	13. more than two but not many	m. order
_____	14. the one liked very much	n. password
_____	15. to put an end to	o. penalty
_____	16. son of a king	p. prince
_____	17. stop	q. purpose
_____	18. another word for "trip"; to travel	r. quit
_____	19. feel with hand or finger	s. several
_____	20. suggestions	t. sorry
		u. study
		v. touch
		w. vacation
		x. wonder

B. Complete each sentence with a word from the list.

1. It's time to ___harvest___ the wheat.
2. Dave asked me for _____.
3. We must _____ for the test.
4. _____ the butter slowly.
5. The storm could _____ the town.
6. Roy _____ his job.
7. He took a _____ to Hawaii.
8. I smelled the _____ odor of garlic.
9. We will _____ to faraway lands.
10. Don't _____ the stove.
11. The _____ is "pudding."
12. Explain the _____ of this meeting.

13. Put these jars in the _____.
14. Chocolate is my _____ flavor.
15. The _____ is five cents.
16. Lee was _____ for his actions.
17. I stirred the _____ of soup.
18. The _____ is heir to the throne.
19. Angie won the essay _____.
20. _____ students volunteered.
21. Dr. Andrews is my _____.
22. The cost will _____ in January.
23. I _____ what he will do.
24. Put these pages in _____.

The Willow Ptarmigan

Study the spelling and meaning of each word. These words are used in today's story. Connect each word with its definition.

1. adapted
2. defenseless
3. invisible
4. plumage
5. protection
6. surfaces

a. not able to be seen
b. without protection
c. feathers
d. made fit or usable
e. exteriors of something
f. defense from harm

Read the story carefully and remember the details.

The willow ptarmigan is a small Arctic bird. It is gifted with nature's best protection — changing plumage.

In the winter the willow ptarmigan's white coat matches the surrounding snow. Its feathers are tightly packed and well-oiled. The bird is protected from the cold winds and wet snow. Its feet are also well adapted to the Arctic conditions. The bird can walk in the snow without sinking in. Its long and sharp claws prevent it from slipping on wet surfaces.

In the summer the bird's plumage changes to reddish brown. The coloring blends in perfectly with the surroundings. On the ground the willow ptarmigan is practically invisible. Its color has saved the bird from many dangers in which it would have been defenseless.

A. Underline the correct answers about today's story.

1. Where does the ptarmigan live?   (a) Arctic   (b) Europe   (c) Asia
2. In the winter the bird is   (a) brown   (b) gray   (c) white.
3. What prevents the bird from slipping?   (a) feathers   (b) big feet   (c) claws
4. What protects the bird?   (a) size   (b) color   (c) claws
5. On the ground the bird is almost   (a) invisible   (b) helpless   (c) transparent.

B. Reread the story and write the answers to these questions.

1. What is the willow ptarmigan's protection?

_____

_____

_____

2. Why can the bird walk on snow?

_____

_____

_____

3. What does the bird match during the winter?

_____

_____

_____

4. What color is the ptarmigan in summer?

_____

_____

_____

Unit 162 cont'd 🖝

An Exercise in Vocabulary I

amusement	cafeteria	delicious	liberty	mischievous
future	necessary	guitar	persuade	stubborn
museum	scheme	volunteer	evidence	wizard
unite	repeat	yacht	recent	frequently
solution	forfeit	content	elevator	counterfeit

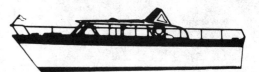

A. Write the word from the list which fits each short definition.

1. to join together ___ *unite* ___
2. not easily handled ___
3. to do again ___
4. a pleasure ship ___
5. troublesome ___
6. what lies ahead ___
7. to be needed ___
8. proof ___
9. a machine that lifts ___
10. a synonym for "tasty" ___
11. to lose as a penalty ___
12. to do willingly ___
13. a synonym for "freedom" ___
14. a musical instrument ___
15. happens often ___
16. has magical powers ___
17. contains collections of the past ___
18. not genuine ___
19. to cause to believe ___
20. a synonym for "entertainment" ___
21. answer to a problem ___
22. satisfied ___
23. a plan ___
24. happened lately ___
25. a place where lunch is served ___

B. Complete each sentence with a word from the list.

1. Let's go to the ___ *amusement* ___ park.
2. They must ___ the game.
3. We will eat in the ___.
4. He is as ___ as a mule.
5. Jack was a ___ child.
6. We rode the ___ to the roof.
7. What are the ___ developments?
8. It is ___ to be present.
9. There was no ___ of his guilt.
10. I spent my vacation on a ___.
11. Carl visits us ___.
12. Ann is ___ to stay at home.
13. The money was ___.
14. Dinosaur bones are kept in a ___.
15. What will happen in the ___?
16. Do you have a ___ to the problem?
17. Can he play the ___?
18. May I have a ___ from the audience?
19. This meal tastes ___.
20. Would you ___ the question?
21. Our forces must ___.
22. I could not ___ him to come.
23. What ___ have you devised?
24. Bob is a ___ at math.
25. The Revolutionary War was fought for ___.

Witches

Study the spelling and meaning of each word. These words are used in today's story. Connect each word with its definition.

1. associated
2. evil
3. magic
4. pictured
5. superstition
6. supposedly

a. excessive reverence or fear
b. presumably
c. connected in thought
d. causing pain or trouble
e. making things happen in an unnatural way
f. depict; shown as

Read the story carefully and remember the details.

Witches have always been associated with magic and evil powers. Most are pictured as old and ugly and riding a broomstick.

People still believe in witches today although we now know how to explain many of the superstitions which are associated with witches. People still jump at the sight of a black cat because witches supposedly changed themselves to cats.

In olden days witches were believed to meet twice a year. The first meeting was April 30, the day before May Day. The second meeting was October 31, which is now celebrated as Halloween. On these two nights witches had special powers given to them by the Devil.

Would you like to see a witch? Next Halloween put your clothes on wrong side out, and walk backwards to a crossroads. At midnight you'll see a witch.

A. **Underline the correct answers about today's story.**

1. Witches are associated with   (a) evil   (b) kindness   (c) good.
2. Witches often change themselves to   (a) dogs   (b) trees   (c) cats.
3. Witches are pictured as   (a) beautiful   (b) old and ugly   (c) young.
4. October 31 is   (a) Halloween   (b) Thanksgiving   (c) Valentine's Day.
5. Witches have powers given to them by   (a) the dead   (b) Zeus   (c) the Devil.

B. **Reread the story and write the answers to these questions.**

1. What two days did witches use to meet?

_____

_____

_____

2. What can you do on Halloween to see a witch?

_____

_____

3. Why do people jump at the sight of a black cat?

_____

_____

_____

4. What do witches supposedly ride?

_____

_____

Unit 163 cont'd

An Exercise in Vocabulary II

airport	history	question	zero	discover
breakfast	journey	remember	piano	guest
country	hospital	umbrella	reason	practice
dessert	leaves	straight	idea	autumn
enormous	protect	vacation	key	daughter

A. Choose the word from the list which best fits each definition.

1. musical instrument ___*piano*___
2. why you do something _____
3. less than one _____
4. a welcome visitor _____
5. out of the city _____
6. girl child _____
7. used to unlock a door _____
8. very large _____
9. place where sick stay _____
10. to watch over _____
11. studying the past _____
12. grows on a tree _____
13. used in the rain _____

14. a place where planes land _____
15. sentence that asks something _____
16. meal at morning _____
17. to do again and again _____
18. opposite of "forget" _____
19. to find _____
20. a thought _____
21. another word for "trip" _____
22. not crooked _____
23. season before winter _____
24. trip for rest and pleasure _____
25. something sweet after dinner _____

B. Complete each sentence with a word from the list.

1. You should ___*practice*___ the drums.
2. I passed the _____ test.
3. Draw a _____ line.
4. They live in the _____.
5. We had pie for _____.
6. That's a good _____!
7. The _____ needs tuning.
8. You are our _____.
9. Next week is our Easter _____.
10. I can't _____ her name.
11. His _____ is my neighbor.
12. This _____ unlocks the door.
13. Planes land at the _____.

14. Did he _____ America?
15. My dog will _____ me.
16. For what _____ did you quit?
17. I had toast for _____.
18. In _____ the leaves turn brown.
19. Sick people go to the _____.
20. When it rains, carry an _____.
21. One minus one is _____.
22. The _____ are turning green.
23. We embarked on a long _____.
24. The dinosaur was _____.
25. Here's the answer to your _____.

Wombats

Study the spelling and meaning of each word. These words are used in today's story. Connect each word with its definition.

1. clumsy
2. complex
3. damage
4. dense
5. playful
6. strict

a. made of many parts
b. destruction
c. thick
d. awkward
e. never changing
f. lively; full of fun

Read the story carefully and remember the details.

A wombat is a bearlike animal which lives in the dense forests of southern Australia. It has a heavy body, short stubby legs, sharp claws, and strong teeth. The wombat is a clumsy animal.

The wombat has small eyes. The animal spends much of its time in dark underground tunnels. The wombat digs long, complex tunnels. It digs while lying on its side. The wombat digs quickly, shoveling the dirt out with its feet.

When dark, the wombat comes out to look for food. It is a strict vegetarian.

In the wild the wombat lives alone. In captivity it makes a playful pet.

People are the wombat's chief enemy. The animal is considered a pest by farmers because of the damage it does to crops.

A. Underline the correct answers about today's story.

1. Which word describes the wombat?   (a) fierce   (b) clumsy   (c) agile
2. Where is the wombat's home?   (a) underground   (b) trees   (c) water
3. The wombat's tunnels are   (a) very simple   (b) plain   (c) complex.
4. What is the wombat's chief enemy?   (a) people   (b) weather   (c) lack of food
5. Farmers consider the wombat a/an   (a) aide   (b) helper   (c) pest.

B. Reread the story and write the answers to these questions.

1. What country is home to a wombat?

_____

_____

_____

2. What does the wombat eat?

_____

_____

_____

3. Where does the wombat spend much of its time?

_____

_____

_____

4. What is a "vegetarian"?

_____

_____

_____

Unit 164 cont'd ☞

An Exercise in Vocabulary III

enough	language	awkward	comedian	replace
asleep	radio	important	frown	piano
between	remember	complete	autumn	habit
bridge	several	shade	teeth	clue
earth	signature	guess	forest	imagine

A. Write the word from the list which best fits each definition.

1. when you sign your name ___signature___
2. not a few, but _____
3. a musical instrument _____
4. the season before winter _____
5. a person who tells jokes _____
6. the plural of "tooth" _____
7. opposite of "smile" _____
8. another word for "hint" _____
9. opposite of "awake" _____
10. to have plenty _____

11. to put back _____
12. in the middle _____
13. to make believe _____
14. the planet we live on _____
15. out of the sunshine _____
16. English is one example _____
17. a wooded area _____
18. the opposite of "forget" _____
19. another word for "clumsy" _____
20. something you do every day _____

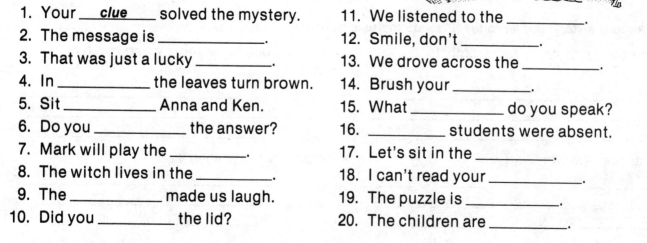

B. Complete each sentence with a word from the list.

1. Your ___clue___ solved the mystery.
2. The message is _____.
3. That was just a lucky _____.
4. In _____ the leaves turn brown.
5. Sit _____ Anna and Ken.
6. Do you _____ the answer?
7. Mark will play the _____.
8. The witch lives in the _____.
9. The _____ made us laugh.
10. Did you _____ the lid?

11. We listened to the _____.
12. Smile, don't _____.
13. We drove across the _____.
14. Brush your _____.
15. What _____ do you speak?
16. _____ students were absent.
17. Let's sit in the _____.
18. I can't read your _____.
19. The puzzle is _____.
20. The children are _____.

Woolly Mammoths   Unit 165

Study the spelling and meaning of each word. These words are used in today's story. Connect each word with its definition.

1. chiefly   a. opponents
2. enemies   b. entirely; really
3. peaceful   c. name; call
4. quite   d. traveled about
5. refer   e. primarily
6. roamed   f. serene

Read the story carefully and remember the details.

Thousands of years ago there roamed an animal which we now refer to as the woolly mammoth. It was not quite as large as an elephant. It had a long trunk and two curved tusks. The woolly mammoth was covered in fur that reached almost to the ground.

The woolly mammoth lived during the Ice Age. It roamed about the northern part of the earth. The mammoth was a peaceful animal. However, it had many enemies, chiefly the saber-toothed tiger and people.

The first mammoth was discovered in 1901 in Siberia. It had been frozen in the ice for over 10,000 years! The food it had eaten was still in its stomach. Today there are no woolly mammoths.

A. **Underline the correct answers about today's story.**

1. The woolly mammoth resembled a/an   (a) dinosaur   (b) tiger   (c) elephant.
2. The mammoth lived during the   (a) Ice Age   (b) Stone Age   (c) Age of Reptiles.
3. Which word describes the mammoth?   (a) dangerous   (b) peaceful   (c) fierce
4. The first mammoth was discovered in (a) Africa   (b) Siberia   (c) South America.
5. The mammoth is now   (a) extinct   (b) smaller   (c) found in zoos.

B. **Reread the story and write the answers to these questions.**

1. Name two enemies of the woolly mammoth.

_____

_____

_____

2. When was the first mammoth discovered?

_____

_____

_____

3. How long had the mammoth been frozen?

_____

_____

_____

4. How many woolly mammoths are there today?

_____

_____

An Exercise in Vocabulary IV

alone	dark	game	know	number	sun
arm	easy	green	life	open	under
book	find	help	little	party	water
bus	friend	home	money	river	wood
city	fun	ice	music	snow	zoo

A. Choose a word from the list which best fits each definition.

1. another word for "small" _little_
2. a place where animals are kept _____
3. the opposite of "close" _____
4. something you ride to school _____
5. a large body of water _____
6. not over, but _____
7. something you read _____
8. another word for "town" _____
9. a word that rhymes with "honey" _____
10. frozen water _____
11. not hard, but _____
12. two _____
13. a group of people having fun _____
14. a family living together _____
15. commonly seen in winter _____

16. the opposite of "lose" _____
17. a color _____
18. someone you like _____
19. a word that rhymes with "wife" _____
20. by oneself _____
21. to understand _____
22. without light _____
23. something that is wet _____
24. a word that rhymes with "came" _____
25. a part of the body _____
26. something trees are made of _____
27. having a good time _____
28. songs _____
29. to give aid _____
30. something that is hot _____

B. Complete each sentence with a word from the list.

1. Detroit is a big _city_.
2. The _____ is closed today.
3. Ralph is my best _____.
4. You can't swim across the _____.
5. The _____ has melted.
6. Is the _____ too loud?
7. It was an _____ test.
8. May I borrow your _____?
9. It will _____ tomorrow.
10. You can't go there _____.

11. I'm going _____.
12. We _____ what to do.
13. The dog hid _____ the bed.
14. She rides the _____ to school.
15. Did you _____ my hat?
16. Have _____.
17. I saw a _____ car.
18. The _____ is too cold.
19. The _____ begins at six.
20. _____ your eyes.

398

Comprehension Check

Ⓐ Match each word with its definition.

_g_   1. neighbor
____ 2. life
____ 3. bus
____ 4. amusement
____ 5. key
____ 6. comedian
____ 7. purpose
____ 8. cafeteria
____ 9. question
____ 10. museum
____ 11. order
____ 12. autumn
____ 13. journey
____ 14. party
____ 15. awkward

a. a person who tells jokes
b. reason for doing something
c. place where lunch is served
d. another word for "trip"; to travel
e. place which contains collections of the past
f. another word for "clumsy"
g. person who lives near another
h. something you ride to school
i. sentence that asks something
j. way one thing follows another
k. a word that rhymes with "wife"
l. a synonym for "entertainment"
m. used to unlock a door
n. the season before winter
o. a group of people having fun

Ⓑ Complete each sentence with a word from part A.

1. The ____journey____ began in New York City on July 27, 1985.
2. Everyday Shawn rides the _____ to Wallace Avenue.
3. We will go to the _____ and see the exhibit from Maori.
4. Andrew is funny; he should become a _____ .
5. Dr. Bennett, our _____ , came here from London.
6. This _____ opens the front, back, and garage doors.
7. In _____ the leaves turn brown.
8. Disneyland is an _____ park in Anaheim, California.
9. Do you have a _____ about today's lesson?
10. In your first paragraph, explain the _____ of the paper.
11. Let's have a sandwich at the _____ at noon.
12. Put the words in alphabetical _____ .

Ⓒ Complete these sentences.

1. In olden days witches were believed to meet on __April 30__ and __October 31__ .
2. A woolly mammoth resembled an _____ .
3. The willow ptarmigan lives in the _____ .
4. The wombat spends most of its time in underground _____ .
5. There are _____ woolly mammoths today.
6. People hunt wild hogs for _____ .
7. A wild hog is quick to _____ .

8. The wombat digs while lying on its _____ .
9. In winter the willow ptarmigan is _____ .
10. Wombats live in _____ .
11. The woolly mammoth lived during the _____ .
12. The willow ptarmigan protects itself by changing _____ .

Test 33 cont'd ☞

Comprehension Check (continued)

D Match these words and their definitions. These words appeared in the reading selections from units 161-165.

d 1. muscular   _____ 7. supposedly   a. awkward   g. seen

_____ 2. comfort   _____ 8. dense   b. opponents   h. feathers of a bird

_____ 3. plumage   _____ 9. clumsy   c. thick   i. not able to be seen

_____ 4. invisible   _____ 10. peaceful   d. showing muscle   j. mainly

_____ 5. defenseless   _____ 11. enemies   e. without protection   k. presumably

_____ 6. pictured   _____ 12. chiefly   f. providing ease   l. serene

E Underline the correct answers.

1. What does a wild hog do at the slightest provocation?   (a) <u>slashes with its tusks</u>   (b) runs away

2. Why are wild hogs hunted?   (a) sport   (b) food

3. Where do willow ptarmigans live?   (a) Arctic   (b) Hawaii

4. What color is the ptarmigan in winter?   (a) gray   (b) white

5. How are witches usually pictured?   (a) young and beautiful   (b) old and ugly

6. What holiday is October 31?   (a) Halloween   (b) Memorial Day

7. Which word describes a wombat?   (a) clumsy   (b) fierce

8. Describe wombat's tunnels.   (a) short and plain   (b) long and complex

9. What animal did the woolly mammoth resemble?   (a) elephant   (b) dinosaur

10. When did the mammoth live?   (a) Ice Age   (b) Age of Reptiles

Choose one of the following topics and write a paragraph.

(1) Many animals we read about are now extinct. What can be done to prevent animals from becoming extinct?

(2) Witches are associated with magic. Do you believe in magic? Why or why not?

_____

_____

_____

_____

_____

_____

_____

_____

_____

_____